*Adapting Mentorship
Across the Professions*

Adapting Mentorship Across the Professions

Fresh Insights and Perspectives

Edited by

Edwin G. Ralph and Keith D. Walker

Adapting Mentorship Across the Professions· Fresh Insights and Perspectives
© 2011 Edwin G. Ralph and Keith D. Walker

Library and Archives Canada Cataloguing in Publication

Adapting mentorship across the professions · fresh insights and perspectives / edited by Edwin G. Ralph and Keith D. Walker.

Includes bibliographical references. Issued also in an electronic format.
ISBN 978-1-55059-410-2

1. Mentoring in business. 2. Mentoring in the professions. 3. Mentoring. I. Ralph, Edwin G. (Edwin George), 1944- II. Walker, Keith D. (Keith Douglas), 1954-

HF5385.A33 2011
658.3'124 C2011-905930-4

Detselig Enterprises, Ltd., recognizes the financial support of the government of Canada through the Canada Books Program.

Also acknowledged is the financial assistance of the Government of Alberta, Alberta Multimedia Development fund.

Government of Alberta ■ Alberta

SAN 113-0234
ISBN 978-1-55059-410-2
Printed in Canada.
Cover design· James Dangerous.

Detselig Enterprises Ltd.

210 1220 Kensington Rd NW
Calgary, Alberta   T2N 3P5
www.temerondetselig.com
temeron@telusplanet.net
p. 403-283-0900 f. 403-283-6947

Contents

Preface

THIS BOOK ON ADAPTING MENTORSHIP across the professions was a direct product of the first national meeting of its kind held in Canada, *The Forum on Mentorship in the Professions*, which took place in Saskatoon, Saskatchewan, June 17–19, 2010. The majority of the authors whose work is featured in this book were attendees at the forum. Each had accepted an invitation from us as book editors to propose and contribute a chapter to the book. We had organized and conducted the forum as one of several components of a project funded by a Public Outreach Grant we had received from the Social Sciences and Humanities Research Council of Canada. The grant was to help disseminate a mentoring model entitled Adaptive Mentorship©, which we had developed, researched, and refined earlier. Through the forum and this edited book we are hoping to disseminate understandings and encourage the sharing of fresh insights on the vital subject of mentorship, across the professions. We have much to learn from each other.

It should be noted here that we also conducted a previous national forum in Saskatoon in June 2008 called *The Forum on Practicum/ Clinical Programs in Professional Education*. This first forum was similarly a product of an earlier SSHRC research grant we received to study the role of practicum and/or clinical education in the preparation of professionals across Canada, and it has similarly spawned an edited book (Ralph, E., Walker, K., & Wimmer, R. [Eds.]. [2010]. *The practicum in professional education: Canadian perspectives*. Calgary, AB: Detselig Enterprises), with chapters written by attendees at the first forum. The focus of that book was on experiential learning across the professions. Again, we believe that we can learn a great deal from other professions that will enhance our own understandings and practices.

The three-day *Forum on Mentorship*, which was also supported by the University of Saskatchewan, attracted 83 attendees representing a variety of professional disciplines from across the nation and sampling an array of fields from government, business, industry, health care, and post-secondary education. The common point of interest among the 2010 forum participants was effective mentorship as typically conducted in the areas of pre-service and in-service professional development, as well as mentorship's philosophical rationales, its theoretical foundations, its key characteristics and principles, its best practices and limiting factors, and its promising future initiatives.

This book is divided into two sections: Part 1 deals with generic mentorship ideas, insights, practices, and experiences; Part 2 addresses the issues, applications, and insights specific to the Adaptive Mentorship (AM) model. Authors of the 15 chapters in Part 1 examine some of the basic philosophical and theoretical underpinnings and the generic conceptual lenses regarding the mentorship process. These chapters are of a rather general nature and deal with broader facets of how our authors believe that mentorship might be best understood and implemented within their respective professional education/training situations. Although several authors in Part 1 present generic perspectives reflecting frameworks used in their own professions, readers will no doubt extract meaningful applications to inform mentorship practice in their own professional or disciplinary settings.

Moreover, the authors of the last two chapters of Part 1 offer two tested ways to bridge the proverbial theory-practice gap that often appears in mentorship discussions and reflections. These techniques are generic enough to relate to any profession and practical enough for anyone with mentoring obligations either to adopt directly or to adapt strategically within their particular contexts. The authors of the nine chapters in Part 2 of the book address the (AM) model specifically. AM and its rationale are described, its research results are summarized, its strengths and limitations are examined, and its potential for future implementation is envisaged.

Several authors pursued the extra provision we had offered to forum attendees who wanted their chapter to undergo an additional double-blind refereeing process. These chapters are identified by a footnote. We are grateful for the willingness of 15 referees (see acknowledgement at end of book) who were provided with the manuscripts of these temporarily unidentified authors and asked to adjudicate the scholarly quality of these contributions. Where accorded sufficient support from referees, the authors were permitted to revise their manuscripts, according to referees' vetting critiques, and after this second submission the editors decided to accord "refereed" status where appropriate.

Both the 2010 mentorship forum and the chapters of this book formally mark the first time a cross-disciplinary group of interested Canadian scholars and practitioners have sought to publicly share and document their ideas and experiences regarding effective mentorship in professional education settings. This book represents their initial efforts to focus on mentorship in an inter-professional venue by describing its key concepts, defining its relevant terms, clarifying mutual understandings, identifying its related strengths and challenges, and exploring its future innovations.

However, in seeking to respond to the many questions that were posed during the forum deliberations and within the writing of the book chapters, the forum delegates and the chapter authors fulfilled what Preston and Walker identified in Chapter 1; namely, they raised as many questions as they might have answered with respect to mentorship. Yet, rather than decrying such a position, we take comfort, because it creates an ideal state for seeking to expand knowledge and understanding of the powerful role of mentorship in professional development. We trust that this book will generate even more interest, dialogue, and research among other interested researchers across the professional disciplines with regard to enhancing mentorship practice and scholarship.

Edwin Ralph and Keith Walker
University of Saskatchewan

Introduction

Part 1: Conceptual, Theoretical, and Contextual Aspects of Mentorship

Part 1 of the book consists of 15 chapters by 24 authors representing diverse cross-disciplinary backgrounds and workplace experiences. Each chapter's author(s) examine the concept and/or practice of mentorship from a unique perspective that reflects their personal and professional interests and traditions. Sometimes they explore mentorship broadly and generically in philosophical or foundational terms or in conceptual and theoretical ways, and sometimes they write in specific and practical terms, catering to readers looking for useful and applicable techniques to enhance everyday mentoring practice. However, what they all did was express their enthusiasm and passion for the key role that mentorship plays both in the pre-service educational preparation and the ongoing professional development of practitioners across the disciplines.

In **Chapter 1**, Jane Preston and Keith Walker describe the first three-day *Forum on Mentorship across the Professions* ever held in Canada. This forum became the key source for the present book. Jane and Keith summarize the forum sessions and activities, and they synthesize the key ideas, experiences, and issues that attendees addressed during the deliberations. No doubt when forum participants begin to read Chapter 1, they will again sense some of the intensity and excitement generated during these times of dialogue on the mentorship process across the professions.

Ellery Pullman, in **Chapter 2**, provides a rich background of the developmental nature of the mentorship processes, rooting mentorship in terms of developmental psychology and adult learning. In keeping with the theme of the book, Ellery emphasizes that it is essential for mentors in any profession or occupation to be able to adapt their mentoring style to appropriately match the changing developmental levels of the protégé(s) with whom they work.

In **Chapter 3**, Kelly McInnes questions some of the traditional approaches to formal mentorship by sharing key findings from her recently completed graduate research on the mentoring experiences of women in higher education administration. She contributes needed understanding on this rarely discussed topic by comparing her results with those reported in the mentorship literature, and she explores the similarities and differences that emerged.

In **Chapter 4**, Dal Lynds and Sarel van der Walt, both employees of Battleford Union Hospital, provide a candid description of the advantages and disadvantages of implementing cross-disciplinary mentorship in an emergency department in a rural Canadian hospital setting. They argue that such venues can provide effective mentorship for health science students, residents, and new staff, provided that leaders carefully plan, organize, and maintain a sound mentorship program.

Michelle Prytula and Linda Ferguson, in **Chapter 5**, combine their professional backgrounds in Education and Nursing, respectively, to illustrate how cross-professional interchange can function. They describe two research projects, one in Education and one in Nursing, which addressed the nature of mentoring cultures within communities of practice. They show how the nature of the communities of practice had significant influence on newcomers in both settings.

In **Chapter 6**, Rosemary Venne draws on her expertise and experience in the Edward's School of Business to propose a mentorship program as a bridge over the generational and career divides. Such a program would result in reduced generational conflict, successful career management, higher levels of employee engagement, a stronger retention rate for the organization, and successful transfer of knowledge from the older to the younger generation of workers.

In **Chapter 7**, Jane Preston (a teacher), Marcella Ogenchuk (a nurse), and Joseph Nsiah (a priest) document their shared, lived mentoring experiences as PhD students in a department of educational administration. Their poignant stories reveal the power of peer mentorship as a means of mutual support and guidance, where members freely adapt between being a mentor and a mentee, as needed. They argue for an institutional approach to peer mentorship, where developmental relationships are directly promoted within the organization.

Norm Dray, in **Chapter 8**, draws on his considerable experience in educational administration and contends that conventional supervision in the education system could be the starting point of establishing mentoring relationships. If developmental, collaborative, and interdependent mentoring approaches match the existing stages of an individual's growth, then ongoing professional growth will be facilitated. He relates cases illustrating that professional development flourishes when communities of learners work together to mentor one another.

Ben Kutsyuruba suggests in **Chapter 9** that one of the most effective ways to bridge the generational gap between novice and veteran teachers is to establish a professional learning community that includes a mentoring system, a collaborative school culture, and a structure of parallel leadership, each unique in its functions. He postulates that such learning communities will promote ongoing collaboration between educators at all levels of their professional careers and will reduce feelings of isolation often encountered by neophytes.

Willow Brown, Andrea Davy, Debbie Koehn, and Denise Wilson in **Chapter 10** describe an alternate teacher mentorship approach using mentorship pairings of teacher candidates with teacher coaches or mentors engaged in assessment-inquiry projects through British Columbia's *Network of Performance Based Schools* (NPBS). The resulting collaboration of teacher leaders and professors facilitated teacher induction to sustain beneficial assessment practices by helping new teachers learn how to provide all children with rich and equitable learning opportunities.

Catherine Neumann-Boxer in **Chapter 11** presents her self-reflections on how she was able to adjust her mentorship role as a District Fine Arts Resource Teacher working with 35 K–7 classroom teachers to build their capacities for music instruction. She traces her professional journey of adapting her mentorship style from a *mentor-as-expert* approach to one that permitted her to respond to individual colleague/protégé needs and changing conditions of the workplace.

In **Chapter 12**, Sabre Cherkowski documents her use of a peer coaching strategy in a graduate educational leadership course. She used a leadership portfolio assignment with an embedded peer coaching component to engage students in critical reflection of their own leadership within their respective school roles. Students reported that the use of peer coaching was a new and effective way of engaging in professional development with colleagues.

Catherine McGregor, Judy Halbert, and Linda Kaser show in **Chapter 13** how coaching in education settings can serve as a distributed-leadership tool in which learning can become the centre of activity among all educational stakeholders. The authors also argue that coaching is an enabling tool, in that it can be used to respond to different contexts, needs, demands, and opportunities of the participants. They also summarize examples from their research to demonstrate this enabling aspect in the shift from best practices to next practices in schools.

In **Chapter 14**, Keith Walker narrates a conversation he had at a restaurant with a younger friend to whom Keith was a mentor. In this dialogue, one can observe a practical approach toward maintaining a developmental mentoring relationship through the pair's dialogue. This mentorship interchange focused on the protégé's personal life and leadership as well as some team development focus. Keith admits to often writing or sketching on a table serviette to record key ideas and thoughts during formal and informal coaching and mentoring, leaving the artifact with colleague for future reference.

Using personal stories as mentees, Kabini Sanga and Keith Walker identify in Chapter 15 the transformative and learning value of mentoring by means of posing relevant questions. In support of their case, they offer a heuristic for the content domain of questions and a strategic compilation of mentoring question types. Both Maieutic and Socratic approaches to questioning and their effective use are considered foundational in mentoring relationships.

Part 2: Implementing and Adapting the Adaptive Mentorship Model

Edwin Ralph describes the Adaptive Mentorship (AM) model, in **Chapter 16**. Although the AM model played a key role in the 2010 Saskatoon Forum on Mentorship across the Professions, and is mentioned several times in chapters throughout this book, he is careful to emphasize that AM is simply one approach to help mentorship participants conceptualize and guide their mentoring practice. He summarizes its rationale and research record, and he invites others to consider implementing this approach in their professional settings.

In **Chapter 17**, Roya Khoii describes a study she recently conducted with a group of post-secondary EAL students in Islamic Azad University in Iran. She examined the effect of her implementation of the Adaptive Mentorship model on the development of the students' writing ability in English-as-a-second language. Results of her carefully designed study showed that the participants improved in terms of self-confidence, attitude to writing in a foreign language, and competence in writing.

Anita Jennings and Brigitte Couture are two Nursing instructors in Toronto, who have recently studied the supervision/mentorship process in the practicum component of their second-year program. In **Chapter 18**, they provide a clear description of the traditional clinical supervision process used in Nursing; and they describe initial results of their study regarding students' perspectives of their preceptorship experiences. The findings indicated that the quality of mentorship was of key importance to students.

Dawna Hawrysh describes, in **Chapter 19**, some of the theoretical background behind the preliminary plans of the University to develop a mentor-training program for the field-based mentorship of their health care students. This training is designed to equip personnel to effectively mentor students from across disciplines; and Dawna argues that the AM model fits well in this new inter-professional (IP) program and promises to enhance the initiative.

In **Chapter 20**, Peter Chin and Ben Kutsyuruba describe the mentorship program used with teacher candidates at the Faculty of Education at Queens University. As was the case in earlier chapters, the authors consider implementing the Adaptive Mentorship model in their program. Its success, they point out, depends on such factors as the frequency of the interaction and the nature of the working relationships between/among the parties in the triad.

In Ellery Pullman's second contribution, **Chapter 21**, he first conceptualizes the mentorship process as resting upon the foundational principles of adult development and andragogy. He then explores the possibilities and theoretical connections of applying the AM model in mentoring programs in professional organizations; but cautions practitioners that whatever approach is adapted, protégés may exhibit an immunity to change, and be simply unwilling or unable to proceed.

Bob Petrick, in **Chapter 22**, also discusses Queen's University teacher-education practicum program (see Chapter 20), but from the perspective of the mentor assuming the role of the teacher candidate's advocate. He grounds his argument in Vygotskian developmental concepts; and he illustrates this position by presenting personal stories from the field that fit into each of the four quadrant-types of the AM model.

In **Chapter 23**, Robert Ralph and Susan Shaw present a unique account that fulfills two core objectives of the mentorship project upon which this book was based: (a) they illustrate that the mentorship process can indeed function successfully across two professions; and (b) they show that the Adaptive Mentorship model can effectively serve as a conceptual framework for both the mentor and the protégé in guiding their respective mentoring practices and responsibilities in the relationship.

In **Chapter 24**, William McKay and Jennifer O'Brien boldly project into the future by offering five new directions for research based upon the Adaptive Mentorship model. They suggest adding dimensions of intensity to the model; second, they offer a study to determine if the Hawthorne Effect might affect AM results. Third, they suggest an approach to cross-cultural AM studies; as well as a fourth study of mentoring within medical simulation contexts. A fifth proposal is to use the AM model in Evolutionary Biology studies of altruism.

Part One

Conceptual, Theoretical, and Contextual Aspects of Mentorship

Chapter One

Mentorship Across Professions: Highlights of the Forum on Mentorship

Jane Preston & Keith Walker

T HE *FORUM ON MENTORSHIP IN THE PROFESSIONS* took place in Saskatoon, Saskatchewan, Canada on June 17–19, 2010, and was supported through a Public Outreach Grant from Social Sciences and Humanities Research Council of Canada. The forum attracted an audience of 83 professionally diverse individuals from the University of Saskatchewan, Queen's University, and the University of British Columbia, as well as several local, provincial, and national organizations from across Canada. Nurses, medical doctors, veterinarians, pharmacists, nutritionists, teachers, engineers, business managers, policymakers, physiotherapists, theologians, scientists, educational administrations, college deans, and professors interacted to share their respective interdisciplinary experiences, perspectives, and insights regarding mentorship. The professional diversity of attendees emphasized the cross-disciplinary nature of mentorship as well as its dynamic and generic scope. The forum was carefully designed as a group-process event, giving 95 percent of the contact time to individual, pairs, and small and large group interaction. The process methodologies of appreciative inquiry, open-space technology, and World Café were adapted and employed, along with other consultative approaches.

This gathering of academics, researchers, policymakers, and practitioners generated a rich assortment of views regarding pertinent meanings, aspects, issues, trends, and challenges related to the process of mentorship across the professional disciplines. The heterogeneity of the forum's audience afforded engaging group discussions and thought provoking question and answer sessions. In this chapter we summarize the event, paraphrase attendees' key ideas and comments, synthesize interdisciplinary definitions of mentorship, identify common challenges faced by mentors, and present attendee suggestions for enhancing mentorship. In an effort to support ongoing discourse and research on mentorship, we pose additional questions to continue the fruitful interchange that occurred at the forum.

Defining Mentorship

An initial group activity during the opening session marked an engaging beginning to the forum. Seated around six banquet tables, attendees were asked to brainstorm a list of words they believed to be closely associated with mentorship. When the results were tallied, the single word that surfaced within all six lists was *relationships*. Four of the six groups included the words *challenging, help, trust,* and *wisdom*; three groups listed *collaboration, growth, leadership, listening, modelling, mutual, reflection, sharing,* and *support*; and two groups suggested *advocate, caring, contextual, empathy, evaluation, generous, nurturing, professional, respect, safe,* and *stretching*.

Building upon this activity, attendees were then requested to create a working definition of mentorship based on their brainstormed word list. In reviewing the results, five of the six groups again incorporated the word *relationship* (or a root thereof) into their mentorship definition. More specifically, the groups defined mentorship as

- ◦: a mutually beneficial relationship;
- ◦: a formative or summative relational process by which mentor and protégé are paired in an apprenticeship model contextualized by the experience, compatibility, and needs of each party;
- ◦: working together to produce growth, professional development, and learning in the context of relationship by guiding, navigating, and nurturing;
- ◦: a relationship of trust, which facilitates mutual growth and understanding through modelling, challenging, friendly critique in working towards building capacity, common goals, and endeavors;
- ◦: a relationship of trust and respect, facilitating professional and personal growth, emphasizing wisdom, firing passion, vision, coaching, mutuality, fun, caring challenge, and rigor; and
- ◦: a process by which a mentor's hindsight becomes a mentee's foresight.

Thus, based on this initial round of interactive dialogue, forum participants appeared to view quality mentorship as centred in active, healthy, productive relationships.

This finding corresponded with definitional and descriptive reports in the literature on mentorship. For instance, Hunter (2002) depicted mentorship as a "learning relationship" (p. viii); and Boston (as cited in Collin, 1988) described mentorship as "a protected relationship" (p. 23) in which learning, experimentation, and growth occurs. Levinson (1978) believed that mentoring was one of the most multi-faceted and developmentally important relationships an individual could have, especially during early adulthood. Forum attendees underscored this notion that "mentoring is principally about relationships between people" (MacCallum & Beltman, 2003, p. 92).

The Mentorship Experience Personalized

Following the definition session, a get-to-know-your-partner activity involved attendees listening to the person sitting next to them and documenting information about his/her mentorship experiences. The roles were then reversed, and the pairs subsequently generated thematic ideas from their personal conversations.

A few attendees made the point that their most nostalgic memories of mentorship originated from a mentor-protégé relationship that had happened naturally. In those experiences, quality mentorship was not the outcome of some pre-arranged, formal assignment. Rather, they explained that such harmonized relationships had evolved because two people, professionally and socially, were brought together "at the right place at the right time." One attendee stated, "Mentorship might not be a person, but a condition that results from chemistry." In turn, this chemistry resulted in the co-production of a mutual learning environment.

Other attendees shared their experiences specifically related to their role as a mentor. One attendee explained how he was stimulated by his protégé's ideas and enthusiasm, making the experience rewarding for him. An attendee described the most gratifying aspect of being a mentor was witnessing his protégé change due to a revolutionary "aha" moment of self-discovery. Another participant said that her most prominent mentoring experience was with a colleague who assumed a similar responsibility and role as she had. This non-hierarchical relationship developed somewhat organically, partially due to a similar style of thinking and to common social and family interests. For her, the mentorship metamorphosed into a friendship. Other attendees described similar "good fit" experiences and referred to them as learning partnerships.

Through their stories, several attendees suggested that mentorship was most effective when it produced synergistic and reciprocal outcomes for both partners. Transformative mentorship experiences were described as those where the mentor and protégé grew from the teaching and learning that occurred. Other attendees believed that personal learning and growth was expedited if the mentoring partnership was punctuated with elements of appreciative processes that acknowledge and utilize the strengths, abilities, accomplishments, and interests of mentor and protégé. A prominent theme that appeared from attendees' stories was that the richness of the developmental experience was dependent on trust, and that a measure of respect permeated the mentor-protégé interactions.

Contextualizing Mentorship

Ralph and Walker (2010) believed that leaders are responsible for adjusting their mentorship style based on the levels of confidence and competence of their protégés. Of the many discussions that occurred during the forum, one such subgroup dialogue was particularly in tune with Ralph and Walker's assertion. Those participants agreed that a core component of quality mentorship was that the mentor needs to assume an adaptive leadership style, contingent upon the contextual needs of the protégé. The career stage, ethnic background, and professional interests of the protégé were deemed to be important contextual considerations that would directly affect the professional focus and social nuances of the response of the mentor. This group postulated that, ideally, one's mentoring style was to complement the culture, age, first language, past experiences, socio-economic status, profession, professional development, and expectations of the protégé.

Although many forum discussants agreed that it was important to be able to differentiate mentoring styles, they at the same time suggested that such a responsibility was a daunting endeavor. A few participants believed that to successfully facilitate a needs-based approach to mentorship, the mentor would have to be privy to a considerable amount of personal information about the protégé, such as his/her interests, talents, life accomplishments, life misfortunes, and family hardships. The extent to which a protégé would divulge this type of personal and often emotionally heavy information would also be contextually based on the level of social comfort pervading the relationship. The sharing of personal details would also be dependent upon the protégé's personality and individual choice to share his/her background information.

Forum attendees identified a number of additional aspects that would complement differentiated mentorship. Participants mentioned that the element of trust must be infused within the mentoring relationship and, if achieved, would take time. That is, ideal learning contexts are sanctioned when a mentor has the capacity to dedicate care and attention to the protégé. As well, in some cultural environments, mentorship may need to incorporate a component of storytelling as a means of professional growth for both partners. Forum contributors commented that success with differentiated mentorship would also be dependent on the protégé's willingness to accept the responsibility for his/her personal growth. In sum, there was a belief that effective mentorship incorporates leadership that is differentiated based on individual needs, but that this adaptive form of mentorship also brings myriad challenges, which mentors and protégés alike must address.

In subsequent sessions throughout the three days, discussion continued regarding adaptive mentorship. A point emphasized was that the environment in which mentorship occurs has a definite influence on the relationship. For example, discussants agreed that mentors would typically be empowered to adapt a learner-focused role if immersed in an organization that valued a variety of mentoring efforts and welcomed transformative learning of its protégées. An organizational culture that was aligned with the concept of adaptive mentorship and professional development would be well positioned in a global economy that valued employee growth and diversity.

By contrast, a few discussion groups described certain organizational environments wherein adapting one's mentorship was difficult. For instance, some attendees from the health professions mentioned high-pressure environments such as a medical triage, in which a mentor /supervisor/manager/preceptor commonly assumes a higher hierarchical status than the protégé. In such life-and-death environments, the protégé's professional development is often characterized by the expectation to follow precise orders and to observe and copy his/her mentor in enacting exact medical procedures. In these and other professional education situations, protégé experiences may be affected by other factors such as the mood of the mentor, the expectations of customers, and the immediate service demands. Attendees also indicated that lack of basic resources, persistent bureaucratic barriers, or difficult/abusive organizational cultures also influence protégé development regardless of the mentor's efforts to adapt his/her leadership style.

Mentorship Considerations and Challenges

In order to promote solid mentorship experiences, forum delegates identified individual and organizational supports that were necessary, such as physical resources (a meeting space, chairs, computers, and email), financial support, and recognition that mentorship is valued. Such endorsements are mandatory despite today's reality of employee and resource cut-backs and increasing demands for personnel to do more with less. A common comment was that in such environments, it is vital that mentorship responsibilities are not merely added to a leader's already burgeoning workload. When mentoring is viewed simply as an extra insignificant task, then mentorship responsibilities become "a counterfeit check-in-the-box" set of procedures, as one attendee described it. Another participant stated, "Merely promoting 'Mentorship Monday' is not an effective approach to mentorship." Another prominent theme emerging from these discussions was that not only do mentors need time to mentor, they also need time to reflect on their mentorship practice and to articulate plans for improving their mentoring capacities. In this vein, one attendee suggested that good mentorship becomes devalued and abused when mentors do not have such time to reflect and implement improvements.

Another point raised by some attendees was that in order to promote authentic mentorship, quality professional development for mentors needs to occur. Participants observed that some organizational leaders often presume that the mentors they assign somehow automatically know how to mentor, how to adapt their leadership skills, and how to deal with mentorship problems. They believed that these assumptions were seldom true and suggested that mentorship programs would be unsuccessful if clear professional development and mentorship training were not included by design.

A further theme that emerged during the forum interactions was that quality professional development must involve effective communication among the partners. The purpose of the mentorship process and its roles must be understood by all concerned. Legal and ethical aspects should be openly discussed, and the provision of genuine support must be seen as an avenue of moral and professional strength that will enhance mentor and protégé confidence. An additional professional support tool that two attendees thought was often overlooked was a provision for written and oral feedback about the mentor given by the protégé. Through such constructive assessment, mentors would be able to recognize their leadership competencies and target areas for continued personal development.

Attendees also identified specific organizational barriers that may prevent rich mentorship experiences from transpiring. One attendee commented that at her current career stage, her focus was on mentoring students; however, the culture of her workplace fostered individualized competition among its employees. This difficulty raised a related question, "How can a mentoring culture co-exist in a system that is inherently competitive?" Also emerging from this mentorship-versus-competition issue was the topic of evaluation or assessment of performance. Mentors are often formally responsible for evaluating the progress and performance of the protégé. When a mentor is required to conduct such assessment, a hierarchical power imbalance within the relationship becomes evident. The danger is that when power-role realities and/or highly competitive undercurrents are present, the mentorship experience may not be transformative for the partners.

During both formal and informal forum discussions, we heard our colleagues express their view that high-quality mentorships are the result of a combination of factors. They provided several examples of this conviction, including the view that effective mentoring partnerships seemed to be dependent on the pre-existence of complementary mentor-protégé personalities. One contributor suggested that harmonious partnerships may be fortified through the use of Myers-Briggs personality workshops. Another person, spotlighting the current *zeitgeist* of globalization within private and public sectors, believed that mentorship aptitudes are becoming highly dependent upon the cultural and ethnic acumen of the mentor. Due to increasing demands for integration in the workplace, mentors also need to be versatile in their ability to work collaboratively with different interest groups such as youth subcultures, community organizations, immigrants, and executives. A third perspective was that, in order to be effective, all mentors need to possess an elevated level of emotional and/or social intelligence and good interpersonal skills. Fourth, quality mentorship relationships were described by some attendees as a subjective entity. For example, a person who may be an ineffective mentor for one protégé might be incredibly effective with another person. Conversationalists further perceived that there are a core set of mentoring proficiencies a mentor needs in order to be effective, but there are aspects of being an effective mentor that are also learnable. One attendee stated, "Mentorship skills can be taught, enhanced, and facilitated, but if the connection to the other person is not in existence, the skills are not sufficient in and of themselves."

World Café Discussions

World Café is commonly understood as a form of social constructionist learning that operates among people who are drawn together because of a similar interest. We adapted this process during a forum session to provide a platform for deepening the conversation. We posted a number of mentorship questions on chart paper on the walls around our meeting room. These questions were generated by delegates during earlier forum sessions. Participants then perused all the questions on the walls and selected one station of interest, each of which quickly attracted members holding similar views. Each group then designated a scribe to write the group's paraphrased ideas on a large paper. After a set amount of time, people changed groups by selecting another station of personal interest. One member of each group was left behind to reiterate for the newly formed group the ideas that were presented by the prior group. The new table group then continued to discuss the given question(s), and the scribe duly noted the additional considerations contributed by the new group.

One of the World Café discussions addressed the question, "How do we recognize organizations that emanate a rich mentorship culture?" Those in this conversation explained that one characteristic of such a culture was that employee success stories are communicated between colleagues and throughout the organization. To assist in the dissemination of such positive information, socialization among employees was deemed valuable. Moreover, a socially affluent environment was valued as assisting in the creation of effective partnerships and/or joint research ventures. An organization that regularly organized staff potlucks was identified as one of many examples on how to promote social/group coherence within an organization. Another important characteristic of a welcoming mentorship culture that was mentioned by Café groups was the presence of leaders committed to nurturing mentorship throughout the organization. Such leaders also seek information from minority groups by asking for their feedback on how to meet their particular needs. As well, mentorship resources must be provided for new people to ensure that they do not feel overwhelmed or isolated in their position; they need to be welcomed and provided with the resources required to be productive. The Café groups also wrote that in a mentoring culture, people are able to transcend individual competition structures and openly ask for help when needed. Moreover, the groups mentioned that implementing an external audit or other assessment mechanism may help an organization create or improve its focus on mentorship. In sum, the World Café participants believed that an organization is fortified when it uses the concept of mentorship to foster the benefits commonly attributed to socially right communities.

Another World Café question that delegates addressed was, "What is the role of power in mentoring relationships?" Attendees explained that role power may be synonymous with influential power, in that both are represented through a person's position, status, experience, wisdom, knowledge, skill, gender, culture, and race. Attendees reiterated that with great power comes great responsibility, and, in order for mentors to effectively use this influence, they need to possess self-awareness and humility so as not to intimidate or abuse the protégé during the mentorship experience. On a positive note, attendees indicated that mentors possessing greater influence may be beneficial for a protégé because such leaders also typically possess a large amount of social capital, which may assist in helping position the protégé within a network of professional contacts that may further enable the protégé's future career development and employment opportunities.

A further topic explored during the World Café discussions was a philosophical question regarding mentorship and trust: "How do we build trust in a mentoring relationship, and why is it important?" Participants said that trust in a relationship is enhanced if both parties possessed shared values related to such elements as work ethic, religion, culture, or family values. They described trust in a relationship as a journey along a continuum from tentativeness to confidence between the partners. Creating trust within a relationship requires the determination from both partners to form a positive, respectful relationship. Trust also requires that both persons be open-minded to each other's differences and be committed to lifelong learning. Café groups also suggested that trust contains an element of risk, a fear of the unknown, and a certain level of discomfort. Trust is built upon knowing the ground rules delineating the specific entities that are to be within the scope of the relationship and those items meant to stay outside of the relationship. Interdependence upon each other is a form of trust, and it involves the recognition and exploration of each other's talents and skills. A note of caution raised by one Café group was that a mentoring relationship, which is infused with trust, is fragile. They reported that trust takes a long time to build but only minutes to destroy.

Promising Ideas for Innovation in Mentorship

In an effort to improve and advance mentorship across the professions, forum attendees provided a number of innovative suggestions. One person stated that mentorship is frequently epitomized by a traditional dyad model with one mentor and one protégé. In this conventional situation, an older and more experienced person often advises, supports, and encourages a younger or less experienced individual; in this dichotomous relationship, there is a knower and non-knower, a power figure and a follower. As an alternative to this traditional model, one attendee called for a greater focus on triad relationships that include a senior mentor, a junior mentor, and a protégé. Here, not only does the protégé have opportunities to learn from two mentors, the junior or neophyte mentor is also mentored by the senior mentor. An effective triad mentorship also requires the seasoned mentor(s) to be open to the idea of being protégés and growing from the relationship experience. Another consideration for enriching the potential resulting from triad mentorships is that the junior and senior mentors would typically have more of an interdisciplinary focus. Such mentorship opportunities would exemplify a mini learning community focusing on the growth and development of all three parties in the mentorship environment.

Improvements to the traditional dyad model of mentorship may also incorporate a triangulated version of mentorship in which protégé development is reinforced by a variety of supports and academic inputs. Triangulated mentorship may or may not incorporate three-way mentorship; however, triangulated mentorship would welcome a *network* of mentors and mentees to be interconnected during the mentorship experience. Triangulated mentorship is a type of group mentorship, where a single dominant leader does not direct the mentorship experience. Triangulated mentorship may or may not incorporate mentor and protégé connections with outside organizations; it ideally situates the protégé within a web of peer mentorship opportunities, where peers provide support and growth for each other. This mentorship network is highly suited for "decolonized" organizations or societies, and it would foster differentiated learning while honoring the power of learning communities.

Attendees also identified mixing technology and face-to-face aspects when creating relevant mentor protégé partnerships. For example, mentors and protégés could create professional profiles that would then be electronically accessible to both parties. This information would assist organizers to generate ideal matches for mentorship programs. In some existing programs, protégés self-select their mentors based on similar interests, while, in others, a central office independently assigns protégés to mentors. These days, such an idea may be enabled through combining mentor and mentee. Some attendees believed that mentorship screening through the use of e-portrait technology would assist in creating positive mentorship experiences where the expectations and needs of the protégés are revealed before the start of the program, thus possibly side-stepping compatibility issues before they arise. Another attendee agreed, saying that forced mentorships are often ineffective, and that a process involving the matching of mentor-mentee profiles and providing an element of choice would be worthwhile.

A further form of e-mentoring using chat rooms was identified, in which mentor and protégé could access personal support among from peers. Such support could be in the form of testimonials or discussions pertaining to personal issues or difficulties encountered during the mentorship. A key advantage of e-mentoring described by attendees was that it is a convenient, flexible, and individualized process.

Concluding Questions to Ponder

At the close of the forum, one attendee stated, "A personal victory I take from this forum is that before yesterday I thought almost nothing at all about mentorship." We were pleased that the *Forum on Mentorship in the Professions* proved to be a dynamic event. The forum raised as many questions as it might have answered for persons attending. Though limited by time, the forum did provide an opportunity for a diverse set of participants to contemplate the concept of mentorship and articulate their ideas and personal experiences pertaining to it. The forum also offered a safe medium for posing questions and exploring various facets of the philosophy, principles, and practices of mentorship, some of which need further consideration and attention.

There are many lingering questions: How is mentoring different from instructing, coaching, teaching, indoctrination, and supervision? Is the purpose of mentorship different than the purpose of education? How is mentorship like a marriage? Does everyone need a mentor? Should everyone in an organization be a mentor? How can mentorship be sanctioned through a holistic approach to professional growth?

How does an individual balance his/her mentorship responses to address the academic, physical, emotional, and spiritual well-being of the protégé? Do mentorship experiences need to consider aspects associated with the matching of baby-boomer mentors and millennial protégés? If cyber-mentoring is to be fully embraced, what aspects of online mentoring need further consideration?

How can one gracefully exit a workplace mentorship that isn't working? How can one manage in a short-term mentorship that isn't working? How do mentors look after themselves when they have been working diligently and feel the mentorship has been a failure? How do we build confidence in a new mentor? How will these deliberations and questions lead to an action plan in promoting effective mentorship across the professions?

We hope that further and ongoing conversations will begin to address these questions.

References

Collin, A. (1988). Mentoring. *Industrial and Commercial Training, 20*(2), 23–27.

Hunter, M. A. (2002). *Getting connected: Making your mentorship work.* Sydney, NSW: Australia Council for the Arts.

Levinson, D. (1978). *The seasons of a man's life.* New York, NY: Alfred Knopf.

MacCallum, J., & Beltman, S. (2003). Bridges and barriers in Australia's youth mentoring programs. In F. L. Kochan & J. T. Pascarelli (Eds.), *Global perspectives on mentoring: Transforming contexts, communities, and cultures* (pp. 73–103). Greenwich, CT: Information Age.

Ralph, E., & Walker, K. (2010). Enhancing mentors' effectiveness: A promising model. *McGill Journal of Education, 45*(2), 205–218.

Chapter Two

Mentorship from a Developmental Perspective

Ellery Pullman

McGINNIS (1985) STATED, "There is no more noble occupation in the world than to assist another human being – to help someone succeed." This assertion represents the essence of mentorship. Several influential works have been fundamental in shaping the field of mentoring scholarship. For instance, Levinson, Darrow, Levinson, Klein & McKee's 1978 examination of the developmental trajectory of forty men provided early insight into the important role that mentors play in an individual's life. Merriman's (1983) review of mentorship in adult development, business, and academic settings illustrated similarities and differences across various conceptualizations of mentorship. Kram's (1985) qualitative research on organizational mentorship also became an important anchor for much of the subsequent research on mentoring.

Given that mentoring experiences exist across a person's lifespan, research has begun to examine how sequential and concurrent mentoring relationships, within and across developmental stages, help shape the personal, social, academic, and professional outcomes for protégés and mentors alike. Mentors and protégés do not function within a vacuum but rather within the context of relationships and how each individual's view of self in turn impacts those mentoring relationships. More work is needed to more clearly understand how such developmental dynamics enhance the potential outcomes of such relationships. In this chapter, my intention is to develop a basic understanding of how these developmental dynamics affect the mentoring relationship. I believe that the background information I share here will provide essential foundational knowledge for individuals in mentorship roles, which in turn may serve to enrich their holistic understanding of their protégés' attitudes and ways of thinking.

Mentorship from a Developmental Psychology Perspective

Theoretical perspectives dealing with college student development generally fall into several broad categories – namely, *psychosocial*, *cognitive-structural*, and *typological* models. Common to each of these theories is the assumption that individuals face unique challenges at each stage of development in their lives, and that they can draw on various social resources to help them successfully overcome these developmental challenges.

A developmental theory or perspective not only attempts to describe and explain changes in behavior as people develop, it also attempts to show the uniqueness of the process from one stage of development to another. Developmental theory also takes into consideration that differences exist in terms of gender, race, and place/status in society and that at various times, development is cyclical as well linear in nature. Although an individual may progress to more advanced stages of development, there will be times when he/she may revisit an earlier theme of development as new challenges and opportunities are encountered.

Psychosocial Theory

Psychosocial theories address developmental issues or tasks and events that occur throughout one's life. These tasks and events tend to occur in a sequential manner and are correlated with chronological age. Psychosocial theory represents human development as an outcome of the interaction of individual needs and abilities with the societal expectations and demands that affect the individual.

Erikson's Theory of Psychosocial Development

An influential theory for understanding lifespan development was developed by Erik Erikson, who described human development as unfolding over eight stages: the first five spanning infancy, childhood, and adolescence; and the last three relating to adulthood. In an attempt to address the emergent changes in society and how they impact human development, Erikson's original work has been expanded to eleven stages. The most notable change was the addition of an "Emerging adult" stage (ages 18 to 24 years) as well as the addition of a revised perspective on "very old age" (75 years of age until death).

Erikson (1982) identified a series of issues or psychosocial crises that must be encountered and resolved if the person is to develop in a healthy manner. A developmental crisis arises when one must make adjustments to the demands and expectations of one's environment at each stage of development. Adjustment might call for the acquisition of new information, the development of a new skill, or the refinement of personal goals. The word *crisis* in this context refers to a normal process of understanding and adjusting to a new set of expectations rather than to an extraordinary event in one's life. Each developmental encounter may result in a positive or negative outcome. In keeping with the purpose of this chapter, I describe the last five stages in Table 1.

Emerging Adulthood

Social scientists have observed that the late teens and early twenties form a period of transition into adulthood characterized by greater exploration of one's preferred future. Arnett (2000) proposed a new theory of development encompassing the ages of 18–25. He argued that this period is neither adolescence nor young adulthood but is theoretically and empirically distinct from both. He postulated that the emerging adult years are often characterized by a growing sensitivity to the process of identity development.

Table 1

Psychosocial Crises in Adulthood as Identified in Erikson's Theory

Life Stage	Age	Psychosocial Crisis
Emerging Adulthood	18–25	Individual identity vs. Identity confusion
Young Adulthood	25–40	Intimacy vs. Isolation
Middle Adulthood	40–65	Generativity vs. Stagnation
Later Adulthood	65–80	Integrity vs. Despair
Very Old Age	80 until death	Immortality vs. Extinction

The concept of individual identity versus role confusion was one of Erikson's most famous concepts, and it was within the stage of adolescence that most of Erikson's research attempted to clarify our understandings of this psychosocial crisis. However, other research has shown that identity achievement is rarely reached by the end of high school (Montemayor, Brown, & Adams, 1985; Waterman, 1982), and that identity development continues through the late teens and twenties and often into adulthood (Pascarella & Terenzini, 1991; Valde, 1996; Whitbourne & Tesch, 1985)

Identity development during that period was considered a cornerstone of the unique individuality of adulthood. With the ever-increasing choices and life roles that face the emerging adult today, with the fact that more emerging adults are living at home longer than ever before, and with their delaying of many decisions related to education, vocation, and marriage, the issue of identity seems to be more important today than ever before. Identity formation among emerging adults tends to involve experimenting with various roles and moving gradually toward making enduring decisions (Arnett, 2000).

One of the most influential interpreters of Erikson's concept of identity development has been James Marcia (1980, 1994, 2002; Peterson, Marcia, & Carpendale, 2004). Marcia classified identity into four statuses: *diffusion, moratorium, foreclosure,* and *achievement.* This system of four categories has become known as the *identity status model.* As shown in Table 2, each of these classifications involves a different combination of exploration and commitment.

Table 2

The Four Identity Statuses of Marcia's Identity Status Model

		The Four Identity Statuses	
		Commitment	
		Yes	No
Exploration	Yes	Achievement	Moratorium
	No	Foreclosure	Diffusion

~: *Identity diffusion* is a status that combines no exploration and no commitment.

~: *Identity moratorium* involves exploration but not commitment. This is a stage of actively trying out different personal, occupational, and ideological possibilities.

~: *Identity foreclosure* is a status experienced by those who have not experimented with a wide range of possibilities but who nevertheless committed themselves to certain choices (i.e., commitment, but no exploration). This status is often the result of strong parental influence.

~: The classification of *identity achievement* represents those who have made definite personal, occupational, and ideological choices. By definition, identity achievement is preceded by a period of moratorium in which exploration takes place. If commitment takes place without exploration, it is considered identity foreclosure rather than identity achievement.

In recent years, the concept of a postmodern identity status has emerged, which is composed of diverse elements that do not always form a unified, consistent self (Schachter, 2005; Schwartz, 2005). From this perspective, a postmodern identity would change across contexts so that people may show a different identity to friends, family, coworkers, and others. It also changes continuously, not only throughout adolescence but also into the young adult years as people continue to add new elements to their identity and discard others.

Chickering's Vectors of College Student Development

According to a well-known college student development theory (Chickering, 1969; Chickering & Reisser, 1993; Evans, Forney, & Guido-Dibrito, 1998), student development occurs sequentially along seven stages or vectors. Chickering's (1969) theory suggested that if the right mix of institutional support exists on college and university campuses, and if students are influenced or impacted by these services, students will be more likely to complete the following tasks during their college experience:

~: developing competence,

~: managing emotions,

~: developing autonomy and moving toward interdependence,

~: establishing an identity,

~: developing mature interpersonal relationships,

~: developing purpose, and

~: developing a greater sense of integrity.

Chickering (1969) proposed that students will progress through the first three vectors simultaneously during the freshmen and sophomore years. Some progression along the first three vectors is a prerequisite for the fourth vector. Students generally progress through the fourth vector during their sophomore and junior years and often at different rates. Development is not simply a maturation process but requires some measure of stimulation through challenge and support. Chickering's theory provided college personnel with useful descriptors of the emotional and psychological transformation that students experience in college (Reisser, 1995; Thomas & Chickering, 1984; White & Hood, 1989). Chickering also addressed the theory of Mattering vs. Marginality (Schlossberg, Lynch, & Chickering, 1989), which posited that if students believe that they matter to someone else, that they are the objects of someone's attention, and that others care about and appreciate them, then they are more likely to persist and to succeed in their assigned tasks. On the other hand, if students do not feel that anyone cares about them or their success, or if they feel ignored by the mainstream and not accepted, then they will feel marginalized, and as a result, be less likely to succeed in their college or university experience.

Young Adulthood

Between the ages of 25 and 40, the psychosocial task of intimacy versus isolation represents a stage when individuals seek to develop close and meaningful relationships with others. If individuals have attained a greater sense of personal identity in the previous stage, they are then able to share themselves with others on a greater personal and interpersonal level. According to Erikson (1963), intimacy is the ability to experience an open, supportive, and caring relationship with another person without fear of losing one's own identity in the process. The negative outcome of this crisis is isolation. People unable or unwilling to share themselves with others will suffer a sense of loneliness and distance and a fragile identity.

Levinson's Theory of Life Structure

Daniel Levinson (1977) sought to trace the course of adult development and suggested that humans' adult lives are divided into eras of approximately 25 years each, beginning at about 17 years of age and ending with the transition to middle adulthood in their early 40s. During the early adult transition, from the ages of 17 to 22 years, an individual must leave behind adolescent life and begin to prepare an adult life structure. During the period from the age of 22 to 28 years, the individual is transitionng to what Levinson referred to as *entering the adult world*. Early adulthood is a time for building the structure of one's life. According to Levinson "the life structure is the pattern or design of life, a meshing of self-in-world" (1977, p. 278). He identified four major tasks of this period:

1. forming a dream and giving it a place in the life structure,
2. forming mentor relationships,
3. forming an occupation, and
4. forming a love relationship, marriage, and family.

The emerging and soon to be young adult would have to understand what it means to be an adult, find work, and create relationships. The mid-life transition in the early 40s age range would have to deal with another set of issues – an awareness of mortality and the realization that certain dreams may not come to fruition.

I contend that mentors who are aware of these stages will be better equipped to understand the backgrounds of the protégés in their charge and consequently be able to work more effectively with them within the mentorship relationship.

Cognitive-Structural Theories

Cognitive-structural theories all tend to address a sequence of meaning-making structures through which the individual perceives, organizes, and reasons about their experiences. The stages identified in the theories tend to be hierarchical, and each successive stage incorporates the functional parts of the preceding stage.

Several cognitive-structural theorists have been influential in helping increase society's understanding of the stages that college students typically pass through. I mention the works of Perry, Kohlberg, and Gilligan, as well as the more recent works of King and Kitchener in this regard.

William Perry's Scheme of Intellectual-Ethical Development

Perry's (1970) model or "scheme" asserts that college students progress in a sequential fashion through four defined stages of intellectual-ethical development.

1. Dualism. They view the world in polar terms.
2. Multiplicity. They begin to see the possibility of several right positions.
3. Relativism. They identify themselves with sources of authority and values.
4. Commitment. They make value choices from among various alternatives and commit themselves to personally owned choices.

According to Perry, the majority of college freshman fit into the *dualism* category. This position carries with it certain attitudes that have considerable impact on students' learning styles. At this stage, students will seize upon structure and organization as supports to help them make sense of their learning. They may become somewhat overwhelmed by expectations that call for more abstract thinking and reasoning.

It is in the students' best interest to move beyond the dualistic stage. Mentors working with students at this stage of development can help them by designing strategies that consciously help them advance to another level, beyond black and white perspectives. These strategies would accommodate the students' developmental stage and entry to the next stage of intellectual development.

A second group identified by Perry consisted of students falling into a broad category he called *multiplicity*. He found that most graduating seniors progressed only to this position during their time in college. A few students reached what Perry referred to as a stage of *relativism* by graduation. In that stage, students understood that knowledge and values depended on context and individual perspectives. Only rarely did students reach the upper level of development. Perry and later King (1978) identified that stage as one of *commitment and relativism*. Characteristically, students at that level made commitments based on personal values.

Perry (1981) concluded that development was recurrent: the discovery and reconstruction of "forms" that characterized the development of college students could also be experienced at later points in their lives.

King And Kitchener's Reflective Judgment Model

Dewey (1938) observed that reflective thinking was called for when people recognized that some problems could not be solved with certainty. Drawing from this observation, King and Kitchener (1994, 2002) chose the term *reflective judgment* to describe the kind of epistemic cognition that included the recognition that real uncertainty exists about some issues. The reflective judgment model described development in reasoning during late adolescence through adulthood.

The conceptual framework for reflective judgment was that of a stage model characterized by seven distinct but developmentally related sets of assumptions about the process of knowing and how it was acquired. The stages were:

~: *Pre-reflective Reasoning* (Stages 1–3). These stages reflect the belief that "knowledge is gained through the word of an authority figure or through firsthand observation, rather than, for example, through the evaluation of evidence (King & Kitchener, 2002, p. 40).

~: *Quasi-Reflective Reasoning* (Stages 4 and 5). These stages recognized

> that knowledge, or more specifically, knowledge claims, contain elements of uncertainty, which [people who hold these assumptions] attribute to missing information or to methods of obtaining the evidence. Although they use evidence, they do not understand how evidence entails a conclusion (especially in light of the acknowledged uncertainty), and thus tend to view judgments as highly idiosyncratic. (King & Kitchener, 2002, p. 40)

~: *Reflective Reasoning* (Stages 6 and 7). Individuals who held these assumptions accepted "that knowledge claims cannot be made with certainty, but [they] are not immobilized by it; rather, [they] make judgments that are 'most reasonable' and about which they are 'relatively certain,' based on their evidence of available data" (King & Kitchener, 2002, p. 40).

Kohlberg's Theory of Moral Development

Although Perry and King and Kitchener recognized the relationship between cognitive development and moral reasoning, they emphasized cognition and learning outcomes. Lawrence Kohlberg, in contrast, focused specifically on moral development, or more specifically on moral reasoning (Kohlberg, 1981). Kohlberg sought to describe the nature and sequence of progressive changes in individuals' reasoning processes when making moral judgments. His primary concern was not with the content of the moral choice but with the modes of reasoning; that is, with the cognitive processes employed whereby moral choices were made.

Kohlberg's theory is a cognitive "stage" theory that identified six stages of moral reasoning grouped into three levels. Each level represented a fundamental shift in the social-moral perspective of the individual. At the first level, the *pre-conventional* level, a person's moral judgments were characterized by a concrete, individual perspective. Within this level, there was an orientation toward avoidance of breaking rules, leading to punishment; obedience for its own sake;

and avoiding the physical consequences of an action to persons and property. There was also the early emergence of moral reciprocity in the form, "You scratch my back and I'll scratch yours." The Golden Rule became, "If someone hits you, you hit them back." Here one would follow the rules only when it was beneficial to someone's immediate interests. What was right was what was fair in the sense of an equal exchange, a deal, or an agreement.

Individuals at the *conventional* level of reasoning, however, had a basic understanding of conventional morality, and they reasoned with an understanding that norms and conventions were necessary to uphold society. They tended to be self-identified with these rules and upheld them consistently, viewing morality as acting in accordance with what society defined as right. This position held the "member of society" perspective in which one was moral by fulfilling the actual duties defining one's social responsibilities within the various contexts where individuals found themselves.

Finally, the *post conventional* level was characterized by reasoning based on principles, using a "prior to society" perspective. Individuals in this stage reasoned based on the principles that undergirded rules and norms but rejected a uniform application of a rule or norm. In essence, this level of moral judgment entailed reasoning rooted in the ethical fairness principles from which moral laws would be devised. Laws were evaluated in terms of their coherence with basic principles of fairness rather than being upheld simply on the basis of their place within an existing social order.

Gilligan's Model of Women's Moral Development

Carol Gilligan (1982) proposed that a morality of care can serve in the place of the morality of justice and rights espoused by Kohlberg. In her view, the morality of caring and responsibility was premised in non-violence, while the morality of justice and rights was based on equality. Another way to look at these differences is to view these two moralities as providing two distinct injunctions: the injunction not to treat others unfairly (justice), and the injunction not to turn away from someone in need (care). She presented these moralities as distinct, although potentially connected.

Further research has suggested, however, that moral reasoning does not follow the distinct gender lines that Gilligan originally suggested. The preponderance of evidence is that both males and females reason based on justice and care. While this gender debate is unsettled, Gilligan's work has contributed to an increased awareness that care is an integral component of moral reasoning.

Other Cognitive-Structural Models

Other cognitive-structural models have also contributed an understanding of the college student/emerging adult and his/her developmental journey. James Fowler (1981, 1996), drawing on the works of Erikson, Piaget, and Kohlberg, developed a model to describe the faith or spiritual development of an individual. Viewing meaning-making as a spiritual endeavor, his model was concerned not with the particular beliefs the individual held but with the process by which the individual took ownership for them. Fowler proposed a series of stages, with each stage more differentiated and complex than the preceding one.

Sharon Daloz Parks (1986, 2000) examined the development of a sense of purpose in life as the development of an understanding faith. According to Parks, faith development proceeded through a series of stages, each shaped and influenced by forms of knowing (cognitive processes), dependence (affective aspects focusing on relationships), and community (social and cultural contexts).

Typological Models

Psychosocial and cognitive-structural theories emphasize the nature and processes of change encountered by an individual, whereas typological theories focus on the relatively stable differences among individuals, and therefore tend to categorize individuals according to these differences. Typological models do not explain how a person changes or what he/she believes, but rather they emphasize individual differences and the characteristics that are distinctive to each person, with the idea that these differences influence development.

Three of the more widely known theorists in this camp were David Kolb (1981), who dealt with learning styles and experiential learning; John Holland (1977), who studied people's vocational preferences, and Katherine Briggs and Isabel Briggs Myers (Myers 1980, Myers & McCaulley, 1985), who delineated various personality types. Other researchers were Howard Gardner (1993), and Daniel Goleman (1995).

All of the above mentioned writers have contributed valuable information and insights with respect to broadening educators' understanding of the process of adult human development. I maintain that being familiar with this body of knowledge would only enhance the effectiveness of personnel working with adolescents or young adults – be they counsellors, teachers, supervisors, managers, ministers, coaches, trainers, instructors, or anyone else in a mentorship role.

No one theory is adequate in and of itself to provide a complete understanding of development at any given stage. However, when viewed from different points of reference, each of these frameworks contributes to understanding the educational, professional, and personal needs and issues of individuals in a protégé role. Being knowledgeable of these developmental perspectives would allow mentors to be more deliberate in their planning and implementation of various mentoring strategies.

The Mentor from a Developmental Perspective

Those mentors who tend to be the most successful are often 10 to 15 years older than their protégés. When viewed from a developmental perspective, this difference would put most mentors in their later young-adult years or into their middle-adult years (approximately 30–45 years of age). From a psychosocial perspective, the psychosocial task of middle adulthood is that of generativity vs. stagnation or self absorption (Erikson, 1963). These years bring with them a new capacity for directing the course of one's life and the lives of others. Generativity implies the desire to attain a sense of sharing, giving, or productivity. Caring about the well-being of future generations and the world in which they live is embodied in the concept of generativity.

Generativity is found in different types of selflessness, which may extend to whatever one might leave behind after passing on and may be operative in virtually any situation in which one is called upon to be responsible for others. McAdams, Diamond, de St. Aubin, and Mansfield (1997) proposed that generativity reflects a combination of needs for agency (expanding and asserting the self) and for communion (merging the self with a larger environment of which the self is a part).

Central to this concept of generativity is the interdependency between the one being cared for and the caregiver, or between the younger generation and the older. The generative adult transmits personal and social values to the new generation, acts as a mentor and model, and sets the stage for continuance of cultural symbols and traditions. Furthermore, developmental benefits are experienced not only by the individuals being guided but also by those engaged in the generative pursuits (Erikson, 1963).

The force counteracting generativity is stagnation. Stagnation suggests a lack of psychological growth, which may take the form of egocentrism or self-indulgence. Stagnation and self-absorption imply caring exclusively for oneself. A sense of emptiness often characterizes such a self-centred life, and that person's abilities are not used to the fullest extent.

In light of the various developmental perspectives addressed in this chapter, the middle adult mentor should see him/herself as being readily equipped to come alongside a younger protégée. Levinson et al. (1978) noted several aspects and responsibilities of the mentoring relationship that the middle adult should feel confident in fulfilling. The mentor may act as a teacher to enhance the protégé's skills and intellectual development. Serving as a sponsor, the mentor may use his/her influence to facilitate the protégé's growth and advancement. The mentor might also serve as a host and guide, welcoming the initiate into a new occupational and social world and acquainting him/her with its values, achievements, and members. Through his/her personal virtues, achievements, and way of living, the mentor may be an exemplar that the protégé can admire and seek to emulate.

The mentor may also provide counsel and moral support in times of stress. The mentor has another crucial function: to support and facilitate the realization of the Dream – that vague and growing sense of purpose and mission of one's life (Levinson et al., 1978,

p. 96). This successful facilitation requires not only the transmission of information but also the care and encouragement of persons. To the extent that mentors are able to accomplish these goals, they will promote their protégés' learning and development. This entire process is reminiscent of Erikson's concept of generativity noted earlier.

In this chapter I have argued that a developmental focus is essential to maximize the benefits of mentorship not only for protégés but for mentors as well. In this light, effective mentorship must be tailored to the appropriate developmental needs of the person in the protégé role. I contend that effective mentorship today also calls for a thorough grounding in skills for processing the deeper concerns of human beings as well as a sound knowledge of oneself. Knowledge of how to mentor adults in leadership skills for managing their lives and for reaching their highest levels of impact within their spheres of influence is also an essential asset to the mentoring process. In conclusion, I believe that one of the key mentoring skills needed to accomplish all of these objectives is for the mentor to be able to adapt one's mentoring responses to appropriately match the existing developmental levels of the protégé(s) with whom he/she is working.

References

Arnett, J. A. (2000). Emerging adulthood: A theory of development from the late teens through the twenties. *American Psychologist, 55*(5), 469–480.

Chickering, A. W. (1969). *Education and identity.* San Francisco, CA: Jossey-Bass.

Chickering, A. W., & Reisser, L. (1993). *Education and identity* (2nd ed.). San Francisco, CA: Jossey-Bass.

Erikson, E. H. (1963). *Childhood and society* (2nd ed.). New York, NY: Norton.

Erikson, E. H. (1982). *The life cycle completed: A review.* New York, NY: Norton.

Evans, N. J., Forney, D. S., & Guido-Dibrito, F. (1998). *Student development in college: Theory, research, and practice.* San Francisco, CA: Jossey-Bass.

Fowler, J. (1981). *Stages of faith: The psychology of human development and the quest for meaning.* New York, NY: Harper Collins.

Fowler, J. (1996). *Faithful change: The personal and public challenges of postmodern life*. Nashville, TN: Abingdon.

Gardner, H. (1993). *Multiple intelligences: The theory and practice*. New York, NY: Basic Books.

Gilligan, C. (1982). *In a different voice*. Cambridge, MA: Harvard University Press.

Goleman, D. (1995). *Emotional intelligence: Why it can matter more than IQ*. New York, NY: Bantam Books.

Hadjioannou, X., Shelton, N. R., Fu, D., & Dhanarattigannon, J. (2007). The road to a doctoral degree: Co-travelers through a perilous passage. *College Student Journal, 41*(1), 160–177.

Holland, J. (1977). *Making vocational choices: A theory of vocational personalities and work environments*. Englewood Cliffs, NJ: Prentice-Hall.

King, P. (1978). William Perry's theory of intellectual and ethical development. In L. Knefelkamp, C. Wildick, & C. Parker (Eds.), *Applyng new developmental findings. New Directions in Student Services* (Vol. 4). San Francisco, CA: Jossey-Bass.

King, P., & Kitchener, K. (1994). *Developing reflective judgment: Understanding and promoting intellectual growth and critical thinking in adolescents and adults*. San Francisco, CA: Jossey-Bass.

King, P., & Kitchener, K. (2002). The reflective judgment model: Twenty years of research on epistemic cognition. In B. Hofer & P. Pintrich (Eds.), *Personal epistemology: The psychology of beliefs about knowledge and knowing* (pp. 37–62). Hillsdale, NJ: Erlbaum.

Kohlberg, L. (1981). *Essays on moral development: Vol. 1. The philosophy of moral development: Moral states and the idea of justice*. New York, NY: Harper Collins.

Kolb, D. (1981). *The Learning Styles Inventory: Technical manual*. Boston: McBer.

Kram, K. E. (1985). *Mentoring at work*. Glenview, IL: Scott Foresman.

Levinson, D. (1977). The mid-life transition: A period in adult psychosocial development. *Psychiatry, 40*(2), 99–112.

Levinson, D. J., Darrow, D., Levinson, M., Klein, E. B., & McKee, B. (1978). *Seasons of a man's life*. New York, NY: Academic Press.

Marcia, J. E. (1980). Identity in adolescence. In J. Adelson (Ed.), *Handbook of adolescent psychology* (pp. 159–187). New York, NY: Wiley.

Marcia, J. E. (1994). The empirical study of ego identity. In H. A. Bosma & L. G. Tobi (Eds.), *Identity and development: An interdisciplinary approach* (pp. 69–80). Thousand Oaks, CA: Sage.

Marcia, J. E. (2002). Identity and psychosocial development in adulthood. *Identity, 2,* 7–28.

McAdams, D., Diamond, A., de St. Aubin, E., & Mansfield, E. (1997). Stories of commitment: The psychosocial construction of generative lives. *Journal of Personality and Social Psychology, 72,* 678–694.

McGinnis, A. L. (1985). *Bringing out the best in people: How to enjoy helping others excel.* Minneapolis, MN: Augsburg Fortress.

Merriam, S. B. (1983). *Themes of adulthood through literature.* New York, NY: Teachers College Press.

Montemayor, R., Bown, B., & Adams, G. (1985). *Changes in identity status and psychological adjustment after leaving home and entering college.* Paper presented at the biennial meeting of the Society for Research in Child Development, Toronto, ON.

Myers, I. (1980). *Introduction to type.* Palo Alto, CA: Consulting Psychologists Press.

Myers, I., & McCaulley, M. (1985). *Manual: A guide to the development and use of the Myers-Briggs Type Indicator.* Palo Alto, CA: Consulting Psychologists Press.

Parks, S. (1986). *The critical years: The young adult search for a faith to live by.* San Francisco, CA: Harper & Row.

Parks, S. (2000). *Big questions, worthy dreams: Mentoring young adults in their search for meaning, purpose, and faith.* San Francisco, CA: Jossey-Bass.

Pascarella, E. T., & Terenzini, P. T. (1991). *How college affects students: Findings and insights from 20 years of research.* San Francisco, CA: Jossey-Bass.

Perry, W. (1970). *Forms of intellectual and ethical development in the college years.* New York, NY: Holt, Rinehart, & Winston.

Perry, W. (1981). Cognitive and ethical growth: The making of meaning. In A. Chickering & Associates (Eds.), *The modern American college: Responding to the new realities of diverse students and a changing society* (pp. 76–116). San Francisco, CA: Jossey-Bass.

Peterson, D., Marcia, J. E., & Carpendale, J. (2004). Identity: Does thinking make it so? In C. Lightfoot, C. Lalonde, & M. Chandler

(Eds.), *Changing conceptions of psychological life* (pp. 113–126). Mahwah, NJ: Erlbaum.

Reisser, L. (1995). Revisiting the seven vectors. *Journal of College Student Development, 36,* 505–511.

Schachter, E. P. (2005). Context and identity formation: A theoretical analysis and a case study. *Journal of Adolescent Research, 20,* 375–395.

Schlossberg, N., Lynch, A., & Chickering, A. (1989). *Improving higher education environments for adults: Responsive programs and services from entry to departure.* San Francisco, CA: Jossey-Bass.

Schwartz, S. J. (2005). A new identity for identity research: Recommendations for expanding and refocusing the identity literature. *Journal of Adolescent Research, 20,* 293–308.

Thomas, R., & Chickering, A. W. (1984). Education and identity revisited. *Journal of College Student Development, 25,* 392–399.

Valde, G. A., (1996). Identity closure: A fifth identity status. *Journal of Genetic Psychology, 157,* 245–254.

Waterman, A. L. (1982). Identity development from adolescence to adulthood: An extension of theory of and a review of research. *Developmental Psychology, 18,* 341–358.

White, D. B., & Hood, A. B. (1989). An assessment of the validity of Chickering's theory of student development. *Journal of College Student Development, 30,* 354–361.

Whitbourne, S. K., & Tesch, S. A. (1985). A comparison of identity and intimacy statuses in college students and alumni. *Developmental Psychology, 21,* 1039–1044.

Chapter Three

Understanding the Mentoring Relationships of Women in Higher Education Administration[*]

Kelly McInnes

IN THIS CHAPTER, AN EXTRACTION from my master's thesis (McInnes, 2010), I compare and contrast my findings with those of Kram (1985, 1988), who is one of the most widely cited authors related to workplace mentoring.

Background

Dougherty, Turban, and Haggard (2007) stated that Kram's work "is probably the most widely cited piece by a mentoring scholar with over 275 citations to date" (p. 142). Research conducted since the publication of her original book has explored such topics as mentoring functions (Jacobi, 1991; Sosik & Lee, 2002), types of mentoring relationships (Chao, Walz, & Garner, 1992; Ragins & Cotton, 1999), mentoring models (Haring, 1997; Wasburn & Crispo, 2006), the benefits of mentoring for protégés (Burke, 1984; Allen, Eby, Poteet, Lentz, & Lima, 2004) and for mentors (Allen, Poteet, & Burroughs, 1997), women and mentoring (Scanlon, 1997; Gibson, 2004), and new mentoring conceptualizations (Higgins & Kram, 2001). However, twenty years later, Chandler and Kram (2005) reported that "to date, multiple definitions of a mentor have been advanced, but researchers in the field have not unconditionally accepted any specific one" (p. 5).

Through my own research, I confirmed that mentorship has several definitions, such as a one-to-one relationship (Kram, 1988), one of a number of development relationships that might also include peers, sponsors, allies, and friends (Higgins, 2007), or as a network

[*] After an academic review process, this chapter was accepted as a "refereed contribution" by the editors.

of virtual relationships between individuals anywhere in the world via e-mentorship (Ensher, Heun, & Blanchard, 2003). Lack of definitional and conceptual clarity has hampered research efforts and rendered research vulnerable to criticism (Jacobi, 1991; Allen & Eby, 2007; Gibb, 1994 as cited in Friday, Friday, & Green, 2004). From a practical standpoint, the lack of clarity has made it difficult to duplicate the benefits attributed to mentoring (Burke, 1984; Allen et al., 2004; Allen, Poteet, & Burroughs, 1997) because the source of the benefit was not clear. In this light, I believed that society's understanding of the concept of mentoring had become so ambiguous that mentoring relationships were either so specific they were virtually non-existent or so vague that every relationship could be construed as mentoring.

In addition to my academic interest in mentoring, I was intrigued by its myths. References to the mythical figure Mentor in Homer's *Odyssey* abounded, and yet two important points had gone largely unnoticed. First, Mentor was actually a woman, Athena. That Mentor embodied both male and female characteristics could be reinterpreted to suggest that features of both genders are necessary for mentoring. Second, Mentor was only one of the disguises Athena wore to provide advice and guidance to Odysseus, Penelope, and Telemachus. This point could suggest that more than one kind of person or relationship is necessary to provide the full range of support that an individual requires over the course of their career.

My research was guided by a simple desire to learn more about mentoring from the perspective of administrative women in higher education who had experienced mentoring relationships. I anticipated the findings of the study would be significant in three ways: to address the lack of definitional and conceptual clarity, to focus on understanding participants' recollected experiences of effective mentorship, and to investigate a population of administrative women in higher education, which had been understudied in mentoring research.

Methodological Overview and Study Design

I conducted my study within a qualitative paradigm that "assumes that social reality is constructed by the participants in it" (Gall, Gall,

& Borg, 2007, p. 32). The methodology I used adapted elements and features from the grounded theory work of Corbin and Strauss (2008), who used the term grounded theory in a general sense to "denote theoretical constructs derived from qualitative analysis of data" (p. 1). While grounded theory was originally conceived as an approach to theory development, Corbin and Strauss suggested that it was also appropriate for "researchers who are interested in thick and rich description, concept analysis, or simply pulling out themes" (p. xi). I thus determined it to be an appropriate theoretical perspective for my study.

I collected the data for my study through focus-group discussions. I designed the focus-group questions according to the Appreciate Inquiry (AI) approach (Cooperrider, & Whitney, n.d.). I recruited 21 women whose role was predominantly administrative in nature (i.e., they either supported the work of academic staff who dealt with students on non-academic matters, or they worked in an administrative function themselves) (Szekeres, 2007, pp. 7–8). I conducted four focus groups over the course of one month: two of which had six participants, one had five participants, and one had four. Each focus group session ran between 60 and 90 minutes. Audio recordings of the focus-group discussions were transcribed to become the data for my study.

Creswell (2007) stated, "data analysis in a qualitative paradigm is inductive and establishes patterns or themes" (p. 37). Creswell recommended a data-analysis spiral to depict how data is analyzed in a qualitative study, which I used to guide the analysis phase of my research. My world view underlying the methodological orientation was best described as constructionist, in which I assumed that individuals constructed knowledge as they tried to make sense of their experiences in the context of conversing with others. As I listened to the voices of the women, I reflected on the original work of Kram (1985). I present the key findings of my study by comparing/contrasting them with Kram's results.

Summary of Findings

Kram (1988) identified mentoring functions as "those aspects of a developmental relationship that enhance both the individual's growth and advancement" (p. 22). The voices of the women in my study reflected the psychosocial and career functions as described by Kram. Agreement amongst scholars with these mentoring functions was evident in the literature (Jacobi, 1991), and my data also reflected these functions. The findings of my study suggested that acquisition of self-knowledge and career-knowledge enhanced both the individual's growth and development; however, this acquisition was not necessarily accomplished in the same ways Kram identified in her study. In summarizing my findings, I first compare/contrast psychosocial functions with the acquisition of self-knowledge and then compare/contrast career functions with the acquisition of career knowledge.

Psychosocial Functions and Acquisition of Self-Knowledge

Kram (1988) defined psychosocial functions as "those aspects of the relationship that enhance a sense of competence, clarity of identity, and effectiveness in a professional role" (p. 22). Activities considered psychosocial functions include role modelling, acceptance and confirmation, counselling, and friendship (p. 23). In my study, acquisition of self-knowledge was reflected in an increased awareness of "who am I" as an individual. Acquisition of self-knowledge included the concepts of reflection, challenge, and tolerance. The voices of the women suggested that an increased emphasis on the intrapersonal perspective might apply to mentorship because participants highlighted the importance of relationships that led to an increased knowledge of themselves.

Role modelling. The women in the study referred to role models; however, most of the persons to whom role modelling was attributed were family or like family to them. One woman acknowledged, "even though we may not be blood relatives there's that kind of genuine closeness so that I think of them like family."

> The first one [relationship that came to mind] is my mother and well that's an obvious relationship. I think hers was a modelling as I was growing up; she was always in the workforce and progressively advancing in her career.

But, they [the individuals] were always sort of the stewards
of my integrity ... they were very good role models that way ...
they taught me to be a risk-taker and to have confidence and
be able to always hold you head up wherever you go.

Kram (1988) stated that "role modeling succeeds because of the
emotional attachment that is formed" (p. 34). The existence of an
emotional attachment may help explain why the comments that related to role models were attributed to family or those like family.
While Kram identified role modelling as an activity within the category of psychosocial functions, other research identified role modelling as a separate function (Burke, 1984; Sosik & Lee, 2002) distinct from other psychosocial functions. My data suggested that role
modelling was a separate function and that it may be more readily
available outside the workplace.

Friendship. Some of the women voiced a desire to maintain
some distinction between friendly relationships with colleagues at
work and friendships with people outside of work. One woman observed that although it was not necessary to have one's best friend
at work, it was necessary to have a best friend at work. The activity
of friendship described by Kram (1988) as "social interaction that
results in mutual liking and understanding and enjoyable informal
exchanges about work and outside work experiences" (p. 38) is consistent with the notion of having a best friend at work.

I don't know I would describe each of these as friends – they're
mentors. I'd like them to be friends, but I suspect they were
here for a particular reason.

The term that keeps popping in my head is best friend. I
guess that's because the relationship that I have with my
best friend is very much like this. But the only thing missing
from that relationship compared to this is that they're not
necessarily giving me career advice, but when I look at the two,
the relationships are the same, it's just the content is different.

The fact that the women spoke of friendships within and outside
of the workplace and made a distinction between these two kinds
of relationships would suggest that there is a difference between the

two and that both are important. Listening to the women speak of best friends outside of the workplace led me to believe that there may be an emotional attachment formed in those relationships that may be similar to the emotional attachment that is formed in role-modelling relationships.

Acceptance and confirmation. Kram (1988) indicated that through acceptance and confirmation, "both individuals derive a sense of self from the positive regard conveyed by the other" (p. 35). Comments by the women suggested that when others recognized talents that they themselves did not acknowledge, they experienced acceptance and confirmation.

Several women described relationships with a person who either provided recognition of a talent or helped them to recognize it for themselves. The talent that was recognized was typically something positive that the individual felt good about, so not only did they receive positive regard, but learning something new about themselves helped them derive a positive sense of self. Peoples' most unique talents are often so much a part of them that they become blind to them, and people often take their own talents and abilities for granted and do not value them. Several women acknowledged that having others acknowledge their abilities contributed to their self-worth, increased their confidence, and sparked personal reflection.

> She saw things in me that I didn't see in me and that was very helpful. Like for instance she once remarked that she thought I was really good at making connections between people and things and ideas, being able to network and put somebody in touch with somebody.

> [He] recognized that I had this business mind and it wasn't something that others could see.

> She often sees what I can't in terms of what my abilities are.

One aspect of acceptance and confirmation that Kram (1988) observed was reciprocity, in which both individuals derived a sense of self. Although my study focused on only the mentee or protégé side of the mentoring relationship, some of the women freely spoke of their experience as mentors.

> One of the experiences I find very rewarding is working with people – younger people and people that are developing their own careers. They're powerful relationships when you get to work with people and sort of serve as their mentor, but you learn so much from those relationships – just as much as you might learn from a powerful mentor that you have.

> When I work with younger individuals, it's amazing how all of the sudden they'll say something and I'll think well how did I miss that one, you know, and I'll have a shift that enables me to grow . . . I know what you mean about when we switch the roles and I remember the first time someone said "well, you're my mentor."

These comments reflected the reciprocity Kram had observed.

Counselling. The counselling function "enables an individual to explore personal concerns that may interfere with a positive sense of self in the organization" (Kram, p. 36). The importance of being able to explore personal concerns that may interfere with self was evident in the appreciation women expressed for others who engaged in this exploration with them. The women spoke of being encouraged to explore opportunities, to decide for themselves what was right for them, and to take some risks.

> They were supportive and not necessarily pushing in one way or another – it's whichever way you wanted – it was more supporting me in whatever decision I wanted to make.

> He taught me about exploring opportunities that might be really far off from where I am right now and to really expand my world.

> What I found was how supportive they were in allowing me to take risks, allowing me to go and maybe try something that

they weren't totally sure was going to be a success or not and allowing me to learn and to experiment.

The discussion amongst the women suggested the importance of retaining control over their career and over the decisions that they made in that regard. The fact that the other person in the relationship was willing to relinquish control so that they could explore and learn together appeared to the women to be a powerful exhibition of trust in them.

Being challenged. One area that Kram (1988) did not identify within the range of psychosocial activities was that of being challenged or pushed. While Kram did acknowledge being given challenging assignments as a career function, what I heard described by women in my study was different. Kram stated that being given challenging assignments, "characterizes effective boss-subordinate relationships. It relates to the immediate work of the department" (p. 31). The comments women made about being challenged or pushed did not relate to success on a particular project or developing a specific skill. Rather, the women identified being challenged to work outside their comfort zone as an important component of them becoming who they were as individuals. Thus, being challenged contributed to their career development because it enhanced their knowledge of self.

> In each case, the relationship was a challenge and I don't mean that in a negative way, but because of the challenges put to me I was able to grow and learn.

> These people all pushed me to be who I am now . . . whether it was good or bad pushing, they still pushed me to my limits.

> This person has pushed me a lot to work outside my comfort zone, to try things that I haven't done before and to be much more reflective about myself and the work that I do.

I have observed an increased emphasis on the intrapersonal perspective in the recent leadership literature. For example, Hatala and Hatala (2005) stated that "the first commandment of life and leadership is to 'know thyself'" (p. 67). Women highlighted the importance of relationships that led to increased knowledge of themselves through reflection, being challenged, and acceptance of their choices. In my opinion, this emphasis on the intrapersonal element was one of the most striking differences between my study and Kram's (1988). The psychosocial functions Kram identified focused on the individual in a professional role in the workplace. Acquisition of self-knowledge shifted attention to the individual in the world, not just in the workplace.

Career Functions and Acquisition of Career Knowledge

Kram (1988) defined career functions as "those aspects of the relationship that enhance learning the ropes and preparing for advancement in the organization" (p. 22). Activities considered career functions included sponsorship, exposure and visibility, coaching, protection, and challenging assignments (p. 23). In my study, acquisition of career knowledge was reflected in the women coming to know and understand "what I do." Acquisition of career knowledge included concepts of deciding on a career path and developing career-specific skills. The significance of these relationships was in what and how the relationship contributed to the individual's career knowledge.

Coaching. Several women described relationships with an individual who had helped them learn the procedures of their profession. The experiences the women described aligned most closely with the activity of coaching that "enhances the junior person's knowledge and understanding of how to navigate effectively in the corporate world" (Kram, 1988, p. 28). Because of the positive nature of the focus-group questions, the women described success as a result of having these relationships as opposed to describing failures resulting from a lack of them.

> Coming into the U from private industry and being mind-boggled by the level of complexity in the organization and really going through the ropes, how you have to do the consultation process, how you have to approach getting something done. So how do you write up a specific document to make a proposal

... and the level of consultation through committees that had to be done and mentoring me through that role of how you do the consultation across the organization, how you prepare submissions was also invaluable.

The relationship was very negative, but this individual was very prominent in her field of work, very intelligent, taught me a lot in regards to business, but very negative relationship.

The voices of the women reinforced the importance of these relationships particularly for individuals who were new to the workforce or the organization.

Challenging assignments. The women also described relationships that seemed to align with the assignment of challenging work. Kram (1988) stated, "the assignment of challenging work, supported with technical training and ongoing performance feedback, enables the junior manager to develop specific competencies and to experience a sense of accomplishment in a professional role" (p. 31). One woman recalled a conversation with an individual about a recent promotion that was not going well. Another woman described a relationship that provided opportunities to develop and in which there was ongoing feedback.

When I started in my new position it was a big jump in terms of what I was doing and all of the sudden you get thrown into a lot of new stuff that you have no idea what to do with. I had three key relationships that tanked and I really began to question why I was doing this and if I should stay doing this. I remember sitting down and talking to her about this and her saying that the reason I was promoted was because she knew I had the confidence to develop that skill set and those relationships. That was a turning point for me.

The person in this relationship was committed to my success, provided plenty of opportunities to develop and there was ongoing feedback and goal-setting. It was very open and honest in that I knew where I stood and what my strengths and weaknesses were.

Through these relationships, the women recognized that it takes time to become proficient in a professional role, and that while they were not fully proficient, they had the potential to be. The conversations with others seemed to give them permission to acknowledge their shortcomings. Once acknowledged, the conversation could then focus on the support required to address the shortcomings and become proficient.

Sponsorship. Women in this study also acknowledged specific opportunities being made available to them. These experiences were aligned with sponsorship that "involves actively nominating an individual for desirable lateral moves and promotions" (Kram, 1988, p. 25). One woman mentioned a particular person who had provided opportunities for her to move up within the organization. She recalled that he did not have to provide these opportunities and that he did not necessarily provide them to others. Another woman recalled the offers she received from a senior executive to work or be trained to work anywhere in the organization. She also recognized that these opportunities were not given to many people. As the women spoke of opportunities that had been provided for them, there seemed to be a sense of wonder that might be summed up as "why me?"

> One [person] in particular provided a number of opportunities to move up within the organization that he didn't necessarily have to do and didn't necessarily do with other people.

> He paid attention to my career and where I was going. He made an offer to work, or be trained to work, wherever I wanted in that company and it was an opportunity not many people are given.

The women recognized that not everyone received these kinds of opportunities, and I observed that they almost felt guilty for being singled out for that kind of attention.

Kram (1988) reported that sponsorship was the most frequently observed career function and that without it individuals would likely be overlooked for promotions (p. 25). I believe that this finding reflected the career context that existed at that time in which career attainment was important (Hall, 1996, p. 4). In contrast, the relationships women in my study described as most powerful in terms of acquisition of career knowledge were ones that acted as a catalyst for a change in their career path.

> I talked about challenge and how each of these individuals have challenged me and this was a very difficult conversation and it was one of those where you pull back the layers and look inside and I didn't know that the barriers were even there and so it was a eureka or aha moment where the learning is being pushed so hard that you're being forced to look deeper than you've ever looked and I think it allowed me to grow professionally.

> I had that conversation when I was 29 or 30 . . . so that is at least five years ago . . . it was a pivotal change for me and it altered how I related to customers in a very concrete way and it's a learning that changed how I work with individuals.

> I think the relationships also contributed to increasing my confidence and my ability to take on new things and the faith that these people demonstrated in me. For each of them, I think I would say were life changing in some way and that's probably why I think of them or why they come to mind.

This finding is consistent with the new-career context described by Hall (1996) as protean. The protean career is shaped more by the individual and may be realigned on occasion to meet the needs of the individual. Although Hall identified this new career context in the late 1970s, due mainly to the economic bust in the 1980s, it was not until 1996 that there was a noticeable shift from the organizational career to the protean career.

Protection and exposure and visibility. What was absent from the comments of the women in my study was any reference to being protected from damaging contact with key people or being assigned responsibilities that would allow relationships with key figures in the organization to develop. Again, the absence of comments in this regard could be interpreted as reflecting the shift in the career context where people are less interested in advancement, therefore less concerned about relationships with senior administrators and more interested in careers that have meaning and produce value (Hall, 1996, p. 5).

Reflections on Findings

The voices of the women in my study reflected alignment with the psychosocial functions and career functions that Kram (1988) attributed to mentoring relationships, particularly in the acquisition of self-knowledge and the acquisition of career-knowledge. This alignment reinforces the observation by Higgins and Kram (2001) that "who provides such support and how such support is provided are now more in question" (p. 267).

The number of people identified by participants as having contributed to their career development suggested to me that mentoring relationships are pervasive. The question is why not all of these relationships are thought of as mentoring relationships. I think there are two reasons, one of which is that individuals believe the myth of Mentor, the wise and trusted advisor that Odysseus left to care for Telemachus. The act of providing advice, support, and encouragement related specifically to career development became synonymous with the figure Mentor. Without a clear definition or conceptualization of mentoring, individuals may continue to define it in terms of the myth. The second reason is that mentoring scholars have not offered a viable alternative to this mythical relationship for individuals to consider.

I offer the following alternative. I see that mentoring relationships are not unique relationships but that they are relationships characterized by those attributes identified both in the mentoring literature and by the views of the women in my study. The question is not whether or not individuals have had mentors, but rather how to recognize with whom they have had or could have mentoring relationships.

In a review of research that has shaped how scholars view mentoring, Eby, Rhodes, and Allen (2007, p. 10) identified five attributes that differentiated mentoring from other types of relationships. The five attributes were that mentoring relationships (1) are unique and are shaped by the individuals in the relationships, (2) focus on acquiring/developing new knowledge or skills, (3) are processes defined by the support provided, (4) are reciprocal, but with benefits to mentor and protégé not necessarily accruing equally, and (5) are changeable over time.

The voices of the women in this study provided confirmation of all of these attributes. Thus, much of what is known about how mentoring is provided remains relevant, but I believe that the question of who provides mentoring needs reconceptualizing to include everyone who has provided advice, support, and encouragement related specifically to an individual's career development. I also believe that this reconceptualization has begun, but as long as people continue to emphasize *mentors* rather than *mentoring relationships*, then it is probable that individuals will continue the untenable search for that one elusive relationship.

Revelations about Mentoring

I had made a conscious decision not to use the phrase "mentoring relationship" with participants in my discussions. Although I did not make any reference to the terms *mentor, mentoring, mentorship*, or *mentoring relationships*, participants often spoke of mentors and mentoring relationships in response to two of my questions. The first instance was at the very beginning of the discussion when they described relationships that had provided advice, support, and encouragement to their career development. My first observation was that the women who spoke specifically of mentoring relationships intuitively defined them in the traditional sense: a dyadic relationship with an individual within the organization who was older and wiser. However, as I proceeded with the analysis of the data, I noticed participants reflecting an intuitive understanding of peers being mentors and a recognition among them of informal relationships being mentoring relationships.

The mentoring relationships described by most of the women who spoke specifically of mentoring appeared to refer to a more traditional definition (an older and wiser guide). As well, the person of whom they spoke was often within the same organization. However, only one woman in this study made specific reference to a formal mentoring relationship, and it had been through a program that was available to her as an undergraduate student in a school of business.

One individual explicitly stated that she had never experienced formal mentoring, but acknowledged that there had been considerable mentoring responses along the way. I interpreted this comment to be reflective of her intuitive understanding of informal mentoring relationships. There were two comments by women that I also believe demonstrated an intuitive understanding of peer mentoring. In one instance, a woman described a relationship with a colleague as a "mutual mentoring relationship." In the second instance, a woman made reference to mentorship from colleagues in a professional association.

I found it interesting that not all of the relationships described by the women were construed as mentoring relationships. For example, not once did any of the women identify a familial relationship as mentoring. In fact, several women lamented the lack of a mentor when they were growing up and speculated on how things might have been different for them had they had one. I also noted that all the relationships identified were in the same context, which was relationships that provided advice, support, and encouragement to their career development. Yet only a subset of all the relationships described in this context were referred to as mentoring.

What was clear, however, from the women's descriptions of their mentoring experiences was the belief that a mentoring relationship was important to career growth. Women who identified a mentoring relationship described it as transformational or life changing. Alternatively, women who could not or did not identify a mentoring relationship believed things might have been quite different for them had they experienced that particular relationship. It is impossible to know whether or not events would have turned out differently if a mentor had been present, but their perception was that it would have. This finding was consistent with an observation made by Kram (1988) that "the popular press has done a disservice by implying that the key to career success is finding a mentor. This is an oversimplification of a complex web of work relationships that could be made available to individuals in organizational settings" (p. 4). Twenty-five years later, I confirmed that there was still a sense that a mentor relationship is an important relationship.

Conclusion

My academic interest in mentoring was complemented by my intrigue in the myth that seemed to lie behind mentoring, Homer's *Odyssey*. The myth continues to interest me, and one of my hopes for the study was some reconciliation of the myth of Mentor with the reality of mentoring. I believe that this hope has begun to be realized. I have reconciled the myth with the reality as follows: Athena was everything to everyone, she embodied many personas, and she could do that because she was a goddess. However, we are human beings and it is a rare human being who could be everything to everyone. Each individual must therefore look to many people to provide the advice, support, and encouragement that will contribute to his/her career development and growth. Interpreting relationships this way can help align reality with the myth.

In terms of providing conceptual clarity, I believe that my study honored and extended the original work of Kram (1988) and other mentoring scholars by helping to broaden the conceptualization of mentoring relationships to be more inclusive. I also believe that this broadened conceptualization honors the voices of the women who participated in this study. Several women spoke of a journey. One comment, in particular, captured this notion: "a career is a journey of learning and self-discovery." What I now understand is that mentoring relationships are not embodied in a single person or relationship as personified by Mentor, but mentorship encompasses all of the persons and their relationships, who, like Athena, journey with us in learning and self-discovery.

References

Allen, T. D., & Eby, L. T. (2007). Overview and introduction. In T. D. Allen & L. T. Eby (Eds.), *The Blackwell handbook of mentoring: A multiple perspectives approach* (pp. 139–158). Malden, MA: Blackwell.

Allen, T. D., Eby, L. T., Poteet, M. L., Lentz, E., & Lima, L. (2004). Career benefits associated with mentoring for protégés: A meta-analysis. *Journal of Applied Psychology, 89*(1), 127–136.

Allen, T. D., Poteet, M. L., & Burroughs, S. M. (1997). The mentor's perspective: A qualitative inquiry and future research agenda. *Journal of Vocational Behavior, 51,* 70–89.

Burke, R. J. (1984). Mentors in organizations. *Group & Organization Studies, 9* (3), 353–372.

Chandler, D. E., & Kram, K. E. (2005). Applying an adult development perspective to developmental networks. *Career Development International, 10*(6/7), 548–566.

Chao, G. T., Walz, P. M., & Gardner, P. D. (1992). Formal and informal mentorships: A comparison on mentoring functions and contrast with non-mentored counterparts. *Personnel Psychology, 45,* 619–636.

Cooperrider, D. L., & Whitney, D. (n.d.). *A positive revolution in change: Appreciative inquiry.* Retrieved from http://appreciativeinquiry.case.edu/uploads/whatisai.pdf

Corbin J., & Strauss, A. (2008). *Basics of qualitative research: Techniques and procedures for developing grounded theory* (3rd ed.). Thousand Oaks, CA: Sage.

Creswell, J. W. (2007). *Qualitative inquiry and research design: Choosing among five approaches* (2nd ed.). Thousand Oaks, CA: Sage.

Dougherty, T. W., Turban, D. B., & Haggard, D. L. (2007). Naturally occurring mentoring relationships involving workplace employees. In T. D. Allen & L. T. Eby (Eds.), *The Blackwell handbook of mentoring: A multiple perspectives approach* (pp. 139–158). Malden, MA: Blackwell.

Eby, L. T., Rhodes, J. E., & Allen, T. D. (2007). Definition and evolution of mentoring. In T. D. Allen & L. T. Eby (Eds.), *The*

Blackwell handbook of mentoring: A multiple perspectives approach (pp. 7–20). Malden, MA: Blackwell.

Ensher, E. A., Heun, C, & Blanchard, A. (2003). Online mentoring and computer-mediated communication: New directions in research. *Journal of Vocational Behavior, 63,* 264–288.

Friday, E., Friday, S. S., & Green, A. L. (2004). A reconceptualization of mentoring and sponsoring. *Management Decision, 42*(5), 628–644.

Gall, M. D., Gall, J. P., & Borg, W. R. (2007). *Educational research: An introduction* (8th ed.). Boston, MA: Pearson Education.

Gibson, S. K. (2004). Being mentored: The experiences of women faculty. *Journal of Career Development, 30*(1), 173–188.

Hall, D. T. (1996). Long live the career: A relational approach. In D. T. Hall & Associates (Eds.), *The career is dead, long live the career: A relational approach to careers* (pp. 1–14). San Francisco, CA: Jossey-Bass.

Haring, M. J. (1997). Networking mentoring as a preferred model for guiding programs for underrepresented students. In H. T. Frierson, Jr. (Ed.), *Diversity in higher education* (pp. 63–76). Greenwich, CT: JAI Press.

Hatala, R. J., & Hatala, L. M. (2005). *Integrative leadership: Building a foundation for personal, interpersonal and organizational success.* Calgary, AB: Integrative Leadership Institute.

Higgins, M. C. (2007). A contingency perspective on developmental networks. In J. E. Dutton & B. R. Ragins (Eds.), *Exploring positive relationships at work: Building a theoretical and research foundation* (pp. 207–224). New York, NY: Lawrence Erlbaum Associates.

Higgins, M. C., & Kram, K. E. (2001). Reconceptualizing mentoring at work: A developmental perspective. *Academy of Management Review, 26*(2), 264–288.

Jacobi, M. (1991). Mentoring and undergraduate academic success: A literature review. *Review of Educational Research, 61*(4), 505–532.

Kram, K. E. (1985). *Mentoring at work: Developmental relationships in organizational life.* Gelnview, IL: Scott Foresman.

Kram, K. E. (1988). *Mentoring at work.* Lanham, MD: University Press of America.

McInnes, K. (2010). *Understanding the mentoring relationships of women in higher education administration* (Unpublished master's thesis). University of Saskatchewan, Saskatoon.

Ragins, B. R., & Cotton, J. L. (1999). Mentor functions and outcomes: A comparison of men and women in formal and informal mentoring relationships. *Journal of Applied Psychology, 84*(4), 529–550.

Scanlon, K. C. (1997). Mentoring women administrators: Breaking through the glass ceiling. *Initiatives, 58*(2), 39–59.

Sosik, J. J., & Lee, D. L. (2002). Mentoring in organizations: A social judgment perspective for developing tomorrow's leaders. *Journal of Leadership & Organizational Studies, 8*(4), 17–32.

Szekeres, J. (2004). The invisible workers. *Journal of Higher Education Policy and Management, 26*(1), 7–22.

Wasburn, M. H., & Crispo, A. W. (2006). Strategic collaboration: Developing a more effective mentoring model. *Review of Business, 27*(1), 18–25.

Chapter Four

Mentoring In Rural Emergency Departments: Challenges and Opportunities

Dal Lynds & Sarel J. van der Walt

EMERGENCY DEPARTMENTS IN RURAL HOSPITALS face unique challenges and offer innovative opportunities in terms of the mentorship of professionals and students in the health sciences. The expectation of rural health facilities to participate in distributive-learning programs with universities has led to an increased demand for mentors in rural health systems. Mentorship in health care has historically been limited to the academic hospital environment, where faculty members formally supervise students in clinical training settings. Many rural health facilities have been required to accommodate students and residents in the health sciences without being adequately prepared for mentorship responsibilities. The renewed focus on mentorship for student and resident training in rural areas has also highlighted the potential impact that mentorship can have on continuous quality-improvement approaches in these settings. In this chapter we examine the unique challenges, opportunities, and recommendations regarding the mentorship process in rural emergency departments.

The Rural Mentoring Environment

Each rural health facility is characterized by unique strengths and limitations in terms of its ability to deliver quality mentorship. Challenges in rural emergency departments include the different roles that health professionals must fulfill while delivering the mentorship program, including being assessors, role models, employers, coaches, or sponsors. Adequate time is also required for a meaningful mentoring relationship to develop between mentor and protégé. Visiting students and residents rarely have sufficient time to establish a strong relationship with their mentors during a typical clinical training rotation. Additional barriers to successful mentorship in most rural health facilities include: the lack of incentives for health professionals to volunteer for mentorship, the broad scope of practice that characterizes rural health care, the interdisciplinary environment of the emergency department, and the lack of a structured mentorship program.

Potential benefits of encouraging and implementing mentorship in the rural emergency department include: the increased awareness of continuous quality improvement and education, the existence of recognized behavior modelling and good bedside skills in a personal and secure environment, the wide scope of practice and exposure to a range of situations, and exposure to the unique setting of rural health care. We believe that, rather than adding to the workload of overstretched rural health facilities, mentorship could be seen as a valuable process through which all participants involved could benefit.

Challenges to the implementation of mentorship in rural emergency departments are related to the mentoring process itself, the challenge of appropriately matching mentors and protégés, and the health system within which it occurs. Previous research on mentorship has suggested that personality characteristics play an important part in the success of a mentoring relationship (Okereke, 2000). In a small rural emergency department, provisions for freely choosing mentors, for easily changing or discontinuing mentorship relationships, and for suitably matching mentors according to protégés' learning needs are not always possible. Therefore, we believe that a well-structured mentoring program with specific goals, expectations, exit strategies, and troubleshooting strategies will create the environment in which effective mentorship could take place. The different styles of mentoring and the various influences affecting the mentorship dynamics all help explain the unique challenges to successful mentorship that arise in the rural emergency room (ER).

Facilitating Mentoring in the Rural ER

The rural ER is a fast-paced environment that poses unique learning challenges to mentors and protégés alike. The demographic features of rural ER health workers, the ER culture, and the accepted standards of professional conduct are potential sources of conflict that can inhibit the mentorship of specific groups of protégés. However, as is the case with all mentorship situations, responding to protégés' professional needs will ensure a satisfying and productive mentoring experience for both partners in the relationship (Coates et al., 2004; Garmel, 2004; Okereke, 2000).

Research suggested that female protégées and foreign-trained graduates have the highest risk of describing their mentoring experience in negative terms (Coates et al., 2004; Garmel, 2004; Okereke, 2000). Women tend to have more positive mentoring outcomes when mentored in a group and when being able to have a female liaison as part of the mentorship process. Creating a mentoring program that would enable female students to freely associate with mentors of a similar demographic background or that would facilitate group mentorship would stimulate productive and satisfying mentoring experiences. However, the limited resources and lower numbers of health workers in rural environments would tend to restrict the free association between mentor and protégé based on these demographics and would limit participation in group mentorship programs.

In addition, international medical graduates who enter the Canadian health system are often expected to participate in a mentorship program to facilitate their adaptation to and integration into Canada's context. Many of these international medical and nursing graduates start working in the rural facilities, but the mentorship process available in these settings is hampered by challenges such as differing communication styles, difficult language barriers, contrasting concepts of professional conduct and patient interactions, and opposing cultural habits and expectations. International medical graduates have a higher likelihood of having a negative mentorship experience if there is inadequate facilitation of their specific mentoring needs (Garmel, 2004).

Pairing international graduates with health professionals from the same demographic and cultural background could have a positive impact on their mentorship experience. The rural ER could be an effective entry point for internationally trained mentees to be exposed to Canadian health care procedures. One of strengths of the rural health system is the existing wide array of health workers from different demographic and cultural backgrounds. The unique mentorship relationships that could develop between mentors and protégés from the same culture and heritage would facilitate adjustment and integration of newcomers on a level that would not be possible in settings where minimal appreciation of cultural differences existed. The influence of shared culture and demographics on mentorship dynamics and outcomes in the rural ER deserves further inquiry to guide integration of internationally trained health workers.

Mentoring Dynamics in the Rural Environment

The multidisciplinary nature of the emergency department provides a unique mentorship environment. Often health care students or residents will interact with health workers from a variety of disciplines, and informal mentoring relationships will be established. The informal sharing of practical wisdom in the rural emergency department will allow students to encounter different perspectives and acquire additional knowledge and skills within a multidisciplinary setting. We believe that conventional, single-discipline structures should be expanded to include formal interdisciplinary mentoring relationships, and that formal mentoring programs should be arranged to facilitate interdisciplinary interaction between mentors and protégés across the health disciplines. Being aware of different types of mentoring should remind protégés and mentors of their varying roles and responsibilities (e.g., mentorship, preceptorship, coaching, supervision, teaching, assessing, or offering friendship).

Rural emergency departments' ability to facilitate effective mentorship has also been restricted by a lack of resources, insufficient time for one-on-one mentoring, a limited range of emergency medicine procedures, a low number of available patients (with a resulting reduced range of medical conditions), a narrower range of personnel with specialized knowledge and expertise, and a decreased number of health care professionals available to assume mentorship duties. Four potential solutions to these challenges that could be established throughout a rural health region would be (1) to focus on involving as many rural hospitals as possible to decrease the mentor-protégé ratio by involving more rural ER physicians, (2) to coordinate student and resident rotations among several emergency departments according to each jurisdiction's ability to facilitate protégés based on staffing and workload considerations, (3) to facilitate group mentorship sessions in order to balance each hospital's mentoring workload, and (4) to create an environment where participants could share experiences and peers would be encouraged to support one another.

As mentioned, the interdisciplinary work environment and high degree of health-worker interaction in a rural emergency department has the potential to enhance mentoring. However, a negative consequence of this interdisciplinary contact in the ER would be the uncertainty among ER personnel regarding the varied mentorship needs of different protégés. To mentor effectively, the ER staff would also need to understand how to discern the developmental and educational needs of the wide array of trainees. Emergency medicine reflects a chain of care that requires excellent interdisciplinary collaboration and communication to ensure success. Being aware of the scope of practice as well as the strengths, limitations, and the personal characteristics of emergency health care colleagues will allow ER personnel to respond appropriately to each link in this emergency medicine chain of care. Involving all disciplines in the mentorship and training process would strengthen the chain of care. Clear delineation of roles and responsibilities of the mentorship partners would be a prerequisite for interdisciplinary mentoring.

Ideally, mentoring relationships would be established through free association in a secure environment with an infinite amount of time and resources; obviously this is impossible. However, we believe that a mentorship program could be developed to help simulate these conditions. One way to accomplish this goal would be to encourage a passionate interest in mentoring among a core group of committed mentors. Commitment to the mentorship process is essential for the relationship to be productive. In our view, one cannot mandate mentorship among health workers because the intimate interpersonal interactions necessary for successful mentoring require honest commitment and passion about the educational process. Involving and supporting committed volunteers in a mentorship program will begin to create a mentoring culture in which interested, enthusiastic, and passionate health professionals participate. As a consequence, we envisage not only an increased likelihood of student competence and satisfaction, but a subsequent increase in the program's appeal and popularity among other health care workers in the field

With respect to the protégé side of the mentoring relationship, it is obvious that protégés must be willing participants in the process. Yet, if they are uncomfortable with the mentoring relationship they are in, if they feel they are a burden, or if they feel intimidated about asking questions or seeking help, then their learning will be stifled and patient care could be jeopardized. We recognize that some of these constraints may be due to the personality characteristics of the protégé and mentor, which may not be changeable. However, what is possible to change is the design and context of the entire mentorship program to facilitate effective learning. In such a program the roles and responsibilities of protégés and mentors must be clearly de- lineated, with the mentor's main goals being: to provide the protégé with ongoing and adequate feedback on his/her progress, to appro- priately guide him/her to assume increased degrees of responsibility, and to allow him/her to deal with conflicts and tensions that emerge in the real world of practice. These areas will be the source of the learner's professional and personal development.

The mentorship relationship in health care is unique in the sense that it develops from a shared commitment to education and profes- sional development, it is facilitated by organizations such as hos- pitals or medical universities, and its methods are rooted in inter- personal interactions that may result in system-wide change. Both the protégé and mentor are aware of the expectations that regulate their interactions and the standards that determine whether their relationship is deemed successful and constructive. The primary methods through which the mentorship interactions take place is basically through sharing knowledge, demonstrating and practicing skills, and providing feedback on protégé performance.

Giving and receiving feedback appears to be a negative or stress- ful experience for protégés and mentors alike (Marco & Perina, 2004; Okereke, 2000; Yeung, Nuth, & Stiell, 2010). Mentors may fear that they will be challenged or disliked by protégés, that their own weaknesses or lack of expertise will be exposed, or that they will be judged negatively. Incorporating an honest discussion about medical error and awareness of human limitations should help es- tablish a productive mentoring relationship. Both partners being open to constructive feedback and being aware of the content and method of communicating feedback should be part of the preparation for entering a mentoring relationship. Encouraging constructive feedback will limit the perceived threat of failure for both the mentor and protégé.

The effectiveness of rural emergency departments is shaped by their ability to face up to complex challenges, to deal constructively with failure, and to strengthen the system by reducing or eliminating weaknesses. This environment of sharing and open discussion should also influence the mentorship partners to view experience and growth as being the result of confronting identified limitations and committing to improve weak areas. The mentor should be able to guide the protégé through this confrontation of his/her limitations and to model a commitment to self-improvement, moral integrity, and loyalty to professional standards of care.

Health System Challenges

The emergency department has served as a training ground for many health professionals including physicians, nurses, and paramedical professionals. Historically, facilities that accommodated student and resident training have been connected to tertiary hospitals and larger universities; however, the increasing reliance on rural hospitals to play a role in this training has identified the inadequacy of existing mentorship and support systems in rural health districts. Therefore, addressing these organizational factors that negatively impact mentorship in rural emergency department will increase the likelihood of improving the professional preparation of new practitioners.

The lack of incentives for health care providers to undertake mentorship duties has been highlighted as an important health-system failure (Marco & Perina, 2004). Time and resource constraints often inhibit health professionals from volunteering as mentors. Students and residents are often well aware of the stressful environment and heavy workload in the ER and are consequently reluctant to approach seemingly overburdened mentors. Some institutions have attempted to increase incentives for mentors by giving academic credits and other forms of official acknowledgement (Yeung, Nuth, & Stiell, 2010).

Because most health professionals in rural emergency departments are not connected with academic institutions, their potential encouragement in the form of official acknowledgement may rather need to focus on continuous medical-education recognition. Innovative incentives that could encourage personnel to volunteer for mentorship might include earning credit for rural health facilities, which in turn could be accumulated and submitted for rewards such as funding for equipment and facility improvements. Future research on mentorship programming should focus on identifying the most effective incentives to encourage rural health care workers to volunteer.

We assert that such commitments by rural health districts to reward mentors for their work will benefit all stakeholders. By contrast, within the urban emergency departments close to university academic venues, most health professionals accept the responsibility of being involved in student and resident education as part of their job description. The challenges of the rural environment have negatively impacted the ability to attract and retain skilled health professionals in rural emergency departments. Most health professionals working in rural or remote environments have a strong sense of responsibility, hold high professional standards, and are already involved in training and informal mentoring on a daily basis. Furthermore, to add increased formal mentorship responsibilities on top of their high-pressure workload seems questionable. However, possible compensation for mentors in these over-stressed systems could include such initiatives as: offering financial rewards, building in specific time periods during the work day for mentorship activities, or reducing workloads for those who are involved in mentorship. Yet, our experience has shown that the health professionals committed to the mentorship process in rural emergency departments, more often than not, are individuals who are overworked but passionate about sharing their knowledge with neophyte colleagues, and who in many cases have little interest in compensation.

With regard to current conditions in rural emergency departments, the first introduction between mentor and protégé occurs at the beginning of an ER shift, with little time for the pre-establishment of any foundational preparation for meaningful mentoring. However, we feel that a formally structured mentorship program would have arrangements in place to allow prospective students to pre-select their mentor, to communicate their expectations ahead of time, and to have reviewed the procedures surrounding the mentorship process. These planned mentoring programs would include specific guidelines regarding the elements of communication, the pair-matching process, the education and training expectations, the troubleshooting mechanism, the exit strategies, the monitoring and evaluation procedures, and the methods for ensuring continuity.

In our view, such mentorship programs would reflect the characteristics of successful mentoring practices such as giving/receiving feedback, catering to minority groups, ensuring confidentiality, and facilitating free movement between/among units. The traditional mentoring approaches that previously characterized academic institutions will need to be adapted to the unique environment of rural emergency departments. Care would be needed to restructure these new mentorship programs to become more dynamic and responsive by promoting more free association, greater confidentiality and security, and increased collaboration and sharing of ideas among participants. We suggest that such modifications will enhance the receptivity of the program among personnel and thus stimulate their motivation to participate.

Mentorship and Continuous Quality Improvement

We think that if health care systems would support the mentorship enterprise in the ways we have described, then these efforts will also translate into increased emphasis on continuous quality improvement in rural emergency departments. Currently, rural health care facilities may be at risk for becoming complacent regarding maintaining the standard of health care because of their distance from tertiary health care centres and their often unique set of dynamics connected to rural or remote environments. We have observed that when rural medical personnel are exposed to the ideas and ideals of visiting students and residents, the local workers begin to critically review some of their traditional practices and routines that may be outdated and/or less effective. We have witnessed that this critical awareness that was stimulated by the distributed-learning and mentorship programs can be translated into innovative and continuous quality improvement efforts that serve to recharge the climate of the unit. Two such initiatives were peer mentoring and practice-based research.

We believe that effective mentoring practice would lead to professional and personal growth of the mentor as well as the protégé, which in turn would produce improvements in the level of emergency care and eventually the entire health facility. A good mentorship program may often lead to the staff's identification and acknowledgement of errors and mistakes, which in turn would promote quality improvement efforts. We have seen that a new perspective of a visiting resident or a fresh insight gained from an interdisciplinary mentorship discussion can result in making improvements in the delivery of quality health care.

Another advantage of developing strong mentorship programs in rural districts is the creation of important communication networks between university faculty and rural health professionals. Because the majority of emergency medicine research has been conducted in tertiary centres, the practice of emergency medicine in rural centres may offer a significantly different research venue compared to the common urban settings often portrayed in the academic literature. This gap between urban-centred research and rural practice could be narrowed through an improved connection between rural and tertiary centres that would be facilitated by including rural mentoring programs with distributed-learning models. Inviting rural districts to participate in research would stimulate new research questions and approaches and would encourage dialogue among health professionals from different environments. Positive consequence of such initiatives would accrue to all stakeholders: protégés, mentors, rural emergency departments, rural health districts, and the research community.

One other benefit of using mentorship as an educational model in rural settings is that it could be employed as a work philosophy. The high stress environment of the emergency department can negatively impact staff morale and standards of care, but developing a mentorship system that would encourage peer-to-peer mentorship would help local health workers. It would assist them to better manage their own work-related demands and to cultivate a commitment to the professional and personal development of themselves and of their colleagues. We contend that creating a culture of mentorship in the rural emergency department would not only improve staff morale, but would help improve staff retention and attraction of new graduates.

Conclusion and Recommendations

The increasing reliance on rural health facilities to participate in student and resident training has highlighted the unique challenges and opportunities for mentoring in the rural ER. Mentorship in emergency medicine has been the topic of only a few published studies and many questions remain to be answered. Moreover, the unique environment of the rural ER offers fertile ground for future mentorship research, which in turn will have implications for broader mentorship inquiry.

Some of this research related to rural emergency department mentoring programs could investigate the needs of minority groups, female students, and foreign-trained health workers. Another possible area would be to study how programs encourage free association between protégés and mentors based on personality characteristics, demographic features, and professional background. Researchers could also investigate if and how such programs increase the likelihood of productive mentoring relationships.

We have also argued that rural health districts should develop rural ER mentorship programs that facilitate interdisciplinary mentoring relationships, that encourage constructive feedback within the secure environment provided by a well-designed mentorship program, and that clearly describe the roles and responsibilities of mentors and protégés. Research could investigate how such programs are developed and maintained.

We indicated that inadequate compensation for health care professionals serving as mentors was a barrier for rural mentorship programs. We assert that a priority exists for research to identify effective and sustainable ways to compensate mentors in rural ER sites. We also charged health care facilities and organizations to support and encourage mentorship in rural ERs by providing extra time and resources for mentorship partners to facilitate the process. The programs should have structured meeting times for partners to discuss the components of the mentorship program (e.g., training outcomes, expectations for conduct, evaluation methods, feedback procedures, and troubleshooting procedures). Health care organizations and rural ER directors should encourage the development and implementation of locally adapted formal mentoring programs. The key is to first identify a critical mass of interested individuals in rural health facilities who are committed to building a strong mentorship program. They then should collaborate with similarly committed professionals from the universities and health districts system with the goal to design, implement, and evaluate mentorship programs that incorporate the elements we have outlined in this chapter.

We feel strongly that the culture of mentorship should be cultivated among all rural health care professionals, even though starting with a smaller core group would be more prudent. We have suggested that this core group of program enthusiasts work at creating a culture of support, continuous learning, constructive feedback, and personal development. This culture would in turn improve worker morale as well as improve quality of patient care. By extension, the effects of such a mentoring culture would not only influence the mentor/protégé pair but would add to the continuous quality improvement efforts of the department, institution, and district. We are convinced that establishing sound mentorship in rural health facilities would have positive repercussions for all stakeholders in the health care system, and perhaps beyond.

References

Coates, W. C., Ankel, F., Birnbaum, A., Kosiak, D., Broderick, K., Thomas, S., Leschke, R., & Collings, J. (2004). The virtual advisor program: Linking students to mentors via the world wide web. *Academic Emergency Medicine, 11*(3), 253–255. doi:10.1197/j.aem.2003.11.002

Garmel, G. M. (2004). Mentoring medical students in academic emergency medicine. *Academic Emergency Medicine, 11*(12), 1351–1357.

Marco, C. A., & Perina, D. G. (2004), Mentoring in emergency medicine: Challenges and future directions [commentary]. *Academic Emergency Medicine, 11*(12), 1329–1330.

Okereke, C. D. (2000). Mentoring: The trainee's perspective. *Journal of Accident & Emergency Medicine, 17,* 133–135.

Yeung, M., Nuth, J., & Stiell, I. G. (2010). Mentoring in emergency medicine: The art and the evidence. *Canadian Journal of Emergency Medicine, 12*(2), 143–149.

Chapter Five

Becoming: The Role of Mentorship in Integration of Newcomers into Communities of Practice*

Michelle Prytula & Linda Ferguson

THE TRANSITION FROM STUDENT TO new practitioner in a profession is typically a tumultuous one, often fraught with anxiety, concerns about practice, and a questionable sense of belonging. As graduates assume their professional roles, they often encounter challenges in entering, understanding, and functioning effectively in the new practice culture. Both the professions of teaching and nursing have attempted to reduce these challenges through various mentorship and induction programs and, most recently, through the cultures of communities of practice. In this chapter, we examine the transition from student to professional from a cross-disciplinary perspective, and we explore the impact of mentoring and mentoring cultures on these newcomers within the two different communities of practice. Our perspectives arise from two research projects: one in education addressing the impact of communities of practice/learning on newcomers at various stages, and the other in nursing addressing the nature of mentorship and mentoring cultures in nursing communities of practice. In both instances, the nature of the community of practice has significant effects on newcomers.

The Community of Practice

Learning cannot simply be transferred in a discrete package, no matter how flexible or well designed; rather, it has to be learned on site, actively and in participation and community with others (Hargreaves, 2003). Communities of practice, described by Etienne Wenger (2004), consist of groups of people who share a concern or

* After an academic review process, this chapter was accepted as a "refereed contribution" by the editors.

a passion for something they do and who learn how to do it better through interaction. The theory of communities of practice is based on the knowledge that learning takes place through authentic tasks embedded in real life (Lave, 1988; Webster-Wright, 2009). Research on learning, however, reveals that not only does learning take place *in situ* (on-site) through practical experiences, but that reflection and mediated discussion have a valuable role in the process as well (Lieberman & Pointer Mace, 2008).

Since Wenger (1998; Wenger, McDermott, & Snyder, 2002) first developed the concept of communities of practice, it has also been utilized and researched in a number of disciplines such as nursing (Andrew, Tolson, & Ferguson, 2008), education (Jawitz, 2009; Warhurst, 2008), and business (Nagy & Burch, 2009; Scarso, Bolisani, & Salvador, 2009). The community of practice concept, while not always named as such by those within the community, provides understanding of the importance of the work environment to newcomers in any practice setting.

As groups of professionals working collaboratively with and learning from one another, the community of practice has the power to create lasting impact and change in an organization. This impact is not simply achieved through the adoption of the structure of the learning community but rather through a transformation in the knowledge, growth, and practice of and among the members involved (Prytula, Makahonuk, Syrota, & Pesenti, 2009). This transformation is largely due to the activities that the members undertake, such as the practices of collaboration, strategy building, and shared accountability. In teaching, working collaboratively in a learning community includes setting instructional or learning goals, measuring their attainment, and monitoring and planning for further or sustained improvement (DuFour & Eaker, 1998). In nursing, it means providing resources in terms of support, information, and discussion to achieve the best decisions in different contexts. Members of communities of practice do not work in isolation but, through the opportunity for discussion and dialogue, they share their practices, support one another, and contribute to each other's learning.

Our exploration of the role of the community of practice in service professions entails a deeper look into two distinct studies: one in education and one in nursing. Following a description of each study we illustrate significant parallels and their implications for the teaching and nursing professions.

The Teaching Study

After conducting a study of beginning teachers, Hellsten, Prytula, Ebanks, and Lai (2009) proposed a model for internship that moves teacher induction from the apprenticeship model to a holistic, constructive model. This model departed from the linear and sequential learning type of approach (Frid, Reading, & Redden, 1998; McNeil, Hood, Kurtz, Thousand, & Nevin, 2006) and rather proposed that the beginning teacher was a novice in some areas and an expert in others. In relationship with proximal zones of development (Vygotsky, 1978), the constructive model for teacher induction assumed that all teachers are learners and inquirers and that all teachers enter teaching both with influential, valuable experiences as well as learning gaps. The constructive model for teacher induction eliminates the need to formally match a mentor with a mentee because it assumes that all members of the community are at the same time mentors, teachers, and learners. The most valuable difference in the model, however, is that at its heart is student learning rather than mentee learning, which coincides with the focus of the professional learning community (PLC) in a pre-K to 12 school.

Teacher Mentorship through a Community of Practice

Situated in a community of practice in a pre-K to grade 8 elementary school, one group of teachers engaged in action research to explore the constructive model as an effective alternative to the existing internship model that was already in use in Saskatchewan. The goal of the study was to explore induction and mentorship through membership in a PLC, and the researchers investigated whether or not the PLC could be used as an alternate model for teacher induction, and if so, what its effects would have on the people involved.

The focus of the PLC in the school was on improved student learning in reading and writing. Regular meetings, assessments, and reporting were part of the learning improvement plan and PLC processes. Research took place over a 10-month period. Data were collected using semi-structured interviews and written responses from teacher candidates, interns, and beginning teachers in the school. Common themes were aggregated and the themes were reported as findings for the study.

Findings

Two key findings emerged from the study, the first being that the PLC was found to be an effective model for teacher induction. The second finding was that learning through the PLC appeared to create a positive departure from the traditional linear model of teacher learning, yielding a better approach that was more holistic in nature.

Factors Leading to Effective Mentorship

The constructive model of induction through the PLC was found to exhibit the attributes of effective mentorship (Salinitri, 2005) necessary for effective teacher induction. These factors or categories that we describe below were: (a) developing confidence, (b) bridging learning, and (c) working in collaboration.

Developing confidence. Regardless of their position or induction stage (i.e., teacher candidates, interns, or first year teachers), the members reported experiencing a general feeling of belonging and active involvement within the PLC. The participants described their moving from a lower level of confidence to a higher one, and much of this confidence appeared to have emerged from dialogues that occurred in the PLC meetings. One first-year teacher noted that "a conversation that happened at one of our last [meetings] meant a lot to me just to make sure that I was on the right page and I found out that I was, and that meant a lot." This confidence also developed though the activities that the participants experienced in the PLC.

Other participants expressed that the PLC meetings provided them with a level of comfort to share their thoughts and feelings, as well as an opportunity for teacher candidates, interns, and first-year teachers to develop relationships with one another and other school personnel. One intern stated that "if I wasn't in this program I would feel as though I was not as involved and that I wouldn't have much of a relationship with any other teacher other than the one I was working with." Rather than simply developing a close relationship with the co-operating teacher, she was able to learn from and relate to several other colleagues as well.

Bridging learning. Because the goals of the PLC had been pre-set, the meetings and conversations focused on those goals and on related strategies. Beginning teachers recognized that the PLC provided direction for their teaching, as illustrated by one of them who said, "It gives me more responsibility in what exactly my assessment is for the kids . . . it gives me more of a concrete idea of how I'm teaching and what I'm teaching." The process of learning together was central in the operation of the school's PLC, and the mentees recognized what they needed to do to improve student learning. Knowledge acquired was not simply program or resource based, but it came from clarifying their understanding of the learning process. Another mentee stated, "I felt as though I was included in a real grassroots formation of knowledge constructed by a community of professionals." Mentees seemed to realize that learning was central to the success of a teacher, and that the mutual learning component provided access for everyone to acquire information that was experiential, authentic, and reciprocal. The dialogue in the PLC explored ideas that were solicited from all members of the group – not only from the experienced teachers. One participant commented "if more (people) could have this experience, I think the art of teaching would change dramatically."

Working in collaboration. As newcomers to the school, the teacher candidates, interns, and first-year teachers reported feeling supported and encouraged. The feeling of importance and trust was illustrated by one intern who said, "Together, just being able to trust – trustworthiness – is a big thing. Having people to talk to and people you can rely on and depend on and go to for anything, advice, comfort, work related or not." Interns made use of that support network outside of the PLC as well, applying the advice received to other aspects of their work.

Induction through the PLC provided further supports, as exemplified by another intern who commented, "It's like having five different co-operating teachers instead of just one." Increasing the numbers of mentors for a newcomer increases the likelihood that they will receive the help that they need. Also of primary concern to the mentees as they began their year was how well they would transition from the university setting to employment in the classroom. One participant noted that "it was a huge connection between the practical and the theoretical." Another one of her peers said that she had learned strategies in her university classes that she saw not working in the classroom and had "always kind of had that scepticism but I'm also learning that some of the things that we are being taught that I didn't think would work, will work if you put in that effort to do it."

PLC participants benefitted from the collaborative nature of the group, deriving solutions to problems together. One intern commented "It has helped me understand the value of teamwork within the school and how that teamwork can affect your teaching."

Stages of Teacher Induction

According to the four-phase linear model of teacher induction (Frid et al., 1998), one would expect that beginning teachers would progress through the stages sequentially: from the first phase where they are focused on themselves, to the second phase where they start to notice their competence and incompetence, to the third stage

Figure 1

The stages of teacher growth in a constructive induction model, such as the professional learning community, where each stage may be developed simultaneously.

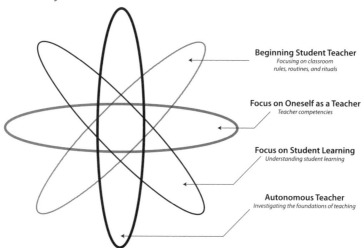

Beginning Student Teacher
*Focusing on classroom
rules, routines, and rituals*

Focus on Oneself as a Teacher
Teacher competencies

Focus on Student Learning
Understanding student learning

Autonomous Teacher
Investigating the foundations of teaching

where they start to focus on student learning, and to the last stage where they become more complete, autonomous teachers. However, with respect to the data collected from this study, there was evidence that teacher candidates in the PLC project progressed beyond the first stages quite rapidly and at times showed characteristics of having achieved the fourth stage. The fourth stage is expected later in the induction process, but one intern stated, "It helped me progress from thinking solely about myself and how my performance is looking to superiors to taking the time to consider the situations and feelings of students and parents/guardians." This study indicated that the stages of learning through the PLC may be less linear, and more holistic, as shown in Figure 1.

Visualizing the stages in a holistic manner implies that induction through the learning community model allows the learner to move in and out of each stage, building on each stage almost simultaneously as each learner is exposed to the thinking and understanding of others.

Education students in this project were engaged in deep learning as they designed lessons, participated in instruction, and learned from their and their peers' successes and challenges. We contend that the typical professional development seminar or instructional lecture could not produce the level of cognitive change that was evident in the participants in this study.

We now focus on the nursing profession and the related communities of practice study, and then highlight the importance of community of practice in mentorship within the social sectors of education and nursing.

The Nursing Profession

Because nursing students' abilities to function within real-life settings are essential to their practice as registered nurses, the apprenticeship model had been prominent in pre-service clinical education. The commonly used one-to-one model of learning, the preceptorship, was based on a formal time-limited learning relationship between a nursing student and a more experienced practitioner. The preceptor was to teach, coach, supervise, and evaluate the performance of the student (Firtko, Stewart, & Knox, 2005; Ralph, Walker,

& Wimmer, 2008; Yonge, Myrick, Billay, & Luhanga, 2007; Udlis, 2008; Zilembo, & Monterosso, 2008).

During the typical clinical preceptorship, student nurses enter a community of practice as temporary members of the community. Their engagement in that community varies, moderated in part by the short duration spent within the community. They are in an apprenticeship relationship with the preceptor, which involves critical and creative thinking, questioning, and innovation in the three areas of knowledge: science, skills and clinical reasoning, and ethical comportment (Benner, Sutphen, Leonard, & Day, 2010). Having undergone such preparation before transition into professional practice, nurses are assumed to be able to navigate the transition with ease. Yet, novice graduates still regularly report high levels of anxiety on entry to nursing practice. In our view, a process is needed in the workplace to facilitate this transition into practice, and mentorship is such a process.

The Nursing Study

In a grounded-theory study, Ferguson (2006) explored the experiences of new nurses in developing their clinical judgment, clinical reasoning, and practice knowledge over the first two years of professional nursing practice. Twenty-five nurses with between two and three years of full-time nursing practice experience were interviewed up to three times. These participants worked on five different types of general hospital units and were graduates from five different four-year baccalaureate nursing programs in two Canadian provinces. Despite this level of diversity, their issues were remarkably similar.

Findings included the creation of a theory of the development of clinical judgment in nursing practice. The core integrating variable in the theory was *Seeking Learning*, reflecting the desire of new nurses to be in communities of practice that value, encourage, and support continuing learning. Distinct stages in the development of judgment and reasoning were evident. As soon as new nurses assumed full responsibility for patient care, they entered the *Learning Practice Norms* phase, which often lasted four to six months, and which was characterized by learning how to fit into the existing workgroup or the community of practice, learning practice norms and in-depth knowledge, and establishing effective working relationships. That period was the most stressful of the new nurse's working career.

At that stage, new nurses used a variety of strategies to build their knowledge base. New nurses spoke of the learning network or community of practice in which they learned to practice nursing more effectively. Their more experienced nursing colleagues answered their questions, used narratives to illustrate their clinical judgment, and provided suggestions for improvements in nursing care. Most new nurses recognized a transition point where they moved to the next stage, *Developing Confidence*. As one new nurse described, "I kind of got inklings of it around six months. You kind of get over the terror of 'Oh my God, there's so much to do. I hope I don't kill anyone,' to feeling at the end of the day, 'You know, I really did a good job today.'" That stage, which extended from six to twelve months of practice, was characterized by continuing development of judgment and practice skill associated with developing confidence. Confidence in one's ability was both a requirement for effective judgment and an indicator of developing competence.

The third stage, *Consolidation of Professional Relationships*, from about twelve to eighteen months of practice, was characterized by a desire for consolidation of professional relationships with other health care professionals. The novices engaged in discussions of patient care with other members of the health care community. By approximately eighteen months of practice, new nurses entered the fourth stage, *Seeking Challenge in Clinical Practice*. They perceived themselves as being resources to other members of the community.

Development of Thinking

All participants identified the importance of the social learning network in their community of practice. It was within this network that their thinking as nurses and their practice knowledge, clinical judgment, and clinical reasoning were fostered. Most new nurses identified their early-practice thinking processes as linear, task-focused, and simplistic. One respondent said, "Mainly I would do it from an approach of the simple things that were happening with that patient. I could pick out the major categories of changes and status or whatever, but I would have never been able to put it all together at that time." Most new nurses identified daily judgment decisions as challenging, needing the assistance of their more experienced colleagues. All respondents, however, recognized that their lack of experience contributed to their lack of multi-tasking and holistic and anticipatory thought. They expressed the need for interactions with more experienced colleague to facilitate their own development and acquiring passed-down knowledge.

New nurses indicated that their initial focus was on themselves as nurses and what they *should* be doing as opposed to a focus on patient outcomes and what they *could* be doing. Their practice was guided by formal knowledge learned in their educational preparation. Through interactions with their colleagues, and through experiences made meaningful through reflection and dialogue (Figure 2), new nurses developed confidence in their own practice knowledge and decision-making abilities. As an indicator for the end of the *Learning Practice Norms* stage, most new nurses indicated that they could intervene in the commonly encountered patient

Figure 2

Constructing practice knowledge through experiential learning in nursing practice.

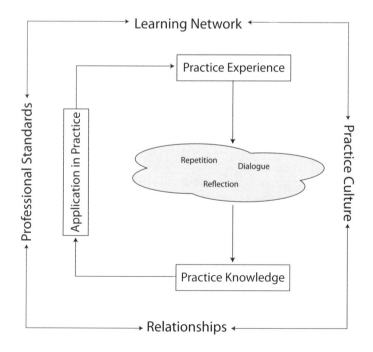

situations with increased confidence. At approximately a year into practice, they felt they could be a resource to newer nurses within their learning communities.

The Community of Practice

Most new nurses indicated that the welcoming atmosphere of the nursing unit was important to their sense of belonging in a specific workplace. In fact, most had chosen the workplace based on the quality of the work environment.

New nurses indicated the need for a trusting learning environment wherein their colleagues were open to questions and willing to provide them with support as well as information. In addition, the quality of care provided within the nursing unit was very important to new nurses.

They sought more experienced nurses within the unit who did practice nursing as they expected, and in many cases, these former became their mentees.

The Role of Mentors

All new nurses in the study expressed an interest in having a mentor, since as one new nurse indicated, being mentored by a respected person within the community facilitated entry into that community: " I found that it was easier to fit in when you had an 'in' with an experienced knowledgeable nurse – it really helped." New nurses were specific about their choices of mentors, indicating that they were looking for mentors who were strong practitioners and role models. "I really admired her skills and the way she went about her nursing. She was just very good at what she did." New nurses also recognized the importance of their mentors having current knowledge. In addition, the mentoring nurses anticipated the needs of new nurses, recognizing their developmental levels and offering the appropriate type of support, knowledge, or guidance as needed. However, exemplary practice was not sufficient in and of itself. As one mentee indicated,

I would seek out those nurses that I knew were receptive to teaching. I think that once I built that relationship with several of the nurses, that it just kept on that way. I developed some informal mentors that way. Nothing was ever formalized. It was kind of an unspoken thing.

In many instances, no formal agreement had ever been established and the relationships evolved over time into what have described as a mentoring relationship.

In addition, new nurses needed a relational connection with those whom they sought out or accepted as mentors. Potential mentor behaviors included being welcoming, friendly, supportive, encouraging, and open to questions. Many mentoring relationships started slowly over time, often developing within the context of a social relationship in the workplace. In describing their mentoring relationships, most new nurses agreed with one of their peers who said, "They care about you as a person . . . and you care about them, whether there's ten years' or thirty years' difference in age." New nurses, who had mentors, indicated that the relationship was characterized by trust and reciprocity, in which the mentee's willingness to learn was essential to the initiation and sustainability of the relationship.

In summary, the establishment of a mentoring relationship between an entry-level nurse and a more experienced Registered Nurse in the workplace appeared to facilitate the development of the novice, and likely the mentor, as well. The concept of a learning community within the community of practice provided an explanation of the learning network that new nurses needed for the development of professional practice.

Discussion

Although situated in discrete disciplines, these two studies of mentorship through communities of practice revealed several significant similarities. By highlighting the parallels in these two service professions, we may shed further light on the opportunities and challenges of mentorship and induction in non-profit service professions.

Apprenticeship in Holistic and Non-Linear Environments

Although teachers and nurses acquire foundational understanding of their disciplines via coursework, they develop practical knowledge in the application phase. Learning through practice in nursing and education is different from training provided in a purely technical apprenticeship model because there is a larger degree of uncertainty to the work. Although teachers and nurses practice techniques in advance, difficulty arises because of the variability in ways that students or clients may respond to a lesson or treatment. Consequently, the judgment and subsequent reaction by a teacher or nurse to such variable responses may largely determine the ultimate success of the event. The discourse regarding this adaptive phenomenon in teaching and nursing is common in that these professionals mention "getting a feel for it" or "figuring it out."

In both teaching and nursing, theory and research are important; however, a portion of their professional learning is tacit and cannot be achieved without experience. Such learning must be learned *in situ*, in community with others, and in sharing stories of successes and failures. The success of the work in teaching and nursing is made uncertain because of human behavior, and there is seldom a predictable day. The idea of perfecting one's work in these disciplines is perhaps unreachable, but the concept of mastery is not. Mastery in the service professions includes being able to apply knowledge, experience, and good judgment to solve unique problems in practice.

These two studies of education and nursing mentioned here refer to learning that was non-linear and eclectic. Although both studies discussed stages of professional learning, teaching included different kinds of learning that occurred simultaneously, requiring different information at different times depending on the situation. Similarly, nursing embodied linear and sequential learning as an initial problem-solving strategy whereby novices reviewed textbook information but quickly realized that situations required a holistic network of information. Teachers and nurses learned to consult certain people for specific cases. The concept of community of practice matched the holistic, flexible, and dynamic environment.

The Community of Practice and Relationship Building

In both studies, participants identified the need to develop relationships that promoted communication with others in order to help understand work roles and responsibilities. Newcomers needed to learn how to fit in, acquire knowledge, develop relationships, and advance their practice. In both professions there was a formal component to the mentorship process where teachers, as interns, were formally paired with a co-operating teacher and where nurses, as mentees, were formally paired with a preceptor in their initial weeks of training. These formal relationships, although valuable for ensuring relative consistency and for assigning assessment responsibilities, were often not those partnerships through which the newcomer developed the strongest relationships. Although these formal relationships were appreciated, it was in the informal relationships developed through the communities of practice where mentees were able to advance their learning and build strong connections. These pairings often occurred because a newcomer identified an experienced professional's strength, because they had compatible personalities, or because needed information was available at the right time and place. The increase in numbers of informal mentors appeared to fill a learning void, to reduce fear and anxiety among newcomers, to enhance routine practice, and to prevent the likelihood of overload and tension from damaging the newcomer's entry into the profession.

Need for Induction beyond Mentorship

The community of practice appeared to offer more than effective mentorship in both education and nursing studies. As Wang, Odell, and Clift (2010) indicated, there is a need for induction beyond the mentorship stage. Because in education and nursing newcomers are not fully responsible for their charges until after the internship/preceptorship, their learning may be not as deep or meaningful than it would be if they were in their first job. Once they entered their first employment, often in complex and hectic environments, they would have to make professional decisions quickly, and the necessity for mentorship at this stage would also be critical. However, within the professions of nursing and teaching today, such mentorship is neither certain nor consistent. These two studies have revealed that as the formal mentorship arrangements elapsed at the end of the practicum programs, the importance of the community of practice increased, and it became vital to the success of the newly hired professional.

In our view, induction into the profession through the community of practice before, during, and after this formal mentorship stage would ensure that newcomers will have access to information and support during the critical period of their career journey. It is imperative that the newcomer develops relationships as soon as possible with mentors whom they can trust and from whom they can learn as they are immersed in professional practice. Such mentorship will help prevent novices from feeling unprepared or overwhelmed. They will be able to access resources through this developed network in order to adapt to their new roles.

From Confidence Building to Reciprocal Learning

Experiencing the community of practice had a significant impact on the confidence of the newcomers in both the teaching and nursing professions. This confidence emerged from the dialogue and discussions that the newcomers had with multiple members of the learning community. These conversations either provided them with information and answers to questions or with affirmation of the work that they were already doing. Having the affirmation *in situ* reinforced their learning immediately when it was needed, making it current, relevant, and concrete. Participants described experiencing a heightened comfort level and a relationship of trust with others.

In the education study, participants achieved a relatively early stage of reflecting on their influence on the student and the student's family prior to making decisions. In nursing, the newcomers had to overcome initial fears of making a fatal error and to develop in their role as competent caregivers. The role that the community of practice filled for new professionals was one of continual support through provision of information and experience.

As newcomers developed their professional confidence and skills, they eventually found that they were able to reciprocally contribute to the community of practice. At times, and depending on the context, this situation put them in a position of expertise, however brief, and it served to deepen their learning, their skills, and their desire to continue learning. In education, their involvement in the community of practice meant taking an occasional role as leader in the group and engaging members in strategies that brought about successful results. In nursing, this involvement meant taking on more responsibilities, moving to another unit to further their skills, fine tuning their skills on the same unit, or occasionally mentoring others. It also meant that they could be resources to other members of the unit. The reciprocity factor also allowed for new information and practice to enter the profession, and it provided newcomers with the confidence that they were not only learners, but were contributors to the profession.

The community of practice not only provided a place where newcomers could access information from multiple members in a timely and efficient manner, but it allowed all members to benefit. Because the entire community was advancing their learning and seeking to improve their practice, newcomers were enveloped in an environment of trust and learning, allowing them a place to ask, learn, and share. The reciprocity of support, trust, and learning benefitted both new and experienced members, and it fostered more effective professional teamwork.

Summary and Implications

The costs of ineffective induction, including stress, burnout, or dropout, are high. In recognizing that teaching and nursing present newcomers with stressful, hectic, and often overwhelming environments in which they must learn, we contend that educational institutions must examine the type of structures and supports that induct newcomers into the professions. Through these two studies in education and nursing, we have indicated that the community of practice is a valuable component that plays a central part in the success of both the transition from student to professional and the learning that occurs before and after the transition.

In these studies we have suggested that the linear, progressive models of newcomer induction stages may no longer be suitable for today's social sectors. Mentee learning through induction via communities of practice has the potential to foster different types of learning simultaneously (e.g., mentor learning and organizational learning). However, if the communities of practice do not exist in an organization, we believe that it would not be possible for this type of mentorship to be developed. Further research needs to be done on the effects of a community of practice on newcomer induction for a clearer understanding of the formation and sustainability of the community of practice in multiple service environments.

The holistic and eclectic environments of teaching and learning require induction programs that are flexible and sustainable. Although participants in these studies began to appreciate the learning and experiences that they underwent in their transition to the professions, in their training, students are not usually made aware of the concept of communities of practice or what learning through such a community might entail. Perhaps by sharing with students the concept of learning communities they may be better able, in practice, to take advantage of the rich environments in which they learn and work, which in turn will help reduce the stress and anxiety they encounter as they enter the workforce. This awareness may also ensure that newcomers into both teaching and nursing have the opportunity to benefit from these rich environments.

References

Andrews, N., Tolson, D., & Ferguson, D. (2008). Building on Wenger: Communities of practice in nursing. *Nurse Education Today, 28*(2), 246–252.

Benner, P., Sutphen, M., Leonard, V., & Day, L. (2010). *Educating nurses: A call for radical transformation.* San Francisco, CA: Jossey-Bass.

DuFour, R., & Eaker, R. (1998). *Professional learning communities at work: Best practices for enhancing student achievement.* Bloomington, IN: National Education Service.

Ferguson, L., & Day, R. (2006). Challenges for new nurses in evidence-based practice. *Journal of Nursing Management, 15*(1), 107–113. doi:10.1111/j.1365-2934.2006.00638.x

Firtko, A., Stewart, R., & Knox, N. (2005). Understanding mentoring and preceptorship: Clarifying the quagmire. *Contemporary Nurse, 19*, 32–40.

Frid, S., Reading, C., & Redden, T. (1998). Are teachers born or made? Critical reflection for professional growth. In T. Maxwell (Ed.), *The Context of Teaching* (pp. 325–350). Armidale, NSW: Kardoorair Press.

Hargreaves, A. (2003). *Teaching in the knowledge society: Education in the age of insecurity.* New York, NY: Teachers College Press.

Hellsten, L. A., Prytula, M. P., Ebanks, A., & Lai, H. (2009). Teacher induction: Exploring beginning teacher mentorship. *Canadian Journal of Education, 32*(4), 703–733.

Jawitz, J. (2009). Academic identities and communities of practice in a professional discipline. *Teaching in Higher Education, 14*(3), 241–251. doi:10.1080/13562510902898817

Lave, J. (1988). *Cognition in practice.* Boston, MA: Cambridge University Press.

Lieberman, A., & Pointer Mace, D. (2008). Teacher learning: The key to educational reform. *Journal of Teacher Education, 59*(3), 226.

McNeil, M., Hood, A., Kurtz, P., Thousand, J., & Nevin, A. (2006, November). *A self actualization model for teacher induction into the teaching profession: Accelerating the professionalization of beginning teachers.* Paper presented at the annual meeting of the Teacher Education Division (TED), Council for Exceptional Children (CEC), San Diego, CA. Retrieved from http://www.eric.ed.gov/ERICWebPortal/detail?accno=ED493951

Nagy, J., & Burch, T. (2009). Communities of practice in academe: Understanding academic work practices to enable knowledge building capacities in corporate. *Oxford Review of Education, 35*(2), 227–247.

Prytula, M., Makahonuk, C., Syrota, N., & Pesenti, M. (2009). *Successful teacher induction through communities of practice.* Saskatoon, SK: Dr. Stirling McDowell Foundation for Research into Teaching.

Ralph, E., Walker, K., & Wimmer, R. (2008). The clinical/practicum experience in professional preparation: Preliminary findings. *McGill Journal of Education, 43*(2), 157–172.

Salinitri, G. (2005). *Teachers' interfaculty mentorship efforts (T.I.M.E.): A study evaluating the effects of a formal mentorship program on first-year at-risk students*. Windsor, ON: University of Windsor Press.

Scarso, E., Bolisani, E., & Salvador, L. (2009). A systematic framework for analysing the critical success factors of communities of practice. *Journal of Knowledge Management, 13*(6), 431–447. doi:10.1108/13673270910997105

Vygotsky, L. (1978). *Mind in society*. Cambridge, MA: Harvard University Press.

Wang, J., Odell, S., & Clift, R. (Eds.). (2010). *Past, present, and future research on teacher induction: An anthology for researchers, policy makers, and practitioners*. Lanham, MD: Rowman and Littlefield Education and the Association of Teacher Educators.

Warhurst, R. P. (2008). Cigars on the flight-deck: New lecturers' participatory learning within workplace communities of practice. *Studies in Higher Education, 33*(4), 453–467.

Webster-Wright, A. (2009). Reframing professional development through understanding authentic professional learning. *Review of educational research, 79*(2), 702.

Wenger, E. (1998). *Communities of practice: Learning, meaning, and identity*. New York, NY: Cambridge University Press.

Wenger, E. (2004). *Communities of practice: A brief introduction*. Retrieved from http://www.ewenger.com/theory/communities_of_practice_intro.htm

Wenger, E., McDermott, R., & Snyder, W. M. (2002). *Cultivating communities of practice*. Boston, MA: Harvard Business School Press.

Yonge, O., Billay, D., Myrick, F., & Luhanga, F. (2007). Preceptorship and mentorship: Not merely a matter of semantics. *International Journal of Nursing Education Scholarship, 4*(1), Article 19.

Zilembo, M., & Monterosso, L. (2008). Towards a conceptual framework for preceptorship in the clinical education of under-graduate nursing students. *Contemporary Nurse, 30*, 89–94.

Chapter Six

Mentoring: Bridging the Generational and Career Divide[*]

Rosemary A. Venne

ENTORING HAS ALWAYS BEEN RECOGNIZED as a valuable tool in the business world. It serves the interests of organizations in a multitude of ways. Mentoring has been used as a means to retain valuable knowledge and to increase both employee satisfaction and employee retention. For example, it is an excellent way to ensure that all team members feel committed to the organization, which ultimately aids in the competition for talent (Cranwell-Ward, Bossons, and Gover, 2004). Also, in the current environment marked by the exit of the large baby-boom generation from the workforce, mentoring has been suggested as a way of guaranteeing that critical knowledge is preserved in the workplace (DeLong, 2004).

In this analysis I contend that mentoring is more crucial than ever to organizations today, given recent career-pattern upheaval and demographic change. These two factors are often acknowledged human resource issues in terms of recruiting and retention, and mentoring is a vital aspect in dealing with them. Among its numerous benefits for individual employees and organizations, mentoring can be used as a tool to help deal with career-management issues and generational diversity. For example, with respect to careers, mentoring is of great importance in dealing with the changing psychological contract and the absence of lifelong jobs (Cranwell-Ward et al., 2004). Also, mentoring has been recommended to improve cross-generational communication (Sabattini, Warren, Dinolfo, Falk, and Castro, 2010).

The importance of mentoring to organizations has received considerable attention among scholars. However, what is missing from the mentoring literature is a recognition of the relationship between

[*] After an academic review process, this chapter was accepted as a "refereed contribution" by the editors.

career change and generational diversity, and it is this gap that I seek to address in this analysis. Mentoring is discussed here in the context of work relationships, specifically in terms of changing career dynamics and generational diversity. Mentoring is characterized as a dynamic process in a learning partnership where the unique relationship is reciprocal yet somewhat asymmetrical (Eby, Rhodes, & Allen, 2010). A further objective is to demonstrate that this learning process is ideally suited to the interrelated issues of career management and generational diversity.

In terms of organization of this analysis, I begin by discussing generational issues. What are generations and why is this issue of generational diversity so important today? Then I summarize changes in career patterns in the postwar period, specifically addressing the overlooked relationship between generational groups and career patterns. Finally, I discuss some examples of how mentoring can help deal with career management and generational diversity. I conclude that specific, goal-oriented mentoring programs are ideally suited to deal with the interrelated issues of career pattern change and generational conflict.

Generational-Diversity Issues

The sense of generation has been heightened in the postwar period. In this section I use demographic terms to define generations in the sense of age-based cohorts drawn from boom and bust cycles in fertility. I present why the issue of generational diversity is so important in the workforce today and argue that mentoring is needed to deal with this diversity.

Trovato (2009) noted that every member of a population belongs to a birth cohort who generally experiences formative life-course events and transitions at similar times. For example, members of birth cohorts tend to encounter similar conditions and circumstances, including important events such as graduation, entry into the labor force, marriage, or home ownership. Thus a cohort experiences similar conditions at similar life-cycle stages as it moves through its lifetime, and it is this sharing of events that sets off a cohort. A cohort's shared experiences (e.g., living through a war or a major economic depression) may create unique sentiments and even a unique world view among its members that the members of other cohorts may find difficult to appreciate. For example, the baby boom generation has been said to be responsible for the counterculture movement of the 1960s (Trovato, 2009). There has been some recent discussion in the media of how the so-called great recession of 2007–2008 and its aftermath will affect younger people living after that event (e.g., the baby-boom echo group).

The sense of belonging to a generation has become heightened over the postwar period due to a number of factors. Owram (1996) asserted that society's postwar school experience became more universal with people's regular school attendance and their more prolonged period of education. Taken together, these factors meant that the sense of peer group (here beginning with the postwar baby boomers) was accentuated, and as a result, individuals' daily contact with people of differing ages and experiences tended to be postponed. At this time there tended to be a prolongation of youth where the transitional period of youth that individuals passed through became elongated.

Ricard (1994) asserted that people did not always define themselves in terms of age groups. He noted that demographic equilibrium or the distribution of age groups is usually so stable that the influence of generations is barely perceptible. He described the postwar baby boom as a profound upheaval and defined it as the rapid and sustained increase in the number and rate of births that took place in Canada and in some other countries after World War II. Today the demographic or cohort factor influences individuals' identity as people come to regard their generation as a fundamental aspect of themselves. Ricard (1994) stated that age has become a new source of division between groups, and that this division determines in large part the nature of relationships between different cohorts.

To further understand these demographic cycles, one could refer to the concept of fertility, defined as the average number of children that a woman has. Boom groups make up a large cohort associated with increases in fertility rates or a large supply of babies. Bust groups, in contrast, are smaller cohorts associated with a decrease in fertility or a smaller supply of babies. Generational influences include the formative experiences mentioned above as well as the size of the cohort that will have an effect on a group. Boom groups, for example, face greater within-group crowding and competition because their members overwhelm school systems in their youth, compete for jobs and housing in adulthood, and eventually crowd seniors' homes in their later years.

A particularly large boom group can cause upheaval or shock to society's institutions by virtue of its generational size. One such cohort is the postwar baby-boom group, which was a defining demographic feature of the twentieth century. Owram (1996) described the large postwar baby boom cohort as a shock wave, forcing adjustments on society's institutions. Ricard (1994) even referred to the baby-boom group as cataclysmic in terms of its effect on society. Bust groups, on the other hand, often face more favorable conditions in terms of lessened within-group competition.

After postponed fertility throughout the Depression and WWII periods, the most significant baby boom occurred over the two postwar decades. Consisting of people born from 1947 to 1966, this cohort comprises approximately one-third of the Canadian population (Foot, 1996) and is commonly referred to as "the boomers" despite the fact that there were several boom groups born during the twentieth century. The postwar boom was preceded and followed by bust groups. The next bust group was born from 1967–1979. The boom group born from 1980 to 1995 is often referred to as the "baby-boom echo" or "baby boomlet" because they were the children of the postwar baby boomers. The latter boom is not as large or as prolonged as their parents' group. To place this concept of generations in terms of the workplace, today's workforce is mainly comprised of the following three demographic cohorts or generations: baby boom, baby bust, and baby-boom echo. Most of the preceding baby bust (i.e., the Depression and WWII bust) have moved out of the labor force through retirement, although some of its youngest members may still be working.

The factor of generational diversity in the workforce has received much attention from scholars. For example, Lancaster and Stillman (2002, 2010) and Zemke, Raines, and Filipczak (2000) discussed how to deal with the different values and expectations of these diverse generations in the workplace. Zemke et al. acknowledged that there have always been multiple generations employed in the same organization; however, they also indicated that in the past these cohorts were largely sequestered from each other due to traditional organizational stratification and structure. For example, middle-aged employees were most likely in mid-management positions and older employees were in command positions. Generational mixing was not common in past workplaces, where formality and protocol were the rule. Today, however, because of new technologies and the increased focus on team-based approaches in most workplaces, different generations and age groups have begun to interact and work together more than ever before. Yet, at the same time, Lancaster and Stillman (2002) made the point that multiple generations in today's workplace also have wider attitudinal and value gaps than ever before due to the accelerated pace of change. They further suggested that these gaps are of greater strategic importance to organizations in terms of recruitment, retention, and succession policies.

Zemke et al. (2000) also noted that today's information-centred workplaces have become more horizontal (i.e., showing trends towards fewer hierarchical levels due to de-layering and/or removing mid-management positions) and spatially compact, leading to greater opportunities for generational mixing. They postulated that diversity can be a source of creativity as well as a source of conflict. Sabattini et al. (2010) discussed the challenges of integrating a multi-generational workforce as a form of workforce diversity. These researchers referred to such challenges as a relatively new and under-developed aspect of workplace life. At the same time, there has been a corresponding growth of interest in the process of mentoring in organizations as a viable means of dealing with these intergenerational differences.

Generational workshops or training seminars have been relatively recent additions in the workplace (Belkin, 2007; Silverman, 2007). These seminars are meant to teach the members of the workforce about the younger incoming workers, in order to be proactive in dealing with any potential generational conflict between/among groups. The learning process is also meant to enhance mutuality, whereby each generation will learn about the others. The use of mentoring has proven useful in bringing together the different generations.

Career Pattern Changes

What is sometimes missing from discussions of mentoring, however, is any analysis of how career patterns have evolved since the end of WWII. More importantly there is a lack of recognition of the connection between generations and career pattern change. In this section I will begin with a discussion of career change in the postwar period, followed by linking this change to generational groups, and ending with the importance of career mentoring.

It has been well established that careers in the postwar period have changed considerably beginning in the last few decades of the twentieth century (Egan, 1994). During the second half of the twentieth century there appears to have been a career divide or schism that began in the late 1970s and early 1980s. The immediate postwar period has been depicted as a period of unparalleled prosperity, marked by a steady rise in the standard of living and an acceleration of technological development (Ricard, 1994). The stable career patterns of the early postwar decades came to be viewed as the norm during that time, although those careers evolved during a period of economic buoyancy and muted competition in North America. Betcherman and Lowe (1997) further speculated that future historians would characterize the last few decades of the twentieth century as a period when North America struggled with the transition from a long and prosperous postwar period of industrialism to a new post-industrial age. During the 1980s, with the rise in global competition, industry entered a period of restructuring and downsizing (Craig & Hall, 2006). Though there was an initial expectation of a return to normalcy in terms of business and career patterns, it became apparent that firms would be in some form of continual transition, and that stable career patterns would be the exception rather than the norm.

In her book *The Death of the Organization Man*, Bennett (1990) documented the change in careers after the end of the postwar golden age. The one-company-for-life philosophy essentially developed out of the three-decade-long heady growth period following WWII. During that extraordinary period of postwar expansion, North America went through a period of rapid organizational growth in which there was a disproportionate increase in white-collar and middle-management jobs, and in which employees enjoyed stable and often promotion-centred careers (Bardwick, 1986). With the shortage of experienced managers, low unemployment, and muted competition during that period, many corporations in North America focused on keeping their employees within their firms (Bennett, 1990). Employees were hired at entry level, trained, and groomed for lifetime employment at one workplace through internal job markets (Cappelli, 2006). Cappelli (2008) referred to those types of long career ladders and low rates of turnover as the golden age for talent management.

Lifelong stable career patterns of the early postwar decades have given way to less stable and more varied career patterns – organizational de-layering and downsizing, creeping credentialism, and lifelong learning as issues. For example, Leana (2002) pointed out that being with a single firm matters less now in that most employees will work for a greater number of employers with shorter periods of tenure over the course of their careers. Cappelli (2006) also documented how modern careers have broken the attachment between employer and employee that was observed in previous generations. Thus, a major change in workplace life has been the switch to external from internal hiring and the decline in job tenure.

What often goes unnoticed is the interaction effect between the previously discussed demographic cohorts and their career patterns. A crucial point here is that career patterns and cohorts went hand in hand. It was mentioned in an earlier section that small cohorts typically have better access to jobs and employment opportunities (Trovato, 2009). Of course a major factor affecting these demographic boom and bust groups is the economy which in turn will affect their labor-force experiences. In fact, interaction effects between demographic and economic factors also help account for career pattern changes in the postwar period. This trend especially applied to the Depression baby bust, whose members entered the labor force during a period when the economy underwent rapid growth with intense demand for workers. For that smaller cohort, the situation presented a fortuitous combination of circumstances (Trovato, 2009). I refer to these busters as being doubly blessed because they formed a small labor force that was in high demand during buoyant economic times.

In contrast, the larger postwar baby-boom cohort was raised during a prosperous period with high aspirations, yet it faced challenging economic conditions after the late 1970s with more tenuous job and career prospects that produced an unfavorable conjunction of demographic and economic conditions (Trovato, 2009). The influx of the larger baby boom cohort into the labor force occurred during a period of increased global competition coupled with technological change, which together led to the elimination of many entry-level and mid-management jobs (Bardwick, 1986; Bennett, 1990). While strong service-sector job growth helped the front-end boomers, job saturation was especially felt by the post-peak or tail end of the larger baby-boom generation (Gaudet, 2007). In contrast with the Depression busters who were doubly blessed before them, some members of the baby boom were in a sense doubly cursed by virtue of being part of a larger generation during a period of economic and career-pattern upheaval.

The study of career patterns revealed dramatic change beginning in the last decades of the twentieth century (Driver, 1985). The two career patterns most prevalent in the immediate postwar decades had been the steady-state career (a stable career path with a life-long commitment to a profession) and the linear career (climbing a promotion-centred ladder within a tall organizational hierarchy). However, the two career patterns more prevalent today are the spiral and the transitory patterns (Foot & Venne, 1990). The spiral career involves a moderate number of changes in occupation over a number of firms. The transitory pattern has the most variation, with frequent occupational change and lateral mobility. These latter two career patterns involved employees being in charge of their more varied careers, having less internal job markets, and having increased demand for education. If careers in the earlier postwar period could be characterized as paddling a canoe down a slow-flowing stream, careers today are more likely to be compared to white-water rafting down a thundering river with numerous rapids and turns along the way.

One notable change in career management today is that increasingly the work environment has shifted the responsibility of an individual's career from the organization to the self (Venneberg & Eversole, 2010). In the immediate postwar decades, it was the organization that decided who would move to what job in order to serve the needs of the firm –the individual had little choice in the matter (Cappelli 2006). Lancaster and Stillman (2002) referred to career changes as the difference between job security and career security. The former was where Depression/WWII busters and early boomers worked their way up the career ladder of a lifetime-employment firm, and the latter was where mid-to-late boomers, current busters, and the echo build their expertise and guide their careers themselves. Individual employees are now told that one's growth and career are one's personal responsibility (Egan, 1994). Career mentoring and management has moved from being rigid or heavy handed under the old career patterns to being non-existent at many firms today. Thus, Cranwell-Ward et al. (2004) noted that mentoring today is needed more than ever because employees need guidance navigating their careers through the changing psychological contract. I explore the importance of mentoring with respect to careers and generational diversity in the following section.

An Emerging Model of Mentoring

In this section I provide examples of how mentoring can be used to deal with changing career patterns and generational diversity. The benefits of mentoring are crucial to organizations as they navigate the changing psychological contract and an emerging model of career management. Also mentoring can improve cross-generational communication and alleviate conflict between cohorts in the workplace.

Cappelli (2008) observed that the shift in career management has gone from the traditional model, in which career plans were managed entirely for the employer's interests, to a situation in which no planning and no help occurred – employees were on their own – and now to an emerging model in which employers seek to help employees figure out their career interests. This latter model uses processes of mentoring and career coaching. It increases employee engagement and retention while decreasing uncertainty, which is especially important with today's tighter labor markets. In essence, the employee is given more of a sense of control.

Firms that provide career development guidance through mentoring have the benefit of developing human assets for the firm.

Mentoring aids in the retention of valued employees by seeking to create a bond and enhancing job satisfaction (Harvard Business Essentials, 2004). For example, Lancaster and Stillman (2002) found in their research that over 40% of Xers (current busters) reported that having a mentor directly influenced their decision to stay at their current company. Mentoring was found to be in demand because two thirds of employees in their survey complained of a lack of mentoring in their careers. DeLong (2004) provided an example of one firm's career development program that helped to reduce attrition, and Dougherty, Turban, and Haggard (2010) reported that those employees who were mentored enjoyed greater career success.

Another important function of mentoring is to help transfer important tacit knowledge from one set of employees to another. This area relates to career pattern change as well as to generational diversity because the transfer is usually from older to younger employees from different cohorts with dissimilar career experiences. Mentoring has also been suggested as a way to deal with the exit of the large baby-boom generation from the workforce. DeLong (2004) predicted that many organizations will be overwhelmed with threats of lost knowledge due largely to baby-boomer retirements over the next few years. He described mentoring as one of the most effective ways of directly transferring critical, implicit, and tacit work-related knowledge from one person to another. Mentoring can support the sharing of the broadest range of knowledge from detailed technical skills and tacit cultural values all the way to career development advice. However, he acknowledged that certain barriers exist to mentoring when dealing with knowledge transfer between the generations.

Training of both mentors and protégés and creating effective infrastructure to support mentoring are essential to ensuring that critical knowledge is passed on. Furthermore, in mentoring relationships where there is specific knowledge transfer from more senior to more junior employees, Delong (2004) recommended adequate two-way interaction between mentors and protégés, and training should involve encouraging this interchange. In terms of generational diversity and mentoring, Erickson (2008) was one of the most sanguine of the experts. She identified the close relationships that the baby-boom echo cohort has with their parents and expects that these relationships will transfer to their baby boomer colleagues. In effect she noted that echos are happy to be mentored and feel comfortable with their parental-aged colleagues. Indeed, Scandura (2002) discussed the mentor role as a balance between parent and peer. Regarding the demand for mentoring, Lancaster and Stillman (2010) indicated that the younger generation was in search of mentors because they have been coached all their lives. In her optimistic book, Erickson (2008) noted that the younger cohorts have been accustomed to team learning and are comfortable working with boomers. She also suggested that the mentoring relationship is collaborative in that it has the dual benefit of re-engaging mid-career or late-career workers (the mentors) while boosting the organizational know-how of less experienced employees (the protégés or mentees). Mentoring as a two-way street is a recurring theme among experts.

Other scholars were not as optimistic as Erickson regarding how the generations interact in the workplace. Delong (2004) characterized the baby boomers as highly competitive and anxious to gain respect for their experiences and achievements. Important ingredients for effective knowledge transfer are trust, mutual respect, and specific training in mentoring. Both Lancaster and Stillman (2010) and Delong (2004) further suggested that another key factor was to reassure older workers that fear of losing one's value by sharing expertise with younger colleagues is an almost universal emotion in organizations today, and that they should rather see themselves as unique possessors and important contributors of accumulated wisdom. Generational knowledge and sensitivity training for all members of the organization would help everyone deal effectively with generational diversity and with the facilitation of the mentoring relationship (Zemke et al., 2000).

There are numerous examples of how mentoring can bring the generations together and aid in career management in workplaces today. For instance, Lancaster and Stillman (2002) described a non-profit program called *Women across Generations* that encouraged cross-generational mentoring. Such programs placed a value on generational diversity, which they considered to be diversity at its finest. One example involved a program in the state of California in which retired state employees returned to the workplace on a part-time basis to serve as mentors and to ensure that their expertise and wisdom were passed on to the upcoming cadre.

Another example involved the 3M mentoring program whereby one high-level director was paired with several younger employees from outside his or her reporting structure. This mentoring program enhanced generational understanding in that the director (usually a baby boomer) taught the busters or echo boomers "the unwritten rules" regarding 3M's culture while the mentor also heard the perspectives and ideas of younger employees. Another innovative program, called *Two-in-a-Box*, partnered older and younger engineers. The program was designed to prevent losing knowledge and had the added benefit of improving retention of those who shared key information (older engineers) as well as those receiving the information (younger engineers). That is, both groups realized the value of sharing their respective bodies of knowledge in a two-way fashion as the younger was also able to share their own thoughts as well.

There are also examples of the two-way benefits of so-called reverse mentoring. Sabattini et al. (2010) described a bank's program of reverse mentoring (referred to as *Engaging Generational Differences*) where senior leaders were paired with junior employees to cultivate opportunities to educate senior employees about diversity, provide visibility to junior employees, and improve cross-generational communication. Lancaster and Stillman (2010) found that reverse mentoring could be used to enhance the younger employees' skill sets, which in turn resulted in increased understanding of generational differences among all subgroups. Another benefit of reverse mentoring involved younger members teaching technical skills to older workplace members. Though research on the benefits of mentoring for the mentor had been minimal, Ramaswami and Dreher (2010) asserted that awareness of generational differences and knowledge of the latest trends in one's field were two observed benefits for mentors. Cranwell-Ward et al. (2004) concluded that although mentoring may offer challenges for both mentor and protégé alike, it was a good way to ensure that all team members feel committed to the organization, a fact which would ultimately aid in the competition for talent.

Concluding Comments

As with any workplace program, the best interventions are purposeful or strategic. So organizations need to determine why they need a mentoring program, what goals they have for the program, and what success will look like (Tardy, 2011). In this chapter I have proposed mentoring programs as a bridge to the generational and career divide. With these twin goals in mind, a successful mentoring program would result in lessened generational conflict and successful career management resulting in high levels of employee engagement and a strong retention rate for the organization. Other measures of achievement might include the successful transfer of knowledge from the older to the younger generation of workers.

In terms of dealing with career management and generational diversity, mentoring can prove to be a valuable tool. Savickas (2010) highlighted the seismic shift of the new boundary-less career with its repeated transitions and identified mentoring as the prime form of career assistance in the information age. Zemke et al. (2000) noted that generational-friendly workplaces allow for accommodation of employee differences and for creation of workplace choice in terms of careers that no are longer regimented. Mentoring has been shown to enhance generational understanding and to help ensure that diversity is a benefit rather than a source of conflict. The use of mentoring in the modern workplace, when applied strategically and purposefully with appropriate resources (e.g., training), can be highly effective in dealing with the related concerns of career change and generational diversity.

References

Bardwick, J. (1986). *The plateauing trap*. New York, NY: Amacom.

Belkin, L. (2007, July 27). When Herbert met Matthew: The generation clash. *The Globe and Mail*, p. C2.

Bennett, A. (1990). *The death of the organization man*. New York, NY: William Morrow.

Betcherman, G., & Lowe, G. (1997). *The future of work in Canada: A synthesis report. Canadian Policy Research Networks*. Ottawa, ON: Renouf. Available from http://www.cprn.org/doc.cfm?doc=454

Cappelli, P. (2006). Changing career paths and their implications. In D. Lawler & J. O'Toole (Eds.), *America at work: Choices and challenges* (pp. 211–224). New York, NY: Palgrave Macmillan.

Cappelli, P. (2008). *Talent on demand: Managing talent in an age of uncertainty*. Boston, MA: Harvard Business Press.

Craig, E., & Hall, D. (2006). Bringing careers back in: The changing landscape of careers in American corporations today. In D. Lawler and J. O'Toole (Eds.), *America at work: Choices and challenges* (pp. 131–152). New York, NY: Palgrave Macmillan.

Cranwell-Ward, J., Bossons, P., & Gover, S. (2004). *Mentoring: A Henley review of best practice*. New York, NY: Palgrave Macmillan.

DeLong, D. (2004). *Lost knowledge: Confronting the threat of an aging workforce*. Oxford, UK: Oxford University Press.

Dougherty, T., Turban, D., & Haggard, D. (2010). Naturally occurring mentoring relationships in the workplace. In T. Allen & L. Eby (Eds.), *The Blackwell handbook of mentoring: Multiple perspectives approach* (pp. 139–158). Malden, MA: Wiley-Blackwell.

Driver, M. J. (1985). Demographic and societal factors affecting the linear career crisis. *Canadian Journal of Administrative Studies*, 2(2), 245–263.

Eby, L., Rhodes, J., & Allen, T. (2010). Definition and evolution of mentoring. In T. Allen & L. Eby (Eds.), *The Blackwell handbook of mentoring: Multiple perspectives approach* (pp.7–20). Malden, MA: Wiley-Blackwell.

Egan, G. (1994, January). Hard times contract. *Management Today*, 48–50. Retrieved from http://www.managementtoday.co.uk/news/410141/uk-hard-times

Erickson, T. (2008). *Retire retirement: Career strategies for the boomer generation.* Boston, MA: Harvard Business Press.

Foot, D. K. (1996). *Boom, bust & echo: How to profit from the coming demographic shift.* Toronto, ON: Macfarlane, Walter, & Ross.

Foot, D. K., & Venne, R. A. (1990). Population, pyramids and promotional prospects. *Canadian Public Policy, 16*(4), 387–98.

Gaudet, S. (2007). *Emerging adulthood: A new stage in the life course; Implication for policy development* [Discussion Paper]. Ottawa, ON: Policy Research Initiative. Available from http://publications.gc.ca/pub?id=320569&sl=0

Harvard Business Essentials. (2004). *Coaching and mentoring: How to develop top talent and achieve stronger performance.* Boston, MA: Harvard Business School Press.

Lancaster, L., & Stillman, D. (2002). *When generations collide.* New York, NY: Harper Collins.

Lancaster, L., & Stillman, D. (2010). *The M factor: How the millennial generation is rocking the workplace.* New York, NY: Harper Collins.

Leana, C. (2002). The changing organizational context of careers. In D. Feldman (Ed.) *Work careers: A developmental perspective* (pp. 274–293). San Francisco, CA: Jossey-Bass,

Owram, D. (1996). *Born at the right time: A history of the baby-boom generation.* Toronto, ON: University of Toronto Press.

Ramaswami, A., & Dreher, G. (2010). Benefits associated with workplace mentoring relationships. In T. Allen & L. Eby (Eds.), *The Blackwell handbook of mentoring: Multiple perspectives approach* (pp. 211–232). Malden, MA: Wiley-Blackwell.

Ricard, F. (1994/1992). *The Lyric generation: The life and times of the baby boomers* (D. Winkler, Trans.). Toronto, ON: Stoddart Publishing Company.

Sabattini, L., Warren, A., Dinolfo, S., Falk, E., & Castro, M. (2010). *Beyond generational differences: Bridging gender and generational diversity at work* [Research report]. Available from http://www.catalyst.org/publication/446/beyond-generational-differences-bridging-gender-and-generational-diversity-at-work

Savickas, M. L. (2010). Foreword: The maturation of mentoring research. In T. Allen & L. Eby (Eds.), *The Blackwell handbook of mentoring: Multiple perspectives approach* (pp. xvii–xix). Malden, MA: Wiley-Blackwell.

Scandura, T. (2002). The establishment years: A dependence perspective. In D. Feldman (Ed.), *Work careers: A developmental perspective* (pp. 159–185). San Francisco, CA: Jossey-Bass.

Silverman, C., (2007, June 25). Attack of the fresh-faced go-getters. *The Globe and Mail*, p. L3.

Tardy, A. (2011). *9 Best practices for creating powerful mentoring programs* [Online Article]. Retrieved from http://www.lifemoxie. com/documents/9BestPracticesforCreatingPowerfulMentoring Programs_000.pdf

Trovato, F. (2009). *Canada's population in a global context*. Don Mills, ON: Oxford University Press.

Venneberg, D., & Eversole, B. (2010). *The Boomer retirement time bomb: How companies can avoid the fallout from the coming skills shortage*. New York, NY: Praeger Publishers.

Zemke, R., Raines, C., & Filipczak, B. (2000). *Generations at work: Managing the clash of veterans, boomers, xers and nexters in your workplace*. New York, NY: Amacom.

Chapter Seven

Peer Mentorship: Narratives of PhD Attainment*

Jane P. Preston, Marcella J. Ogenchuk, & Joseph K. Nsiah

O NE AFTERNOON IN EARLY SEPTEMBER, we ten new PhD students had just sat down in a small university classroom and were glancing nervously at one other. Although most of us had never met, we had made the same decision to enter the graduate program in educational administration, and now it was time to embark on the journey. As we waited for the professor to enter the room, we awkwardly began to make small talk in an effort to ease the discomfort. Over the next two years, we neophyte scholars would work closely together to complete our courses and face the challenges that would punctuate our academic campaigns. Both collectively and individually, we would experience confusion, frustration, mental fatigue, self-doubt, and other intellectually, physically, spiritually, and emotionally taxing circumstances. Unbeknownst to us that first morning, we would soon discover that we would need each other as we adjusted to the new academic lifestyle and its related pressures. Moreover, as that first semester passed, we would come to increasingly trust and rely on one another, and for some of us, we were to find that the stranger sitting next to us that first day would become a best friend and confidante. In this chapter, three of us share some personal reflections of that journey in which we were able to mentor one another.

In generating our narratives, each author independently reflected upon his/her experiences as a doctoral student, and that method of documentation allowed for common themes and differentiated topics to naturally emerge from our experiences. Writing our individual stories first, later permitted us to collectively analyze our narratives and identify the overarching themes threaded throughout the pieces.

* After an academic review process, this chapter was accepted as a "refereed contribution" by the editors.

A noteworthy aspect of our independent reflections was that they were in line with the principles of narrative inquiry research. As Connelly and Clandinin (1990) suggested, collecting information through an individual story is an alternate way to think about an experience. Riley and Hawe (2004) stressed that personal narrative methods give new and deeper insight into the complexity of professional practices. Following Riley and Hawe, we believe that one of the most powerful attributes of our PhD narratives was the idea that they *portrayed* rather than *told* the reader what peer mentorship means. Our stories were three separate descriptions showing how peer mentorship positively influenced our paths toward the attainment of our PhDs.

We provide definitions and characteristics traditionally associated with mentorship, but we also explain how our perception of peer mentorship differs from other forms of mentorship commonly described in the literature. By communicating our lived experiences, we give examples of how and why our cohort of graduate students succeeded academically and flourished socially. We describe how the culture of our cohort, with its aspects of reciprocity, synergy, and trust, helped individual classmates become a cohesive learning family. We believe that our story illustrated that effective peer mentorship can honor the intellectual, emotional, spiritual, and physical well-being of graduate students, and in doing so, it can also enhance a sustainable institutional culture of learning. The overarching purpose of the chapter was to identify the power of informal peer mentorship and how it contributed to the attainment of our academic goals.

Defining Mentorship and Peer Mentorship

Although multiple descriptions of mentorship exist, it is commonly characterized as a process whereby experienced individuals guide or teach less experienced individuals (Achinstein & Athanases, 2006; Fresko & Wertheim, 2003; Shaw, 1995; Shea, 2002; Smit, 2003). Trorey and Blamires (2006) indicated, "The classic portrayal [of mentorship] is of an older and wiser individual influencing the personal and intellectual growth of a younger protégé" (p. 167). In such traditional capacities, mentors are often referred to as a teachers, coaches, counsellors, advisors, guides, role models, sages, or resource persons. Mentorship typically involves relationships created via assigned mentor/mentee pairs or groups of individuals. In its traditional sense, mentors and mentees often meet during pre-arranged times to discuss mentee development and any concerns or challenges a mentee might face. Mentorship is often generated through a formal structure where protocol or regulations define the mentor-mentee relationship and determine the hierarchy and distribution of power. For example, mentor responsibilities frequently include the creation of written professional targets for the mentee (Cullingford, 2006; Zachary, 2000). Mentors are assigned to evaluate a mentee's work or academic progress, and Allen and Eby (2007) found that much of the research on mentorship focused on assigned youth-adult mentorships, student-faculty mentorships, or mentor-mentee partnerships formally established within the workplace.

In contrast, our focus on peer mentorship was different. First, by clarifying what peer mentoring was *not*, we were able to describe this distinctiveness. In our experiences, peer mentorship was neither premeditated nor formally structured. Novice and experienced students were not officially paired in a traditional buddy system, for example. Our reference to peer mentorship did not involve mentors' and mentees' predetermined goals or job descriptions, but rather it referred to a natural process of friends nurturing each other. It was an informal process where mentees and mentors communicated verbally and non-verbally, and where tacit knowledge between these individuals was generated and shared. Any distinctive responsibilities of mentor and mentee were blurred; a peer at any time could assume the role of mentor, mentee, or both roles simultaneously. We considered the concept of peer mentorship to be somewhat elusive and yet characterized by trusting, synergistic relationships that had the potential to transform a cohort of individual students into a team of academic comrades. To us, peer mentorship turned out to be a socially unifying practice that provided us with guidance, confidence, direction, and experiential learning opportunities. Furthermore, it became a strand within a learning cultural-web, which involved affable relationships with specific faculty members, which in turn led to student empowerment in an enriched learning experience. These points are threaded throughout our peer mentorship accounts.

Jane's Story

At the beginning of my graduate program, although I was committed to the academic challenge, certain feelings of self-doubt permeated my thoughts, such as: Did I have what it would take to finish? Would I be able to contribute to scholarly conversations with fellow students and professors? Was I "PhD worthy?" My classmates appeared more intelligent than I was. They sounded articulate and appeared confident as they expressed their ideas and convictions regarding their research; while in comparison, I had not even chosen a research topic in time. As I sat with my classmates during our early graduate classes during the first term, I remember feeling uncomfortable and intimidated by them and by the unknowns of the program.

Although it may have been normal for graduate students to feel uneasy at that stage, I found that such emotional barriers could be surmounted when I realized I was not alone on my academic journey. I believe that the first step in generating peer-mentorship opportunities was to have a cohort of students who were socially comfortable with each other. It was during the first few weeks of school that we were the most impressionable and open to meeting new people. Freshly-enrolled in a new graduate program, we were optimistic, inquisitive, enthusiastic, and excited about the newness of process. At that time, our workload was lighter, but it grew in intensity as the first semester progressed.

Our department recognized that this period was a social window of opportunity. Consequently, just before the official launch of September courses, the department sponsored a graduate orientation for all PhD students, followed by a graduate student/professor luncheon at the faculty club on campus. During these occasions we introduced ourselves (and any accompanying family members) to our peers and instructors. Professors reciprocated with self-introductions, they identified the classes they taught, and they articulated their research interests.

During the luncheon, I remember feeling honored to dine in a facility frequented by academic scholars, and I felt accepted and valued by my department and its professors, as if I was in some way their "newest sibling." I learned about fellow graduate students and their families and the professors who were going to be my academic guides for the next few years. Those initial social events provided physical and emotional nourishment for me.

However, to encourage a cohort of students to develop trust in each other requires more than an orientation seminar and luncheon date. Establishing a peer mentorship culture would necessitate many more relationship-building opportunities, and our professors were attuned to these requirements because they provided several occasions where our cohort of students could socially bond. For example, during one of our morning courses that was three hours in length, the professor personally invited and accompanied us to the faculty lounge during the break. Not only was the walk from our classroom to the lounge a type of social recess for the group, but sitting in the lounge gave us opportunities to interact with other professors who had congregated there as well. Sometimes we brought cake, candles, and song as we celebrated student and professor birthdays or other special events such as Valentine's or St. Patrick's Day. Regardless of the occasion, I looked forward to sharing fifteen minutes with a group of people who were fast becoming my university family. I believe that our regular visits to the faculty lounge were an integral component of inducing and fostering peer mentorship within our cohort.

As we progressed through our courses, other professors encouraged our cohort to unite academically and socially, such as the one who threaded our group assignments and off-campus weekend retreats into his course requirements. To prepare for many of these classes, students were required to meet outside of normal class time. As is typically the case, meeting to discuss a co-written assignment often involves students engaging in conversations that are off-topic from the allocated task. In preparation for one such co-generated assignment, Jack* and I met to discuss how we were going to complete our work. As he walked into the computer lab, he greeted me and asked how I was doing? I confessed that I was feeling overwhelmed by the workload. I said, "I feel like I am on a sinking ship." He responded, "Yeah, me too. It's called the Titanic!" It was comforting and even empowering to know that my feelings of anxiety were shared by a fellow classmate who I thought was a genius with no

* All names in this chapter are pseudonyms.

problems. I continued to talk with him about the stresses I was feeling. Later, I realized that this cathartic exchange did wonders for my spiritual well-being. As I continued to meet with other peers regarding assignments, I soon recognized that no one understood the tribulations of my academic program better than the students of my cohort. The socialization, trust, laughter, and constructive learning that my peers and I shared while working on our co-assignments were part of the peer-mentorship process.

Not only did the students in my cohort bolster each other socially, emotionally, and spiritually, they complemented each other's academic strengths. For example, the diverse cultures and professions that were represented within our cohort supported the intellectual growth of each student. In terms of countries, our cohort represented Bangladesh, Canada, China, Finland, and Ghana, and the majority of us were conversing in a second or third language. In terms of profession, we represented teachers, nurses, librarians, priests, and managers in a variety of capacities. With such an internationally and professionally dynamic group, class discussions were enriched with a plethora of ethnic, political, religious, and vocational views being continuously contributed. Moreover, because we respected and were open to each other's unique nationality, culture, religion, and belief systems, our heterogeneous backgrounds helped create a type of group homogeneity. We benefitted from each other's knowledge, and cognitively we grew through our assimilated learning experiences. We did not always agree with each other, but because we respected each other, we created a safe environment conducive to intriguing discussions enhanced by divergent philosophical perspectives and thought-provoking questions. Experiencing such a learning culture was highly advantageous in improving the academic growth of individual students, which is a central outcome of quality peer mentorship.

Marcella's Story

Unlike other academic pursuits in which I needed a degree for future employment purposes, my decision to enter into a doctoral program stemmed from a desire to learn about a topic for which I had much passion. However, nervousness set in when I realized that my PhD dream was beginning to materialize. I started to wonder if I had the ability to fulfill the program requirements. In addition, I was feeling intimidated by my lack of experience in academia. Did I even know what was necessary to complete this journey?

Prior to classes starting, my first warm recollection was a welcome email from one of our professors. The email was personal in nature and included a genuine invitation into his course. Later, upon meeting this professor face-to-face for the first time, I recall having a conversation where he displayed a sincere interest in who I was and why I had decided to pursue a PhD. I walked away from our meeting feeling assured that I was where I needed to be. The personable and social aspect of our meeting secured in me a sense of hope that I would find the support I needed from the department. As I look back, his sincerity that I felt during that initial interaction was the genesis of the professional trust that developed between him and me.

From that point in the PhD experience, there were other opportunities within the department that focused on welcoming graduate students and making us feel valued. Most of these events were informal in nature, which enabled me to be more relaxed and to be myself. I felt there was a sense of sincerity from faculty members that permeated the atmosphere and further established a culture of trust within the department. Faculty members were sure to attend graduate student orientations and welcoming sessions, and professors, along with the seasoned students, sat around the tables *with* us, the newcomers. There was food and coffee and plenty of humor that often lightened the seriousness of the task at hand. Time set aside for coffees and celebrations provided us all with opportunities to become acquainted. I soon realized that the "ritual" of taking the time to get together on an informal basis was a norm of the department – a part of the culture of the group. I now believe that these social events were as important as attending classes and completing assignments. The peer mentorship that took place among our student cohort during these times was valuable because together we shared our trepidation as well as our excitement. We not only learned about each others' families but often became a part of each other's lives. Largely because of these events, we gradually developed a strong bond throughout our cohort, which was characterized by a collective expectation of needing to be there for each other.

Planned orientations and regular social and academic gatherings were instrumental in modelling the culture of the department. These meetings provided me assurance that I was not alone in my concerns about completing my academic journey. As a part of this culture, I noticed that the faculty literally kept their office doors open, and when I met professors in the hallway, they took the time to greet me and ask me how I was. This practice grew as faculty members occasionally stopped by our offices to say hello or to inquire if we had questions or needed clarification about assignments. The faculty members made themselves available to us. Our cohort of students watched and learned from our professors, and, in turn, we began to make ourselves available for each other.

As the program workload increased, so did our reliance upon each other. It was not until I was well into the first year that I realized that some of our cohort members knew each other and the professors from previous academic pursuits. Even though some of these relationships pre-existed, I felt as much a part of the group as those who had been there before me. Consequently, it became even more apparent to me that regardless of the similarities or differences of the group members and their backgrounds, the caring outlook we developed for each other was authentic. We kept each other's best interests in mind and maintained mutual respect for each other.

As our program progressed, each student's academic demands, workload changes, and home/employment situations all began to add stress to our lives. Receiving and giving support within our cohort became a way to survive and thrive in many areas of life. When life-changing events occurred for anyone in our cohort, professors showed understanding and flexibility. Some students tragically lost family members or struggled with family health challenges. I learned that just because I was pursuing an academic goal important to me, life did not stop happening for me or for other cohort members. Respect and support for each other was extended through emails, attending religious ceremonies, and providing time to listen. We also freely shared our coping mechanisms with one another. Some members of the cohort seemed naturally adept at dealing with life-changing events through the use of mental and physical strategies such as running. These healthy activities proved to be valuable coping models for the other cohort members to try. Additional selfless acts of our peers provided needed support in other capacities, such as sharing meals, taking time to teach each other necessary skills, or providing transportation to friends without it. These gestures of kindness permeated our PhD environment. Upon reflection, I realized that over the course of our program each one of my cohort members had provided me with something that I needed in order to complete the PhD journey. A lesson taught to me by one of my professors and by the members of my cohort was that life-changing events naturally happen to everyone. I found that such events cannot be avoided or postponed, but they can be experienced while simultaneously succeeding in a doctoral program.

I acknowledge that in my PhD experience, the department orientations and the various opportunities for informal communication were instrumental in building an inclusive, supportive learning culture necessary for peer mentorship to exist and flourish. The support that existed among my cohort allowed me to focus on my primary purpose that had led me to the program, which was to learn more. Trust was established through sincere actions, revealing that our cohort's interest was as much collective as it was individualistic. The professors in the department modelled behaviors that the students in our group began to emulate. I feel fortunate to have had been a part of that peer mentorship culture because it proved to be vital to the completion of my doctoral dissertation. The entire experience enriched my life, provided me with lasting friendships, and offered me a valued learning model that I could use in my future working and teaching environments.

Joseph's Story

We were an apprehensive cohort of 10 students from different backgrounds, each with unique experiences. We were fortunate to be in the hands of caring and knowledgeable professors who not only facilitated our intellectual growth during class but also showed genuine interest in us after class. We represented the continents of North America, Asia, and Africa; we were a veritable United Nations. Early in our program, we came to the understanding that our different backgrounds bolstered each other's intellectual growth. We shared the belief that we had come together to acquire knowledge, nurture relationships, and support each other in obtaining the PhD degree.

At the start of the program, all the students in our cohort were excited and positive about being together. Nevertheless, each student still faced his/her individual challenges during the program. For me, one of those challenges was getting sufficient sleep. For almost two months after entering the PhD program, sleep eluded me! A multitude of reasons accounted for this insomnia, but the main cause was best captured by the nagging question, "What is your dissertation topic?" Initial topics I proposed did not seem to interest or resonate with professors or fellow students, so I quickly abandoned them. My restlessness worsened as professors continued to stress the need to define our research topics as early in the program as possible. As my classmates confidently and excitedly talked about how they were planning to approach their research, my angst increased. I began to ask myself whether or not I had made the right choice enrolling in a PhD program. My peers listened to me as I continued to discuss my tentative research plans. They also recommended that I schedule appointments with the professors in the department to discuss my future research. Equipped with a handful of vague ideas, co-generated from peer discussions, I made appointments with several professors. It was during one such meeting that my research agenda finally became lucid. During this perplexing period of topic search, I am thankful that my peers and professors were there for me. Upon reflection, I believe that the peer mentorship I experienced during that early timeframe played a major role in helping me complete my doctoral program.

As a result of the regular social interaction among the students in our cohort, we began to develop trust in each other. Because of this emerging trust, Susan, one of my classmates, candidly asked me a question one day: "Joseph, we never see you during our coffee breaks. Why aren't you joining us? Is there a problem? Don't you like us?" Truthfully, I did not like drinking coffee and was indifferent to such time-consuming breaks. So, I regularly rejected offers to socialize. Furthermore, I had come from a culture where peer fraternization together with professors was uncommon and somewhat uncomfortable. I explained my feelings and cultural inclinations to Susan. She replied, "I understand that is the way it might be in your country, but here it's not viewed in that way. In fact, you may be considered antisocial if you don't join us once in a while." This forthright advice revealed an important facet of Canadian culture that I later found relevant to my PhD studies. After becoming accustomed to partaking in coffee breaks, I discovered that sitting at a table in the faculty lounge with classmates, professors, and students from other programs created priceless *aha* moments for me. The intriguing ideas and advice I gained while informally talking to my peers and professors enabled me to improve the quality and expedite the completion of my dissertation.

Repeatedly, throughout our time together, our group of 10 demonstrated that knowledge, per se, was not to be monopolized but to be shared for the growth of all. That point was fostered by the fact that our department provided shared office space for its PhD students. The close proximity of all of our offices was convenient for dispersing information and for permitting us easy access to one another to answer course-based questions, to borrow/lend materials, or to seek clarification on assignments. Our willingness to share knowledge, resources, and talent were epitomized during various group-work tasks and when we volunteered to read or to provide editorial comments on our peers' papers. Some students with specific subject expertise presented workshops for our entire cohort. As we prepared for our comprehensive examinations in the second year of our program, we provided emotional and intellectual support for each other in many ways. In particular, we would invite our peers to conduct slide presentations to practice for the pending comprehensive examinations because we found that presenting information in front of peers was less intimidating than facing a group of professors. On several occasions, students invited cohort members to observe and critique the quality of peers' presentations created for a conference, examination, or job interview. By means of such activities by the students in our cohort, the process of peer mentorship emerged, and as a result we recognized our individual academic strengths and talents and were gradually willing to offer these self-contributions to any of our peers who needed what we could supply. It proved to be a mutual and collaborative exchange that energized and benefitted all of us.

For me, one of the things I needed from my peers was computer assistance. Because I had minimal computer skills, I estimated that it took me five times longer than my classmates to access useful information and to complete assignments. Cognizant of the fact that my survival in the PhD program depended on my computer skills, I did not hesitate to ask my peers to assist me in this area. My peers taught me how to navigate Microsoft Word, Microsoft Publisher, and PowerPoint, how to create a table of contents, how to create tables and figures, and how to format documents using computer shortcuts. As a result of their patience and direction, I gradually gained in these technical skills, and I was able to personally type my dissertation without hiring the services of a professional typist. This accomplishment would not have been possible had I not been a recipient of peer mentorship.

By the mid-point of my program, as I was becoming increasingly comfortable being a PhD student, I was to take a mandatory course that I nicknamed *Almighty Statistics*. Because statistics was compulsory and the stakes were high, I needed to pass the course to obtain the PhD. For me, having to complete this course meant revisiting and reliving the mathematical anxiety and humiliation I had experienced throughout my elementary and high school grades. I asked several classmates for help. One peer, who was also enrolled in the course, provided me with the typed notes that he created after every class, and another peer provided me with moral support. I regularly met with a homework group to complete our statistics assignments. It seemed strange that with all the support I had, I still did not understand many of the concepts being discussed. While discussing my statistics frustrations with one particular classmate, I said, "Dorothy, before you stands the most obtuse mind when it comes to calculating figures. If you discuss statistics, consider me not only as tabula rasa but as a grade one student." From the day I confided in her until the end of the statistics course, Dorothy dedicated approximately three hours a week to re-teaching the course-content for me, individually. Every week, we found an empty classroom, and, on the chalkboard, we worked through the assigned problems. She also created homework assignments and mock exams for me. I found her to be especially gifted at simplifying complicated concepts. Thanks to Dorothy's and other peers' mentorship, I passed the statistics course.

I was thrilled when Dorothy told me that she had developed a better understanding of statistics because of this teaching/learning period. This experience emphasized the reciprocal potential of peer mentorship.

The cohesion and solidarity that developed within our cohort was also manifested in other ways, including the home invitations that my peers extended to each other as we celebrated birthdays and special occasions. Invariably, during these social events, we conversed with each other, exchanging useful ideas that directly or indirectly affected our PhD journey. For our group, there was little separation between our academic pursuits and our personal lives. We expressed acts of sympathy and condolence towards our peers who had been bereaved at various times during their programs, we listened and offered family/domestic advice to each other as needed, and, on occasion, laughed at our shortcomings. For me, peer mentorship was evident in our department made up of a caring group of professors and a selfless, encouraging, and supportive cohort of peers. I believe that these relationships are a key reason why I humbly boast of a PhD degree today.

Implications and Concluding Thoughts

"Mentoring is best when it is free of pressure, and when it feels reciprocal" (Cullingford, 2006, p. 9). A key characteristic of the above stories is that each student had the freedom to both mentor their peers and be mentored by their peers in ways that addressed their differentiated needs and abilities. Such dynamic process is in a continuous stake of flux because the roles of mentor and mentee are interchangeable and flexible, as the situation warrants. This two-way symbiotic relationship is not something that can be coerced into existence. Instead, we feel that peer-mentorship relationships need to be nurtured within a type of learning-focused microcosm that accentuates and utilizes the strengths and skills of each of its members. This relationship-dependent environment has characteristics typically found within learning communities. The strength of a graduate student learning community can be further fortified by the unit's administrators and professors who provide graduate students with opportunities to co-learn, co-teach, and support each other.

Capra (2002) stated, "For an organization to be alive, the exist-ence of social networks is not sufficient; they need to be networks of a special type" (p. 108). We contend that promoting peer mentor-ship in graduate student programs requires the formation of a spe-cial type of social network that attends to the intellectual, emotion-al, spiritual, and physical realms of student well-being. Honoring growth within these four areas cultivates a holistic and intercon-nected atmosphere that promotes success in graduate studies. The professional and academic development of graduate students must be attuned with addressing the challenges of balancing academic and personal fulfillment. We believe individuals best gain know-ledge by observing and participating in relationships that create and stimulate their learning/work environment. Quality peer mentor-ship is the formation of a relationally constructed education that emphasizes experiential learning, a type of immediate application for theory-based knowledge.

Promotion by universities, professors, and graduate students to take advantage of peer mentorship possibilities will enhance gradu-ate programs. The benefits accrued by having graduate students immersed in a peer mentorship culture are too powerful to ignore because it has great potential to endorse academic self-confidence, cognitive growth, a social safety-net, and, ultimately, greater gradu-ate success. By contrast, graduate students encounter heightened feelings of isolation and distress when enrolled in programs that are devoid of a peer mentorship spirit.

Perhaps one of the most powerful aspects of peer mentorship is its prospects of sustainability. Although organizations work at developing and maintaining mentorship programs, some of these programs enjoy limited success, while others are dynamic and thriv-ing. We assert that the difference between mediocre mentorship programs and vibrant sustainable ones relates to the existence of an institutional approach to peer mentorship, where it is directly pro-moted within the organization. At its core, sustainable peer men-torship pertains to forging positive student-student and student-faculty relationships that in turn positively inspires student morale and learning. Our collective experience has shown that when the teaching and learning enterprise in a graduate program takes into account students and their unique needs, sustainable peer mentorship is enabled.

Metaphorically, we conceptualize that the united strength reflected through peer mentorship is similar to a type of academic and emotional banking system in which anyone involved in peer mentorship can make a deposit or withdrawal. For example, when a student provides guidance and advice to another student, deposits are made, or when a peer accepts the help of another student, withdrawals are transacted. The best aspect of this peer mentorship banking system is the lack of formal record keeping because deposit and withdrawal slips are never required. In our three stories we have attempted to describe some of the wealth contained in one such peer mentorship depository.

References

Achinstein, B., & Athanases, S. Z. (2006). Introduction: New visions for mentoring new teachers. In B. Achinstein & S. Z. Athanases (Eds.), *Mentors in the making: Developing new leaders for new teachers*. New York, NY: Teachers' College Press.

Allen, T. C., & Eby, L. T. (2007). Overview and introduction. In T. C. Allen & L. T. Eby (Eds.), *The Blackwell handbook of mentoring: A multiple perspectives approach* (pp. 3–6). Malden, MA: Blackwell.

Capra, F. (2002). *The hidden connections: A science for sustainable living*. New York, NY: Random House.

Connelly, F. M., & Clandinin, D. J. (1990). Stories of experience and narrative inquiry. *Educational Researcher, 19*(5), 2–14.

Cullingford, C. (2006). Mentoring as myth and reality: Evidence and ambiguity. In C. Cullingford (Ed.), *Mentoring in education: An international perspective* (pp. 1–10). Aldershot, UK: Ashgate.

Fresko, B., & Wertheim, C. (2003). Building cultures of caring and empowerment for Israel's at-risk youth. In F. L. Kochan & J. T. Pascarelli (Eds.), *Global perspectives on mentoring: Transforming contexts, communities, and cultures* (pp. 23–38). Greenwich, CT: Information Age.

Riley, T., & Hawe, P. (2004). Researching practice: The methodological case for narrative inquiry. *Health Education Research, 20*(2), 226–236.

Shaw, R. (1995). Mentoring. In T. Kerry & M. Shelton (Eds.), *Issues in mentoring* (pp. 259–267). London, UK: Routledge.

Shea, G. F. (2002). *Mentoring: How to develop successful mentor behaviours*. Menlo Park, CA: Crisp.

Smit, P. (2003). Women, mentoring, and opportunity in higher education: South African experiences. In F. L. Kochan & J. T. Pascarelli (Eds.), *Global perspectives on mentoring: Transforming contexts, communities, and cultures* (pp. 129–148). Greenwich, CT: Information Age.

Trorey, G., & Blamires, C. (2006). Mentoring new academic staff in higher education. In C. Cullingford (Ed.), *Mentoring in education: An international perspective* (pp. 167–182). Aldershot, UK: Ashgate.

Zachary, L. J. (2000). *The mentor's guide: Facilitating effective learning relationships*. San Francisco, CA: Jossey-Bass.

Chapter Eight

Mentoring and Teacher Supervision in K to 12 Schools: Parallel and Related Processes

Norm Dray

I GOT OFF THE PHONE AT 10:30 one evening after a long conversation with a colleague who I believe would call me his "mentor." Conversing with him caused me to reflect on the relationships that I have had in my career and the implications of these relationships for the mentorship process. I consider myself fortunate that there are many people with whom I have worked, or more recently taught in graduate school, who have called me to discuss career or life challenges. The mentorship process is one in which I have often engaged as a mentor, but very few times have I had the opportunity to be a protégé. Over the years I have reflected on the mentoring process and the impact it may have had on some people and perhaps on the school divisions in the provinces where my family and I have lived. Some of my recent conversations and readings have helped me to frame my perspectives on mentorship, especially as it relates to my own working life.

As a long time educator and administrator in Kindergarten to Grade 12 (K–12) school systems, I see a close relationship between mentorship and the process of teacher supervision, which was a critical part of my duties, both when I was a school principal and when I was a system-level senior administrator. Before elaborating on these insights, I share a brief autobiography to contextualize my perspectives, I provide an overview of the chapter, and I describe the teacher supervision process that exists in many K–12 school systems.

Autobiographical Sketch

I had the pleasure of serving as a principal for eight years in several K–12 schools of various sizes. In all of them I had direct responsibility for teacher supervision and for writing supervisory reports regarding teachers' performance. After my time as principal in a relatively large school, I served as CEO or Director of Education for three school divisions in Canada. The first division was a small system serving approximately 1000 students in a rural area, the second district was a larger suburban system, and the third was a system with 16,000 students and 43 schools. My career as Director/CEO of these school systems spanned almost 22 years. During that period, I was responsible for supervising and evaluating teachers for 18 years and was responsible for supervising and evaluating principals for all 22 years. Consequently, my interest in the mentorship and supervision processes, and my perspectives on them, stem from the extensive, practical, and predominantly positive experiences I have had being immersed in these activities throughout my 30 years as an educational administrator.

In addition to school-system-based experience, I had the opportunity to study teacher supervision and mentorship from an academic perspective. My doctoral studies supported and developed my understanding of supervisory/mentoring practice. Through my graduate-studies research with successful principals, I became convinced that teacher supervision needed to be conducted within a "Community of Learners" (Sackney & Mitchell, 2002), or a "Community of Practice" (Wenger, 1999). My research led me to reflect on supervision and to relate it to the mentoring process.

Overview of Chapter

I argue in this chapter that teacher supervision is best understood as part of a larger mentorship process, and that some of the theoretical work regarding supervision could be applied to gain a deeper understanding of mentorship within K–12 education. I use Glickman's (1981) *Paradigm of Teacher Categories* as a framework for distinguishing between different teacher types. I refer to my professional experience as a mentor to illustrate these concepts, and I relate them to the literature.

To contextualize this discussion, I describe the teacher supervision process based on a developmental approach, particularly Glickman's (1981) model. Next, I share stories of supervision and mentorship from my professional career to illustrate connections between the supervisory and mentorship processes. Then I refer to Glickman's teacher categories as a frame to analyze my personal experiences and other approaches to teacher supervision. As I review these elements, I relate them to my evolving conception of mentorship.

Teacher Supervision

Teacher supervision is the process of supervising and evaluating the work of teachers in the performance of their instructional and professional duties. These duties primarily involve the teaching act; the planning, preparing, and assessing components; and the professional/ethical aspect of their role. Appraising teachers' ability to keep current with teaching methods, to manage student behavior, and to achieve prescribed educational outcomes is also part of this supervision and appraisal process. As with most aspects of the educational enterprise, a variety of theories exist regarding how to conduct the supervision/mentorship. I believe that, at its best, teacher supervision is closely related to mentorship because both processes focus fundamentally on fostering the professional growth of an individual.

The traditional supervision process usually involves a type of pre-conference, a classroom observation of performance or some collection of data over a specified period of time, and a post-conference where the results of the observation are reviewed and goals set for future development. From insights gained from my educational experience, I contend that this post-conference stage of the process is critical because it is where the mentorship relationship can begin to be fostered. Post-conferences can take on a wide-ranging focus in which the aspirations of the teacher and the needs of his/her students can be discussed in a collaborative manner and future initiatives can be collegially explored.

Supervision and Mentorship

I focused on teacher supervision for my doctoral dissertation, and as I reflected on my related reading and my previous practical experience, I learned more regarding the relationship between mentoring and supervision. During my own supervision practice, I had varied my approach based on the experience, ability, and commitment of the teacher or administrator with whom I was working. The literature supported this approach. For instance, Glickman, Gordon, and Ross-Gordon (2001) and Glickman (1981) suggested that supervision should be conducted differently according to the level of abstraction and the level of commitment of the teacher involved (see Figure 1). Glickman (1981) described abstraction as the ability to think through how a strategy or plan might work in a classroom, while he referred to commitment as a person's concern for the welfare of the profession, as evidenced by his/her willingness to spend extra time and energy to help students and other teachers. The goal of instructional supervision should be to help teachers learn how to increase their own capacity to facilitate their students' achievement of learning goals (Glickman et al., 2001; Glickman, 1981).

Teachers often work alone in their classrooms but are, at the same time, part of a larger educational community at the school level (Joyce & Showers, 1987; Senge, 1990). Smith (2003) has cited Lave and Wenger's notion of "community of practice" (pp. 73–84), which is described as a joint enterprise or a mutual engagement focused on generating a shared repertoire of appropriate ideas, commitments, and memories. A community of practice also needs to develop various resources (e.g., tools, documents, routines, vocabularies, and

Figure 1
Glickman's paradigm of teacher categories from Glickman (1981, p. 48)

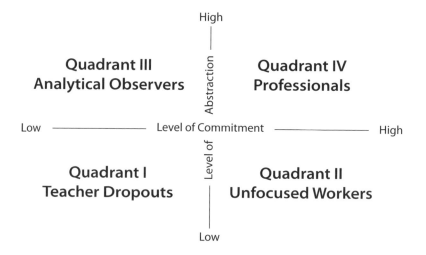

PARADIGM OF TEACHER CATEGORIES

symbols) that represent accumulated knowledge of the community (Lave & Wenger, 1999; Wenger, 1999; Wenger, McDermott, & Snyder, 2002). For example, such groupings could be a community of joint professional practice through the teacher supervision process or a community of mentorship.

Within K–12 school systems, school communities often work together to support staff members who are new to the profession or who may be experiencing challenges in their roles. During my administrative career, I often worked with teachers and administrators who needed guidance through the supervisory and evaluation process. In this capacity, I often collaborated with school-based administrators, other teachers, and district office consultants to access and provide the resources and/or support that these individuals needed.

Glickman's Quadrants

In my mentor or supervisor role, I did not treat all protégés in the same manner. For some individuals, my primary role was to provide encouragement or to serve as a sounding board. For others, I may have had to provide specific directions or advice. The style which I conveyed in those relationships was contingent on the frame of mind, the expressed needs, and/or the ability level of the particular protégé.

Ralph (2000) conducted a study of contextual supervision, in which supervisory style was matched to supervisee readiness. The study demonstrated that when there was a match between supervisor style and supervisee performance on a developmental grid, teacher skill development was enhanced. The later work of Ralph and Walker (2010) reframed contextual supervision as Adaptive Mentorship©(AM), which postulated that protégés should be treated differently depending on their task-specific competence and confidence levels. For instance, mentors working with protégés low in confidence should respond with high levels of support, and similarly, provide protégés low on competence with a more directive response. On the other hand, protégés high in confidence and competence would need little direction and support from the mentor.

The AM model seemed to be similar in approach and findings to the work of Glickman regarding the developmental supervision of teachers. These models emphasized the symbiosis between supervision and mentorship. While Glickman suggested different approaches to supervision based on protégés' level of abstraction and level of commitment, Ralph suggested using different approaches to mentorship based on protégés' levels of skill-specific confidence and competence. Both approaches employed a model with four quadrants and recommended varying supervisor/mentor responses depending on the existing performance of the supervisee/mentee.

Glickman suggested that any teacher fitting the descriptors for Quadrant I was a *Teacher Drop-out*. Such teachers have a low ability to abstract and a low commitment level or who have no ability to analyze their own teaching and no drive to be an effective teacher. He suggested that these people needed directive supervision and were likely to be counselled out of the profession if their commitment level did not change. I would consider that Quadrant I teachers were not suitable candidates for an ongoing mentoring relationship.

Glickman identified a Quadrant II teacher as an *Unfocused Worker*, with low ability for abstraction but a high commitment level – they are not sure what to do, but work diligently. Neophyte teachers often fit into this category because they need some direction, but their motivation to do well is high. They just need help to analyze their teaching and to improve, and such assistance can be provided in a collaborative manner. Teachers in Quadrant II can move into Quadrant IV with support and encouragement. A mentorship relationship can likely be formed with a teacher in Quadrant II, but it will probably not be a lasting relationship if the teacher cannot develop the ability to analyze his or her own teaching. There will be no progression into Quadrant IV.

A Quadrant III teacher type was an *Analytical Observer*, who had high ability to abstract but had a low commitment level – they knew what to do but were not doing it. These people need directive supervision with timelines or occasionally ultimatums to help them enhance their teaching. Because they do not have strong motivation or commitment, I believe that a mentoring relationship on a long term basis with a highly committed mentor is not likely sustainable. I feel that before a lasting relationship with a protégé is possible, he/she would need to be at least progressing into Quadrant IV.

Glickman's Quadrant IV: The Professional

According to Glickman's continuum, the most fully developed stage was Quadrant IV, *The Professional*. This protégé has the ability to both analyze his/her teaching and the commitment to follow through with needed changes to enhance their effectiveness in promoting student learning. Sackney and Mitchell (2002) affirmed that teaching and learning are at the heart of educational leadership. They stated, "Leading is not about telling others what to do but rather about opening spaces for people to learn about what matters to them" (p. 909). Individuals in Glickman's Quadrant IV would find the facilitation approach most useful in the course of their work because they require little direction and consistently analyze and reflect on their own teaching. This philosophy of leadership and learning led Sackney and Mitchell to assert that schools can be communities of learners and possibly even communities of leaders. Senge (2000) described a community of learners as a group working in an environment that is nurturing, supportive, understanding, and challenging. The group shares a mutual understanding and commitment to its own development and the development of children in its jurisdiction. This characteristic seemed consistent with how Glickman described *The Professional* in Quadrant IV and how mentorship might be fostered to suit their needs.

Most of the colleagues who called me for advice or council over the years were people whom I met through the supervisory/mentorship process. We first interacted within a subordinate/superordinate relationship but since then have become friends and colleagues. When I think of the phenomenon of "mentorship" from this personal perspective, I see myself as having been a supporter for them as they built their careers. In my role as an administrator, I conversed with many individuals regarding their strengths, and I encouraged them to consider seeking formal leadership positions. If these people later moved into a leadership position and began to see themselves as leaders, they often recalled our initial conversations or "shoulder tapping" with respect to being encouraged to pursue promotions. If they became formal leaders in the system, the mentor relationship often grew and developed as the initial bond of trust was solidified.

Some Mentoring Stories

I present three accounts of interactions and relationships that I identify with the mentorship process. These relationships were fostered within what Lave and Wenger (1999) described as a community of practice, in which professional support and sense of a "joint enterprise" were present.

Story One: The Large-School Administrator

I became CEO of a school district that seemed like a positive place for adults to work but where student learning was not always the focus. There was genuine camaraderie among adults in the district but no clear vision for the district to foster student learning. According to large-scale assessments, the academic achievement of the students was lagging compared to most other school districts in that province.

The principal of one of the larger schools was focused on relationships and, consequently, was widely respected by parents, students, and staff. He was especially well regarded by his principal colleagues who viewed him as a leader and sometimes as a role model. When I joined the district, I began to speak of instructional and learning improvement and began asking the principals to pay more attention to their role as instructional and learning leaders. This vision became clearer over time. But while it was accepted on the surface, the shift from a relationship-based approach to an approach based on student learning was not embraced by everyone and I believe at times was viewed as an impractical, unattainable "pipe-dream." In particular, the large-school principal I mentioned seemed convinced that positive relationships should be at the centre of the educational enterprise, and that teaching and learning would take care of themselves.

I assigned myself to conduct a performance appraisal with this principal, and as it progressed, I chose a data-based approach. When confronted with achievement data from his school that showed it lagging considerably behind other comparable schools, he and I began a constructive dialogue. Over time, he accepted the merit of an approach that set student learning as the ultimate goal, and he also recognized that positive relationships could still exist in a climate where high expectations were maintained for teachers and students. I was consistently encouraging in my discussions with this principal, even through difficult conversations that focused on the necessity of classroom visits and collaboration with teachers on improving instruction.

I viewed this principal as having strong leadership skill and potential but also as one who needed to refocus the goal of his daily work. Gradually, he adopted the vision of improving student learning and he began calling me regularly for advice and support. His focus changed and his concern for instruction and learning became more obvious, including the development of a school-wide plan to enhance student learning. When a position became available in the division office for supporting principals and schools, I encouraged the principal to apply. He was successful and subsequently became a key advocate for the district's learning-focused vision.

I maintained contact with this individual after I left the district and I continued to encourage him and to support his career path. I believe I had become a mentor to him, even though we had begun our relationship at different places philosophically and educationally. However, we were fortunate to have built our relationship on honesty, and over time we were able to strengthen that relationship based on mutual trust and shared vision. As that bond of trust deepened and our professional roles altered, our relationship became more collegial. The initial "supervisory" relationship morphed into a "peer-mentorship" relationship, which still exists.

Story Two: A Case of Growth and Change

Another account concerns a young teacher who came to a small district where I was CEO. He became a both a highly successful teacher and a well-liked member of the community. The school in which he taught was known for its excellence and innovation, even though it had not always been so. It became known for regularly documenting high student achievement in all subject areas and at all grade levels. I worked with this teacher on a collaborative supervisory plan that gave us the opportunity to explore and expand his teaching repertoire. When the principal of the school retired, this teacher was the staff's choice to fill the position, and it was an easy decision to reach for those of us on the selection committee. Under his leadership the school continued on its trajectory toward excellence.

I left that district and moved to a larger district near a metropolitan centre. This principal called me a year or two later and asked if a job I had advertised was one for which I would consider him. I answered affirmatively, and, after an interview and selection process, he was appointed as a vice principal. During his first year at that school, a situation arose in which the principal vacated the position abruptly, and as a result the vice principal was thrust into the role of principal of the large school, first in an acting capacity and then permanently. He helped resolve one difficult situation and made some decisive changes to refocus the school on its primary responsibility for student learning. Over his time as a VP and then as a principal, the relationship between he and I grew and we became peer mentors. He eventually became a school district CEO. We still speak regularly and offer each other advice and support. Our mentoring relationship grew, and the mutual trust we have developed still supports an ongoing relationship of respect, dialogue, and peer mentorship. Again I note that we began our initial relationship through the supervision process. He had a high level of ability to abstract early in his career and he was always a conscientious worker. I found over the years that he needed little supervisory direction; often only a listening ear and some reflective questions was all the support he required.

Story Three: Working through Challenges

A teacher whom I hired and supervised (first as a teacher and then as a principal), later became a close friend. I have supported her through many work and life challenges in the ensuing years, and as was described in the above two cases, the relationship in this third account also began through the supervision process. Early in her time as a teacher, and later a novice principal, she needed very little directive guidance. I observed that as her confidence grew, she accepted more ownership for her own learning and professional development. She reflected the Quadrant IV attributes, with a high degree of ability to assess her own work and a constant drive to do what was best.

This individual recently experienced a trauma in her career and has left the principalship in favor of a teaching position. She has approached me for advice and support, and according to the AM model, her current confidence level is low (Ralph & Walker, 2010) and needs to be rebuilt. My approach to our mentorship relationship will therefore need to be different as she endeavors to regroup and chooses her path forward. A gentle mentorship response will be important as this rebuilding process takes place.

Teacher Supervision and Mentorship: More Parallels

In the examples above, the protégés developed and changed, and because of this growth, the AM (Ralph & Walker, 2010) model suggested that they should be mentored differently, depending on their levels of competence and confidence to perform specific skill sets or tasks. At certain times they may require direct and close supervision, at others they may require little direction and support.

The research of Siens and Ebmeier (1996) compared the developmental supervision process to a more traditional, purely clinical model. The researchers found that developmental supervision substantially enhanced the reflective thinking skills of teachers. There was also some evidence that when teachers set their own direction for instructional change through a reflective process, there was more commitment to the change and to follow through. In the AM model, people low on confidence but high on competence would benefit most from a mentor with a highly supportive response (to help bolster the lagging confidence), but a less prescriptive or directive task response in favor of a more delegating style in which the mentor backs off and encourages the protégé to set his or her own goals (because of the latter's high level of competence).

To enhance the learning of teachers, there must be significant commitment to the mentorship/supervision process among the participants involved. All stakeholders (administrators, team leaders, and teachers) must co-operate in providing mentoring services that result in frequent feedback to teachers, focus on instructional improvement, emphasize student achievement, and foster collaboration and co-operation (Glatthorn, 1990). Glatthorn, like Glickman, looked at a differentiated model of teacher supervision. He defined self-directed supervision as a process wherein teachers direct their own professional growth (p. 149) and this definition seems to be quite workable in a district where I was CEO for a number of years.

Rettig (1999) examined a case study of a school system that moved to a differentiated model of supervision. He argued that by implementing a differentiated model, the district made major strides in ameliorating the traditional shortcomings of teacher supervision and evaluation approaches. He wrote, "with the flexibility of the differentiated supervision, teachers and administrators are beginning to work together for professional development and teachers are working together more as colleagues and professionals" (p. 39). Similarly, it could be argued that through adaptive mentorship and other differentiated approaches, professionals can work together for mutual growth and development in an effective manner.

Collaborative Models of Supervision

Good and Brophy (1987) noted that classrooms are active places and teachers are so busy responding to a myriad of demands that they have little time to think deeply about what they are doing. They stated, "Teachers are seldom observed on any systematic basis. Consequently, they seldom get valuable information about ways to increase their effectiveness, and when they are observed it is typically for purposes of evaluation" (p. 50). Good and Brophy suggested that observation in classrooms can help to address some of these issues through the development of language to identify specific classroom practices. They felt that peer observation and collaborative practices were underutilized as mechanisms to enhance the instructional process.

It is my belief, born out of my experience, that Good and Brophy's work is still relevant because sometimes as educators we are still too isolated as we carry out our duties. Teachers close the classroom door and seldom get feedback on their work, and principals are often alone within their schools, without access to any meaningful voice for consultation or advice. Mentorship can help to rectify some of these challenges identified by Good and Brophy.

The work of Joyce and Showers (1988) identified the importance of coaching in the classroom for the implementation of change. Their work on the transfer of changes or implementation of new instructional strategies into teaching practice emphasized the benefits of instructional coaching, mentoring, and supervision. They stated that "coached teachers generally practice new strategies more frequently and develop greater skill in the actual moves of a new teaching strategy than do teachers who have experienced identical initial training" (Joyce & Showers, 1988, p. 88). They also stressed the importance of classroom coaching visitations. The relationship between coaching and supervision depends on the nature of relationships and power differentials in the school district. In many districts, the imbalance of power is maintained by combining the processes of instructional supervision and evaluation. Decision making often stays in the hands of superiors while teachers are the recipients of the process. Joyce and Showers (1988) found that supervision is not incompatible with staff development, but they believed that there must be separation between the supervision and evaluation components and an amelioration of power and status differentials.

In 2002, Joyce and Showers reaffirmed their original work and described a process that I would call peer mentorship. They stated that the act of planning with someone and of observing each other using a new skill would more likely help the teacher transfer the skill into practice than any amount of in-service training alone. My experience has supported the work of Joyce and Showers. I have found that coaching, coupled with professional learning opportunities, is a powerful tool for the implementation of change.

A case study of teacher evaluation and supervision at a high performing urban elementary school found that four themes emerged from the data. These themes described characteristics that were perceived to have the greatest impact at the school site on student achievement (Hillyer, 2005). They were staff collaboration, high quality leadership, meaningful professional development, and an emphasis on student achievement. Varley (2005) drew the link between principal leadership, collaborative supervision, and student achievement. She said, "By being visible in classrooms via informal and formal observations, the instructional leader can improve teaching and learning through supervision" (p. 15). Florence (2005) added, "Collaborative supervision also enables teachers to evaluate their own instructional effectiveness and to solve instructional problems" (p. 17). She also stated that:

A significant body of research suggests that teacher quality can positively impact student learning and teacher supervision programs can improve teacher quality. These teacher supervision programs are collaborative and emphasize formative over summative feedback. (p. 167)

A number of studies have shown a strong link between instructional supervision and the learning of students. This potential link emphasizes the importance of the mentorship/supervision process in schools.

Interdependent Models of Supervision

For effective supervision or mentoring to be enacted in a school, I believe that a collaborative culture needs to be in place. Neither independence nor dependence is the right model to pursue. Rather, when the staff of a school is working together in a productive manner, there is a culture of interdependence that fosters collaboration and professional growth.

Fullan (2001) and Hargreaves (2003) emphasized the need for this kind of collaborative cultures in schools. Fullan noted that many corporations, and the U.S. Army, espoused that high quality relationships and collaboration are vital to their success (p. 82). Hargreaves (2003) admonished schools to get past "contrived" collegiality and move to true collaboration. At best, when true collaboration was achieved, "collaborative efforts focused on ways to improve teaching and learning, the effects on students' achievement and school improvement were strong" (Hargreaves, 2003, p. 165). The goal of collaboration, for Hargreaves, was to create a professional learning community. Professional learning communities put a premium on teachers working together, but they also insisted that this joint work consistently focus on teaching and learning, and they used evidence from data as a basis for enhancing classroom instruction and informing school improvement discussions.

DuFour (1997; 2004) found that in schools functioning as learning communities, teachers were guided by a shared purpose and they took collective responsibility for student learning. Sergiovanni (1991) asserted that despite good intentions, most teachers perceived supervision as a non-event and a ritual that they participated in according to well-established scripts. To address this issue, Sergiovanni suggested that the metaphor for schooling must be changed to that of a community of learners.

Ralph and Walker's (2010) AM model seemed also to be consistent with the development of professional learning communities. What I call *Communities of Mentorship*, where protégé competence and confidence are fostered and developed, could also lead to the formation of teams of colleagues who would nurture and support each other's professional growth.

I believe that embracing any one of these metaphors referring to communities of learners has the power to effect change in the education system. In fact, my most recent school-district-administrative experience has borne that assertion out. In schools where principals took an active leadership role in supporting the implementation of learning communities among their teachers, we witnessed a growth of effective instructional practices that benefitted students. For example, one principal in a school with many social and economic issues began to spend considerable time in classrooms with teachers and also scheduled time for them to collaborate with their colleagues. These initiatives resulted in higher student achievement results. In another school, which also achieved high results in a geographic area where logic suggested otherwise, the principal had provided learning-community time, and the staff had begun using student achievement data to inform instructional decisions. In both circumstances, the principals were perceived by stakeholders as being instructional leaders and as maintaining high expectations for their respective school staffs.

Conclusion

I contend that conventional supervision in the education system can be the starting point of establishing mentoring relationships, which can be developed and fostered in many ways. Developmental approaches, collaborative approaches, and interdependent approaches to the mentorship/supervision process are all suited to facilitate the ongoing professional growth of all teachers according to their existing stages of growth. I have found that professional development can be best encouraged within some type of community of practice or community of learners. Moreover, an entire community of mentors will not only enhance the growth of those being mentored, but the school-wide effects will also be positive

The personal stories that I have shared in this chapter document events that occurred within systems where I have worked and where learning communities existed to support the individuals with whom I worked. No single person was solely responsible for these successes, but rather the results came from the combined forces of all members of the educational team. The committed individuals (whether mentors or protégés) in the learning community who were working at a high level of abstraction (i.e., Quadrant IV) were able to profit from a variety of mentorship approaches that proved to be effective. With respect to protégés reflecting other quadrants, a more directive approach (e.g., traditional supervision) was needed to enhance their growth. The Quadrant IV people benefitted from collaborative and interdependent models of mentorship and peer-mentorship. I believe that there are very few professions whose overall quality of practice could not be enhanced through the influence a caring community of learners working together to mentor one another in the ways I have described.

References

DuFour, R. (1997). Make the words of mission statements come to life. *Journal of Staff Development, 18*(3), 54–55.

DuFour, R. (2004). What is a "professional learning community?" *Educational Leadership, 61*(8), 6–11.

Florence, G. W. (2005). *Teacher supervision methods in Virginia* (Unpublished doctoral dissertation). Virginia Commonwealth University, Richmond, VA.

Fullan, M. (2001). *Leading in a culture of change.* San Francisco, CA: Jossey-Bass Inc.

Glatthorn, A. A. (1990). *Supervisory leadership: Introduction to instructional supervision.* Glenview, IL: Scott, Foresman/Little, Brown Higher Education.

Glickman, C. D. (1981). *Developmental supervision: Alternative practices for helping teachers improve instruction.* Alexandria, VA: Association for Supervision and Curriculum Development.

Glickman, C. D., Gordon, S. P., & Ross-Gordon, J. M. (2001). *SuperVision and instructional leadership: A developmental approach* (5th ed.). Needham Heights, MA: Allyn and Bacon.

Good, T. L., & Brophy, J. E. (1987). *Looking into classrooms* (4th ed.). New York, NY: Harper and Row.

Hargreaves, A. (2003). *Teaching in the knowledge society: Education in the age of insecurity.* New York, NY: Teachers College Press.

Hillyer, D. (2005). *A case study of teacher evaluation and supervision at a high performing urban elementary school* (Unpublished doctoral dissertation). University of Southern California, Berkeley, CA.

Joyce, B., & Showers, B. (1988). *Student achievement through staff development.* White Plains, NY: Longman Inc.

Lave, J., & Wenger, E. (1999). *Situated learning: Legitimate peripheral participation.* Cambridge, UK: Cambridge University Press.

Ralph, E. G. (2000). Aligning mentorship style with beginning teachers' development: Contextual supervision. *Alberta Journal of Educational Research, 46*(4), 311–326.

Ralph, E., & Walker, K. (Chairs). (2010, June). *Forum on Mentorship in Professional Education.* Forum supported by The Social Sciences and Humanities Research Council of Canada and the University of Saskatchewan, conducted at the Delta Bessborough Hotel, Saskatoon, SK.

Rettig, P. (1999). Differentiated supervision: A new approach. *Principal, 78*(3), 36–39.

Sackney, L., & Mitchell, C. (2002). Postmodern expressions of educational leadership. In K. Leithwood & P. Hallinger (Eds.), *Second international handbook of educational leadership and administration* (pp. 881–913). Dordrecht, Netherlands: Kluwer Academic Publishers.

Senge, P. (1990). *The fifth discipline: The art and practice of the learning organization.* New York, NY: Doubleday Dell.

Senge, P. (2000). *A fifth discipline: Schools that learn.* New York, NY: Doubleday Dell.

Sergiovanni, T. J. (1991). Moral authority and the regeneration of supervision. In C. D. Glickman (Ed.), *Supervision in transition: 1992 yearbook of the association for supervision and curriculum development* (pp. 203–214). Alexandria, VA: Association for Supervision and Curriculum Development.

Siens, C. M., & Ebmeier, H. (1996). Developmental supervision and the reflective thinking of teachers. *Journal of Curriculum and Supervision, 11*(4), 299–319.

Smith, M. K. (2003). Communities of practice. In *The encyclopedia of informal education.* Retrieved from http://www.infed.org/biblio/communities_of_practice.htm

Varley, S. M. (2005). *Supervisory practices of three female principals in the era of no child left behind* (Unpublished doctoral dissertation). University of Pittsburgh, Pittsburgh, PA.

Wenger, E. (1999). *Communities of practice: Learning, meaning and identity.* Cambridge, UK: Cambridge University Press.

Wenger, E., McDermott, R., & Snyder, W. (2002). *Cultivating communities of practice.* Boston, MA: Harvard Business School Printing.

Chapter Nine

Mentorship of Teachers across the Intergenerational Gap[*]

Benjamin Kutsyuruba

ONE OF THE MOST CRITICAL problems facing the teaching profession is how to improve the development of beginning teachers. Indeed, "teaching has been a career in which the greatest challenge and most difficult responsibilities are faced by those with the least experience" (Glickman, Gordon, & Ross-Gordon, 2004, p. 25). Novice teachers in many schools find their first years of teaching a trying experience. Teachers begin their careers facing the most difficult assignment with a lack of time for planning, supervision, and interaction with colleagues (Odell & Ferraro, 1992). Moreover, they encounter a number of environmental difficulties, such as inadequate resources, difficult work assignments, unclear expectations, a sink-or-swim mentality, and reality shock (Glickman et al., 2004; Johnson & Kardos, 2002). The first years of teaching are a "make or break" time, and the metaphor of "being lost at sea" is used by scholars to describe how the new entrants, upon accepting a teaching position in a school, are often left to their own devices to fail or succeed within the confines of their own classrooms (Johnson & Birkeland, 2003). Not surprisingly, teachers who do not receive adequate support in their first years as educators leave schools and abandon teaching in favor of other professions.

Teacher Attrition

Teaching has traditionally been characterized as an occupation with high rates of attrition, especially among newcomers into the profession (Lortie, 1975; Veenman, 1985). One can observe that experiences of beginning teachers from different parts of the world seem to be similar. Recent statistics from the United Kingdom (Smithers

[*] After an academic review process, this chapter was accepted as a "refereed contribution" by the editors.

& Robinson, 2003), Australia (Stoel & Thant, 2002), the United
States (Smith & Ingersoll, 2004), and other countries (Organization
for Economic Co-operation and Development, 2005) have indicated that teacher attrition has become an international problem; most
teachers quit the profession in their first two to five years (some
teachers even dropping out before the end of their first year). As
many as 50% of new teachers leave within the first five years of entry
into the occupation (Hafner & Owings, 1991; Ingersoll & Smith,
2003; Murnane, Singer, Willett, Kemple, & Olsen, 1991). In fact,
nine percent of new teachers do not complete their first year (Black,
2001), and 14% leave after their first year (Ingersoll, 2002). Across
Canada in 2000, only 60% of the 1995 graduates from teacher
education programs were employed as full-time teachers five years
after graduation; of these graduates, almost one quarter did not go
into teaching at all (Canadian Teachers Federation, 2003). In 2004,
teacher turnover was estimated at approximately 30% in the first
five years of service (Federation Canadienne, 2004). A 2008 study
by Karsenti, Collin, Villeneuve, Dumouchel, and Roy reported that
a large proportion of the departures of French Immersion or French
as a Second Language teachers occurred in the first five years of service (with 50% occurring in the first two years).

Along with the issue of teacher attrition, scholars have identified
the repercussion of an aging teaching force. As a result of high turnover of younger teachers, the percentage of teachers nearing retirement is steadily increasing in schools worldwide. In 1982, Watson
and Quazi argued that unless hiring policies advantaged new graduates, the projected teaching force in Ontario would mainly consist of
re-entering mature teachers aged 35 to 55 years, a trend that would
steadily increase. In 1988, Ryan and Kokol (1988) reported that the
teaching force in the United States had been steadily maturing, with
a consequent increase in the number of teachers retiring in the future. Furthermore, the 1995 Labour Force Survey (Tremblay, 1997)
showed that elementary and secondary education in Canada was
facing an aging teaching force, with 60% of them being 40 years of
age or over in 1995. Grimmett and Echols (2000) identified similar
trends in Australia and the UK. Ryan and Kokol viewed teacher attrition as a mixed blessing for schools: on the one hand, it meant
more room for recently trained teachers; on the other hand, "the

people who are most equipped to orient young teachers as mentors and provide day-to-day guidance [would] also be gone" (p. 59). Therefore, the issues of teacher retention, teacher development, and teacher mentorship became increasingly important from a global perspective.

Mentoring

The enhanced use of induction and mentoring programs has become prominent in the effort to retain novice teachers (Wynn, Carboni, & Patall, 2007). Mentorship has become a means to connect new teachers with experienced practitioners. Traditionally defined as "the forming of mutually supportive and learning relationships between two individuals who work together in the same or similar organization" (Daresh & Playko, 1995, p. 373), mentoring has been seen as a way to initiate newcomers to schools by pairing them with more experienced colleagues who can assist others in learning to survive and succeed in their new role. The education community has embraced formal mentoring as a necessary extension of learning the complexities of teaching and learning (Collinson et al., 2009). Moreover, the traditional one-on-one definition of mentoring has been reconceptualized into a "multiple relationships" phenomenon where a protégé has a network of mentors, each providing different functions (Higgins & Kram, 2001).

Mentoring relationships are key to assist novice teachers in adjusting to teaching requirements (Smith, 2002). Individuals who have a new teaching assignment require support from more experienced colleagues, who themselves have a professional and ethical responsibility to assist their neophyte colleagues to develop professionally. Mentorship has become viewed as a collaborative process in which learning, growing, and change become the mutual focus for participating teachers. A culture of collaboration and collegiality, in which best thinking occurs through collective judgment, is considered to be the best way teachers learn (Hopkins-Thompson, 2000).

Mentoring as a form of collaboration is based on a process of being a "critical friend" (Costa & Kallick, 1993). A critical friend provides assessment feedback to a student, teacher, administrator, or group. A critical friend is a trusted person who may ask provocative questions, provide data to be examined through another lens, and/or critique a person's work. "A critical friend takes the time to fully understand the context of the work presented and the outcomes that the person or group is working toward" (p. 50) and is an advocate for the success of that work. Such collaboration engenders reflective practice on the part of protégé and mentor alike.

Novice teachers are considered protégés in this mentoring process, which facilitates instructional improvement wherein an experienced educator (mentor) works with a novice or less experienced teacher (protégé) collaboratively and non-judgmentally to deliberate on ways to improve instruction (Sullivan & Glanz, 2000). Mentors support the development of their protégés, providing advocacy, counselling, help, protection, feedback, and information that the latter would otherwise not have. Reflecting on how a mentor contributed to his professional growth as a beginning teacher, Parkay (1988) defined mentoring as an intensive, one-to-one form of teaching in which a wise and experienced mentor inducts an aspiring protégé into the profession. In this professionalization process, the protégé learns from the mentor not only the content of pedagogical knowledge and skills, but also a "subjective, non-discursive appreciation for *how* and *when* to employ these learnings in the arena of professional practice" (p. 196).

The main mentoring functions are teaching, supporting, assisting, guiding, sponsoring, encouraging, counselling, and befriending. In mentoring, the primary goal is passing on knowledge, skills and values, and this learning process, as Bennetts (1995) suggested, is what distinguishes the mentoring relationship from other relationships. Lankau and Scandura (2002) emphasized the primary role of mentoring in the personal learning of the protégé. Ideally, mentors are respected teachers and administrators highly skilled in communicating, listening, analyzing, providing feedback, and negotiating. They have to be trustworthy and committed to the helping process. They need to believe in personal and professional development and be adept at adjusting their expectations of the protégés (Hopkins-Thompson, 2000). Mentors are the collaborative guides during the initial stage of career-long professional development (Nolan & Hoover, 2008). Supportive and trusted relationships are "paramount to successfully assist novice teachers in adjusting to teaching requirements" (Smith, 2002, p. 47).

Intergenerational Gap

Because mentoring is by nature considered collaboration between experienced and new teachers, intergenerational dynamics often present challenges to those involved in the mentoring process. Each generation has a unique perspective on the world of work; members of each generation hold similar values and beliefs regarding the work environment, the nature of the group they would choose to work with, and preferences for acquiring, digesting, organizing, and distilling information and skills (Bova & Kroth, 2001). Understanding these generational differences is critical to organizations that try to impart the values, philosophy, knowledge, and skills upon which the operation of the organization depends. Because multiple generations in the workforce have differing values and preferences, "the potential for conflict is higher than in days with more of a homogenous workforce" (p. 59). The fundamental differences between generations are often not explicit, but "like death and taxes, they are assumed to be immutable and irreparable, and consequently, they are never openly addressed" (Zemke, Raines, & Filipczak, 2000, p. 12). Furthermore, in both research and policy terms, younger and older generations tend to be problematized and pathologized and are seen as competing for scarce resources (Ellis & Granville, 1999).

The fundamental differences between generations are often ascribed to the differences in age (Finkelstein, Allen, & Rhoton, 2003). With respect to mentoring relationships, researchers have examined age issues in the workplace from a relational demography perspective. Tsui, Egan, and Xin (1995) defined relational demography as "an individual's similarity to or difference from others in a group on specific demographic attributes" (p. 198) and noted that field researchers in this area have examined age and concluded that age heterogeneity may negatively affect communication and group cohesion.

The dynamic of age in the mentor/protégé relationship has been explored as one variable that might influence the effectiveness of the relationship in terms of learning, one of the fundamental purposes of mentoring. For instance, a mentor has often been described by researchers as a senior, experienced employee who serves as a role model and provides support, direction, and feedback to the younger employee regarding career plans and interpersonal development (Noe, 1988). Furthermore, in the early mentoring research, effective mentors were typically characterized as being 8 to 15 years older than their protégés (Levinson, Darrow, Klein, Levinson, & McKee, 1978). Related to age, the dynamic of hierarchical distance has been considered in order to try to identify whether there was an optimum level of distance between the mentor and the protégé to support learning (Hale, 2000). It was considered that if the age gap was too wide then there would be too much psychological distance. Other research on mentoring (Mendelson, Barnes, & Horn, 1989) suggested that average age differences tended to be 16–18 years. Furthermore, Kram and Hall (1991) found that the early-career and late-career managers tended to provide more mentoring to others than did mid-career managers. They also found that younger, non-established mentors under forty tended to use mentoring others as a way of helping build their own reputation, while mentors over 50 tended to provide more intimacy and psychosocial support because they were less concerned with advancement and were more mature and at one with themselves. Mentors in their forties may have been more concerned with their own mid-life anxieties than with mentoring others, unless the organization provided some incentive.

Some of this literature that related to business, management, and organizational theory is applicable to education settings as well. In a school setting, as Johnson and Kardos (2005) noted, veteran teachers nearing retirement and new teachers in their first few years of service differ in their goals and expectations. Therefore, schools often are faced with difficulty bridging the divide or "yawning generation gap" (p. 9) between independent, sometimes complacent, veteran teachers and inexperienced, often distressed, novice teachers. The retiring generation of teachers often prize their classroom privacy and rely on colleagues primarily for social support (Johnson, 1990). Contributing to these practices is the egg-crate structure of schools, with each teacher working alone in a classroom, a practice that discourages the development of specialized roles for teachers (Johnson & Kardos, 2005). On the contrary, the new generation of teachers tends to be surprised by the isolation of a classroom, expecting instead to be able to learn from colleagues, work in teams, have varied responsibilities, and gain increasing influence.

In order to bridge the separation between the cohorts of new and veteran teachers, Johnson and Kardos (2005) offered a number of strategies to integrate the work of these groups. They argued that the hiring process should be treated as the first step of induction, by incorporating in-depth information about the school in order to (a) increase novices' understanding of how the institution works, and (b) increase veterans' investment into the development of the entrants. One-on-one mentoring was considered one of the most significant strategies. Thus, the authors argued that new teachers should be assigned to work alongside experienced teachers across grades or courses so that the novices could tap into the veterans' knowledge and the veterans could become energized by the new teachers' enthusiasm. They believed that schools needed to deliberately allocate time for shared planning, observations, and feedback to ensure that the teachers who should meet together could do so, thus making collaborative work and professional exchange not only possible but likely. Researchers have found that in general, expert mentoring by experienced teachers effectively supports new teachers in their work (Ingersoll & Kralik, 2004).

However, more than one-on-one mentoring processes are needed to bridge the gap and enhance the experiences of neophytes and veterans. Johnson and Kardos (2005) found that often one-to-one mentoring failed due to inappropriate matches, lack of mentors, or lack of mentor training. In order to be effective, one-on-one mentoring should be situated within an integrated professional school culture, should function alongside school-based induction programs led by experienced teachers, and should be coupled with ongoing professional development and teacher leadership opportunities (Johnson & The Project on the Next Generation of Teachers, 2004; Kardos, 2004; Smith & Ingersoll, 2004).

Bridging the Intergenerational Gap through Mentorship

In order to bridge the generation gap among staff and ensure retention of novice teachers in schools, it is necessary to position one-on-one mentoring as an initial step in an enhanced system of mentoring. This system should assist novice teachers to participate in communities of practice (or learning communities) characterized by knowledge management and transfer of learning between generations of educators. The intersection of a learning community's framework and teacher retention is complex. Researchers (Hord, 1997; Morrissey, 2000) identified five dimensions that characterize a school as a learning community: supportive and shared leadership, shared values and vision, collective learning and application of learning, supportive conditions, and shared personal practice. These dimensions are able to be meshed with themes in teacher retention research, which suggests that mentoring, school climate, and principal leadership are able to impact beginning teacher retention (Wynn et al., 2007). I expand on this claim and contend that a broader *system* of mentoring (as opposed to sole one-on-one mentoring practice), collaborative culture (as opposed to school climate alone), and parallel leadership, or a combination of administrative and teacher leadership (as opposed to sole principal leadership) should all be considered holistically as factors necessary to stem teacher turnover and attrition.

To begin with, one-on-one mentoring is a first step to establish a systematic practice of mentoring in which protégés will have a network of mentors from which to draw support and advice. Smith and Ingersoll (2004) distinguished between having a mentor ("basic induction"), basic induction plus collaboration ("enhanced induction"), and basic induction plus collaboration plus teacher network plus extra resources ("comprehensive induction"). Similarly, Danis (1999) argued for a mentorship model that would allow an inductee to become a "teacher of record" through one-on-one mentoring coupled with a support team that builds a safety net around new teachers, thus providing a foundation for content and pedagogy. In a recent study (Kutsyuruba, 2010), I identified the divide between generations of teachers in cases where mentorship had not become systematic in schools and had been informal and random in nature (i.e., it had only occurred when there was a problem or an urgent need). Furthermore, mentoring relationships can serve as a means to promote ongoing dialogue and collaboration between educators at all levels of their professional careers. Mentoring programs have the potential to transform schools from being lonely places where staff members work in isolation from other adults (Daresh & Playko, 1995) to more collaborative places.

Bridging the generation gap is necessary to help experienced teachers "bestow a legacy of skills and knowledge on the school and on their successors" (Johnson & Kardos, 2005, p. 14). To ensure that generations of teachers work together, schools must become learning organizations and be more flexible and collaborative in nature (Johnson & Kardos, 2005; Wynn et al., 2007). However, despite the growing rhetoric about the importance of schools becoming learning organizations, many schools continue to function without practices or norms that sustain ongoing development for all teachers.

In learning organizations, the nature of mentorship is changing; mentors are no longer required only to teach, coach, and impart knowledge, but they also need to be open to the exchange of ideas that protégés bring to the relationship. As an integral part of a learning community, protégés help drive the relationship and also take responsibility for outcomes of the development that occurs in the relationship. The need for such systems of mentoring is congruent with the emphasis organizations are placing upon developing "learning organization attributes" (Senge, Kleiner, Roberts, Ross, & Smith, 1994), becoming increasingly sophisticated in creating and utilizing knowledge management repositories, supporting communities of practice, and facilitating the transfer of learning (Davenport, De Long, & Beers, 1998). The community of learners is important for the development of collaborative relationships among generation cohorts in schools. Collaboration and learning are benefits inherent in the intergenerational exchange or solidarity that can help shape an organization or a society, which is respectful of the development and social needs of all its generations (Ellis & Granville, 1999; Newman, Ward, Smith, Wilson, & McCrea, 1997).

Effective mentoring can reflect both collective learning and application of learning, as well as shared personal practice. Wynn et al. (2007) posited that school climate reflects the supportive working conditions that include both the physical and the human dimensions necessary for a learning community. Climate can be seen as "the enduring characteristics that describe the psychological makeup of a particular school, distinguish it from other schools, and influence the behavior of teachers and students, and as the 'feel' that teachers and students have for that school" (Sergiovanni & Starratt, 1998, p. 177). Working conditions of teachers that meet their instructional needs (e.g., appropriate space, material, and support) have been shown to influence beginning teachers' decisions to remain in the profession (Ingersoll & Smith, 2003; Johnson & Birkeland, 2003). However, meeting teachers' working condition needs is not sufficient to bridge the generation gap. What is also necessary is that schools provide collaborative cultures where teachers can share ideas, materials, problems, and solutions in order to foster student learning.

Scholars (Deal & Peterson, 2009; Firestone & Seashore Louis, 1999; Fullan & Hargreaves, 1996; Levine & Lezotte, 1990; Little, 1990) have delineated several common functions of a strong, positive, and collaborative culture and its effects on schools. These functions include (a) building of trust, knowledge, and commitment of staff to each other and to the school through joint work; (b) fostering school effectiveness and productivity; (c) improving collegial activities that foster communication and problem-solving practices; (d) fostering successful change and improvement efforts; (e) building commitment and identification of staff, students, and administrators; (f) amplifying the energy, motivation, and vitality of a school staff, students, and community; and (g) increasing the focus of daily behavior and attention on what is important and valued. Collaborative culture affects every aspect of school life, from the casual interactions in the halls, to the type of instruction that is valued, to the importance of professional development, and to the effectiveness of the learning/teaching processes in school. Collegial relationships among staff members of different age and experience groups are an important feature of collaborative school cultures. Such norms and school structures provide the purpose and the opportunity for deeper involvement and interaction on professional issues of importance to teachers. When these qualities are present in a school, then it is obvious that the mentorship process that functions among staff members will also be enriched and enhanced.

Finally, Wynn et al. (2007) argued that principal leadership is key for teacher retention because it provides for the supportive and shared leadership and creates the opportunity for shared values and vision. Researchers (Darling-Hammond, 2003; Leithwood, Leonard, & Sharratt, 1998) argued that successful learning communities in schools have principals that share power, authority, and decision making in a democratic way with teachers. In the same vein, I contend that more than just principal leadership is needed to bridge the gap between generations of teachers. What schools require is strong *parallel leadership* (Andrews & Crowther, 2002; Andrews & Lewis, 2004; Crowther, Ferguson, & Hann, 2009; Hargreaves, 2001; Harris, 2004; Heifetz & Laurie, 1997) that regards teacher leaders and school administrators alike as parallel entities engaging in collective action to build school capacity.

Parallel leadership involves teachers and administrators working collaboratively (in complementary but different ways) to build the capacity of the school to enhance its outcomes, particularly in relation to teaching and learning. The notion of parallel leadership emerged from perspectives on educational leadership that is shared or distributed across the school. However, as Crowther et al. (2009) pointed out, it is distinct in two significant ways: (1) it sees the leadership of principals and teachers in school reform as similar in significance (they are different but equivalent) and (2) it recognizes schools as learning organizations and assumes an inextricable link between school-based leadership and the enhancement of educational outcomes.

According to Crowther et al. (2009), parallel leadership embodies three distinct qualities: *mutual trust, shared purpose,* and *allowance for individual expression. Mutual trust,* through a dynamic interplay of respect, competence, personal regard for others, and integrity, creates an environment where individuals share a moral commitment to act in the interests of the collectivity (Bryk & Schneider, 2002; Elmore, 2000). Trust relationships are based around the following facets: benevolence, honesty, openness, reliability, competency, wisdom, educational ideals, and care (Day, 2009; Hoy & Tschannen-Moran, 1999; Tschannen-Moran, 2004). Where trust is nurtured, practiced, and valued, teachers feel less isolated, share in the collective responsibility for student success, and have higher morale and lower absenteeism (Crowther et al., 2009). Furthermore, trusting relations positively influence teacher job satisfaction and increase the probability of teachers remaining in the school and in the profession (Leithwood & McAdie, 2007).

A sense of *shared purpose* tends to develop most effectively in contexts characterized by transparent decision processes, collaborative problem solving, and positive communications (Andrews & Lewis, 2004), and it takes the form of an alignment between the school's stated vision and teachers' preferred approaches to teaching, learning, and assessment (Crowther et al., 2009). Furthermore, collaboration fosters a clear sense of shared purpose and helps to define roles and responsibilities in schools (Cowan, 2006). *Allowance of a significant degree of individual expression* by respective leaders may seem contrary to concepts such as teamwork, collegiality, and consensus decision-making; however, research indicated that highly successful parallel leaders manifest strong convictions about individual values as well as a capacity to accommodate the values of co-leaders and to work collaboratively with them (Andrews & Lewis, 2004; Crowther et al., 2009). In contrast to individualism, which connotes isolation and solitude, individuality emphasizes personal independence and self-realization (Hargreaves, 1994). Successful parallel leadership is associated with strong, skilled, autonomous individuals and with collaboration among them (often with discrepant voices) rather than with consensus or groupthink. Limerick, Cunnington, and Crowther (1998) argued that collective processes that obscure individuality are more likely to contribute to the perpetuation of questionable practices than are processes that recognize individual action and the legitimacy of dissent. For generations of teachers, such collaboration was valued due to the emphasis on "acceptance of otherness and cooperation within difference" (Furman, 1998, p. 307).

All three qualities that underpin parallel leadership are essential in relationships between teachers and administrators to help foster intergenerational exchange, professional growth, and leadership development – including mentorship relationships both formal and informal.

Parallel leadership allows administrator leaders and teacher leaders to engage in collaborative action and at the same time fulfill their individual capabilities, aspirations, and responsibilities; it leads to strengthened alignment between the school's vision and teaching and learning practices; it facilitates the development of a professional learning community, culture building, and school-wide approaches to teaching and learning; and it enhances school identity, teachers' professional esteem, community support, and students' achievements (Crowther, Andrews, Dawson, & Lewis, 2001).

In summary, a mentoring system, a collaborative school culture, and a structure of parallel leadership, each unique in its functions, can together be considered aspects of an overall professional learning community that has the potential to bridge the generational gap between beginning and experienced teachers. Such learning communities promote ongoing dialogue and collaboration between educators at all levels of their professional careers and reduce the problem of isolation. For both experienced and novice teachers, learning communities provide support for the development of joint work, mutual trust, shared purpose, individual expression, and collaborative culture.

References

Andrews, D., & Crowther, F. (2002). Parallel leadership: A clue to the content of the "black box" of school reform. *International Journal for Educational Management, 16*(4), 152–159.

Andrews, D., & Lewis, M. (2004). Parallel leadership for 21st century schools. *Access, 18*(4), 5–8.

Bennetts, C. (1995, June). The secrets of a good relationship. *People Management, 29,* 38–39.

Black, S. (2001). A lifeboat for new teachers. *American School Board Journal, 188*(9), 46–48.

Bova, B., & Kroth, M. (2001). Workplace learning and Generation X. *Journal of Workplace Learning, 13*(2), 57–65.

Bryk, A., & Schneider, B. (2002). *Trust in schools: A core resource for improvement.* New York, NY: Russell Sage Foundation.

Canadian Teachers Federation. (2003). Teacher supply and demand series: Volume 3. *CTF Economic and Member Services Bulletin,* (2003–3). Retrieved from http://ctf-fce.ca/documents/publications/Bilingual/annual_report/2004AnnualReport/Economic.pdf

Collinson, V., Kozina, E., Kate Lin, Y., Ling, L., Matheson, I., Newcombe, L., Zogla, I. (2009). Professional development for teachers: A world of change. *European Journal of Teacher Education, 32*(1), 3–19. doi:10.1080/02619760802553022

Costa, A. L., & Kallick, B. (1993). Through the lens of a critical friend. *Educational Leadership*, 50(1), 49–51.

Cowan, D. F. (2006). Creating learning communities in low-performing sites: A systemic approach to alignment. *Journal of School Leadership*, 16(5), 596–610.

Crowther, F., Andrews, D., Dawson, M., & Lewis, M. (2001). *IDEAS facilitation folder.* Toowoomba, Queensland, Australia: University of Southern Queensland and Education Queensland, Leadership Research Institute.

Crowther, F., Ferguson, M., & Hann, L. (2009). *Developing teacher leaders: How teacher leadership enhances school success* (2nd ed.). Thousand Oaks, CA: Corwin Press.

Danis, R. (1999). Of hair stylists and master teachers. In M. L. Donaldson & B. Poon (Eds.), *Reflections of first year teachers on school culture: Questions, hopes, and challenges* (New Directions for School Leadership Series, Vol. 11, pp. 65–74). San Francisco, CA: Jossey-Bass.

Daresh, J. C., & Playko, M. A. (1995). *Supervision as a proactive process: Concepts and cases.* Prospect Heights, IL: Waveland Press.

Darling-Hammond, L. (2003). Keeping good teachers: Why it matters, what leaders can do. *Educational Leadership*, 60(8), 6–13.

Davenport, T. H., De Long, D. W., & Beers, M. C. (1998, Winter). Successful knowledge management projects. *Sloan Management Review*, 43–57.

Day, C. (2009). Building and sustaining successful principalship in England: The importance of trust. *Journal of Educational Administration*, 47(6), 719–730.

Deal, T. E., & Peterson, K. D. (2009). *Shaping school culture: Pitfalls, paradoxes, and promises* (2nd ed.). San Francisco, CA: Wiley.

Ellis, S. W., & Granville, G. (1999). Intergenerational solidarity: Bridging the gap through mentoring programmes. *Mentoring & Tutoring: Partnership in Learning*, 7(3), 181–194.

Elmore, R. (2000). *Building a new structure for school improvement.* Washington, DC: The Albert Shanker Institute.

Fédération canadienne des enseignantes et des enseignants (FCE). (2004). Recrutement et maintien du personnel enseignant: Pourquoi les enseignants et enseignantes entrent dans la profession, y restent ou la quittent. *Bulletin des services économiques et services aux membres, 5,* 1–20.

Finkelstein, L. M., Allen, T. D., & Rhoton, L. A. (2003). An examination of the role of age in mentoring relationships. *Group Organization Management, 28*(2), 249–281.

Firestone, W. A., & Seashore Louis, K. (1999). Schools as cultures. In J. Murphy, & K. Seashore Louis (Eds.), *Handbook of research on educational administration* (2nd ed., pp. 297–322). San Francisco, CA: Jossey-Bass.

Fullan, M. G., & Hargreaves, A. (1996). *What's worth fighting for in your school.* New York, NY: Teachers College Press.

Furman, G. C. (1998). Postmodernism and community in schools: Unraveling the paradox. *Educational Administration Quarterly, 34*(3), 298–328.

Glickman, C. D., Gordon, S. P., & Ross-Gordon, J. M. (2004). *SuperVision and instructional leadership: A developmental approach* (6th ed.). Boston: Allyn and Bacon.

Grimmett, P. P., & Echols, F. H. (2000). Teacher and administrator shortages in changing times. *Canadian Journal of Education, 25*(4), 328–343.

Hafner, A., & Owings, J. (1991). *Careers in teaching: Following members of the high school class of 1972 in and out of teaching* (NCES Report No. 91–470). Washington, DC: U.S. Department of Education, National Center for Education Statistics.

Hale, R. (2000). To match or mis-match? The dynamics of mentoring as a route to personal and organizational learning. *Career Development International, 5*(4), 223–234.

Hargreaves, A. (1994). *Changing teachers, changing times.* New York, NY: Teachers College Press.

Hargreaves, D. (2001). A capital theory of school effectiveness and improvement. *British Educational Research Journal, 27*(4), 487–503.

Harris, A. (2004). Teacher leadership and distributed leadership. *Leading and Managing, 10*(2), 1–9.

Heifetz, R., & Laurie, D. (1997). The work of leadership. *Harvard Business Review, 75*(1), 124–134.

Higgins, M. C., & Kram, K. E. (2001). Reconceptualizing mentoring at work: A developmental network perspective. *Academy of Management Review, 26,* 264–288.

Hopkins-Thompson, P. A. (2000). Colleagues helping colleagues: Mentoring and coaching. *NASSP Bulletin, 84*(617), 29–36.

Hord, S. M. (1997). *Professional learning communities: Communities of continuous inquiry and improvement.* Austin, TX: Southwest Educational Development Lab.

Hoy, W., & Tschannen-Moran, M. (1999). Five faces of trust: An empirical confirmation in urban elementary schools. *Journal of School Leadership, 9,* 184–208.

Ingersoll, R. M. (2002). The teacher shortage: A case of wrong diagnosis and wrong prescription. *NASSP Bulletin, 86,* 16–31.

Ingersoll, R. M., & Kralik, J. M. (2004). *The impact of mentoring on teacher retention: What the research says.* Denver, CO: Education Commission of the States.

Ingersoll, R. M., & Smith, T. M. (2003). The wrong solution to the teacher shortage. *Educational Leadership, 60*(8), 30–33.

Johnson, S. M. (1990). *Teachers at work: Achieving success in our schools.* New York, NY: BasicBooks.

Johnson, S. M., & Birkeland, S. (2003). Pursuing a "sense of success": New teachers explain their career decisions. *American Educational Research Journal, 40*(3), 581–617.

Johnson, S. M., & Kardos, S. M. (2002). Keeping new teachers in mind. *Educational Leadership, 59*(6), 12–16.

Johnson, S. M., & Kardos, S. M. (2005). Bridging the generation gap. *Educational Leadership, 62*(8), 8–14.

Johnson, S. M., & The Project on the Next Generation of Teachers. (2004). *Finders and keepers: Helping new teachers survive and thrive in our schools.* San Francisco, CA: Jossey-Bass.

Kardos, S. M. (2004). *Supporting and sustaining new teachers in schools: The importance of professional culture and mentoring* (Unpublished dissertation). Harvard University, Cambridge, MA.

Karsenti, T., Collin, S., Villeneuve, S., Dumouchel, G., & Roy, N. (2008). *Why are new French immersion and French as a second language teachers leaving the profession? Results of a Canada-wide survey.* Ottawa, ON: Canadian Association of Immersion Teachers.

Kram, K., & Hall, D. (1991). Mentoring as an antidote to stress during corporate trauma. *Human Resource Management, 28*(4), 493–510.

Kutsyuruba, B. (2010, May). *Teacher collaboration, mentorship, and intergenerational gap in post-Soviet Ukrainian schools.* Paper presented at the Canadian Society for the Study of Education Annual Meeting, Montreal, QC.

Lankau, M., & Scandura, T. A. (2002). An investigation of personal learning in mentoring relationships: Content, antecedents, and consequences. *Academy of Management Journal, 45,* 779–790.

Leithwood, K., Leonard, L., & Sharratt, L. (1998). Conditions fostering organizational learning in schools. *Educational Administration Quarterly, 34*(2), 243–276.

Leithwood, K., & McAdie, P. (2007). Teacher working conditions that matter. *Education Canada, 47*(2), 42–45.

Levine, D. U., & Lezotte, L. W. (1990). *Unusually effective schools: A review and analysis of research and practice.* Madison, WI: National Center for Effective Schools Research and Development.

Levinson, D. J., Darrow, D., Klein, E., Levinson, M., & McKee, B. (1978). *Seasons of a man's life.* New York, NY: Knopf.

Limerick, D., Cunnington, B., & Crowther, F. (1998). *Managing the new organization* (2nd ed.). Sydney, Australia: Business and Professional Publishing.

Little, J. W. (1990). The persistence of privacy: Autonomy and initiative in teachers' professional relations. *Teachers College Record, 91*(4), 509–536.

Lortie, D. C. (1975). *Schoolteacher.* Chicago, IL: University of Chicago Press.

Mendelson, J. L., Barnes, A. K., & Horn, G. (1989, July). The guiding light to corporate culture. *Personnel Administrator,* 70–72.

Morrissey, M. S. (2000). *Professional learning communities: An ongoing exploration.* Austin, TX: Southwest Educational Development Lab.

Murnane, R., Singer, J., Willett, J., Kemple, J., & Olsen, R. (Eds.). (1991). *Who will teach? Policies that matter.* Cambridge, MA: Harvard University Press.

Newman, S., Ward, C. R., Smith, T. B., Wilson, J. O., & McCrea, J. M. (1997). *Intergenerational programs: Past, present and future.* Washington, DC: Taylor & Francis.

Noe, R. A. (1988). An investigation of the determinants of successful assigned mentoring relationships. *Personnel Psychology, 41,* 457–479.

Nolan, J. F., & Hoover, L. A. (2008). *Teacher supervision and evaluation: Theory into practice* (2nd ed.). New York, NY: John Wiley & Sons.

Odell, S. J., & Ferraro, D. P. (1992). Teacher mentoring and teacher retention. *Journal of Teacher Education, 43*(3), 200–204.

Organization for Economic Co-operation and Development (OECD). (2005). *Teachers matter: Attracting, developing and retaining effective teachers.* Paris, France: OECD Publishing.

Parkay, F. W. (1988). Reflections of the protégé. *Theory into Practice, 26,* 195–200.

Ryan, K., & Kokol, M. (1988). The aging teacher: A developmental perspective. *Peabody Journal of Education, 65*(3), 59–73.

Senge, P., Kleiner, A., Roberts, C., Ross, R. B., & Smith, B. J. (1994). *The fifth discipline: The art and practice of the learning organization.* New York, NY: Doubleday.

Sergiovanni, T., & Starratt, R. (1998). *Supervision: A redefinition* (6th ed.). New York, NY: McGraw-Hill.

Smith, S. J. (2002). Teacher mentoring and collaboration. *Journal of Special Education Technology, 17*(1), 47–48.

Smith, T. M., & Ingersoll, R. M. (2004). What are the effects of induction and mentoring on beginning teacher turnover? *American Educational Research Journal, 41*(3), 681–714.

Smithers, A., & Robinson, P. (2003). *Factors affecting teachers' decisions to leave the profession.* Nottingham, UK: DfES.

Stoel, C. F., & Thant, T.-S. (2002). *Teachers' professional lives: A view from nine industrialized countries.* Washington, DC: Milken Family Foundation.

Sullivan, S., & Glanz, J. (2000). *Supervision that improves teaching: Strategies and techniques.* Thousand Oaks, CA: Corwin Press.

Tremblay, A. (1997). Are we headed toward a teacher surplus or a teacher shortage? *Education Quarterly Review, 4*(1), 53–85.

Tschannen-Moran, M. (2004). *Trust matters: Leadership for successful schools*. San Francisco, CA: Jossey-Bass.

Tsui, A. S., Egan, T. D., & Xin, K. R. (1995). Diversity in organizations: Lessons from demography research. In M. M. Chemers, S. Oskamp, & M. Costanzo (Eds.), *Diversity in organizations* (pp. 191–219). Thousand Oaks, CA: Sage.

Veenman, S. (1985). Perceived problems of beginning teachers. *Review of Educational Research, 54*(2), 143–178.

Watson, C., & Quazi, S. (1982). The aging Ontario teacher force. *Interchange, 12*(1), 39–52.

Wynn, S. R., Carboni, L. W., & Patall, E. A. (2007). Beginning teachers' perceptions of mentoring, climate, and leadership: Promoting retention through a learning communities perspective. *Leadership & Policy in Schools, 6*(3), 209–229.

Zemke, R., Raines, C., & Filipczak, B. (2000). *Generations at work: Managing the clash of veterans, boomers, Xers, and nexters in your workplace*. New York, NY: American Management Association (AMACOM).

Chapter Ten

Beyond Prepositions: Learning Assessment with Teacher Mentors

Willow Brown, Andrea Davy, Debbie Koehn, & Denise Wilson

AN IMMEDIATE PROBLEM OF PRACTICE can be a powerful catalyst for inquiry. The collection of formative assessment practices known as *Assessment for Learning* (AFL) is resonating with teachers and becoming increasingly endorsed by school districts to raise student achievement. As a result, teacher education programs and schools are challenged with inducting new teachers into an assessment culture different from what they experienced as students. However, teacher candidates' (TCs') frames of reference can be persistent, powerful, and limiting. By drawing only on their previous student experience, they may miss the urgency of building engagement and ownership of learning for less successful students through formative assessment.

An opportunity to craft alternate visions arose when Debbie Koehn suggested a mentorship pairing of TCs with teacher coaches or mentors engaged in AFL-inquiry projects through British Columbia's *Network of Performance Based Schools* (NPBS). The resulting collaboration of teacher leaders and professors brought two perspectives to our action-based inquiry: as teacher leaders we were concerned with new teacher induction to sustain the assessment practices beneficial for our young students; and as teacher educators, we sought ways for TCs to learn how to provide all children with rich and equitable learning opportunities.

Our goal was to help TCs learn more than the definitions of assessment described by the prepositions: assessment *of*, *for*, and *as* learning (Western and Northern Canadian Protocol for Collaboration in Education, 2006). They needed values and skills that they were not developing through texts and classroom exercises. In this chapter, we review the literature that informed our understanding of teacher learning in partnerships and communities, and we describe the contexts that influenced our study. We tell the story of our learning using a professional inquiry platform that drew on the learning community principles of *wholeness, awareness, meaning,* and *commitment* (Brown, 2004; Davy & Brown, 2006) as phases of action and reflection. Finally, we summarize our findings and describe the next steps for our learning.

Problem Framing: Learning More than Prepositions

We, Willow Brown and Andrea Davy, were university instructors of a compulsory teacher-education course in classroom assessment. For five years, our course texts have balanced assessment for learning, which provided achievement information for students themselves, with traditional assessment of learning, which provided information for parents and school systems (Stiggins, 2008; Black & Wiliam, 1998). However, some teacher candidates were skeptical of practices different from how they were taught; others accepted the information without the understanding needed to apply it. Most TCs seemed indifferent to the potential of student-involved assessment to re-engage discouraged learners. We knew from Argyris and Schon's (1978) notion of *single-* and *double-loop* learning that new instructional practices are unsustainable without corresponding changes in teachers' beliefs (Fullan, 2007). We therefore began this inquiry wondering if TCs' relationships with teacher mentors who embraced the beliefs and practices of AFL would help the novices develop a new vision of assessment and consequently gain confidence to begin aligning practices with those beliefs.

We, Debbie Koehn and Denise Wilson, were teacher leaders in a school recognized for improving student learning through formative assessment. We found that TCs and early-career teachers were often unaware of the connection between assessment theory from university courses and the practices we used to empower elementary school students to guide their own learning. As advocates for our elementary students, we knew their continued academic progress would depend on our ability to mentor new teachers. We also believed that the community of teachers who learned formative assessment through NPBS inquiries could be expanded to include TCs.

We envisioned mentoring relationships as being mutually beneficial, in which teacher coaches could deepen their knowledge and perhaps critique their own practices as they responded to TCs' questions. Based on the coaching approach presented in our master's program (Robertson, 2009), we saw learning partnerships as a natural, personalized way to support professional learning for all participants.

Mentoring: A Theory-into-Practice Solution

As a *learning team* of four, we paired 33 TCs in the assessment course with volunteer teacher coaches from the local NPBS group. TC reflections based on interaction with these learning partners were an optional component of a graded portfolio assignment. Although only about one-third of our class accessed the mentorship opportunity, outcomes for those students were encouraging in that they had "aha" moments that connected course content with events in the classrooms of their teacher coaches. AFL seemed to come alive when they visited their mentors' classrooms and saw children understanding learning intentions, responding to descriptive feedback based on criteria, and articulating what they would like to work on next.

Analysis of the data turned our initial question into a conviction: learning relationships *can* indeed address both the *why* and *how* of AFL by transmitting values and demonstrating steps for implementation that become refined through ongoing inquiry. We also saw evidence of the potential of modelling the mentoring roles we hoped TCs would assume as they, in turn, became educational leaders. Specifically, we were encouraged by two developments in TCs' thinking: (1) they gained a new respect for students as agents in their own learning and (2) they began to forge their own professional identities as lifelong learners and leaders within a supportive and inquiring professional community.

Literature on Teacher Learning

Convictions and commitments (i.e., strong, internalized beliefs and corresponding practices) emerged from this inquiry as we integrated our collective, action-based experience with related academic literature. We synthesized the research that we have found accessible, compelling, and useful, in order to scaffold readers into the common language and mental models that our learning team used.

Our theoretical framework for interpreting teacher learning was Mitchell and Sackney's (2000; 2009) vision of sustainable learning communities. These authors showed that profound improvement in learning can occur when collaborative dialogue makes individual teacher learning accessible and embeds such learning in the school culture. More recently they have focused on an ecological understanding of enduring learning communities and have identified interdependence and networks as foundational structures of learning and renewal. We saw the interpersonal aspect of Mitchell and Sackney's capacity building as supported by intrapersonal leadership mindsets that Kaser and Halbert (2009) drew from work with the NPBS. Our integration of these authors' ideas emphasized the notion that how leaders think is foundational to the way they (a) interact with colleagues, (b) create social conditions for professional inquiry and dialogue, and (c) initiate the shift from a *sorting* to a *learning* system that values academic success for all students.

The heart of a learning community is the moral imperative to facilitate learning for both adults and students (Mitchell & Sackney, 2000), and as such, mentoring relationships are part of the process by which personal learning becomes accessible to the group and characterizes its culture. This suggests that attention to adult learning is essential for two reasons: (1) as valued human beings and not merely instruments of the state, the well-being of teachers is important in its own right, and (2) there is a relational symmetry to teaching in that teachers need to experience, for themselves, the social learning conditions they are expected to create for students (Brown, 2004).

Our understanding of the purpose and function of collegial relationships as learning partnerships was enriched by Robertson's (2008) three Rs of *reciprocity, relationship,* and *reflection-on-reality* in leadership coaching. These principles resonated with our respect for human beings and their right to be active agents in their own learning. Robertson's technical emphasis on active listening and reflective questioning was foundational for our practice of learner-centred mentorship within a democratic environment (Davy & Brown, 2006). Robertson's view of coaching connected our interest in learning community development with mentorship: "Coaching is a learning relationship, where participants are open to new learning, and engage together as professionals equally committed to facilitating each other's leadership learning development and well being (both cognitive and affective)" (p. 4).

Robertson's (2006) coaching theory began with "the coach as learner," learning "based on real experiences in leaders' daily work, reflective observation of those experiences by oneself and with others, feedback from others, opportunities to question, problem-pose, problem-solve and analyze" (p. 1). Robertson (2009) further believed that peer coaching provides learners with the challenge essential to professional learning, "to understand and reflect on how changing their practice will make a difference" (p. 6), which is even more effective when shared with other partnerships in learning communities.

Other research supported our premise that learning occurs when teachers have multiple, ongoing opportunities for reflection and engagement in conversations about theory and practice with colleagues. For example, Pedder, James, and McBeath (2005, p. 209) described four ways that teachers learn:

> Teachers' learning is an *embedded* feature of teachers' classroom practice and reflection. Teachers' learning is *extended* through consulting different sources of knowledge. Teachers' learning is *expanded* through collaborative activity. Teachers' learning is *deepened* through talking and valuing learning. (p. 209)

Moreover, Desforges (2005) introduced three key-knowledge theories that emphasized the complexities of teacher learning and underpinned how teachers apply and adapt theory and practice. He described (a) knowledge that was *public* or embedded in theoretical models, (b) knowledge that was *private and personal* or encompassed by individuals' understanding of their beliefs, values, background knowledge, learning style, and identity, and (c) knowledge that was *collaborative* or created in the interactions between colleagues in working practices (p. 148).

Similarly, McLeskey and Waldron (2004) cited Cochrane-Smith and Lytle's typology of teacher learning, with *knowledge-for-practice* as the predominant form presented in readings and lectures in teacher preparation courses, compared to the *knowledge-of-practice* and *knowledge-in-practice* most effective for translating theory into daily activity. Teachers acquiring knowledge-in-practice "learn and become better teachers through experience, reflection on their practice, participation in collaborative teacher groups, [and] inquiry into their experiences in the classroom" (p. 8). Conversely, teachers engaged in knowledge-of-practice typically work together to construct and share knowledge. Knowledge-in-practice and knowledge-of-practice involve teacher construction and reconstruction of knowledge to improve classroom practice and student learning, and teachers are committed to work together with their colleagues in partnerships.

Finally, Kelly (2006) explored a socio-cultural perspective for teachers as they developed from novice to experts to engage in collaborative opportunities in order to create, reflect on, and share knowledge (p. 514). In this way a spiral of deeper learning is created as more experienced peers not only create change for themselves but become agents of change for other learners, who in turn adopt the role of mentor as it has been modelled for them.

Mentorship Context

A provincial teachers' learning network and an outstanding school were integral aspects of this study's context. The NPBS provided a cadre of teacher leaders and mentors, and successful implementation of AFL at Glenview Elementary School grounded our beliefs in the potential of formative assessment to enhance learning.

The *Network of Performance Based Schools* (NPBS) was initiated by Dr. Judy Halbert and Dr. Linda Kaser in 1999 in the belief that teams of teachers and formal leaders could work together to improve student learning through inquiry-based implementation of AFL practices. Described as a grassroots organization, the NPBS has obtained top-down funding for its bottom-up initiative, which included regular local meetings and annual regional learning fairs where teachers showcased the results of their inquiries. Research from over four hundred participating schools has confirmed that student learning is enhanced when teams work together "across roles on behalf of learners" (Halbert & Kaser, 2006, p. 43). These authors identified effective teamwork to include developing a reflective inquiry focus, encouraging shared leadership, implementing specific assessment strategies and ideas, establishing a strong internal accountability that includes actively sharing AFL practices with parents, and attending to the sustainability of improvements. Because participating schools and individuals have learning partners, more experienced mentors bring the benefit of their experience to new members.

Glenview Elementary School, where Debbie Koehn and Denise Wilson taught and where they participated in this study as teacher coaches, has shown exceptional gains in student achievement. TCs placed at this school for their practicum understood the practices and potential of formative assessment. The power of their conviction, as revealed in classroom discussions about what they had experienced, began to transform the textbook theories of formative assessment into realistic practice.

Teachers and a past principal of Glenview credited the profound change at Glenview to Debbie Koehn's inspired and dedicated teacher leadership. Debbie, in turn, credited her development as a learner and leader to the mentorship received from Linda Kaser and Judy Halbert in her graduate studies and NPBS training. Dismayed by the low quality of student work and social interactions when she arrived at Glenview, Debbie began sharing her use of AFL with colleagues. They were receptive to her practice because the writing quality displayed by her primary students surpassed that of older students. Over time, collaborative, inquiry-based, and practice-embedded professional learning became a way of life at Glenview, and the students began to take responsibility for their own behavior and learning. Team teaching in cross-grade groupings supported both a culture of personalized learning and the development of a common language among teachers and students. Through purposeful inquiry, the use of basic formative assessment strategies at Glenview developed into a school-wide focus that empowered learners not only to identify and pursue next steps in their own learning but to coach each other.

Similar to Mitchell and Sackney's (2000) vision of schools as sustainable learning communities, Glenview's focus on learning for teachers as well as students was foundational. Denise Wilson (2009) documented the development of Glenview's learning community and attributed the growth to five factors, which were that teachers (a) created multiple opportunities to collaborate with each other and with students, (b) learned, applied, and adapted pedagogical content knowledge and effective formative assessment processes and strategies in daily practice, (c) inquired and reflected on theoretical and pedagogical knowledge and practice, (d) embraced personal and contextual beliefs and values that focused on learning for all, and (e) shared with formal leaders to be knowledgeable regarding how to improve teacher and student learning by facilitating deep learning throughout the school.

Although such learning conditions may not exist at every school, the Glenview experience may inspire teachers to seek to pursue similar mentorship efforts. If so, they will be able to create inquiring cultures that educators want TCs to embrace through mentorship and to recreate it in other contexts.

Research Method

Our research method was based on a *professional inquiry platform* (Brown, 2004; Davy & Brown, 2006) that brings characteristics and values of a sustainable professional learning community (Mitchell & Sackney, 2000; 2009) to an action-research cycle. The process is designed to improve practice, generate knowledge, and empower participants (Carr & Kemmis, 1988; Sagor, 1992). The platform adapts a plan-do-reflect-revise cycle to correspond with learning community characteristics of *wholeness, awareness, meaning,* and *commitment.* These four new terms frame a platform for inquiry that provides guiding questions in flexible steps. Inquiry starts with the wholeness of systems thinking and collective vision and ends with personal convictions and commitments that are a transformational synthesis of public, private, and collaborative knowledge (Desforges, 2005). In the process, teachers alternate between collecting and analyzing data to create awareness and meaning. We chose this method because it was familiar and meaningful to us and coherent with our theoretical framework for building sustainable learning cultures through professional dialogue.

Wholeness

In this planning stage, learning teams identified or developed a common purpose and envisioned a preferred future. The inquiry was understood as an incremental step toward the overall vision, the collective gifts of the group were assembled, and the work was situated within a body of informing literature. For example, we understood our goal to improve assessment learning for teacher candidates as a step toward empowered human agency in a democratic learning community (i.e., to achieve the profound moral purpose of schools as learning and not sorting systems) (Kaser & Halbert, 2009). The gifts that each member brought to the group, in terms of theoretical knowledge, values, skills, and experiences, were woven together over time through dialogue and collaboration to create a wholeness or synthesis of understanding broader and richer than individual members possessed at the start.

Awareness

In this phase, learning teams developed *creative tension* (Lewin, as cited in Senge et al., 2000), a heightened awareness of the difference between the existing situation and the wholeness vision. Creative tension pulled the team toward action and increasing awareness of the effects of the action. In this study, we first became aware of our shared dissatisfaction with the responses of teacher candidates to our existing methods of teaching and with the ability of new teachers to embrace formative assessment in their own classrooms. Later, analysis of the data heightened our awareness of the impact of mentoring, which in that round of inquiry focused on teacher candidates.

We drew data from class discussions and questions, written excerpts from portfolio assignments, including email correspondence between candidates and coaches, and end-of-term questionnaires and interviews. We found that one third of our TCs communicated with their teacher coaches at least three times, and that six teacher candidates engaged in the classroom visits and dialogues we had envisioned. Several coaches were disappointed that they were not contacted by their TCs and thus had little to report. At least one candidate contacted her coach but did not receive a reply in time to create a journal entry. Teacher candidate journals had an overall focus on familiar alternatives to the mentoring relationships, such as reflections on readings or in-class activities. However, 19 entries revealed emerging patterns in TC thinking that we found encouraging. Video-taped discussions between two students and their mentor/ coaches also provided examples of the rich discussions characteristic of collegial relationships and professional growth.

Specifically, teacher candidates who entered into a successful mentoring relationship showed that they had begun to develop (a) belief in the potential of AFL and confidence in their own ability to implement practices successfully, with ongoing inquiry and collaborative support, (b) respect for children as agents in their own learning, and (c) an identity as learners/leaders within a community of professional inquiry. The following selection of candidates' comments illustrates these findings.

Valuing AFL and Knowing Where to Begin

TC questions, in initial emails to their coaches, were tentative and general, such as, "How do you choose an assessment?" Most correspondence showed a single question and response pattern followed by an unrelated question – although more prolonged dialogue on a single topic sometimes occurred in face-to-face discussions. Questions and responses often focused on specific single-loop issues of implementation, such as how to make learning intentions relevant to young children, how to write learning intentions for process as well as outcomes, or how to use rubrics effectively. TCs' belief in the potential of assessment seemed to grow with their own self-efficacy, when they witnessed specific examples of it during classroom visits. For example: "[My mentor's] example allowed me to see how easy and beneficial it would be to incorporate this type of assessment into a language arts writing assignment in my own lesson plans." However, the reverse was also evident, particularly when the mentorship relationship was not fully utilized: "I think that assessment for learning is a wonderful tool, but I just wish that I felt more comfortable using it. I wish that I had examples of how to include it in my lessons."

Teacher coaches appeared open with TCs regarding their evolution as AFL practitioners and the struggles they faced, such as difficulties with report card formats. For example: "[My coach] reports that formative assessment has become her way of life, but also that it was a slow and difficult process." Occasionally, TCs' reflection deepened to double-loop learning, revealing the shifts in perspective that undergirded changed practices: "I suppose . . . there must be a balance to where life just does need to be let go of and control given over to knowing when things need to be learned or taught. I can only hope that in my classroom one day I will always have the child's greater good over my lesson plan, no matter how hard I worked on it." One TC used his journal to voice a concern: "How can different teacher's ideas of assessment for learning better transfer between grades and individual students while maintaining some form of continuity?" However, his discussion was speculative and did not appear to draw on any dialogue he experienced with an experienced mentor. Nevertheless, we acknowledged his focus on a central question as a first step toward inquiry.

Classroom visits and observations of teaching, when they occurred, seemed to have a powerful effect, in that TCs gained confidence and strengthened their values. For example, one said, "Every child is celebrated and his or her strengths are highlighted during the day. The teacher uses . . . multi learning styles in each lesson so all students are given optimum learning opportunity. Assessing where each child is, what needs to be addressed, and empowering the students to reach their potential is evidently visible through [the teacher's] descriptive feedback to the students."

One TC, who found her own mentor (a principal), responded with a logical rationale for AFL: "It is my responsibility to try to teach in a way so that all students will be successful, and when the research shows that assessment for learning increases achievement, then I need to incorporate it into my own teaching." She also outlined steps toward making a difference with formative assessment. She balanced an existing reporting system of numerical scores with intention, criteria, self-assessment, and goal setting, and she separated feedback on students' work habits from their academic grades. These steps, which drew on the NPBS featured strategies, were common in many journal entries.

Respect for Children as Agents in Their Own Learning

In some journal entries, TCs identified their mentor's respect for children who were active agents in their own learning. One said, "Students are learning to be knowledge builders, not knowledge tellers. I learned that to focus on this it is important to work on the following questions: What do you know? What do you need to know? How are you going to get there?" Another TC commented, "I learned that the depth of young students' thinking is quite amazing. Their capabilities are great when the right questions and thought-provoking material is posed;" a third wrote, "I think the most important resource I cannot forget about is my students. I need to consult them about assessment practices and guidelines in words they can understand. I need to value their opinions and invite them to be an active part of their own assessment."

One TC remarked on the shift in relationship that occurred when assessment was a joint venture between teacher and students: "I especially respect that relationships are also huge for [my mentor], and first she likes to build caring and trusting relationships with her students by showing them personal regard and revealing herself to be a fellow learner." Another candidate demonstrated movement beyond a concern for how to implement strategies to a vision for students as partners in assessment: "I want my students to feel empowered by assessment and not frightened by it. I want them to feel capable and in control of their learning. I want them to have the skills in life to look at their performance critically and decide what they have done well and what they want to do next." Yet another TC described her transformative, "aha" moment: "What caught me right away was that she described assessment for learning as 'respectful learning'. This revolutionized my thinking about AFL practices. Already a believer in AFL, I found it empowering to hear that we can guide, assess, and respect our students all at once!" She continued to show how this new vision differed from her previous experience: "Throughout my schooling, I found that we were always expected to learn on our own without the help of peers or other adults. I am now excited to teach in a world in which compromise and team learning can and is taking place."

Learners and Leaders within Inquiring Communities

A common theme in the journals was that TCs began to see themselves as learners and/or leaders in professional communities, as illustrated by this record: "The best way for me to keep going and get where I want and need to go further in regards to assessment is to keep a varied and mixed group of learning partners in my network of colleagues and personal friends. . . . Keeping the dialogue going and learning and practicing techniques and strategies are important for me."

Other candidates provided the following observations: "We are in a profession where sharing information is essential and vital for the success of the students," and "Being a new teacher, it is reassuring that there are teachers in the school district who are willing to help you." One teacher candidate expressed empowerment as a teacher leader: "I will continue to increase my connections with educators and peers that know and want to know about formative assessment. It is the future of assessment and I am confident that I will be fully involved in shaping it."

Meaning

In the meaning phase, we talked, thought, and wrote about the responses of TCs and mentors and why they mattered to us. Here, we extended the awareness we developed though observation and analysis, and we increased our understanding by linking our experiences back to the research literature.

Employing the four ways that teachers learn (Pedder, James, & McBeath, 2005), we were helped to understand the types of learning that were evident and the capacities that were developed. TCs seemed to *extend* and deepen their learning through a wider range of sources of knowledge and talk that valued learning. Through mentor modelling, we believe they built capacity for learning that would later become *embedded* in their classroom practice and *expanded* through ongoing collaborative activity. Desforges (2005), and Kelly's (2006) socio-cultural perspective, helped us see that *public*, theoretical knowledge was insufficient for transformation. However, *collaborative* knowledge, created in interactions, was an important step toward internalizing the knowledge of more experienced peers. Through the work of McLeskey and Waldron (2004), we have understood the value of blending the knowledge-for-practice evident in most university classes with knowledge-of-practice provided by mentors. We also have a new appreciation of how TCs can use their synthesis of knowledge from texts and mentors to apply and construct new knowledge-in-practice by means of their own inquiries. One TC illustrated that process: "Three months ago I didn't even know what assessment for learning was. One and half months ago I was unsure how to put it into practice. Today I feel fairly confident using assessment for learning. I have read about it in text books, I have talked about it with my learning partner, I have put it into practice in my practicum, and I am still having 'ah ha' moments about it."

Overall, we believe this mentoring project was of value because we have helped initiate TCs into the world of learning teams and leader-rich professional communities characterized by ongoing inquiry. Through our application of various typologies of teacher learning, we have increased our appreciation of the potential of blending text-based background knowledge with focused learning experiences guided by mentors. We recognize that inquiry and dialogue are essential to an ecology of learning in which strong communities nurture effective teachers and effective teachers strengthen their communities (Starratt, as cited in Mitchell & Sackney, 2000).

Commitment

In that phase, inquirers move the *convictions* developed in the meaning phase toward sustainable *commitments* to altered practice. TCs' confidence grows, but this confidence must also be questioned in a reflexive way. Furthermore, inquiry begins to deepen in plans for a subsequent round, beginning the cycle again from an expanded wholeness that includes the promising solutions and remaining mysteries emerging from the initial inquiry.

As teacher educators, we believe our practice has been altered in that we have learned to supplement text-based learning with focused classroom observations and follow-up dialogue. We have brought our espoused theories of learning community into greater alignment with our practices. We have also confronted an unexpected bias: our reluctance to trust the learning of our students to the greater community and to relax our control of their learning.

However, we equally recognize the importance of designing learning structures that contribute to culture building. Now we are curious about the potential that could be achieved if all teacher candidates were "scaffolded" into mentorship, using required participation, face-to-face meet-and-greet sessions, and focus groups where newly constructed knowledge is shared with other mentor pairs. Although the analysis reported here has focused on TC learning, we believe an important next step is to encourage teacher mentors to examine the effect of mentoring on their own learning and leadership development.

As teacher leaders, we have been encouraged by a collegial relationship with professors, and we have enjoyed the intellectual companionship that has been rare in our daily school routines. We have expanded our professional network to include previously untapped resources (i.e., university space for meetings, facilitators for conferences, and greater access to joint authorship and publication). Our relationship with the university will remain part of our vision for ourselves as creators and members of a non-hierarchical community in which contributions from all levels of experience are valued.

As a team of four, we are committed to formative assessment and action-based, collaborative inquiry in pursuing the goal of an educational system focused on nurturing learning rather than sorting. We have learned to be more focused and more specific in our data collection and analysis and yet to remain open to the energizing delight of "learning in the face of mystery" (Ghalardi, as cited in Mitchell & Sackney, 2000). However, even as our single-loop strategies improve, we still question our basic assumptions and consider whether further double-loop learning is appropriate.

We have further questioned whether culture can be altered intentionally, and whether formative assessment will deliver on its promise or, as many failed innovations have done, contribute to teacher cynicism and disillusionment. We have wondered if we could be doing teachers a disservice by cultivating their capacity for leadership within a hierarchical system that may stifle and disappoint them. We are also concerned that our actions may not always appear to align with our espoused appreciation for diversity and our belief in non-instrumental treatment of teachers. In our roles as educational leaders, models, and mentors, we fear perceptions that may undermine the values we want most to share. Finally, we understand that our emphasis on the beliefs and strategies of formative assessment may have caused us to overlook other important aspects of the moral purposes of education.

However, in weighing all of these elements for our final commitments, we remember that one test of the implementation of a new idea is whether relationships have improved. By this test, we believe that our inquiry has succeeded and that it promises more success if we persevere. We are willing to share our imperfections and development with other educators, in subsequent rounds of inquiry because we believe that the integrity of beliefs and actions that we develop will support the trust that is essential for healthy communities. Through this research we realize our responsibility, as educational leaders, involves sharing our knowledge and constructing new knowledge. We also reaffirm our commitment to continue to develop knowledge of formative assessment, as expressed in the prepositions *of*, *as*, and *for*, and to maintain an orientation to inquiry in sustainable harmony because the well-being, development, and growth of everyone involved in the educational enterprise: professors, teachers, teacher candidates, and students, benefit through such work.

References

Argyris, C., & Schon, D. (1978). *Organizational learning: A theory of action perspective*. Reading, MA: Addison Wesley.

Black, P., & Wiliam, D. (1998). Inside the black box: Raising standards through classroom assessment. *PHI Delta Kappan, 80*, 139–148.

Brown, W. (2004). *Building a learning community through restitution: A case study* (Unpublished doctoral dissertation). University of Saskatchewan, Saskatoon, SK.

Carr, W., & Kemmis, S. (1988). *Becoming critical: Education, knowledge, and action research*. London, UK: Falmer Press.

Davy, A., & Brown, W. (2006). Turning show 'n' tell into democratic dialogue. *Networks: An On-line Journal for Teacher Research, 9*(1). Retrieved from http://journals.library.wisc.edu/index.php/networks/issue/view/20

Desforges, C. (2005). On teaching and learning [Online article]. *Networked Learning Communities: National College for Leadership Online*. Available from http://networkedlearning.ncsl.org.uk/knowledge-base/programme-leaflets/on-learning-and-teaching-desforges-2005.pdf

Fullan, M. (2007). *The new meaning of educational change* (4th ed.). New York, NY: Teachers College Press.

Halbert, J., & Kaser, L. (2006). Deep learning: Inquiring communities of practice. *Education Canada, 46*(3), 43–45.

Kaser, L., & Halbert, J. (2008). From sorting to learning: Developing deep learning in Canadian schools. *Education Canada, 48*(5), 56–59.

Kaser, L., & Halbert, J. (2009). *Leadership mindsets: Innovation and learning in the transformation of schools*. Oxon, UK: Routledge.

Kelly, P. (2006). What is teacher learning? A socio-cultural perspective. *Oxford Review of Education, 32*(4), 509–519.

McLeskey, J., & Waldron, N. L. (2004). Three conceptions of teacher learning: Exploring the relationship between knowledge and the practice of teaching. *Teacher Education and Special Education, 27*(1), 3–14.

Mitchell, C., & Sackney, L. (2000). *Profound improvement: Building capacity for a learning community*. Lisse, Netherlands: Swets & Zeitlinger.

Mitchell, C., & Sackney, L. (2009). *Sustainable improvement: Building learning communities that endure*. Lisse, Netherlands: Sense.

Pedder, D., James, M., & MacBeath, J. (2005). How teachers value and practice professional learning. *Research Papers in Education, 20*(3), 209–243.

Robertson, J. (2006). *Coaching leadership: Towards a knowledge of practice* [Online article]. Retrieved from http://www.sst-inet.net/default.aspx?page=2526

Robertson, J. (2008) The 3R's for coaching learning relationships. *Professional Development Today, 11*(2), 6–11.

Robertson, J. (2009) *Coaching educational leadership: Building leadership capacity through partnership*. London, UK: Sage.

Sagor, R. (1992). *How to conduct collaborative action research*. Alexandria, VA: Association for Supervision and Curriculum Development.

Senge, P., McCabe, N., Lucas, T., Kleiner, A., Dutton, J., & Smith, B. (2000). *Schools that learn*. New York, NY: Doubleday.

Stiggins, R. (2008). *An introduction to student-involved assessment for learning* (5th ed.). Upper Saddle River, NJ: Pearson.

Western and Northern Canadian Protocol for Collaboration in Education. (2006). *Rethinking classroom assessment with purpose in mind*. Retrieved from http://www.wncp.ca/media/40539/rethink.pdf

Wilson, D. (2009). *The conditions that facilitate deep teacher learning* (Unpublished master's project). University of Victoria, BC.

Chapter Eleven

Mentorship: A Self-Reflection on a Learning Journey

Catherine Neumann-Boxer

FROM 2006–2009, I HAD THE privilege of being employed as a district fine arts resource teacher for thirty-five K–7 classroom teachers in nine elementary schools in a Western Canadian school division. My assignment was to build classroom teachers' capacities for music instruction. Formally appointed as a mentor, I recognized that in order to build capacity among these teachers, I would probably need to consider using other conceptions of mentorship than a traditional one based on a unidirectional transmission approach. I felt I had to figure out what kind of mentor I needed to be. This reflective stance was sparked by participant comments that were collected at the Forum on Mentorship (J. P. Preston, personal communication, June 2010; Chapter 1 of this volume), and it was based on my prior professional learning experiences. The purpose of my reflection was to articulate how my practice had been informed by mindful attention to my own relationships and professional learning and, in so doing, to raise implications for my subsequent mentorship practice.

Participant Comments and Conceptions

The editors of the present book had organized the Canadian Forum on Mentorship in the Professions in 2010 for the purpose of bringing interested scholars and practitioners together to investigate mentorship and to initialize the process of putting together this book. Participant comments on definitions, purposes and processes of mentorship were collected during discussion activities. I was inspired by the participants' insights into what they perceived mentorship to be and by how their perceptions of mentorship seemed to vary to meet the demands of today's differing workplaces. Within their comments, I found parallels to my own search that I was in the midst of conducting regarding the kind of mentor I wanted to be. The forum comments, and my reflections on them, have prompted me to examine more deeply my own professional practice as a mentor. I list below eight of the comments that I drew from the forum sessions because they resonated with me in my current search for understanding mentorship and for being an effective mentor. These comments are:

1. Mentoring is not automatically a function of older versus younger or more skilled versus less skilled. It may have something to do with how some people value added experience;
2. Mentorship is a relationship of trust and respect, facilitating professional and personal growth, emphasizing wisdom, firing passion, vision, coaching, mutuality, fun, caring challenge and rigor;
3. The process of mentorship is completely driven by relationship. Mentorship is a relational practice;
4. Definitions of mentorship vary greatly among participants (rightly so). We need time to deconstruct our assumptions and contest what it is we mean by mentorship;
5. It's important to have theory before entering into a mentorship relation;
6. A mentorship system or model must begin with principles about learning;
7. The dyad model (expert-learner) for me is too much like knower/non-knower. I prefer the co-learner approach and/or the critical friend interaction route; and
8. There is a developing tension between the traditional idea of mentoring and the notion that we are all mentors and mentees. I am not sure if this is a paradigm shift or not, but I sense it is an important shift, nonetheless.

These attendee comments identified key ideas that I also embraced about the importance of informing one's practice by paying attention to the nature of the relationships that individuals have in their professional learning communities. I also believe that these comments represented a reaction to changing ideas about mentorship. In this vein, Darwin (2000) suggested that "taken-for-granted practices need to be brought to the surface for mentoring to be regarded as a useful learning tool in today's work settings" (p. 1), and he further identified major differences between functionalist and radical humanist perceptions of mentorship. In my initial search for the kind of mentor I wanted to be, I found I tended to favor the radical humanist perspective. Although I was not at first aware of this perspective, I discovered that, by means of my own reflective self-analysis and recent research on mentoring, the humanist view best explained the philosophical framework that has influenced my thinking and shaped my visualization of the type of mentor I wanted to be.

The Experience

As indicated, I had been hired as a teacher-mentor to help build classroom teachers' capacity for music instruction. At that time, the school division had perceived a need for more and better-quality music instruction in classrooms. The task was to build teachers' capacities for music instruction and to mentor the teachers as they sought to enhance their instructional practice. In this assignment, the mentorship process was preconceptualized in a more traditional light in which I, "the expert," was to mentor "the non-experts."

At that time, my professional learning had become an integral part of my ability to understand mentorship and to engage in my freshly assigned mentorship role. Fortunately, during that period I was working on a Masters of Education in Leadership Studies and was actively engaged in exploring school management and leadership learning. Through that concurrent professional learning experience I was able to inform my mentorship practice with my course readings and assignments regarding professional relationships (Bryk & Schneider, 2002; Robertson, 2005) and professional learning (Timperley, Wilson, Barrar, & Fung, 2008; Wiliam, 2004). All of the information I was processing in my program of studies seemed to be vital to my understanding of mentoring relationships and mentorship practice. Upon reflection, I now realize that the effectiveness of my mentoring practice was enhanced as a result of what I was learning in my professional reading and consequent critical thinking about my practice.

Specific concerns about the nature of the relationships that I was experiencing in my real-world mentorship practice and actual questions about how best to promote professional learning in particular cases led me on an authentic search for needed information. One of my key questions for which I sought answers both in the literature and in the learning community of which I was part was: "How do I establish mentoring relationships?"

Mindful Attention to Relationships

As I look back on my journey, I believe that my learning curve in that area was swift and nearly vertical. I started by relying on my prior experiences, vague instincts, and gut feelings, but began searching diligently for information from others. I instinctively knew that mindful attention to building and maintaining positive relationships would be a key to success. For instance, I had already recognized that if another educator had come to me saying, "I am going to build your capacity," I would have asked, "What is wrong with my capacity?" Furthermore, I would have probably angrily avoided the situation, or if I was forced into it, I would have probably just passively "played along" to avoid complicating consequences. I also realized, however, that as a mentor I had the attitude that I knew more or better than others, I would quickly block my ability to form any sort of productive relationship with my protégés.

As a person in a mentoring role, I wanted my colleagues to engage in new learning with me, and I thus needed to find a way to achieve that goal that would be comfortable for the partners. At first, I did not know how to go about being a good mentor, but yet I sensed that a conception of a mentor as the wise more experienced advisor (Shea, 2003; Shaw, 1995) would be inadequate in my particular situation.

I knew that my demeanor as I approached and worked with the teachers would be essential to my ability to affect change. Bryk and Schneider (2003) described "social trust as essential for meaningful school improvement" (p. 94), while Robertson (2005) maintained that relational trust, respect, and affirmation are foundational for professional relationships and defined mentorship as "a process of instilling confidence and creating independence; not as a status or position, but a process shared" (p. 1). These ideas resonated with me because I sincerely wanted to establish a trustful relationship wherein partners felt "confident to actively experiment with different and innovative concepts and ideas" (p. 5). I wanted to be a mentor "well placed to release the potential in others" (p. 4). I operated from the premise that I was a fellow learner – not an authority figure, but a guide. Thus, I entered my new role with a goal of developing trustful relationships.

Through my synthesis of the related literature regarding relationships, I developed a working model that allowed me to remain mindful of those objectives during my everyday mentoring practice. I constructed this model using key concepts and strategies while engaged in my mentoring experiences. I established four relational categories

Figure 1

Key concepts and strategies for everyday mentorship practice

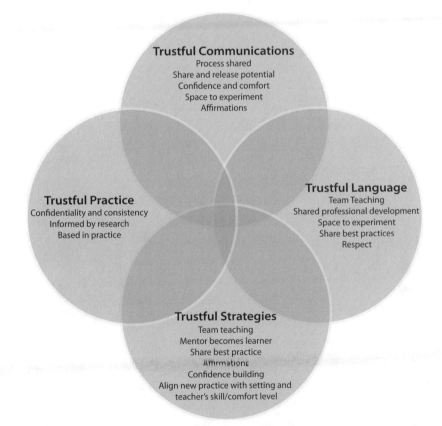

Trustful Communications
Process shared
Share and release potential
Confidence and comfort
Space to experiment
Affirmations

Trustful Practice
Confidentiality and consistency
Informed by research
Based in practice

Trustful Language
Team Teaching
Shared professional development
Space to experiment
Share best practices
Respect

Trustful Strategies
Team teaching
Mentor becomes learner
Share best practice
Affirmations
Confidence building
Align new practice with setting and
teacher's skill/comfort level

within the model: trustful communications, language, strategies, and practice. In each category I embedded key ideas from the literature that I believed would help me build and maintain positive and productive relationships and ultimately help me be the mentor I wanted to be.

Using this model I was able conceptualize and record the particular aspects from the literature that I believed would help me form good mentorship relationships. As I continued to refer to this model during my routine mentoring encounters, I found that the keywords were not distinct to each category but that several of the strategies overlapped and melded together across the categories during our mentorship events. For example, for the category of *Trustful Practice* as well as the other three areas, I knew that teachers had to recognize that I was, in fact, an expert in conducting best practice in music education, but I had to convey my possession of this level of professional knowledge and skill in a sensitive way, not perceived by them as distasteful or arrogant. In like manner, I knew that suggestions I would be making to teachers needed to be easily transferable to their classroom settings.

Consistency was also a vital aspect for creating and maintaining trust in the mentoring relationships. By being consistent in my approach and conduct, I found that the teachers were able to become increasingly comfortable with me because they grew accustomed with what to expect from me. Confidentiality was also a key component to effective mentorship both in my practice and in the research literature. Making changes to practice can make teachers feel vulnerable, but when they were assured that I would maintain privacy and confidentiality regarding any changes they made or attempted, or any discussions about their felt shortcomings or limitations, then their level of trust with our mentorship process increased. I found that this elevated degree of mutuality also helped teachers feel more comfortable about looking more deeply at their teaching practice and making possible changes to it.

For the areas of *Trustful Communications* and *Trustful Language*, I instinctively knew (and the literature confirmed this) that how I communicated with teachers influenced the quality of our mentoring relationships. By approaching teachers with a respectful demeanor and by using supportive language, I found that mutual trust between us was enhanced. Through trustful communication I was able to share my belief with teachers that the mentoring relationship was a collaborative process for mutual professional development. I also used team teaching with several teachers, which further cemented the mentoring relationships that in turn served to promote teacher development in areas that required it.

For the creation and maintenance of *Trustful Strategies*, I recognized that I needed to align any initial new learning with each teacher's unique setting, skill level, and confidence/comfort level. I wanted to avoid making the teachers feel overwhelmed with unrealistic expectations. In order to build professional trust between us and promote their motivation for music instruction, I believed I needed initially to build their confidence by starting with instructional strategies that were easily integrated into their current practice. I also realized that I needed to give teachers time to become comfortable with our relationship and any new strategies that were introduced and to permit them to move at their own pace towards change. In sum, I used the keywords shown in the model to provide me with a tangible way of reminding myself of the mentorship qualities that I wanted to exhibit in order to assist teachers to enhance their instructional practice and ultimately their students' learning.

Professional Learning

Continuing the search to inform my mentoring practice and help with what kind of mentor I wanted to be, I consulted the literature I was studying in my graduate program about how to engage teachers in professional learning. I thus addressed a second key question that emerged from my new mentorship role, which was: "How do professionals learn?"

In my university coursework, I had been introduced to the work of Wiliam (2004) and Timperley et al. (2008). I believed that Wiliam's (2004) *A Model for Teacher Learning* was especially relevant for my mentorship work, and I thus decided to embed it in my mentoring practice with the music teachers with whom I was working. Having been a classroom teacher for a few years, I knew that the everyday demands on teachers are at times overwhelming. Wiliam acknowledged that "classrooms are extremely complex places." (p. 19), and his model seemed to build my own professional confidence and to promote clearer lines of thinking. I believed that it allowed educators to "see through all of the immediate classroom demands to focus on our goals and purpose" (p. 20). The model consisted of small steps, was flexible, provided for choice, and considered accountability. What I especially liked was that it took into account the complexity of teaching and the myriad of activities and obligations teachers are involved in throughout a typical school day. The model provided me with a grounded framework that made sense and was mindful of teachers' highly complex contexts.

Wiliam's (2004) model particularly helped me to better understand my role as a mentor. He indicated that "the leader is not to create teacher change, but to engineer situations in which the teacher change can take place" (p. 20). This statement actually helped me be more relaxed and reduced the pressure I had placed on myself that I was responsible for everything. I combined the principles of Wiliam's learning model with Timperley et al.'s (2008) *Principles of Professional Learning*. Timperley et al. (2008) postulated that (a) a vital component to exposing teachers to new learning is aligning new practices to what was already happening in the school and (b) that not doing so will create "fragmentation leading to the dissolution of trust" (p. 12). The last thing I wanted to do was to isolate the new learning people were engaged in from what was already going on in their classrooms. I knew that I had to begin with elements of the protégés' existing practice.

Threaded through Timperley et al.'s (2008) synthesis of professional development work was the importance of building and maintaining relationships. Timperley et al. (2008) extracted principles that were derived from professional development and learning research studies to provide a framework for effective professional learning. These principles resonated with my own professional experiences and beliefs because they reflected how I as a teacher or protégé could genuinely engage in changing my practice. These principles seemed to sidestep the angry avoiding or playing along I mentioned earlier.

Thus, during my tenure of music mentor in my school district, I developed a chart (see Table 1) to serve as a guideline for developing and sustaining the district music network. In this instance a learning

Table 1

A Mentoring Guide for Developing Teacher Learning in the District Music Network

Principles	Model	Applications
1. FOCUS ON VALUED STUDENT OUTCOMES· Which student outcomes do we value and why?	Small steps and choice. Engage teachers by identifying which outcomes to start with.	Each teacher identifies four Ministry prescribed student outcomes.
2. WORTHWHILE CONTENT· What knowledge and skills do we need to develop in order to be effective in achieving these outcomes?	Choice and accountability.	Network develops rubrics from the four outcomes to assess progress.
3. ASSESSMENT SUCCESS· What will your school work on?	Accountability. Choice in what to change creates more independence and motivation for change (Timperley, 2008).	Choose one outcome, develop measurable plan for action. What data will we collect to assess practices?
4. OPPORTUNITIES TO PROCESS NEW LEARNING WITH OTHERS· How do we share successful practice? Collegial interaction . . . can help teachers integrate new learning into practice." (Timperley, 2008)	Small steps. The "demonstration of effective alternate practice is most effective in motivating teachers to] make small changes to practice." (Timperley, 2008)	Create opportunities in schools to share high quality music instruction. Monthly sharing of successful practice with music network.
5. ACTIVE LEADERSHIP AND MAINTAINING MOMENTUM· How do we actively lead? How do we maintain momentum?	Choice. Accountability. Site based leaders. Continued support in the organizational context of the district.	Form relationships with teachers and leaders in schools centred on maintaining quality music instruction

community consists of one teacher and/or one leader from each of the district's nine elementary schools.

In the chart I combined Timperley et al.'s (2008) principles with Wiliam's (2004) model for teacher learning, and then developed specific applications related to our district's mission and context. The first column of the chart deals with the philosophical principles guiding practice, the second column identifies particular models for practice established to promote professional learning, and the third column details actual applications in practice – specific ways in which we built music programs in our classrooms. I introduced this framework during my initial meetings with the teachers and used it as a vehicle to begin developing the relationships needed to build teacher capacity and sustain our joint-learning journey.

In sharing this framework with the teachers and leaders from the beginning, I thought that being completely transparent about the proposed journey would help to (a) begin to build the trustful relationships we all desired and (b) to provide a possible foundation upon which to engage in further professional learning. The framework allowed the teachers to see the philosophy behind what the district wanted to achieve and why, the possible models we could use and why, and some suggested ideas we could consider regarding what we could do in practice to improve the program, measure its success, and sustain the improvements.

By first assisting teachers to delineate central student outcomes on which to focus, I attempted to convey my belief that starting with small achievable steps, while also allowing for individual choice, would help build trust and commitment among the group. Teachers appreciated the provision to be able to choose the area on which they wished to work. After deciding what to work on, each teacher and I assessed our respective skill sets and determined which areas we needed to develop in order to achieve the outcomes. We sought to collaboratively select worthwhile skills and knowledge to develop, then we designed sensible rubrics relevant for each teacher's context. We used these rubrics as a guide for teacher skill development and as a means with which to assess the success of this development. The rubrics thus provided the teachers with goals to work towards and a way to determine accountability. From these rubrics the teachers developed a measurable plan of action and a method for collecting data to record progress. The teachers assessed the success of their action plans with the rubrics and, in doing so, were holding themselves accountable with the evidence of data collected using the rubrics.

We also brainstormed ideas for communicating this process of new learning with others. We decided as a group that I would team teach with each teacher and her students using the musical instruments. In these settings, both the teacher and I worked together to teach students how to play the instruments. For several of the teachers who did not know how to play the instruments, they had the opportunity to have me (in a temporary role of "expert") to present demonstration lessons and to start to learn how to go about making changes to their practice.

Teachers also reported their appreciation of being able to learn from each other during our monthly team meetings. They used those occasions to freely report on music successes and to analyze what worked, did not work, and why, in our classrooms. I also gained knowledge from these teachers and emphasized that I was a co-learner with them. The group seemed to agree that the entire learning process was facilitated by an atmosphere of trust that we had been able to forge among the community. I requested two colleagues to conduct demonstration lessons for my own classes – in drama from one teacher and in dance from another – both areas wherein I wanted to enhance my instructional capacities. I found that employing this co-learner approach helped to further develop the group climate needed for professional learning.

The last step in this framework focused on leadership and on maintaining momentum. After working through the first steps of the learning framework, the teachers and I believed that the most fitting way to sustain our program was to have site-based music leaders to maintain the momentum we had created. Leaders at each school volunteered to be the site-based contacts for teachers wishing to continue improving the quality of their music instruction. In the end, I actually worked myself out of a job, but ultimately I believe that is what a good mentor should do.

Engaging collaboratively in this framework helped us form helpful relationships and provided us with step-by-step strategies for building capacity. With the learning I had been simultaneously experiencing in my graduate program regarding trustful relationships and the nature of professional learning, I was able to "engineer situations in which teacher change could take place" (Wiliam, 2004, p. 20). Fusing Wiliam's (2004) model with Timperley et al.'s (2008) principles allowed me to facilitate the individuals in the network to co-operate as co-learners, to make changes to their individual practice, to collect data to monitor the effect of those changes, and to maintain the momentum for enhancing music learning in our district's schools and classrooms.

Reflections for Future Mentorship Practice

In the future, I would like to consider incorporating an adaptive approach with the guidelines I described above to enhance my mentorship practice. Perhaps the Adaptive Mentorship© (AM) model proposed by Ralph and Walker (2010) could provide an overall framework that could serve to hold the various facets together with less of a "mentor-centric" aspect (Ralph & Walker, 2010, p. 1) on which conventional approaches seem to focus. The AM model "requires mentors to adjust their helping behaviour" (p. 4) in response to the protégé's developmental needs. What attracts me to the model is that it avoids using a one-size-fits-all approach but instead allows the person in the mentor position to adjust or modify his/her mentoring style and response according to the contextual situation. I believe that the principles of AM could be integrated within the five steps of our guidelines for teacher learning. Furthermore, the AM model seems to situate the work of developing trustful relationships and professional learning within a protégé-specific frame by guiding the mentor to work with the partner by using a synchronized adaptive response to the specific needs of the person in the protégé role.

Incorporating the AM model in my music-mentorship experience may have helped to make my mentoring practice more transparent and trustful. Upon reflection, I believe that utilizing the AM model may have provided the teachers with a greater voice in the process. Too, it may have helped me reduce the somewhat forceful way I began through my initial top-down introduction of the guidelines and my agenda. Using the AM model in the way that the authors suggested would emphasize more differentiated attention to protégé needs – making the whole mentorship practice a more authentic process. I think that incorporating AM in this manner in any future mentorship opportunity in which I am engaged would be a worthwhile consideration.

Implications for Mentor Learning

Similarities between the participant comments at the Forum on Mentorship (2010) and my own experience as a music-education mentor raise implications for broader mentorship practice. By informing his/her practice through mindful attention to relationships and professional learning, it is possible for mentors to increasingly ground their mentoring in the growing body of research-based practices. Findings from both the forum and the research literature indicate the changing nature of mentorship, the importance of relationships, and the place of professional learning. These three themes were also present in my personal experience of beginning to become the effective mentor I envisaged. Yet this image is also evolving as I learn more about the process.

Changing Ideas about Mentorship

As a result of what I have learned in my graduate studies of leadership and learning communities, my personal mentorship experience, and my own action research, I find that my ideas of mentorship are evolving. Comments from the forum participants influence my positions regarding mentorship:

- ~: The conventional dyad model of mentorship (expert-novice) for me is too much like knower/non-knower. I prefer the co-learner approach and/or the critical friend interaction route.
- ~: There is a developing tension between the traditional idea of mentoring and the notion that everyone is both mentor and protégé. I am not sure if this assertion reflects a paradigm shift, but I sense it is an important shift, nonetheless.
- ~: Mentoring is not automatically a function of older versus younger or more skilled versus less skilled. Rather, the concept of mentorship may have more to do with how some people value added experience.

~: Definitions of mentorship vary greatly among participants and in the literature, which is acceptable. I think that all of us who have an interest in the mentorship process – educators, practitioners, and researchers alike – need time to deconstruct our assumptions and continue to examine what mentorship is in its various contexts.

Conceptions about the meaning of mentorship are changing. In my experience as a mentor I moved from more traditional expectations of "mentor as expert and authority" because of an inherent sense of "tension between the traditional idea of mentoring and the notion that we are all mentors and mentees" (Forum comment, 2010). I became more comfortable with adopting a mentor-as-co-learner approach. Using a radical humanist interpretation of mentorship, I was able to work from my belief that I could help effect change through co-learning situations based on trust and professional learning principles. To me, mentorship became what Darwin (2000, p. 8) termed "a collaborative, dynamic, and creative partnership of coequals."

Comments from the Mentorship Forum (2010) aligned with my thinking during the time I was sorting out my understanding of mentorship. For me, the concept of the "dyad model of expert-learner . . . knower/non-knower" (Forum comment, 2010) was inadequate, and the contrast between "*expert* and *learner* become arbitrary delineations" (Darwin, 2000, p. 8). In my current understanding, the "notion that we are all mentors and mentees" (Forum comment, 2010) created a "concept of co-learning [that] suggests individuals transcend roles (or create different roles) and interact as colleagues" (Darwin, 2000, p. 9). I believe with Darwin that mentoring must be "viewed less as a role and more as a character of the relationship" (p. 10), and in that relationship mentor and protégé must first discuss "what it is we mean by mentorship" (Forum comment, 2010) in order to begin developing a less "mentor-centric" (Ralph & Walker, 2010, p. 1) relationship.

At this stage in my journey, I conceptualize mentorship as a coaching relationship that is rooted in trust and respect and that facilitates professional and personal growth. To me, effective mentorship is positive relational practice that emphasizes partners' wisdom and that stimulates their passion and vision for excellence. It is also characterized by mutuality, caring, challenge, rigor, and occasionally fun. In the light of these statements, I believe that all individuals holding mentorship responsibilities should inform their mentoring practice by reflecting on the principles discussed in this chapter.

Mentorship as Mutual Relationship

I now believe that a mentor must pay attention on a daily basis to relationship as a foundation for building capacity and helping protégés enhance their practice. I saw that the approach I took with mentoring experienced teachers in the field, stemming from my belief that building capacity starts with building mutuality, set a foundation for improving classroom practice. In mutuality all of us were able to forge the type of relationship needed to enhance the teaching/learning experience. The initial model I developed prompted me to be ever cognizant of trustful communication and language in my mentoring practice. Through shared professional learning and respectful relationships, mentor and mentees alike were able to collaborate as a learning team and inform and improve our classroom practice.

Mentorship as Professional Learning

I recognize that effective mentors inform their practice with pertinent research-based principles about how professionals learn in order to build capacity and help individuals in the protégé role to improve make their practice. I helped build classroom teacher capacities by facilitating change through provision of teacher choice and flexibility regarding their own action plans. By means of a mutually beneficial approach constructed by my integration of Timperley et al.'s (2008) and Wiliam's (2004) work, I was able to assist teachers to enact manageable changes in their classroom practice and to build in accountability structures to assess these changes. Throughout this process, I was able to inform my ongoing mentoring practice with what I needed to know about how adults learn.

Concluding Thoughts

My learning about the mentor I wanted to be emerged from my fundamental concerns regarding maintaining positive relationships and my questions about how teachers learn. In my mentorship role, I attempted to pay attention to the atmosphere I was creating through the ways I established relationships. In so doing, I was able to facilitate our group of elementary school music teachers to develop into a professional learning community characterized by trust and mutuality. I was able to navigate between the more traditional mentor-as-expert approach and the adaptive-mentor approach in which I responded to individual protégé needs and changing conditions of the work place. In the future, I intend to consider the AM model to help me further ground my practice in adapting my mentoring response and style to appropriately match the task-specific developmental level of the protégé with whom I am working. In sum, I believe that giving attention to developing positive, productive relationships, knowing how professionals acquire new knowledge and learn new skills, and being able to adapt one's leadership responses are three essential components to the informed practice of mentorship in educational settings.

References

Bryk, A. S., & Schneider, B. (2002). *Trust in schools: A core resource for improvement.* New York, NY: Russell Sage Foundation.

Darwin, A. (2000). Critical reflections on mentoring in work settings. *Adult Education Quarterly, 50,* 197–209.

Ralph, E., & Walker, K. (2010). Rising with the tide: Applying "Adaptive Mentorship" in the professional practicum. In W. Wright, M. Wilson, & D. MacIsaac (Eds.), *CELT: Collected Essays on Learning and Teaching,* (Volume 3, pp. 3–8). Hamilton, ON: McMaster University. Available from http://celt.uwindsor.ca/ojs/leddy/index.php/CELT

Robertson, J. M. (2005). *Coaching Leadership: Building educational leadership capacity through coaching partnerships.* Wellington, NZ: New Zealand Council for Educational Research.

Shaw, R. (1995). Mentoring. In T. Kerry & A. Mayes (Eds.), *Issues in mentoring* (pp. 259–267). New York, NY: Routledge.

Shea, G. F. (2003). *The mentoring organization.* Menlo Park, CA: Crisp Learning

Timperley, H., Wilson, A., Barrar, H., & Fung, I. (2008). *Teacher professional learning and development: Best evidence synthesis iteration.* Wellington, NZ: New Zealand Ministry of Education.

Wiliam, D. (2004). Assessment for learning: Why, what and how. *Orbit, 36,* 2–6.

Chapter Twelve

Peer Coaching: Awakening Teacher Leadership

Sabre Cherkowski

AN AWAKENING WAS THE METAPHOR that inspired my reflection on the relationship between peer coaching and an increasing self-awareness of teacher leadership potential in graduate students in an educational leadership course. As I reflected on the students' descriptions of their introduction to peer coaching, through a leadership portfolio assignment, I awoke to the potential of peer coaching for increased teacher leadership. The students themselves were awakened to their leadership potential as teachers through peer coaching. Furthermore, the metaphor reflected the general awakening among educators to the importance of teacher leadership in school improvement initiatives. There is a growing interest in, or awakening to, teacher leadership as an essential element in creating and sustaining learning community cultures in schools.

Teacher leadership is not new. In his research on the connections between teacher leadership and school improvement, Reeves (2006) described the notion of teachers and leaders as having always been inseparable, but there is a growing recognition of the importance of engaging teachers as leaders for sustainable school improvement. In this chapter I describe the use of peer coaching with teachers in a graduate educational leadership course, and I explain the links I forged between this mentoring strategy and teacher leadership for school improvement. It was an awakening to the essentiality of teachers as leaders in building and sustaining learning community cultures.

My examination of student reflections on the use of peer coaching within a graduate level educational leadership program revealed opportunities for awakening and deepening students' sense of teacher leadership in their own school contexts. By means of informal course evaluations and class discussions in the graduate course, I collected students' descriptions of the assigned portfolio and peer coaching activities. Many of the students described how the use of the portfolio as an intentional observation of their leadership practices contributed to a sense of increased empowerment, rejuvenation, and wonder at their leadership effectiveness in their schools. Although they admitted that it was often difficult to overcome certain barriers and obstacles in this peer-coaching activity, students recognized that peer coaching was effective in engaging them in professional development with colleagues. Students reported that they appreciated the use of a partner to both challenge and support their growth as teacher leaders.

I will discuss four key principles within the framework of both the relevant literature and my own observations with respect to peer coaching and school leadership. First, peer coaching can awaken a sense of teacher leadership in the school context. Second, peer coaching can provide a meaningful and contextually relevant form of educator professional development. Third, peer coaching can be integrated into master's level education courses through the use of portfolio assignments. Fourth, peer coaching can present challenges for implementation in graduate education courses.

At the outset, I clarify that a learning community framework infused the overall framework of this graduate course and that peer coaching was used as a tool to promote reflective practice among the students. I describe the theoretical framework, the use of the portfolio, and summarize my observations of the use of peer coaching in a graduate level educational leadership course. I conclude by identifying areas for further inquiry and research.

A Theoretical Framework

I used the learning community model (Mitchell & Sackney, 2000, 2009) as the overarching framework for the course, for the design of the portfolio assignment, and for the development of the peer-coaching component. Inherent in the learning community literature is the assumption of a leader-rich environment where teacher leaders are as influential as formally appointed leaders. Lieberman and Miller (2004) proposed that teacher leaders have a unique role in reshaping school culture from focusing on individualism to reflecting professional community. Creating a coaching relationship between teachers as learners and leaders (Robertson, 2008) can facilitate the shifting of the learning mindsets (Kaser & Halbert, 2009) of individuals in schools as a way of moving towards sustainable learning communities.

Learning Communities: Teachers as Leaders

A learning community exists where members continually expand their capacity to create the results they desire, where new patterns of thinking are nurtured, where collective aspiration is set free, and where people learn together to see "the whole" of a situation. A learning community can flourish when learning mindsets are cultivated and nurtured (Kaser & Halbert, 2009; Mitchell & Sackney, 2009). Flexibility, adaptability, critical reflective thinking, and a sense of curiosity and wonder about the magic of learning all become important elements for establishing learning communities in schools. The formation of learning communities represents a shift in thinking about the ways educators conceive of schools, and such communities reflect an interdisciplinary trend toward a less mechanized and a more ecological ontology regarding the entire school experience.

In a professional learning community, members take an active role in their own professional development that in turn generates increased learning capacity within schools. The culture of the school has to be transformed through shifting or altering institutional structures, attitudes, and beliefs in order to allow authentic learning to occur at all the levels of an organization (DuFour & Eaker, 1998; Kaser & Halbert, 2009; Mitchell & Sackney, 2000, 2009).

Traditionally, educators have emphasized the important role of principals in ensuring that learning communities are built and sustained. Research has established that leadership from the principal was a key to teacher and student learning (Hargreaves & Fink, 2006; Leithwood & Jantzi, 2005; Mitchell & Sackney, 2000; Speck, 1999). However, because of the increasing public demand for school improvement to support student achievement, a growing body of recent research has affirmed that teacher leadership is also a critical component of school improvement (Firestone & Martinez, 2007; Harris & Muijs, 2005; Lieberman & Miller, 2004; Mayrowetz, Murphy, Seashore Lewis, & Smylie, 2007; Muijs & Harris, 2006;

Reeves, 2006). Sustainable changes in schools necessitate that the formal leaders must develop leadership capacity at many levels of the school (Fullan, 2006; Mitchell & Sackney, 2009; Slater, 2008) and that this capacity is built when teachers are engaged as leaders of continuous learning in their workplace (Elmore, 2000).

In his description of the eighth habit of highly effective people, Covey (2004) emphasized the process of leading a group to become an interdependent, high-capacity learning organization or community (Mitchell & Sackney, 2000, 2009). Thus, prospective leaders must not only find their individual leadership voices, but they should also encourage colleagues to find their own as well. My implementation of peer coaching centred on the hypothesis that creating peer partnerships would provide an opportunity for the class members to challenge themselves as leaders while at the same time supporting and encouraging their peers to find their own leadership strengths. I believed that engaging the participants in opportunities for leadership through learning would be the key to unlocking the leadership capacity and commitment of their colleagues.

Portfolio Assignments: A Means for Reflective Practice

Portfolios are used regularly by instructors to encourage their students to demonstrate what they know and are able to do (Elbow & Belanoff, 1997; Lyons, 1998). Portfolios can be seen both as a process, providing a way for students to tell the story of their learning (Fiedler, Mullen, & Finnegan, 2009; McKinney, 1998), and as a product, when used as an assessment tool of learning (Paulson & Paulson, 1991). Moreover, research has highlighted the usefulness of portfolios for helping student teachers develop teaching skills (Beck, Livne, & Bear, 2005; Fiedler et al., 2009; McKinney, 1998; Shulman, 1998). In my case, I similarly designed a leadership portfolio to help develop leadership skills and attitudes among my graduate students. The portfolio enabled the students to engage in the self-observation of, and the peer coaching for, informal leadership growth. The leadership portfolio proved to be an important tool in supporting and awakening teacher leadership through reflective conversations between peer coaches.

Reflective practice "has emerged . . . as the primary tool for professional growth, school and organizational development, and continuous improvement" (Mitchell & Sackney, 2009, p. 24). Reflective practice can be an effective tool for practitioners to discover the gap between what they say they do and what they actually do and between their espoused theories and their theories-in-use. To master this skill is essential for learning-oriented leaders. Within the context of the graduate course in question, the portfolio work provided an opportunity for the students to construct rich understandings or adaptations of the leadership theories discussed in class. These meanings were (a) literature-based, (b) personally meaningful, and (c) grounded in their reflections on their own leadership practices.

Over the period of the six class sessions, students recorded in their portfolios their reflections and self-observations of leadership within the context of their work in the schools. To complete this task, they used a provincially derived set of leadership standards (BCPVPA, 2007). Although these standards had originally been created with administrators in mind, I encouraged the students to reflect on how teacher leaders might use the standards as a learning tool for self-observation of leadership growth. They indicated that as they engaged in discussions and reflections with their peer coaches, they connected the relevance of the theory to their daily practice. They also reported sensing a closer connection to their leadership goals and seeing the leadership portfolio as an important component for creating realistic opportunities for peer coaching within this course.

Peer Coaching in Relation to Mentoring

Mentoring has been an important aspect of educator professional development and teacher induction programs for decades. For me the term mentoring encapsulated an array of professional development activities that would support educators at all levels of a career in ways relevant to their particular needs (Ensher, Thomas, & Murphy, 2001). I conceptualized peer coaching as a strategy within the broad professional development field of mentoring.

Although the terms mentoring and coaching have often been used interchangeably, I saw peer coaching as distinct, based on the assumptions that each partner is a learner, little or no hierarchy is attached to the relationship, and both participants work towards achieving learning goals (Parker, Hall, & Kram, 2008; Robertson, 2009). Further, Hobson (2003) distinguished between mentoring and coaching at the level of process. To him, mentoring was a broadly defined process in which a more experienced individual sought to, or was asked to, assist a less experienced individual. In contrast, he defined coaching as a form of assistance "related more specifically to an individual's job specific tasks, skills or capabilities" (p. 2). Yet, Reiss (2007) suggested that as coaching has become a more prevalent strategy for professional development in education, the boundaries for coaching have expanded to include both general and task-specific coaching.

Although a clear delineation between mentoring and coaching has yet to be identified, research has indicated the contributions of both mentoring and coaching to educator professional development. Knowledge of the mentoring and coaching process is critical in establishing meaningful and relevant professional development and learning for emerging leaders (Reiss, 2007). Robertson (2008, 2009) believed that the coaching and mentoring process is a powerful agent of change for professional development in creating learning leadership in schools.

Peer Coaching: Creating a Learning Partnership

Peer coaching has been described in business as a relational process that can accelerate career learning (Parker et al, 2008). In educational settings, peer coaching was perceived as a learning partnership that can transform school cultures (Muijs & Harris, 2006; Reiss, 2007; Robertson, 2008, 2009). Robertson (2009) argued that the use of coaching helps facilitate desired change through a positive relationship of ongoing support and challenge. Teachers have often experienced their work in isolation, with little discussion or sharing of practices in public forums (Harris, 2001; Lieberman & Miller, 2004). Peer coaching can alleviate this isolation and create an opportunity for teachers to engage in reflective learning with colleagues. Putting teachers and leaders in contact with their own sources of leadership may help to facilitate change through a relational process of ongoing support, challenge, and self-reflection.

Several characteristics are evident in successful peer coaching relationships. Trust and support, mutual respect and authenticity, dialogue, reflection, and feedback are essential for successful coaching relationships (Parker et al., 2007; Reiss, 2007; Robertson, 2008; Veenman & Denessen, 2001). Gewertz (2008) described coaching as an observation-and-feedback loop that can build trust, respect, and collegiality. Coaching relationships are not designed to be personal relationships per se, although the coaching relationship does ebb and flow between professional and personal discussions depending on the context and learning needs of the partners. Reiss (2007) described how the coaching relationship tended to flow naturally into an emotional and personal realm. Often the peer coaching relationship becomes more fulfilling if it includes an emotional component (Hargrove, 2008; Parker et al., 2008). The students in the course I describe did demonstrate that they shifted between the professional and the personal role as they connected within their peer-coach relationships.

Designing the Peer Coaching Process: Meaningful Professional Inquiry

Creating opportunities for meaningful inquiry that leads to teacher growth and development is an important component of establishing a forum in which teachers can practice becoming learning leaders (Blackman, 2009; Gabriel, 2005; Kaser & Halbert, 2009; Reeves, 2009). I used Robertson's (2008) coaching-for-educational-leadership model, as well as Reiss' (2007) coaching model for professional development, to establish a framework for the peer coaching initiative within the course. I designed a leadership portfolio assignment in which I embedded a peer-coaching component. The assignment was to engage students in an inquiry into their leadership practices and attitudes within their own school context and in a reflection with a peer coach regarding their inquiry. Over a 10 week period, the students engaged in six peer-coaching sessions with their partners, and I also encouraged them to communicate informally with each other outside of the formal coaching sessions. The students provided me with oral and written feedback during class discussions and course evaluations regarding this peer coaching process.

The graduate program was a part-time one – designed to accommodate practicing educators on Saturdays – and the group consisted of practicing teachers, new administrators, and other professionals. I presented the coaching model to them during the first class session, and because of time constraints, the students were exposed to only two peer-coaching skills: active listening and the use of different levels of questioning (see for example, Reiss, 2007; Robertson, 2008). Peer coaches were encouraged to use these skills throughout their peer-coaching sessions after they had practiced them with their partners.

I assigned member pairs, who met for the first time at the end of the first class, and who subsequently continued to meet during each class session for at least one hour as well. During the peer-coaching sessions, each partner shared with his/her peer coach the leadership events they had experienced in their own school context. During these sessions, they reflected on what had been learned, on what remained a challenge for them, and on what goals were to be set for the upcoming period. The peer coaches were encouraged to use the active listening and questioning skills that they had practiced earlier.

I structured the course so that the content of each class session aligned with the weekly coaching challenges set out in the standards. For example, on the day that the peer coaches selected goals from the instructional leadership organizer of the BCPVPA Leadership Standards (2007), we discussed in class the various issues, concerns, and theories related to instructional leadership. In this way, the theory and literature discussed during each class were incorporated into their coaching session for that week. At the end of the final session, the peer coaches shared their experiences and reflections regarding the peer-coaching process and how it had been affected through the leadership portfolio.

Selecting a Partner: The Learning Platform Activity

The partner selection procedure is important in the peer coaching process, and autonomy in selection tends to provide greater satisfaction in the relationship (Parker et al., 2008). In this course, students participated in an activity that gave them an opportunity both to describe their values, beliefs, and dispositions with each other as described in their *learning platforms* (Robertson, 2008) – documents which they had previously completed. This exchange gave them an opportunity to clarify their perspectives related to their learning and teaching dispositions. For example, the students were asked to reflect on their beliefs about teacher-student relationships, pedagogy, institutional climate, and parental consultation.

This activity marked the first time in the course that the students made their educational platforms public. Although this event was intended to optimize the selection process, the added benefit was that it initiated a culture of reflective learning within the group as the students began to explore, develop, and later challenge their underlying beliefs, values, and dispositions regarding the concepts of learning and leadership. After they shared their learning platform statements, each student provided me with a list of three people with whom they would like to be paired in a peer-coaching arrangement. I was able to accommodate each student with one of their three choices and by doing so ensured that they had choice and autonomy in selecting the peer coach.

In the section to follow, I describe my observations of the use of peer coaching as a tool for awakening graduate students' awareness of their own leadership potential in their schools. I identify the potential for peer coaching as meaningful professional development for teachers, as well as challenges and obstacles to embedding peer coaching in graduate education courses, and I conclude with suggestions for further research into the use of peer coaching in educational programs.

Awakening Teacher Leadership through Peer Coaching

Coaching can be an effective way of shifting teachers' mindsets to see their own leadership role as they participate in influencing the learning of their peer coaches through their own learning process (Blackman, 2009; Robertson, 2009). The concept of learning in and through practice is viewed as foundational to teacher leadership (Cochran-smith & Lytle, 1999; Cherkowski, 2004; Reeves, 2006; Robertson, 2008; Robinson, 2006). Throughout this graduate course the educators engaged in reflexive learning through the use of peer coaching. As they engaged with their peers in coaching relationships, they expanded their vision of who they were and what they could do as they began to envision themselves as leaders. Self-reflection through the use of peer coaching created opportunities for teachers to shift in an intentional way to a leadership mindset within a trusting and safe relationship.

Students revealed that they sensed a deeper connection to their leadership development goals as they engaged in discussions and reflections with their peer coach, and a few of them began to notice that they were conceiving of leadership in a new way, beyond that associated with a formal role. One student noted that the "assignment provided a format for reflecting upon leadership development and my current disposition as a leader." She mentioned that she had never thought of herself as a leader because she "was only a teacher." However, as she engaged in the portfolio observations with her peer coach, she began to see herself as a leader in many ways and began to envision more ways in which she could exercise her leadership abilities in the school. Several students mentioned that they were surprised to begin to see the ways they engaged as leaders in their work as teachers. For others, the experience became an opportunity to validate through discussions with their peer coaches the important role of informal leadership in their schools.

Overall, the students reported having an increased sense of empowerment and rejuvenation in their work in their schools as they became intentional about identifying and reflecting on their daily leadership as teachers through their portfolio assignment. They also noted that the use of peer coaching engaged them in professional development with colleagues. They appreciated the use of a partner/coach to both challenge and support their growth as teacher leaders.

The students also noticed how the coaching relationship provided an opportunity to challenge their own beliefs and ways of thinking about leadership and learning. They appreciated the safe and trusting climate that developed as their relationship with their peer coach matured. This climate of trust promoted their reflections and insights regarding their beliefs and practices. One student mentioned that "having an objective viewpoint from another person was very valuable" and also said that they were "challenged to think about another person's problem or perspective without it being judgmental." The students learned through their work with their peer coaches how to engage in critical dialogue with, and to accept challenging questions from, their peers regarding their practice. This element is critical in developing sustainable learning communities (Mitchell & Sackney, 2009).

Peer Coaching: Meaningful Professional Development

Meaningful professional development opportunities are essential for creating learning for leadership capacity among educators (Reeves, 2006). If peer coaching is going to become a useful and prevalent tool for professional development, it must respond to the needs of the teachers, who must be given opportunities to determine and communicate their learning needs (Wragg, 2000).

Through the peer coaching process in this course, the students' professional needs became clearer to them as they began to trust the process as it was unfolded in a safe and helpful way. This trusting aspect was reflected in one student's comments: "We sometimes can only learn what we need through the process of identifying and observing our practice." He further stated that "[Coaching is] most useful at the beginning of one's career or when changing roles or when facing a difficult situation. Ok, on the whole, peer coaching is a good idea." Although his reflection resonated with his unique sense of humor, there was a note of seriousness in his inference regarding the importance of being able to identify the needs of teachers at various stages and contexts in their career in order to fulfill the promise of peer coaching.

In general, the students from the course believed that the peer coaching activity was beneficial for exposing them to a new way of professional development, and several expressed interest in continuing to find ways to meet with their coaching partner. One student stated, "thanks for opening us up to something new."

Challenges to Peer Coaching: Timing and Matching

Successful peer coaching relationships require the commitment of both partners to give the time and effort needed to develop skills, to establish relationships, and to dialogue (Reiss, 2007). As was experienced by several peer coaching partnerships in this course, finding adequate time was a challenge to establishing and maintaining effective coaching relationships (Rhodes & Houghton-Hill, 2000; Thompson, 2001).

Another related challenge faced by the students was the short duration of the course. Several students reported that the course was too short for engaging in a meaningful coaching relationship and that more time was needed to implement and then to reflect on the leadership initiatives that they explored with their peer coaches. One student indicated that there was "not enough time to thoroughly address the big issues" with his coaching partner. Overall, the students were interested in the use of peer coaching and believed that it was a "very valuable experience," but they would have preferred more time to have been spent on the coaching sessions. One student wondered if, "we could have an entire course just for coaching." Establishing a meaningful relationship in which peers learn both to coach and to be coached often takes time (Reiss, 2007). In this course, the peer coaches did have prior opportunity for becoming acquainted through previous courses, but they still reported needing time to develop their interpersonal skills to solidify their interrelationships of mutual trust, confidence, support, and respect.

Although they recognized the challenges to peer coach relationships, the students appreciated the time and effort extended to them by their peer coach. However, they did comment that the time commitment was often a demand that became a burden in their busy work world, as similarly reported in the literature (Rhodes & Houghton-Hill, 2000; Thompson, 2001). One student stated that "we were doing this at the end of the day after a whole day of class; we did not have the energy to fully engage in coaching."

Despite the time constraints, the students believed that they had benefitted from the learning opportunity inherent in peer coaching by learning from their partner's experiences as well as their partner's coaching and by having acquired a new source for professional development and growth. One student said, "peer coach(es) help to identify goals for my growth plan and methods to develop my leadership disposition." The students saw the peer-coaching experience as a way of identifying areas of growth for their own leadership as teachers.

A further challenge to peer coaching was related to the matching/selecting of the peer-coaching pairs. A decision to pair with someone in a different school district could be perceived as either positive or negative. For example, some of the students saw the benefit of being matched with a colleague in a different district, as illustrated by one teacher who said, "cross-district is especially powerful." Another student stated "having someone not in your school, who is removed from the immediate situation, can offer a refreshing non-judgmental approach." However, one student suggested that it "would be most valuable to have a peer coach within my district." Overall, the students recognized that within their own school districts, and perhaps across districts, the issue of geographic location would likely be an obstacle to furthering their future peer-coaching relationships.

Similarly, there were both positive and negative perceptions associated with matching peers based on their previous experience. Although in ideal terms there is no presumed hierarchy in peer coaching (Robertson, 2008), in practice, different levels of experience tend to bring different traits and tendencies to the coaching relationship. Similar to the ideas raised regarding geographic proximity, there was a range of views concerning differences in peers' years of experience. While some students indicated having a positive learning experience with a peer at a different career stage, others believed they would have benefitted from a peer at a similar career stage. Because the selection process is an important aspect of establishing successful partnerships, I believe more research is needed to understand the impact of the various aspects of the selection process on peer coaching partnerships.

Despite the challenges, the students were generally positive about the benefits of having participated in an activity that helped their professional growth in the school. The key connections made by some coaching partners illustrate the potential for further inquiries into the journey of peer coaches throughout their graduate program and in their work in the schools. As demonstrated by the students in this course, the use of peer coaching can create opportunities for professional growth as partners mentor each other in their growth in awakened teacher leadership and professional development. Further research is needed to explore how peer coaching in graduate education programs might serve as an impetus for developing peer coaching relationships among teachers in schools.

Finally, students in this course were able to analyze their reflections of their daily experiences with their peer coaches to create learning connections between the course and their daily practice. At the same time, they developed their potential as scholars within the theoretical components of the course. Further inquiry into the use of peer coaching in educational leadership programs would be useful in identifying how this mentoring strategy might serve as a bridge between theory and practice for educational practitioners pursuing graduate work.

Conclusion

Teacher leaders have a unique role to play in reshaping school culture from focusing on individualism to promoting professional community (Lieberman & Miller, 2004). Reflection through peer coaching creates opportunities for teachers to improve practice in an intentional way in a trusting and safe relationship. The use of peer coaching in a graduate level educational leadership program can contribute to an increased sense of teacher leadership in participants' school contexts. Leadership portfolio assignments can be an effective tool for creating a forum for exploring peer coaching for teacher leadership. The challenges to participating in peer coaching are both physical (e.g., time constraints) and attitudinal (e.g., willingness to try a new way of learning). Continued research is needed to explore the benefits, challenges, and obstacles to embedding peer-coaching opportunities in graduate educational leadership programs. The result has the potential for awakening teacher leadership in school contexts.

References

BCPVPA. (2007). *Leadership standards for principals and vice-principals in British Columbia.* Retrieved from http://www.bcpvpa. bc.ca/downloads/pdf/Standardsfinal.pdf

Beck, R. J., Livne, N. L., & Bear, S. L. (2005). Teachers' self-assessment of the effects of formative and summative electronic portfolios on professional development. *European Journal of Teacher Education, 28*(3), 221–244.

Blackman, A. (2009). Coaching as a leadership development tool for teachers. *Professional Development in Education, 1,* 1–21.

Cherkowski, S. (2004). *Teacher commitment: Towards a wholeness view* (Unpublished doctoral dissertation). University of Saskatchewan, Saskatoon, SK.

Cochran-Smith, M., & Lytle, S. (1999). Relationships of knowledge and practice: Teacher learning in communities. In A. Iran-Nejad & C. D. Pearson (Eds.), *Review of research in education* (pp. 251– 307). Washington, DC: American Educational Research Association.

Covey, S. R. (2004). *The 8th Habit: From effectiveness to greatness.* New York, NY: Free Press.

DuFour, R., & Eaker, R. (1998). *Professional learning communities at work: Best practices for enhancing student achievement.* Bloomington, IN: Association for Supervision and Curriculum Development.

Elbow, P., & Belanoff, P. (1997). Reflections on an explosion: Portfolios in the '90s and beyond. In K. B. Yancey (Ed.), *Situating portfolios: Four perspectives* (pp. 21–33). Logan, UT: Utah State University Press.

Elmore, R. (2000). *Building a new structure for school leadership.* Washington, DC: The Albert Shanker Institute.

Ensher, E. A., Thomas, C., & Murphy, S. E. (2001). Comparison of traditional, step-ahead, and peer mentoring on protégés support, satisfaction, and perceptions of career success: A social exchange perspective. *Journal of Business and Psychology, 15,* 419–438.

Fiedler, R., Mullen, L., & Finnegan, M. (2009). Portfolios in context: A comparative study in two pre-service teacher education programs. *Journal of Research on Technology in Education, 42*(2), 99–122.

Firestone, W., & Martinez, M. (2007). Districts, teacher leaders, and distributed leadership: Changing instructional practice. *Leadership and Policy in Schools, 6*(1), 3–35.

Fullan, M. (2006). Leading professional learning. *School Administrator, 10*(10), 63–70.

Gabriel, J. G. (2005). *How to thrive as a teacher leader.* Alexandria, VA: Association for Supervision and Curriculum Development.

Gewertz, C. (2008). California district makes instructional leadership a priority. *Education Week, 27*(27), 1–17.

Hargreaves, A., & Fink, D. (2006). *Sustainable leadership.* San Francisco, CA: Jossey-Bass.

Hargrove, R. A. (2008). *Masterful coaching.* San Francisco. CA: Jossey-Bass.

Harris, A. (2001). Building the capacity for school improvement. *School Leadership and Management, 21,* 261–270.

Harris, A., & Muijs, D. (2005). *Improving schools through teacher leadership.* Berkshire, UK: Open University Press.

Hobson, A. (2003). *Mentoring and coaching for new leaders: Review of literature.* Nottingham, UK: National College for School Leadership.

Kaser, L., & Halbert, J. (2009). *Leadership mindsets: Innovation and learning in the transformation of schools.* New York, NY: Routledge.

Leithwood, K., & Jantzi D. (2005). A review of transformational school leadership research 1996–2005. *Leadership and Policy in Schools, 4*(3), 177–199.

Lieberman, A., & Miller, L. (2004). *Teacher leadership.* San Francisco, CA: Wiley & Sons.

Lyons, N. (1998). Constructing narratives for understanding: Using portfolio interviews to scaffold teacher reflection. In N. Lyons (Ed.), *With portfolio in hand: Validating the new teacher professionalism* (pp. 103–119). New York, NY: Teachers College Press.

Mayrowetz, D., Murphy J., Seashore Lewis, K., & Smylie, M.A. (2009). Conceptualizing distributed leadership as a school reform: Revisiting job redesign theory. In K. Leithwood, B. Mascall, & T. Strauss (Eds.), *Distributed leadership according to the evidence* (pp. 167–195). New York, NY: Routledge.

McKinney, M. (1998). Preservice teachers' electronic portfolios: Integrating technology, self-assessment, and reflection. *Teacher Education Quarterly, 25,* 85–103.

Mitchell, C., & Sackney, L. (2000). *Profound improvement: Building capacity for a learning community.* Lisse, Netherlands: Swets & Zeitlinger.

Mitchell, C., & Sackney, L. (2009). *Sustained improvement: Building learning communities that endure.* Rotterdam, Netherlands: Sense Publishers.

Muijs, D., & Harris, A. (2006). Teacher led school improvement: Teacher leadership in the UK. *Teaching & Teacher Education: An International Journal of Research and Studies, 22*(8), 961–972.

Parker, P., Hall, D. T., & Kram, K. E. (2008). Peer coaching: A relational process for accelerating career learning. *Academy of Management Learning and Education, 7*(4), 487–503.

Paulson, P. R., & Paulson, F. L. (1991). *Portfolios: Stories of knowing.* Paper presented at the 54th Claremont Reading Conference, Claremont, CA.

Reeves. D. B. (2006). Of hubs, bridges, and networks. *Educational Leadership, 63*(8), 32–37.

Reeves, D. B. (2009). *Leading change in your school.* Alexandria, VA: Association for Supervision and Curriculum Development.

Reiss, K. (2007). *Leadership coaching for educators: Bringing out the best in school administrators.* Thousand Oaks, CA: Corwin Press

Rhodes, C. P., & Houghton-Hill, S. (2000). The linkage of continuing professional development and the classroom experience of pupils: Barriers perceived by senior managers in some secondary schools. *Journal of In-Service Education, 26,* 423–435.

Robertson, J. (2008). *Coaching educational leadership: Building capacity through partnership.* London, UK: Sage.

Robertson, J. (2009). Coaching leadership learning through partnership. *School Leadership and Management, 29*(1), 39–49.

Robinson, V. J. (2006). Putting education back into educational leadership. *Leading and Managing, 12*(1), 62–75.

Shulman, L. (1998). Teacher portfolios: A theoretical activity. In N. Lyons (Ed.), *With portfolio in hand: Validating the new teacher professionalism* (pp. 23–37). New York, NY: Teachers College Press.

Slater, L. (2008). Pathways to building leadership capacity. *Educational Management, Administration, and Leadership, 36*(1) 55–69.

Speck, M. (1999). *The principalship: Building a learning community.* New York, NY: Prentice-Hall.

Thompson, M. (2001). Towards professional learning communities. In D. Gleeson & C. Husbands (Eds.), *The performing school: Managing, teaching, and learning in a performance culture* (pp. 253–272). London, UK: Routledge Falmer Press.

Veenman, S., & Denessen, E. (2001). The coaching of teachers: Results of five training studies. *Educational Research and Evaluation, 7*(4), 385–417.

Wragg, C. (2000, February). Failing teachers? *Managing Schools Today, 10*(5), 36–38.

Chapter Thirteen

Coaching: Enabling Leadership Learning Through Integrative Program Design

Catherine McGregor, Judy Halbert, & Linda Kaser

IN 2005 THE UNIVERSITY OF VICTORIA began contemplating the redesign of its educational leadership program. During this process, faculty addressed such questions as: How do we prepare potential school leaders for the increasingly complex work of educational leadership? What programmatic features would enable aspiring leaders to engage in the practices necessary for responding to these challenges? How might a leadership development program be more effectively linked to the best theoretical and empirical scholarship?

In this chapter, we examine the concept of *coaching for leadership*, which was a foundational means of integrating theory and practice in that redesign process. We argue that the idea of *coaching for learning* provided the means for (a) transforming leaders' vision of schooling from one based on *sorting* to one of *learning systems* (Kaser & Halbert, 2009) and (b) enabling creative, theory informed leadership strategies to be consistently practiced. We include a literature review on theoretical foundations of coaching, an overview of the Certificate in School Management and Leadership (CSML) program, and a selection from a program evaluation completed in 2009 (Shaw & McGregor). We illustrate how coaching enabled the "taking up" of learning-centred leadership practices, and we discuss the enabling features of coaching and argue for its capacity to foster what Hannon (2009) described as "next practices." We suggest that coaching develops leadership mindsets (Kaser & Halbert, 2009) and builds ontological commitments to equitable learning.

Mentorship in Educational Leadership Programming

Mentorship has been a popular approach to the preparation of new school leaders and administrators (Daresh, 1995; Juusela, 2004;

Villani, 2006). In recent research on exemplary leadership programs (Darling Hammond, LaPointe, Meyerson, Orr, & Cohen, 2007; Huber, 2004), mentorship is seen as a foundational component for enabling the development of professionally focused school leaders. Similarly, Samier (2000) traced mentorship's use in administrative preparation as a supplement to graduate programs designed to prepare and certify administrators. Protégés benefitted from the experience by being the recipients of new skills, knowledge, and practices related to the work of leadership. Moreover, the support of mentors was seen as advantageous because they informed protégés of the social and political culture in which similarly situated leaders worked.

Coaching as Mentorship

A complete review of the mentorship literature is beyond the scope of this chapter. Instead, we focus on the idea of "coaching," which we consider important within the field of mentorship. We believe that the focus of the partnership between experienced and novice leaders needs to move from leadership knowledge transmission to inquiry and learning dialogically and needs to emphasize the collaborative and reciprocal nature of learning in the coaching partnership.

We see coaching as a means of avoiding some of the problems identified by other authors about the normative nature of the mentoring process. Dahle (1998) explored the limitations of mentorship based on gender, arguing that mentoring reinforces patriarchy and reinforces the "old boy's network." Hansman (2002) similarly argued that mentoring processes can, for marginalized participants, "encourage the unquestioning replication of organizational values and hegemonic culture" (p. 1). Several authors have identified the paired nature of mentoring as problematic. For instance, Hay (1995) suggested developmental alliances as an alternative, indicating that individuals may work with a series of mentors interested in enabling actions focused on self- and organizational-development, while Higgins and Kram (2001) "consider mentoring as a multiple relationship phenomenon" (p. 266). We believe that all three of these limitations (dyad specific, skill and/or transmission specific, and power dynamics) can be resolved, or at least mitigated, by shifting to the concept of coaching. We further believe that in increasingly complex social, cultural, and politically situated educational environments, traditional mentorship models may disadvantage leaders who need to move from past practice to next practice (Hannon, 2009).

Coaching for Educational Leadership

We conceptualize coaching as a process-rich framework focused on emergent inquiry and learning, compatible with understandings of organizations as complex living systems. We see the need for leaders who can take multiple and varied approaches to problem solving and to emergent organizational dynamics. Robertson's (2008) model emphasized coaching as a relational and learning-centred practice between two or more people who work together to set professional goals. Such partners are "professionals equally committed to facilitating each other's leadership learning development and well being (both cognitive and affective), and gain a greater understanding of professionalism and the work of professionals" (p. 4). Robertson further argued that coaching is a dynamic relational process that changes to meet the needs and contexts of participants, including the social and political contexts of their work as school leaders.

Coaching in this sense is an "intervention because it requires people to stop and look critically at the reality of their worlds . . . It [coaching] is concerns-based because it focuses on the issues and difficulties that arise in everyday practice" (pp. 57–58). It is also understood to operate intersubjectively in learning communities; that is, coaches and learners create and maintain multiple partnerships with and among other practitioners and create networks of shared, professionally inspired relationships in which continued cycles of inquiry and action can take place. This process speaks to the complexity in which leadership practices are situated. Moreover, we see coaching as setting out to inquire in order to take action on these issues in ways that transform rather than reproduce agents, practices, and policies that maintain existing social patterns. This perspective is critical to our emphasis on "next" rather than "best" practice because our goal throughout the CSML program was to prepare school leaders ready to produce rather than reproduce knowledge, and to inquire into and problem solve in learning-centred work.

We have situated coaching in this way because we see an articulation of how leadership learning happens as critical to addressing the complexity of educational leaders' work and to developing morally centred change agents. We do not see this process as accidental but rather as designed and supported on an ongoing basis, and we believe that the Robertson (2008) coaching model emphasized this lifelong approach. Our position speaks to one of the primary means for achieving program coherence, a topic we will return to shortly. We emphasize how coaching allowed for a deepened focus on leadership as and for learning, one that is morally centred on creating equity for all learners. Situated learning theories – including our coaching informed approach to leadership development – provide important evidence for how such leadership mindsets (Kaser & Halbert, 2009) "stick" with our leadership students. In other words, we conceptualize coaching as an enabling tool – a versatile, flexible, and adaptable practice that can be taken up by leaders in order to continually focus on learning in a range of settings and contexts.

The CSML Program

The CSML program was designed to provide participants with contemporary understandings of learning and leadership theories and practices alike. Underpinning CSML was the belief that schools and school systems must shift from an industrial model of sorting and ranking students, mainly in relation to post-secondary opportunities, to a knowledge-era model in which all students are coached to the highest possible level in a more personalized and responsive way. This perspective changed our conceptualization of contemporary leadership development and our approach to designing a leadership program that supported the development of conditional and procedural knowledge, conceptual literacy, and knowledge management. Intentionality regarding the development of adaptive leadership expertise (Bransford, Derry, Berliner, & Hammerness, 2005; Donovan, Bransford & Pelligrino, 1999; Heifetz & Linksy, 2002) was foundational to achieving these outcomes. "Adaptive leadership is specifically about change that enables the capacity to thrive. New environments and new dreams demand new strategies and abilities as well as the leadership to mobilize them" (Heifitz et al., 2009, p. 14).

Drawing from the sources cited earlier, from Huber's (2004) study of leadership development programs and from Castells's (2004) work on networked communities, the faculty design team developed a multi-component framework to link theory and practice using field-based learning inquiry. Part of that design included an intensive ten-day summer residency during which time CSML students were introduced to the core ideas undergirding the initiative. Individually and in collaborative teams, they applied to their own settings the learning gained from readings, presentations, problem simulations, and case studies. They also engaged in two days of intensive learning with their coaches, who served as interested, reflective colleagues, jointly identifying and exploring various foci for a year-long action-oriented leadership inquiry. During the school year, while working with their coaches, the students also participated in online course work and discussions and submitted regular journal reflections on the progress of their inquiry. The latter months were focused on their role as leaders of adult learning as they developed a research-informed professional learning plan for their school or school district. Students also prepared a multimedia display of their leadership learning, which they presented during the final three-day summer residency that served as a capstone following the full year of study.

We believe that the programmatic design was strong, based on our research and field knowledge. However, a critical feature of the program was the quality of the partnership that existed between the coach and the CSML learner; we understood that without integrally linking coaching with dynamic, learning-centred leaders, the theory-practice gap common in many leadership programs could persist.

Program Coherence

Program coherence – the ways in which a program's features and design align with program components – is essential for program success. With a high degree of program coherence, learning within a program is expected to more readily transfer to field or practice based experiences, which in turn enhances the leadership capabilities of participants. Leadership program designers want to promote such transferability and avoid what Feiman-Nemser and Buchmann

(1985, as cited in Grossman, Hammerness, McDonald, & Ronfeldt, 2008, p. 274) described as the "two-worlds pitfall." By this phrase they meant the seeming contradiction between the theoretical and research-informed practices promoted in a program and the "real world" experienced by practitioners in their daily routines.

While positive program coherence is expected to enable the application of theory to practice, as Grossman et al. (2008) noted, "most of the assertions about coherence remain unexamined" (p. 278). Their study set out to establish empirically specific ways to measure positive coherence within a teacher education program. They concluded that there was a positive correlation between program coherence and the factors of:

- length and quality of field supervision (including the selection of supervisors by program faculty and number of hours of supervision) that linked content with practice;
- prior experience of field supervisors as lead practitioners; and
- number of course assignments that required field integration.

While we did not attempt to duplicate this empirical methodology in our study, there were some important inferences that we drew from that work and applied to our understanding of how coherence was enabled within the CSML program. In particular, we saw coaching as a central feature that, following the Grossman et al. (2008) framework, enabled positive program coherence. For example, CSML coaches were (a) carefully selected on the basis of the degree to which they met a set of effective leadership for learning capabilities as documented in recent leadership scholarship, (b) expected to meet with their CSML partners regularly throughout a year long course either face-to-face or online, (c) collectively educated about the CSML coaching model, and (d) required to have regular contact with the instructors, who supported the coaching pairs as they completed their leadership inquiry project.

We also noted that all program assignments deliberately set out to integrate theory and practice, and that classroom/online instruction regularly used local case studies drawn from a practitioner-based network[1] that reinforced the links between leadership theory and practitioner application to local contexts. Finally, as with the

Grossman et al. (2008) study, our CSML participants reported their belief that the program had a high degree of program coherence and relevancy.[2]

Our discussion of program coherence would be incomplete, however, without also drawing attention to how the program design also invoked conceptual coherence. As Darling-Hammond (2006, as cited in Grossman et al., 2008) noted "in such intensely coherent programs, core ideas are reiterated across courses and theoretical frameworks animating courses and assignments are consistent across the programme" (p. 306). Core ideas and the shared vision of a program need to be structurally maintained if coherence is to be positive. It is the consistent application of this shared vision – in our case, for a morally centred form of educational leadership – that must be maintained by participants, if they are to alter the culture of education from a sorting to a learning system (Kaser & Halbert, 2009).

Coaches: Catalysts for Learning Leaders

We see two key questions that arise regarding this process: If a goal of a school leadership program is to help develop transformative educators who will work to shift schools towards a learning system (Shields, 2009), then what skills and attributes will their coaching partners be able to demonstrate? What types of colleagues will new school leaders need as they embark on a journey through often ambiguous and shifting terrain?

We believe that the educators who serve as inquiry coaches in such a program need to possess and exercise capabilities in innovative leadership practice. They need to be current in their own educational practice and be open to a reciprocal relationship where they can assist their new leader partner in the inquiry and reflection process and in turn be open to learn from their partner. To help their partner navigate in the rapid white-water-change world, they will need to have a strong moral compass with a well-developed sense of purpose around equity and quality. They will need to be interested in and be familiar with current studies of innovative learning environments and be adept in using an evidence-informed learning repertoire in their own settings. Their restless curiosity and willingness to learn will drive their interest in working with an emergent leader.

In the CSML program, coaches were initially drawn from two sources: leading educators who were known provincially for creating positive and equitable changes in their respective settings and committed educators who had participated in a large, provincially distributed networked-learning community that focused on inquiry, innovation, learning, assessment, and system changes. In the first year of CSML, we identified a pool of one hundred potential coaches, the large majority of which positively responded to our invitation to participate as coaches. As the program evolved, many of the CSML graduates in turn became skilled and committed coaches. Several experienced coaches asked to continue, and some of them have worked with two or three learners over the five years of the program. However, we found that not all partnerships worked equally well, and occasionally changes had to be made. A critical factor to the program's effectiveness was having a strong cadre of coaches to draw upon and having access to faculty-members who were willing to make the necessary changes.

We also considered questions regarding such factors as the coaching partnerships, the individual roles of the partners (e.g., peer or supervisor), geographic location, gender and age, and frequency and mode of contact. We found over the span of the experience that high levels of trust, mutual respect, an inquiry mindset, and consistent communication all characterized the most successful coaching partnerships.

How Coaching Enables Leadership

While we were convinced of coaching's potential as a tool for developing morally centred leaders, we operated more on our tacit knowledge of exceptional leaders and our review of relevant North American/European literature describing exemplary programs rather than on British Columbia or Canadian-informed research evidence. The B.C. Ministry of Education – our partner who funded the new program – was also interested in understanding how the program might enable the development of leaders committed to the goal of transforming schools into learning-centred communities. As a result, they agreed to support an evaluation of the CSML program. While we cannot document the full study here, we draw upon components of that report regarding the effectiveness of coaching and how it enabled commitments to learning-centred leadership.

The study surveyed nearly 100 participants from four different cohorts of CSML students (enrolled between 2005 and 2009) and 45 coaches who answered a series of questions in an online survey. In addition, seven coaches and 16 school leaders from four school districts representing urban, rural, and geographically diverse regions of the province all completed interviews. The interview data were supplemented with field notes collected from ten school sites where CSML leaders worked in 2009. Also, one rural school district was studied as a case in greater depth. It was selected on the basis of the diverse ways in which coaching was being applied by CSML participants and coaches.

What We Heard: Creating Foundations of Trust

We found that coaching was a tool for broadening, applying, and implementing educational leadership practices and was a support for positive program coherence. Moreover, our analysis showed the effectiveness of coaching as a leadership learning strategy was best realized when there were strong, nurturing, supportive, and trusting relationships. This finding was not surprising in that most of the coaching and/or mentorship literature also identified the need for trust. Yet perhaps a more nuanced analysis of those relationships was the degree to which conceptual clarity was achieved through a shared belief in – and a passion for – learning as a means of transforming student, teacher, and community lives. For example, in one interior-B.C. school, one respondent stated: "The coaching program [is] amazing. It's the same for me; my connection with my mentor opened up a whole whack of things, that darned woman! She would have all these connections that we made during our time. And it has to keep happening!"

Another novice school leader in a small interior community described her pre-CSML work as a teacher, and then compared it to her current practice, then in a formal role and after having completed the CSML program:

I've had far more conversations about learning, far more work on student performance as a VP than I did as a classroom teacher. That's what I've been thinking about the past little while ... [for example] I used descriptive feedback in my Grade 12 class for a semester and then in staff meetings I would share the research I was doing in my class. Then I brought in my provincial exam results in the last staff meeting to say, "Look at what happened here. What do you think?" (paused, appeared to be thinking). I think ... it [my coaching approach] removed the threat, they don't view me as coming in to do an evaluative process, they view me as someone who is thinking about students, and for instruction. They don't seem to view that as threatening in any way ... it was all about the kids, and that's what I took from the coaching [experience].

This example also helps illustrate another key point: coaching is not formulaic, but rather it serves as a means to an end. In other words, it was modified, adapted, and reapplied into a form that made sense for a particular setting. In a more northerly community we also heard how one CSML learner applied the coaching model to his school context:

I found that as an administrator now, I'm doing mini mentorships, if that makes sense. I'll have a staff [member] that will come and talk to me about something, and so I coach them ... It is a sort of coaching. They're coming to get an answer, but it's almost like when they ask me how I should do something, or tell me they don't know what to do, I will sit down and talk about it. So they're coming up with a solution that works for them. To me it's like mini mentorship. So some of the mini mentoring might only be one time, but there's been no teacher I know of that I haven't talked to ... two or three times now, about different things. But now when they are coming in – they ask what I think of things, things that they are doing, or ask what else they can do.

This approach to coaching – to apply in principle, but then adapt, modify, or add new applications – is consistent with what Hannon

(2009) described as "next practice." In other words, coaching provides a structured framework, yet simultaneously is flexible enough to allow modifications that creatively address local circumstances. Yet its primary purpose, a focus on learning, remains.

Other CSML learners applied the coaching model to create a series of coaching relationships or networks of support systems. For example, Barbara, an informal school leader, used the term "critical friend" to describe her coaching/networking strategy. For her, the goal was to build a support network for her own leadership inquiry that helped her to deepen her own thinking. Thus, she sought to find an on-site colleague, someone she described as a "second coach," who she could work with in her own school site. At the same time, she created a parallel coaching and partnership network among a group of teachers within her school as part of her own leadership inquiry project. In this example, three forms of coaching relationships operated simultaneously, each of which focused on a commitment to enhancing professional practice for learning.

An important implication that emerged from the conversation with Barbara and colleagues at her school was how this local coaching network enabled the development of trust between teaching colleagues because it was focused on beginning in places/practices where teachers were ready and willing to make change. In other words, Barbara worked from each colleague's strength, continued to model her own learning and efforts to improve student performance, and recognized the multiple ways in which this process might be accomplished. Her school principal was so impressed with how this coaching network functioned, he restructured the school's timetable to provide regularly scheduled collaborative professional learning time for this group of teachers.

Becky, another principal in one of the northern school districts, mentioned how coaching had altered her own practice as a new school leader and also noted the dynamic, contextual and emergent nature of the approach. She said:

I think the coaching component of CSML brings in the more reflective piece . . . . Like, you're doing this inquiry, and you're working with assessment for learners, and you're working with teachers because your teachers have to be part of the process.

So it's all of those things, and you're sort of working on your leadership skills as well. It's kind of mixed together.

Here, the theory of coaching for learning informs how that principal interacted with others. While her approach did not take the form of formally scheduled activity with individual staff members, the reflective processes foundational to coaching informed how she communicated with others.

Nancy, another school administrator, provided examples of how she built reflection into her daily interactions with teachers: "How do you think that is working?" "Why do you think so?" She also framed her own self-inquiry: "How can I best enable learning centered relationships with my staff?" "Where do I want to go with this person?" "How am I going to get there?" "What kind of conversations do I have to have with them to support them and move them ahead?" She attributed this new way of thinking and enacting learning-centred leadership as a direct outcome of the CSML coaching and its learning centred orientation.

Observing Nancy's application of coaching to her work as a formal school leader demonstrated its adaptability in a variety of educational and political contexts. It also illustrated how trusting, interpersonal relationships were established upon a shared commitment to student learning. School improvement scholarship has emphasized creating a shared, safe space is a prerequisite of significant, persistent, and successful school change initiatives (Bryk & Schneider, 2002; Wahlstrom & Seashore-Louis, 2008).

The Coaching Model, District Scaled

One of the notable initiatives that we observed during our field visits was how one central-interior school district had applied the CSML coaching model on a district-wide scale. At every level, from the Superintendent, to school principals, to individual teachers and/or teams of teachers, we heard repeatedly about the ways in which coaching had permeated the culture of the school district. Each participant reported using coaching as a learning-focused strategy to support the attainment of personal, school, and school-district goals.

Our initial meeting was with the District Superintendent, who described how she used the coaching model to develop her executive team (a district-wide school principal network) into a cohesive and professionally oriented group. We also heard how the coaching strategy was applied during all district meetings, where time was allotted for leadership pairs to meet, to report on their progress in meeting personal and professional goals, and to set new interim goals for the future.

What was of interest to us was how this application of coaching enabled and nurtured distributed forms of leadership. For example, school administrators were given responsibility for leading a district initiative in such areas as literacy, numeracy, technology, distance learning, or early learning. This practice is common across many B.C. school districts, but the emphasis on coaching for learning enabled a significant role shift in this particular district. For example, there was less emphasis on the administrative functions of coordination and more emphasis on building leadership teams that both networked throughout the district and focused on professional learning.

Current and former CSML learners also assumed distributed leadership roles within this school district. Many of them were lead teachers who had designed school-based inquiry projects focused on enhancing student learning – projects supported with funds from both the school district and the Network of Performance Based Schools. Of interest to us was the number of these projects that included coaching components, three examples of which were (1) several CSML learners shared how they had developed reading clubs for teachers using coaching as a primary strategy, (2) another CSML participant had established a peer-to-peer student coaching program that focused on teaching formative assessment strategies, and (3) another had designed an inquiry project that used peer-to-peer coaching as a means of implementing strategies for enhancing the literacy skills of boys. The following observation of one CSML coach in this school district highlighted the transformative role that coaching played in influencing the shift to a learning-centred system:

It's just about the right knowledge and constantly helping people to shift their thinking so they can see students differently, and are therefore enabled to support the students' learning more effectively. Ultimately I guess that I want a just and equitable society, and that's my deep motivation . . . But it depends where the person you are coaching comes in. If they come in a place where they're stuck, and they just need to be unstuck for a period of time, they retreat back. And then you help them move forward a bit.

Emergent Design: Enabling Next Practices

Our interviews with CSML program participants also revealed that many of them had created their own informal network of contacts, both within their own cohort of program participants and with other teachers who had participated in the program previously. Other CSML participants reported how they had sought out second and third coaches, such as a school colleague as a coach, or a distant individual with expertise in particular fields. In all of these cases we saw how the idea of coaching was redeveloped into a networked support strategy, not dissimilar to the constellation of mentors described by Higgins and Kram (2001) or advocated by Hay (1995). In each case, however, the CSML learners spoke of the way in which the coach supported their efforts to think through the problem and to set goals and reflect on their actions – not to act as a source of answers. It was clear in our data that those CSML participants had a different mindset to that of the traditional mentoring relationship of expert-to-novice. The CSML learners valued the deeper understanding that emerged from reflection-on-and-in practice.

Our investigation of the case-study district showed that coaching had become a culturally instituted practice at the individual level and had provided a foundation for developing individualized or localized strategies to support the perceived learning needs. In other words, while coaching might be considered a best practice for leadership learning, it could also be a tool that enabled moving from best to next practice (Hannon, 2009) because of its inherent flexibility in supporting different forms of learning in many sites and settings.

We saw that coaching could be adjusted to reflect the size of the group involved; it could be varied to include short-term and longer-term goals; it could be used in engaging members of the community in problem solving on a policy question; and it could be used with adults and students alike. It was practiced at a micro level (between teacher partners), at the meso level (between schools and school leaders), and at the macro level (at the district level).

Our analysis enabled us to conceptualize coaching metaphorically in two ways. One metaphor was a well-woven cloth in that coaching provided the thread that tied together the fabric of the school district both vertically and horizontally. At the same time, it left room/freedom to add new colors, thread sizes, patterns, or designs. Our second metaphor depicts coaching as a toolkit that allowed for creative and innovative approaches, which allowed emergent and authentic responses to particular contexts. Both metaphors illustrate how coaching enabled nearly continuous conceptual and structural coherence, helping us understand the persistence of CSML learning and the strength of our program design.

Cautions in Our Analysis

We have traced the successes of coaching in our program and highlighted its application in one school district, showing how, as a "best practice," coaching has been a means through which the district, its schools, leaders, and learners have been positively affected. However, we do not believe that coaching is the only strategy responsible for developing strong, morally centred school leaders. We know that the CSML program tended to attract a particular kind of learning leader because of the program's reputation and its commitment to learning centred leadership. These program participants typically reflected a mindset already committed to instructionally centred leadership. The ontological frame of the CSML program was situated in embracing a sustained moral commitment to enhancing the learning of all students. This sustained and cross-programmatic theme informed all of the coursework in the program, and it consistently and persistently guided the development of leadership practices towards this goal.

The pedagogical strategies used in the program also incorporated reflection and commitment. They were based on leveraging opportunities and on accepting events as opportunities to learn. The promotion of professional learning communities – another key ontological component – also incorporated the power of shared learning experiences and reinforced the processes of learning more its products. All of these features also characterized how program coherence – both conceptual and procedural – was achieved. We believe that this illustrates that when program coherence is high in a leadership development program, ideas and concepts are more likely to become embedded in practice.

Concluding Thoughts

Coaching is a powerful, strategic means of helping develop learning-centred leaders. In this chapter we described the theoretical context for understanding its potential and we considered its limitations. Using Grossman et al.'s (2008) notion of coherence as a core principle linking field and program features, we framed coaching as a coherence strategy. We found that it enabled greater transferability of learned competencies from the CSML program to the CSML learners' core leadership practices by building learning-centred cultures in schools and the school district.

We also found that coaching was more than a coherence strategy; it offered a dynamic, situated, and contextually responsive means for transforming leadership students into learning-centred leaders. Because of its enabling features, it emphasized and reinforced the relational qualities of all educative experiences among teachers, learners, parents/caregivers, and formal leaders, and it helped build trust and commitment to common goals.

We believe that coaching offers potential as a distributed leadership tool (Robinson, Lloyd, & Rowe, 2008) in which learning can become the centre of activity among all educational stakeholders. Coaching in this sense is an enabling tool; it allows multiple approaches that respond to different contexts, needs, demands, and opportunities. The examples from our study demonstrated this enabling aspect in the shift from best practices to next practices (Hannon, 2009).

Finally, we noted that coaching is a practice that is both performative and constitutive in that it provides a bridge that shifts from a program that is epistemologically focused to one that is ontologically informed. We found that coaching is a catalyst designed to create leadership mindsets (Kaser & Halbert, 2009) focused on the foundational purpose of schooling as improving the life chances of all learners.

Notes

1 The *Network of Performance Based Schools* is a provincially and federally funded initiative designed to support educators in practitioner-based inquiry focused on enhancing student learning.
2 A full discussion of the methodology used for making this assertion is beyond the scope of this chapter. However, readers should be aware that participants beliefs were confirmed by a series of "school colleague interviews." For more details about the methodology, see Shaw and McGregor (2009).

References

Bransford, J., Derry, S., Berliner, D., & Hammerness, K. (2005). Theories of learning and their roles in teaching. In L. Darling-Hammond & J. Bransford (Eds.), *Preparing teachers for a changing world* (pp. 40–87). San Francisco, CA: John Wiley & Sons.

Bryk, A. S., & Schneider, B. L. (2002). *Trust in schools: A core resource for improvement*. Chicago, IL: Russell Sage Foundation.

Castells, M. (2004). *The network society*. Northampton, MA: Edward Elgar.

Dahle, C. (1998). *Women's ways of mentoring*. Retrieved from http://www.fastcompany.com/magazine/17/womentoring.html

Daresh, J. C. (1995). Research base on mentoring for educational leaders: What do we know? *Journal of Educational Administration, 33*(5), 7–16.

Darling Hammond, L., LaPointe, M., Meyerson, D., Orr, M., & Cohen, C. (2007). *Preparing school leaders for a changing world: Lessons from exemplary leadership development programs*. Stanford, CA: Stanford University, Stanford Educational Leadership Institute. Available from http://edpolicy.stanford.edu/publications/pubs/243

Donovan, M. S., Bransford, J. D., & Pellegrino, J. W. (Eds.). (1999). *How people learn: Bridging research and practice.* Washington, DC: National Academy Press

Grossman, P., Hammerness, K., McDonald, M., & Ronfeldt, M. (2008). Constructing coherence: Structural predictors of perceptions of coherence in NYC teacher programmes. *Journal of Teacher Education, 59,* 273–287.

Hannon, V. (2009). The search for next practice: A UK approach to Innovation in schools. *Education Canada, 49*(4), 2.

Hansman, C. (2002). Diversity and power in mentoring relationships. In C. Hansman (Ed.), *Critical Perspectives on Mentoring: Trends and Issues* (Information Series No. 388, pp. 39–48). Colombus, OH: ERIC Clearing House.

Hay, J. (1995). *Transformational mentoring.* New York, NY: McGraw-Hill.

Heifetz, R. A., Grashow, A., & Linksy, M. (2009). *The practice of adaptive leadership: Tools and tactics for changing your world.* Boston, MA: Harvard Business Press.

Higgins, M., & Kram, K. (2001). Reconceptualizing mentoring at work: A developmental network perspective. *The Academy of Management Review, 26*(2), 264–288.

Huber, S. G. (2004). *Preparing school leaders for the 21st century: An international comparison of development programmes in 15 countries.* London, UK: Routledge-Falmer.

Juusela, D. L. (2004). *An analysis of the aspiring principals' preparation programmes provided by Florida school districts* (Unpublished doctoral dissertation). University of Central Florida, Orlando, FL.

Kaser, L., & Halbert, J. (2009). *Leadership mindsets: Innovation and learning in the transformation of schools.* New York, NY: Routledge.

Robertson, J. (2008). *Coaching leadership: Building educational leadership capacity through coaching partnerships.* London, UK: Sage.

Robinson, V., Lloyd, C., & Rowe, J. (2008). The impact of leadership on student outcomes: An analysis of the differential effects of leadership types. *Educational Administration Quarterly, 44*(5), 635–674.

Samier, E. (2000). Public administration mentorship: Conceptual and pragmatic considerations. *Journal of Educational Administration, 38*(1), 83–101.

Shaw, P., & McGregor, C. (2009). *Leadership and learning: A research report.* Victoria, BC: University of Victoria.

Shields, C. (2009). *Courageous leadership for transforming schools: Democratizing practice.* Norwood, MA: Christopher-Gordon.

Villani, S., (2006). *Mentoring and induction programmes that support new principals.* Thousand Oaks, CA: Corwin.

Wahlstrom, K., & Seashore-Louis, K. (2008). How teachers experience principal leadership: The roles of professional community, trust, efficacy and shared responsibility. *Educational Administration Quarterly, 44,* 458–495.

Chapter Fourteen

Serviette Mentorship: A Dialogue about Life and Work

Keith Walker

A CULTURAL *FAUX PAS* ONE CAN MAKE, as a Canadian, visiting with friends in the United States, is to ask for a *serviette*. This term immediately identifies you as a foreigner. Apparently, for those I have met in the United States, the more correct term is *napkin*. Yet, there was a time when to ask for a napkin in the United Kingdom might have been understood to be asking for something wrapped around the bottom of an infant. Despite these cultural distinctions, "serviette or napkin mentorship" is the topic of this chapter. Borrowing from the inspiration of John Wareham (1992), I provide a practical approach to describing a few features of a developmental mentoring relationship through a mentor's dialogue with a young friend. I see this process as mentorship with a focus on a protégé's personal life and her/his leadership development.

My most common use of what I am about to share has been recorded many times on coffee shop or restaurant paper napkins (serviettes) with colleagues and executives in both formal and informal coaching and mentoring situations. One will be able to imagine numerous uses for this approach after I share the basic idea in the form of the following coffee-shop conversation. From a "fly on the wall" perspective, one would have witnessed this dialogue.

Keith: Great to be with you again, Julius! Are you alright? How is your work going?

Julius: All is fine, Keith! It's been a good year. I've been with the company for almost two years; our group's strategies are getting some good traction. Some of the projects have had staggered starts over last months but are proceeding even better than I thought they might: only a few minor bumps on the road thus far. So far, so good, I think.

But Keith, I was glad to touch base with you, today, because it's time to have a personal check-up. I wonder if we could get right to business and talk again about my approach to developing leadership through mentorship. I always benefit from reviewing the basics with you, and I am at a point where I need to do some upgrades on the way I am developing the leaders around me. I want more than anything to help create a leaderful (Raelin, 2003) organization, where everyone is invited into the work of leadership. I want to be a better mentor to the leaders around me. To put it out to you, I want people to see me as a true servant leader, as someone who passionately engages with them in fulfilling the promises and purposes of our company.

Keith: I hear you, Julius. Thanks for this. Well, do you remember a few times ago, I used a stick figure to guide our conversation about your mentoring of leaders? We talked about how the greatest challenge of the servant leader, and your being a servant to mentors, entailed consistently putting the basics into practice.

Julius: Yes, but I'd like to go over that again with you so that I can use it with my new staff-members and team leaders when I meet with them. I've used some of the ideas from our conversations, but my interpretations have probably morphed since your original explanations. I am sure I've added my own understandings to the things we've talked about.

Keith: Well, making this your own is a good thing, Julius. We both know there aren't any scientific orthodoxies or formulas; it depends so much on who you are working with, your roles and relationships, and their circumstances. As you may recall, we talked about a diagram that Wareham (1992) used, though, as you say, we've both adapted it for our own use over time. You have lots of terrific momentum already. It would be surprising if you hadn't re-synthesized the content of our conversations in ways that made the most sense to you, your experiences, and your leaders' various circumstances.

Julius: I can clearly remember the stick figure. I'll draw it on this napkin, just as you did for me.

Keith: That's it.

Julius: Yes. I remember the heart-shaped body represented the leader's capacity for energy and emotion; one leg represented the person's set of interpersonal skill/attitudes; and the other stood for

Figure 1

A basic stick figure representing a leader.

their task competencies and work ethic. The neck was figuratively the maturity that connects the energy (heart) to the head or mind, which has lots of complexities to it (including values, goals, intelligences, personal and social identity, and the spirit of the person). The platform represented the leader's past job and personal history (including psychological stability, critical incidences, and so forth). The hand behind the stick figure was holding a professional resume of past achievements.

I remember you told me that we too often give disproportionate attention to paper resumes when we are hiring or assessing a protégé's development needs. We talked about assessing behavior and competence, as well as good intentions, level of confidence, passion, and promises. This was reinforced when we were putting together one of our development teams: what one person said they were good at, and what looked good on paper, were different from what our experience with that person bore out. We also had at least two people who surprised us, in altogether positive and pleasant ways, with their high quality contributions to the team efforts.

Keith: Interesting that you mention "surprises" (both positive and negative). None of this is exact science. In fact, I am more and more appreciating the complexity, the mystery, the artistry, and the aesthetics of leadership. It is not as simple, predictable, controllable, rational, and even explainable as I once thought, to be sure.

Well, this is excellent. You've about summed it up very well, Julius.

Julius: That's because I've reviewed it a number of times since you first showed it to me. I actually kept the old serviette in my wallet for a few months, and I've sat down with a few other people, just as you did with me, and went through it with them. One of my colleagues at work told me she'd shared it with her husband and, later, with her teenaged daughter. So, the serviette picture is making its way around.

Keith: Well then, you have adapted it, owned it, and given it away. That's great!

Julius: Well, it made sense to me. This was especially so when you explained how the various components fit together.

Keith: What do you remember about that?

Julius: When we last talked, I had been burning the candle at both ends and was basically exhausted with all my long hours on

Figure 2

A sketch representing the heart of a leader.

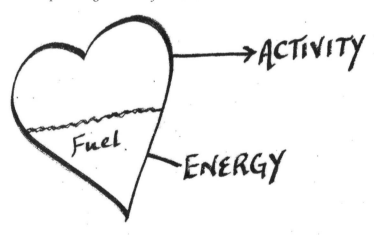

the job. You drew a big version of the heart and asked me, "What are some ways that you get your energy?"

I told you that for me (it might be different for others), proper eating, regular exercising, getting a good night's sleep, and knowing that things are good on the home front were basic to my sense of wellness. You asked how it was going in each of those departments, and as soon as you asked the simple question, I knew why I had less energy and what I needed to do to remedy my situation.

Keith: It's not always that straightforward. Anything else?

Julius: Yes. I went on to tell you that I get energized working with certain kinds of people and when I am doing particular types of work. I find myself renewed, energized, and encouraged by certain aspects of the job, by positive feedback, by recognition of my work by respected colleagues, and by the time I spend with my wife and kids.

You asked me for a barometer reading on these. You even drew a barometer with a one-to-ten scale for me. Then, after I'd responded and reflected on this, you asked me what zaps my energy or depletes my energy stores. We talked about a number of people, circumstances, issues, and emptying situations that were entropy producing. You explained the continuum that you had learned from Gordon MacDonald (2007) about *Very Resourceful People* (VRPs) on one end and *Very Draining People* (VDPs), on the other end. It was interesting to plot the key people in my work and non-work life on this continuum. I realized how important it is to juggle the amount of time that I attend to resourceful and draining sources of inputs and outputs. I tend to be overly heroic and problem-focused. In fact, you asked me if I enjoyed riding into situations to save the day! I realized that I had built a tendency for people to be overly dependent on my ability to put out fires. My continuum was tilted south because of this imbalance.

I remember at the time thinking that I ought to use this to offer my wife some help to get a better balance on her people continuum. She just gets out there and helps everyone. She has a huge heart, but she hadn't found ways to replenish herself with resourceful people or other sources of refreshment. She simply runs herself ragged, without a way to rekindle and refill her own reservoirs. You know, it is so easy to see it in someone else – a bit harder to see it when it's yourself that's running on empty. Then I realized I do exactly the same thing as she does, only in a more ego-driven fashion.

Keith: So, by using the heart (energy capacity or fuel tank) metaphor, you were able to diagnose your own condition – to see what fills your tank and what contributed to emptying it. I guess the key pieces here are that it will be a bit different for everyone, but that our activity or output will never be sustained at a level higher than our energy level. We need to look for ways to reduce unnecessary energy depletion and fitting in ways to fuel our energy tanks. I specifically remember your self-prescriptions, which included taking time every day to renew your goals, focus on what is most important to you, and to develop some "margins" or white space in your life for yourself, your family, and your relationships in your workplace. In particular, I recall you expressing a quiet commitment to guard your own involvement in rescuing and doing certain tasks when there were other capable people around to work on these. Back then, we talked some about your approaches to delegation. It seems like self-leadership and mentoring others to lead are related, as we pass onto others some of our own life challenges. This keeps our developmental relationships "real."

Julius: Yes, exactly. Not surprisingly, I still have to concentrate effort and discipline to leave myself enough time to let some things go and let others work things out. I have this propensity to keep the peace, be in control, have things done in *my* way, and to keep the ship on an even keel. It is sometimes easier to do the work myself than to delegate the work or let others develop the skills. I am trying to learn to be patient; it has not been easy for me.

Keith: I hear you. The ego and inclination to control can be treacherous leadership patterns.

As you said earlier, the first leg of the stick figure had to do with being mindful of your interpersonal attitudes and to polish your people skills.

Julius: Yes. It was really evident with the stick figure that if I wanted a leg to stand on – I needed to develop and sustain relationships of grace and influence with people I was serving. You didn't tell me what these attitudes and skills were but asked me two questions to get these out of me. First, "Julius," you asked, "when you think of someone for whom you have great respect as a servant leader, who comes to your mind?" Immediately I thought of my rugby coach from when I was a teenager.

Second, you asked, "What are the features or the characteristics of this person that brought him or her to mind?" Well, I listed seven or eight one-word descriptions that commended "Coach Shaw" to me. You asked me to write these down on the diagram: respectful, caring, enthusiastic, courageous, forthright, engaged, intense, and passionate. I could give you illustrations of each of these qualities that Coach Shaw possessed.

Keith: Then what?

Julius: Yes, now I could see that these are the interpersonal and attitudinal features that I hold important in a leader. I suppose we form these from our own experiences with positive and negative

Figure 3

A representation of key interpersonal and attitudinal dispositions of a good leader.

exemplars in our lives. Remembering Coach Shaw simply personalizes and concretizes my vision for what it takes to be a genuine and effectual leader. Of course there are other people who have influenced me and have similar characteristics. I've since thought of a few people who I don't want to be like, and these recollections have been a pretty powerful motivator for me, too!

You told me that recalling exemplars was just half the story. You said that the other people in our work setting would not likely disagree with any of my ideal features, but that they might have their own list – a different set of preferred leadership traits or features that I needed to pay attention to. You said the part of the challenge of leadership is to live up to one's own list but also, and perhaps more importantly, to listen to and discern what other people expect of you as a leader. You said it was crucial to know what others had on their lists and to be sure that these features were incorporated into my attitudes and behaviors in the best way I knew how.

The caveat was to never try to be someone else or to cave in to expectations that were against my own moral code. It was sort of like the challenge to meet people more than half way by being true to one's own sensibilities but serving the positive expectations of others with high regard. I have used this approach with two of my newer staff members, who I think have great potential as leaders in our company. This has been an interesting way to engage them in thinking about their own concepts of leadership and related behaviors.

This made sense to me and widened my picture of the ideal leader. It also reminded me that effective leadership is always plural because no one person can meet the ideal expectations of everyone in the organization. If I can encourage others to be leaders and leaders of leaders, I know this will make a major difference in our organization.

Keith: Julius, why don't we go back to the sketch? Please explain to me what you remember about the second leg.

Julius: Well, I know it has a lot to do with work habits and task competencies. You can be great with people, but you also have to be able to contribute to getting the work done well.

Keith: That's a good way of looking at it. What's important is not so much what you remember about how I articulated this during our last conversation but how you've made practical use of the stick figure as a heuristic or tool of understanding – to reflect and to diagnose with it in your own practice of leadership and protégé development.

Julius: I've seen this leg as the one that gives attention to the good standing of the leader who I am mentoring and that provides the person with a way to see the importance of their developing credibility through diligent performance. More than just good, effectual, and proper work happening, it is also the choice of manner and means by which the work is done. Words like industry, orderliness, reliability, resourcefulness, perseverance, interdependence, collaboration, and steadiness are all words that I associate with the way a leader helps the job get done. But also the servant leader needs to act as a steward of the larger purposes and promises associated with this work. I'd just love to see more and more of our staff to develop along these lines. When a staff member isn't performing well, we can do a differential diagnosis together by talking with them about their perceptions of what it takes to do the work.

Keith: So, putting it all together, you have personalized this bipedal approach to describing leadership as getting along well with people by keeping attuned with the ways that encourage each of them to flourish and as facilitating the accomplishment of the work of the organization in ways that are aligned to agreed-upon purposes, priorities, and potentialities. This makes sense. How have you used this on a day-to-day basis, Julius?

Julius: I don't use it every day, but I am sure the basic ideas are always in the back of my mind as I interact and engage in the work I do. Every once in a while when I feel a bit frustrated, anxious, or even angry with my own leadership or with the way things are going, I go back to this diagram. I recall you telling me one time that I should only take responsibility for those things over which I have direct influence. You said that when I was mentoring others and felt frustrated, anxious, or angry that I probably have mixed up my desires and my goals. You told me that a goal might be seen as something that no one can block and something that I can achieve without any impinging external constraints. On the other hand, a desire may be seen as something I might wish for but that requires the support or co-operation of others (who may or may not be willing to offer their part). Switching these up will bring a lot of stress my way. So I focus on what I can do by drawing the stick person and asking myself the obvious questions:

1. What is my energy level right now?
2. What can I do to plug the leaks in my fuel tank?
3. What habits and disciplines do I need to renew to get back into balance and to recharge my batteries (to "sharpen my saw," as Stephen Covey said)?
4. What is working for me in my interpersonal relationships and what isn't?
5. What is working as I engage the tasks before me and what isn't giving us the forward momentum we had hoped for?
6. What and who do I simply need to be more patient with, and what timely changes are required?

These questions have been a help to me. On further reflection, I say to myself, "Here is what I should keep doing, stop doing, and start doing." (I jot my responses down to each of these three questions). If I am going to be, do, and dare with greater attunement and alignment, here is what it is going to have to look like tomorrow compared to what I've experienced today. (I have a short brainstorming session with myself or colleagues). This is how I have used these aspects of the napkin/serviette diagram.

Keith: Great questions, Julius. I presume you'd ask different versions of these questions for different circumstances, but I get the idea.

Julius: And I've found these helpful in my work with colleagues as well. This has set us up for a common approach to problem solving with our business-development teams. We want to be a learning organization. As I am mindful of these questions and the visual model that you and I talked about, I've done the same with other people on their paths of self-discovery, reflection, formation, and problem solving.

Keith: I know we could tell lots of stories and elaborate further on the particulars of each of these elements, but let's move up to the *mind* aspect of the stick figure.

Julius: Yes. We've been talking about the relational and technical aspects of leadership, but these are nothing without the DNA-like code, direction, and intelligence flowing from a person with their head on straight, so to speak. Implicit in all we've talked about are the values, goals, and motivation that come from the mind of the leader. You told me that the neck represents maturity or the capacity of a leader to wisely connect their intelligence with energy to produce meaningful activity on behalf of others. I've come to see this as an important aspect of my mentoring the leaders around me. As the old saying goes, "good theory needs good practice, and good practice needs good theory." Running around mindlessly chasing the demands of the urgent doesn't make sense unless you are a fanatic.

Keith: A fanatic is someone who, having lost his or her sense of direction, doubles their speed, and this can be a problem. These mindless or rogue leaders are downright dangerous. There is a world of difference between the wise and the foolish leader. This may be the distinguishing feature.

Julius: Right. If we see the mind as the origin of our values, conscience, goals, creativity, and multiple intelligences, then we see how these components can govern the wisdom of our actions. How do we purposively use our interpersonal and task acumen to serve the greatest good?

Keith: Say more about this, Julius.

Julius: Leaders must have vision and credibility (virtue in the eyes of their beholders) as they serve with and on behalf of others. I think that one's values and vision need to be connected for internal integrity (in one's own eyes), and one's vision and behavior need to be connected for external credibility (in the eyes of others). In other words, what we think is important should match what we advocate as important; what we envision (say out loud) should be consistent with the actions people see us take. This is obviously easier said than done, but you need people to see that you are trustworthy and reliable to be a person of integrity.

Keith: Beyond being conscious of one's own values (what is important to you), being sensitive to the values of others (social radar or antennae) and being true to one's conscience are also important. I think a person needs to develop their full potential: body, soul, and spirit. Our education (formal and informal), experience, and resultant expertise provide us with the raw material for our intellectual formation (whether emotional, social, spiritual, moral, or whatever facet of intelligence we might consider). We also learn how to reason, create, and judge with increasingly mature processing capacities. And certainly, we strive to combine our physical, social, and psychological needs with our drives to produce goals, which are mediated through our values and intelligences.

Julius: There is a lot to this, isn't there?

Keith: Yes, it is a lot, and of course it's more complex, but your explanation helps us to see how the facets of our mind engage our energies into particular activities. If we can integrate our learnings, our values, and our goals, and express these with our interpersonal and organizational capacities, then we have a chance in our service to make a difference in our work world.

Julius: When I've had occasion, I have often reminded my work colleagues that servant leadership is about servanthood. It is the sweet spot between the negative extremes of servitude, selflessness, and selfishness.

Keith: I see. It sounds like you are talking about the importance of a well-anchored self and social identity in the protégé and in yourself.

Julius: I think you will agree that we have a natural propensity to wear masks, to engage in defense mechanisms, and that there is a tendency to either diminish our own worth or demean the worth of others. I know I oscillate in and out of these zones in my own practice of leadership. This serviette mentorship heuristic that you've introduced me to calls upon me and those I mentor to be authentic, to be reflective, and to be the best we can be, independent of our life stages or circumstances. The persona, or false self, of a leader will always be worn, but we must do all we are able to be our true selves as servant leaders – the more real and the more transparent, the better. I've come to appreciate that so much of leadership and the mentorship of others is self-leadership. It is about *being* so much more than *doing*. It is about the resonance and grace of our both being and doing.

Keith: There is a duality of leadership that we need to keep in mind: What is seen (our doing and performance) and what is unseen (our identity and core person). You are making an important point here. We find it so easy to wear the façade of what I hope other people will see in us. There is this inclination to root my identity in power, prestige, or possessions rather than in the person I am. Seems like half the time I feel guilty of this and half the time I don't even realize I am putting on a show. Faking it is hard work and it's nearly impossible to sustain. I am sure lots of people I work with can see through my self-protective or self-aggrandizing guises, but for some reason I still insist on continuing to wearing my sophisticated costumes. Perhaps I am addicted to my false self.

Julius: Wow, you really are asking for some deep personal reflection here. I've been discovering that mentoring others requires me to grow, too!

Keith: This persona topic warrants several more conversations, Julius – conversations that I am afraid are all too rare. But for now let's move on with the present task, and we can come back to some of this the next time we meet.

Julius: Let's do that.

Keith: If we think of our minds and the head on the stick person as the software that gives direction and drive to the hardware (our energy expressed in behavior), then we need to look more closely at this software.

Julius: In other words, what instructions do my mind, my will, and my emotions give to my body?

Keith: Yes, that's a good way of putting it, Julius. Let's just take one set of responses to this question. We have value commitments, and as leaders I think it is useful to see at least four of these. First, there is a commitment to external moral constraints. This might be laws of the land, general societal mores, or professional codes. These are the well-known public obligations or implicit promises that leaders are assumed to have with their direct constituents and society. In some ways these are like psychological contracts or covenants we have developed as professionals with those we serve. When we agree to assume certain roles, there are moral expectations that we implicitly or explicitly agree to.

Julius: Another value set might be our commitment to common ethical values (such as honest, caring, respect for persons, and so on).

Keith: That's right. One way I like to think about this is to consider the provocative proposition that leaders cannot afford to be naïve relativists, narcissists, or egoists when it comes to ethical principles like the ones you've mentioned, Julius. Those we serve count on us to be honest, caring, respectful, trustworthy, consistent, and reliable. We have to live and serve within the bounds of these ethical principles. There is so much more we could say about this.

Julius: But you said there were four commitments that we would want to see developed through our mentorship?

Keith: Yes, a third commitment is to act in a fashion consistent with our personal conscience. All of these commitments need to work together, but a strong contributor to the leader's integrity is the capacity to engage their conscience to do what is right, good, and virtuous. I'd like to suggest that 90% of a leader's hard choices and most intense moments are not matters of figuring out what is right or wrong, but rather the challenges consist of finding the courage to act in a fashion consistent with one's personal conscience. The

Figure 4

A representation of key elements in the mind of the leader.

other 10% of ethical decision making requires imagination and careful deliberation to figure out what the right, good, or virtuous action ought to be.

Julius: So, you are saying the tough part about being a virtuous leader is to consistently act in accord with your conscience.

Keith: Yes, that's what I am saying. I am not suggesting there aren't sticky, messy, and complex issues that we have to work through, but the real challenges and most intense challenges we face typically consist of living and working with a good conscience and much courage before others, in a fashion consistent with what we know to be the right, the good, and the proper.

Julius: I'll have to digest and ponder that against my own experience. And the fourth commitment you had in mind?

Keith: As a person gains experience and confidence in their area of service and leadership, they accumulate a sense of what the best practices are, and some of these actually become professional convictions, beliefs, or ideals. I am not suggesting we have a long list of these, but leaders will be able to characterize some of their most important decisions as being made on the basis of strong conviction (versus mere preference). For example, we can define and describe best practice in relating to others, and we know when equality, security, or justice is threatened in the workplace, or we know where the lines are between professional and non-professional behavior. Perhaps our set of convictions is related to how people ought to be treated or what tends to work best in team practice. These convictions are composed of our own unique syntheses or composites of principles applied to the practice of work and life.

Julius: Keith, I've got to get back to the office now. This time has given me lots to think through. Thank you. Do you mind if I keep the serviettes?

Keith: Of course I don't mind! Julius, you've given me some things to think about as well. I am grateful for you. It will be good to get together down the road and see how you've developed these ideals of serviette mentorship further. There is lots of room to think further about this.

Julius: Yes, I like this. It gets me thinking and talking about a range of topics that are important to me and that I want to pass onto others so they "grow as persons, become healthier, wiser, freer, more autonomous" (Greenleaf, 1977, p. 27) and more able to reproduce themselves in other leaders. I know we've talked in broad and conceptual kinds of ways, but believe me, I need these perspectives to assess my own practice, and I find these ideas quite easy to pass onto others. So, thank you.

Keith: Call me. We'll do this again!

Julius: Thanks, Keith. Have a terrific day.

Concluding Thoughts

Though some research indicates that although the relationship between mentors and protégés is typically positive (Linn, Howard, & Miller, 2004), in many cases there is a persistent deficiency that arises within the mentorship transaction related to such negative elements as inadequate/inappropriate guidance, unacceptable supervisory interventions, unproductive mentoring responses, or poor leader communication (Taherian & Shekarchian, 2008). There have been many calls for better mentorship and for means by which to enhance these developmental relationships (Asare, 2008; Myall, Levett-Jones, & Lathlean, 2008). As educators and leaders seek to better equip individuals who are mentoring others and to help their clients develop as leaders themselves, the formative advantage of dialogue and the variety of means and tools of interaction should all be given consideration.

As indicated at the outset, I have personally found face-to-face dialogue, as illustrated above, to be an effective tool for engaging mentors and mentors of mentors in a number of different reflective activities. For example, on occasion I have made use of this transcript by asking graduate students or workshop attendees to "pair-up" and assume the two roles as they read through the script. I have asked them to assess the relationship depicted in the dialogue, to critique the content, and to examine the mentorship process going on in the conversation. I have asked them to tap their own experiences and expertise to suggest other mentorship approaches and to consider past clients or circumstances where this type of conversation might be useful. I have also asked workshop attendees to write on some supplied serviettes to role play a dialogue using diagrams or depictions as a part of a simulated mentorship conversation. Because humans gain understanding by visual means, and because they solidify their learning by re-teaching what they have learned to others, I have found this serviette activity to be a useful mentoring approach.

In this chapter I attempted to show what the "serviette mentorship" process actually looks like. Perhaps it simply reflects what has transpired on numerous occasions during mentor/protégé conversations. Whether they use serviettes or other visual media to enhance their communication, the key point is that both mentorship partners are engaged in a mutual learning relationship.

References

Asare, A. (2008, April). A few good faculty: Inspiring and preparing contemporary dental educators. *New York State Dental Journal*, 74(3), 23–27.

Greenleaf, R. K. (1977). *Servant-leadership: A journey into the nature of legitimate power and greatness*. Mahwah, NJ: Paulist.

Linn, P., Howard, A., & Miller, E. (Eds.). (2004). *Handbook for research in cooperative education and internships*. Mahwah, NJ: Lawrence Erlbaum.

MacDonald, G. (2007). *Ordering your private world*. Nashville, TN: Thomas Nelson.

Myall, M., Levett-Jones, T., & Lathlean, J. (2008). Issues in undergraduate education: Mentorship in contemporary practice; The experiences of nursing students and practice mentors. *Journal of Clinical Nursing*, 17(14), 1834–1842.

Raelin, J. A. (2003) *Creating leaderful organisations: How to bring out leadership in everyone*. San Francisco, CA: Berrett-Koehler.

Taherian, K., & Shekarchian, M. (2008). Mentoring for doctors: Do its benefits outweigh its disadvantages? *Medical Teacher*, 30(4), 95–99.

Wareham, J. (1992). *Anatomy of a great executive*. New York, NY: Perennial.

Chapter Fifteen
Mentoring with Questions

Kabini Sanga & Keith Walker

THIS CHAPTER HAS FOUR SECTIONS. The first introduces two personal stories that point to the profound learning that can come from mentors who effectively use questions to encourage, exhort, enlighten, and empower their mentees. These stories illustrate how even the simplest questions can instill courage, bring about growth, teach new truths, and imbue mentees with energy, resources, and power. In the second, we introduce the maieutic and Socratic approaches to mentoring through questioning. In doing so, we suggest that inquiry is a way of creating shared understanding with and developing wisdom in mentees. This shared territory of understanding is the basis of effective communication and a foundation for developmental relationships. Third, we provide a heuristic for thinking about the content domain of questions that mentors might ask their mentees. Some of these foci give attention to the interiority (inside-out or "life-world" focus) and some to the exteriority (wider world and "system-worlds" focus) of mentees. Finally, the fourth section provides various types and kinds of questions mentors might use in their mentoring relationships.

Stories from Two Mentees

Questions have the possibility of drawing out the best or worst of mentees' thinking, feeling, and choosing capabilities in ways likely to be transformative. Everyone has their own stories of mentoring through questions. Here are two of our stories.

Keith's Experience with Walter

One of the most influential men in my life is Walter. I was first attracted to the church where he was a pastor, not because of his popularity as an eloquent preacher but because of the people, programs, and positive climate that he seemed to be animating. I eventually became one of his staff members. It has been over two decades since we last worked together. As of late, we have only had infrequent conversations. Yet, as I reflect on Walter's contributions to my life, I have no doubt about the lasting legacy of our relationship. My mentor had taught me by consistent example, by his wise words, and by his remarkably discerning questions.

I loved to watch Walter with people. He was self-assured, calming, and focused in his interactions. I enjoyed observing him in public settings. He was uniquely dignified, respectful, and profound in his words and extremely effective in connecting with his audiences. In private settings, Walter was devoted, humble, and had a rarely seen friendship with and reverence for God.

I learned from my mentor through his pithy sayings. For example, he would regularly tell me "It's always too soon to quit," "No condition is permanent," "We will always be in transition," "The human spirit fails unless the Holy Spirit fills," "People are down on what they are not up on, so communicate," "Hire right and delegate according to maturity," "I know of no better way to bring people together than food – look for every possible reason to celebrate together," "People vote with their feet," "The problem is never the problem," and "There is never a shortage of money in God's economy – just too few God-inspired ideas – dream and take the first steps." Each of these sayings has special meaning for me, so over the intervening years these proverbs and clichés have been woven into my own vocabulary and their truths into my soul.

Walter's eloquent and highly relevant public oratory skills were well known. People often sought his advice. He was also known for his strong missile-like focus and his ability to cut through the weeds to get us to see the essence of a situation. He was a bit intimidating with his "Socratic inquisitions" during staff meetings. We knew he knew what he knew and what we didn't know or didn't have just right.

But on reflection, I especially learned from his questions. For me, the most profound experiences of learning from Walter were when he didn't tell me but simply asked me a question and let that simple question sit with me – the question was for me to answer. Yes, Walter was willing to ask me the least comfortable of all possible questions.

His mentorship had transforming influence when he asked me well-timed and purposeful questions. Here are just three examples:

- ~: Keith, if today was your last day of work here, what would you be doing and thinking about? Perhaps he was asking me to work towards a definitive purpose, to finish what I'd started or to be sure I was finding people to take over certain tasks, or thinking about leaving situations better than I'd found them.
- ~: Keith, if resources weren't an issue, what should we be doing to accomplish our purposes? Perhaps he was asking me to get more creative, to not be paralyzed by the many "hows" or barriers but to want to get things done badly enough that little frustrations or obstacles didn't impede the way. Sometimes he simply wanted me to think bigger and grander thoughts.
- ~: Keith, if this was your first day at work here, what would you want to be doing? Perhaps he was noticing that my initial energy was flagging or knew that I needed to renew the original vision for what I was doing. Maybe he was providing me with space to rethink my priorities and regain some fresh perspective.

I am not sure that I ever knew exactly what he was hoping to do with the questions. Perhaps it doesn't matter. All I know is that he triggered all sorts of healthy responses when he asked these questions. He made a difference in my life and work through questioning. These are just a few of my recollections of Walter – one of my mentors from years past. Walter is blind now, but he is as sharp in mind and spirit as ever. I hope he sees me living out some of these memorable lessons. I still ask myself and others these same questions.

Kabini's Experience with His Mother

In my tribe, mom was a trail-blazer as an influencer. She was gentle, cultured and of character. She was much loved. As my family knew, mom was also everyone's mother. Her generous spirit was consistently expressed in her compassion, hospitality, and wise counsel to all that came her way. Throughout her life, many had learned much from her "fānanau aroaro lā" (peaceable advice). Often, people spoke of her "goni lana tei boro 'ana" (compassionate embrace) or her "fali aroaro lā sulia rau kini" (respectful conflict solving). In her later years, elders referred to mom as "ai baita" (valued woman), "ai abu" (holy woman), "ai fungu" (abundant woman) and "ai kali' afu" (wholesome woman). Mom was a leader I admired and aspired to emulate.

There were times I felt uncomfortable in mom's presence because of her penetrating questions. She would ask: "Kabini, oe utā" (Kabini, how are you)? In Malaita culture, such a question requires thought. As a cultured Malaita son, I would respond with another question, "utā lau" (what is it that you are asking about)? Mom would further ask, "kusi nē lau to'ona wela nau" (shouldn't I be concerned about my child)? After a pause, I would say, "te'ena e lea ma'ana na, tē" (I have heard you and will ensure all is well, mom). In Malaita culture, "how are you?" is a deep question. It is not asking about one's health or how one feels. If about health, the question is "nonimu e utā" (how does your body feel)? My final response would have assured mom that I clearly knew what I needed to do, and do right or well, without disclosing what may have been wrong, unhealthy, or imbalanced about my life at the time of our conversation.

Every time I showed up in the village, mom would ask "ko nau kini fainia fungo nau gera tō lea ma'agera" (What is the well-being of my grandchildren and my daughter-in-law)? In Malaita culture, this was not a question about health or physical needs. Also, in Malaita culture, mom was not calling Keith and Amalani (my children) or Jennifer (my wife) by name in her question posing. Instead, she established her relationship claims over the subjects of her inquiry by using "my grandchildren" and "my daughter-in-law." By doing so, her question became a more serious inquiry. It was not just my interest that was being enquired about; it was hers as well. In Malaita culture, she was asking if I was caring for her grandchildren and honoring her daughter-in-law. Further, to the Malaita mind, mom was asking whether I was honoring her (my mother) through my parenting and marriage. Mom was asking about the extent to which I was living up to my familial responsibilities.

My mom passed on two years ago. She had lived a full and satisfying twenty years after my dad was called to rest. During the last decade of mom's life, I often went to the village to seek guidance from her. In response to my uncertainties she would ask "liomu e tōēā" (Has your heart hit it? Has your mind encircled the matter of your consideration? Has your heart become one with the matter for your choosing)? At times, she would help me clarify my motives or encouraged me to think further by asking "'aena tā nori" (what is its source or have you established its essence or have you dug to its roots)? During our conversations she would pose a question, "rau mamana boro nē" (how truthful or trusted are you)? As well, this could mean "how firm is your claim, stand or defence?" Often, before I departed from mom, she would ask "oe babatō boro nē?" In Malaita, "babatō" is the foundation sitting plank in a dug-out canoe. This piece is the centre of gravity of the canoe. In posing this question, she was asking me to clarify, establish, and be rooted courageously to my "babatō."

During my last visit with mom, she confided in me in her usual contented manner, "I am a very happy mother and grandmother. You, my children, have blessed me with your lives. Thank you for honoring me." These were wise and deeply meaningful words. Such were her passion-fostering messages; such powerful sentiments of meaning, value, and motivation came to me from her. What protégé would not be inspired to aspire for, sustain, and reproduce a life of honor from such affirmations? Of course, mom had a profound impact on me. Again, what protégé would not allow him/herself to be mentored by such profoundly caring and wise mentor-mother?

Maieutic and Socratic Approaches to Mentoring

Perhaps it is coincidental that Kabini's mother was a mid-wife in the Solomon Islands and who, over the decades, had earned the far-reaching, deep respect of many through her truth-bearing and caring interactions with people. She helped deliver babies and she deeply cared for all those placed along her life's journey. We suggest that the act of mentoring may be seen as an act of mid-wifery, where mentors invite mentees to reflect on what they know from their past experiences and to draw from themselves to discover or put together new ways forward or to analyze their life or workplace circumstances.

In this section we will introduce both maieutic (mid-wife questioning) and Socratic questioning as means by which to mentor (Alder, 1982). These two approaches derive from what we have come to associate with ancient Greek approaches to teaching and learning (associated mainly with Pythagoras and Socrates). In Socratic teaching, the first step or phase is to identify prejudices and wrong thinking by incisive questioning of the learner, their language, and their assumptions. This approach is most commonly associated with Socrates and his methods. Having dealt with presuppositions, prejudices, and biases, the second phase (also evident in Socratic teaching such as in Theaetetus and Meno) was the maieutic approach, wherein the mentor's questions seek to assist in the delivery of stored knowledge and germinating "latent truths" already possessed by the learner but needing liberation and articulation. The maieutic method simply indicates an approach where mentors mediate the birth of ideas, solutions, or understandings. In this sense, mentors are mid-wives for the process of mentees birthing their best responses to particular issues or developmental needs.

For those familiar with the Adaptive Mentorship Model, we would suggest that the maieutic approach is most appropriate for mentoring D2-D4 mentees (with need for confidence or periodic

Figure 1

Adapting the JOHARI Window for Mentoring Through Socratic and Maieutic Questioning.

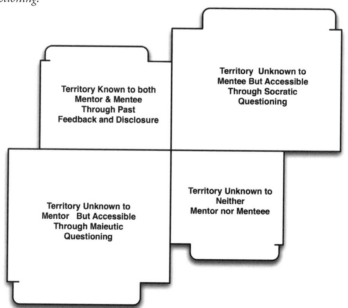

and sustaining encouragement to keep doing a fine job). The D1 (overconfident and incompetent; the unconscious incompetent) mentees may be more usefully provided with direct or deductive mentoring (if open to being told what to do), but often a Socratic approach of questioning will work well with such persons.

The Socratic method is intended for those who think they have everything figured out but are actually ignorant or unable or both. The Socratic method points out error, prejudice, fallacious thinking, overconfidence, or misplaced attention and has a definite critical edge to it. On the other hand, the maieutic approach is intended to come to the aid of those who don't know they know until helped with questions. Mentors help mentees to give birth to solutions that are dormant within them. In essence, the Socratic approach is a deficit approach; whereas the maieutic approach is appreciative of the powerful and latent capacities of the people being mentored. A combination of Socratic and maieutic approaches is likely best. Best is determined by matching the developmental levels of mentees with appropriate mentoring strategies (or questions). The Socratic questions can bring mentees to a place of readiness (that arrogance, pride, unharnessed ego, or overconfidence may otherwise prevent) for digging deeper creatively, coherently, constructively, and critically into the ideas and practices that will later become self-prescriptive or undergirding for their responses to life circumstances, barriers to performance, or work-place opportunities or threats.

Contrary to some practices, mentoring is more about uncovering understandings and intelligence than it is about covering a certain quantity of facts or sets of understandings. Mentoring is about exploring and making known territories of knowledge, understandings, expertise, experience, and practical wisdom that were previously unknown. The JOHARI window (Figure 1), originally developed by Luft and Ingham (1955), is a classic and oft-used metaphor for appreciating the panes of awareness people (mentees) have, do not have, and the role of other people (mentors) to help the former uncover their understandings.

Of course dialogue is the notion of exchanging two sets of understandings or truths (your and my truth). The understandings of mentors are passed along to mentees, and the mentees' understandings are uncovered when expressed for the review of mentors. Whether the focus is on mentors as people, or the exegesis of particular circumstances, or the analysis of tasks to perform, the mentors and mentees know some things the other doesn't know, in addition to sharing certain common knowledge between them.

The mentoring relationship is about knowing, being known, and increasing the knowledge for being, doing, and daring of mentees. It is about enhancing the multiple intelligences and practical wisdom of learners to be more fruitful, fulfilled, and fit for life, work, and leadership. It is the role of mentors to help increase this territory for truth and support in order to enrich mentees' learning experiences and to make space for their incremental personal and/or professional transformation.

The simplest ways to enlarge the territory of common understanding are for mentees to disclosure their unspoken truths, quiet understandings, and "secrets" to their mentors and for mentors to provide direct feedback, opinion, intelligence, and perspectives. Perhaps the greatest barrier to achieving a shared understanding is the false assumption that each knows what the other knows, or when either or both overestimate the size of the shared territory. We argue that one of the most effective ways for increasing the territory of shared intelligence and learning is through dialogue using questions.

Schon (1987), Argyris (1993), and Hargrove (1995) suggested that mentees learn at three levels. They "learn in action" as they do or perform particular tasks and experience life circumstances. This is an obvious place for mentor presence, accompaniment, and co-journeying. Mentees learn when they "reflect on what they've learned in action" (double-loop learning). This is to say, when they look back on their experience and wonder about what happened, might have been, and what might be learned from experience, they learn for the next time. They also learn when they "reflect on the reflections on their learning in action" (triple-loop learning). This is sometimes called "metacognition" or thinking about one's thinking. Mentors serve their mentees well by facilitating these three levels of learning. The second and third levels of learning may be particularly fostered by using maieutic questioning. These maieutic questions may begin from mentors' curiosities and from their due regard for mentees but can evolve to strategically draw out lessons learned from their mentees' experiences. They can dialogue about barriers encountered (or erected) and success patterns that might otherwise remain hidden from or unnoticed by mentees.

With respect to the territory that is not known to mentees, by virtue of mentors' observations, expertise, and experience, these understandings can be unveiled in many ways. Straight out telling, lecturing, or showing will often work well. However, it can be much more meaningful to use the Socratic approach to lead learner-mentees to these understandings. The questions we pose later in this chapter include examples of both maieutic and Socratic questions.

A Heuristic for Thinking about the Content Domains of Mentoring Questions

While there are multitudes of purposes for mentoring activities and relationships, essentially mentors and mentees enter into a psychological contract (Schein, 1988) with each other. This is a tacit, informal, and often taken-for-granted set of mutually held expectations. This socio-emotional bundle of unique terms of reciprocity, promise keeping, trust, modes of exchange, and dynamic qualities of relational values lies in the deep structures of mentor-mentee relationships.

If the layers of such a psychological contract were peeled back, this may reveal a number of foci around which the activities and interactions of mentors and mentees revolve. In Figure 2 we have depicted one such look into the infrastructure of mentors and mentees psychological contract. Our view is that the question-asking initiative of mentors will often relate to one or more of these foci. As well, the questions posed will invite mentees to give attention to certain domains or purposes for the developmental relationship. We have depicted four broad domains of questions together with other abiding dimensions and agenda for questioning. In the wider and purpose-focused sense, mentors may ask questions connected to mentees' identity (being or personhood, community of origin, context for personal hardwiring, etc.), their relationships, or acts and manner of relating to others or to certain causes. Questions may encompass mentees' desire or need to discern, find guidance, be affirmed, or to envision their preferred future or their strategic directions. A third domain may be that of assisting mentees to deeply reflect or to explore possibilities or unfamiliar understandings. And then there is the domain of working with mentees in the performance or doing of particular tasks or perhaps finding the courage to tackle a difficulty or stretch beyond their normal comfort zones – to dare or take a risk. The questions for each of these domains are likely self-evident to the reader.

As Figure 2 depicts, there are also questions that focus on helping mentees to be mindful of what experience, expertise, or even conscience has already told them. Mentees are well served when asked questions about their priorities, convictions, and behaviors that, perhaps, they don't seem to resonate with. Instilling hope, fanning passions, and giving attention to one's strength in association with purposes is a key to success for anyone, as is helping mentees to define and describe what "success" looks like. Mentors can provide the reminders and reinforcement for these alignments.

From time to time, mentees become overly accepting of the status quo, complacent with systemic issues, overly accepting of poor performance, and uncritical in their thinking. Likewise mentees can feel stuck, plateaued, or trapped by seemingly impossible constraints or

Figure 2

Dimensions of Mentoring Through Questions.

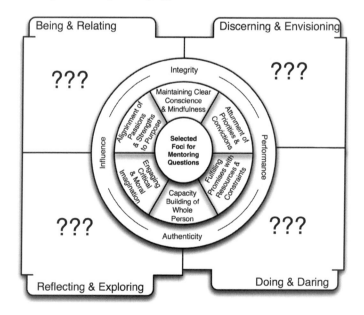

dilemma. Mentors who can ask questions that generate well-timed, critical, and constructive engagement and invite moral and even prophetic imagination will provide great value to their mentees.

As often as not, the fundamental needs of mentees are related to the day-to-day fulfillment of promises and obligations that come with various, and sometimes conflicting, roles in life. They attempt to act with the resources and within the constraints of their context, time, and capacities. The service of mentors is to ask questions that privilege promise keeping and acknowledge or shed light on resources, accentuate driving forces, and minimize restraining factors. Of course, mentors are sometimes said to be persons who coach to task, and mentees are ones who accompany in life's journeys. This may be an artificial distinction, but one can never forget that leaders fail for lack of task competence and/or personal character. So supporting the life journeying of mentees is imperative. Effective mentors will reflect the healthy view that mentees are whole persons, not merely means or functionaries to some ends. Mentors will do so by the range, depth, tone, and persistence of their questions. The spirit, soul (mind, emotions, and will), and physical (behavioral) dimensions of mentees ought to be touched upon by mentors' appropriate questioning.

Mentees' integrity (wholeness), authenticity (true-self), influence (difference-making capacity), and performance will always be sources for the content of mentors' questions.

Twenty Kinds of Questions that Mentors Use

Questions can be incredibly powerful. Just asking a question can create something new and generative for mentees (*poiesis* = creative power). Questions are fateful because they circumscribe the focus of mentees' attention (narrow, wide, specific, general, deficit oriented, or appreciative). Questions can test or challenge assumptions, provide perspective, explore connections, cause focus, generate courage, enable insight, and invite clarity of thinking. Questions can be conversation starters or themes for months of conversations. This section simply offers a few types and examples of questions that mentors can use in mentoring.

Six Servant Questions

Both school children and journalists are introduced and urged to memorize Rudyard Kipling's six servants poem: "I keep six honest serving men. They taught me all I knew. Their names are: What and Why and When ... And How and Where and Who." In the toolkits of mentors, these are powerful words with which to ask:

- ~: What projects are you giving your attention to these days? (Focus of attention)
- ~: Why is this so important to your organization? (Goal affirmation)
- ~: When will the process be completed? (Timeline)
- ~: How will you solve that particular issue? (Problem solving)

Figure 3

Examples of Types of Mentoring Questions.

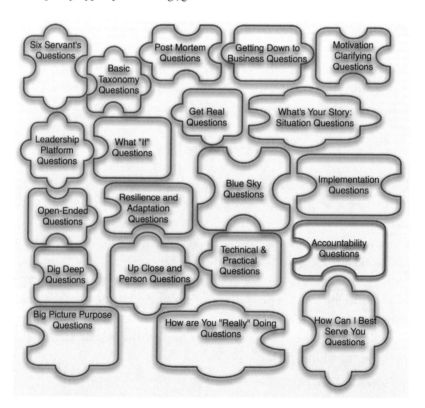

~: Where will you find the information you are looking for? (Research)

~: Who is involved with you in this? (Personal)

Basic Taxonomy Questions

Bloom's taxonomy (Bloom, Englehart, Furst, Hill, & Krathwohl, 1956) is a familiar way of talking about levels of learning and questioning. The taxonomy consists of six levels: knowledge, comprehension, application, analysis, synthesis and evaluation. It is possible to create meaningful questions at all levels:

~: **Knowledge:** What happened after . . . ? How many . . . ? Who was it that . . . ?

~: **Comprehension:** What do you think . . . ? Who do you think . . . ? What was the main idea . . . ? What differences exist between . . . ? Can you provide an example of . . . ?

~: **Application:** Do you know another instance where . . . ? Could this have happened in . . . ? What factors would you change if . . . ? What questions would you ask . . . ? Would this information be useful if . . . ?

~: **Analysis:** What could have happened . . . ? How was this similar to . . . ? What do you see as other possible . . . ? Why did . . . changes occur? Can you compare . . . with that . . . ? Can you explain what . . . when . . . ? What was the problem with . . . ?

~: **Synthesis:** Can you design a . . . to . . . ? Can you see a possible solution to . . . ? Can you develop a proposal which . . . ?

~: **Evaluation:** Is there a better solution to . . . ? Can you defend your position about . . . ? Do you think . . . is a good or a bad thing? What changes to . . . recommend? Do you believe . . . ?

Leadership Platform Questions

In some mentoring contexts, the aim is to come alongside mentees to encourage their growth as leaders or leaders of leaders. This can take place using many of the question types included in this section. However, every once in a while it is good to stand back – to parenthesize the situations, demands, challenges, and circumstances of leading to refresh or reconstruct a platform (place for standing) that will constitute and articulate the ideals or aspirations of mentees' leadership. Here are a series of interconnected questions from which many others may emerge in nurturing conversations of mentorship relationships:

- ❧ Who are your life role models – images of leadership – and what are their qualities?
- ❧ What is your leadership mission?
- ❧ As a leader, what is the difference you want to make – destination?
- ❧ What are the personal values, convictions, ethical positions that drive life and leadership for you – what matters to you?
- ❧ What are your beliefs about motivating, serving, and leading others?
- ❧ What can people expect from you and you from them?
- ❧ How are you going to model and mentor your leadership platform with others?

Open-Ended Questions

Questions that can be answered with a "yes" or a "no" are quite limiting (though not useless). Alternatively, mentors can ask questions that ask for a less summative response and that inspire more rumination.

- ❧ Can you tell me more?
- ❧ What's the up side of this?
- ❧ How do you see the situation?
- ❧ What would it take to . . . ?

Big-Picture Purpose Questions

There are differences in one's views when considering the past, looking at the present, or projecting the future. A view from 50 metres up is different than one from an airplane. Big-picture questions allow mentees to zoom in and zoom out of their perspectives.

~: How will this make a difference?

~: How does this help you get where you want to go?

~: Is this what you really want?

~: Will you be satisfied if . . . ?

How are You Really Doing Questions

Good mentors will ask "second questions" to get beyond cliché interactions.

~: What did you actually do?

~: Where does that idea come from? Tell me more.

~: What do you do best?

~: Are you sure about that?

~: Are there any areas that you struggle with?

Up Close and Personal Questions

Some people play their cards "close to the chest" and others are like an open book. These questions ask mentees to show their cards and to disclose personal and otherwise hidden features of their thinking, feeling, and reflecting.

~: How did that make you feel?

~: What do you do best?

~: Do you like the way your life is shaping up?

~: Why is that so hard for you?

Resilience and Adaptation Questions

Maturity is often determined by our responses to environmental demands. Assessing where we are, where we need to go, and how we will adjust and shift to make things work is crucial to mentees. Questions that give pause and attention to resilience and adaptation are important.

~: How are you going to handle that?

~: What's preventing you from doing that?

~: Why are you behind schedule?

~: What do you need to change to make this happen?

~: What is going to keep you going on this?

Post Mortem Questions

Reflecting on past activities and performances is a vital exercise for growth. Whether there is a sense of success or failure, it is worthwhile to think out loud with another to process what we've experienced.

~: How do you think you did?

~: What could you have done better?

~: If you had it to do all over again, what . . . ?

~: What made that a successful experience . . . ?

What's Your Story: Situation Questions

Questions that invite mentees to tell their stories and to share their journeys provide wonderful pretexts for development.

~: Can you tell me about a time when you felt excited/energized?

~: How are you doing with the goals that are important to you?

~: What have you been learning?

~: What would you say has been the most satisfying aspect of your week?

"What If" Questions

In part, prudence or wisdom is about anticipation, foresight, and taking responsibility for reasonable or predictable outcomes with changes of circumstances.

~: What would happen if . . . ?

~: If you succeed, will you have achieved . . . ?

~: What if the conditions had been different?

~: If you were the other person . . . ?

~: If you get what you want, what will it give you?

Blue-Sky Questions

Imagination is vital for development of potential. Engaging and exploring the imagination of mentees through questions stretches and inspires them.

- ~: What are the best possible outcomes of . . . ?
- ~: Where would you like to be five years from now?
- ~: If you could do what you'd love to do, what would that look like?
- ~: Assuming everything lines up, what are the possibilities?
- ~: What is your vision of success?

Technical and Practical Questions

Mentorship relationships are often set up as knowledge asymmetries (mentors know and mentees don't). In such cases, the exchanges will have a technical, educative, or experiential flavor.

- ~: How will you know you've done it well?
- ~: Does what I've shown you make sense?
- ~: How does that work?
- ~: What do you need to know to do?

Dig-Deep Questions

Penetrating questions to excavate the down-deep parts of our lives are important for our development. Mentors might ask:

- ~: Why does that matter to you?
- ~: Are there any disappointments that have consumed your thoughts this week?
- ~: What is it that makes this situation so important?
- ~: What satisfied you the most about that?
- ~: If you let me inside your thinking on that, what would I see?

Accountability Questions

Sometimes the developmental relationship becomes one that allows for mutual or mentee accountability. Mentees can give mentors permission to ask them hard personal questions that will bring healthy pressures to their life and lifestyles. Mentors might ask, "Since we last met . . ."

- Are there things that we've shared previously that you'd like to talk about?
- How are you maintaining a healthy, balanced schedule (sharpening the saw)?
- Have you invested the proper quality/quantity of time in your most important relationships? What have you done this week to enhance your relationship with your spouse and/or child(ren)?
- How have you been living according to your priorities this week? What's working and what's not?
- Is there anyone you've been disrespectful to or any situations where you've struggled to control your anger?
- What temptations are you facing, and how are you dealing with them?
- In what ways has your life reflected integrity this week? Are the "visible" you and the "real" you consistent?
- Have you exposed yourself to anything that has been unhealthy for you?
- What was your biggest disappointment? How did you handle it?
- What do you see as your number one need for next week?
- In what ways have you stepped out in faith or courage or with conviction since we last met?
- Have you lied to me in any of your answers?

"Getting Down to Business" Questions

Mentors are able to help their mentees to think through situations and strategies in guiding ways.

~: How will you assess that?

~: What do you think you can achieve?

~: What's next for you?

~: What's the bottom line?

"Get Real" Questions

Sometimes mentors are the critical friends that ask the hard questions and bring reality to bear.

~: To what extent have you achieved . . . and how do you know?

~: Do you know that for sure?

~: What's that elephant doing in the room? (unearthing an unspoken or inconvenient truth)

~: Have you tried to . . . ?

Implementation Questions

Of course having good intentions does not guarantee successful or effective actions. It is often helpful for mentees to ponder questions from their mentors about the details of implementation.

~: Who will be involved?

~: Where is the money coming from?

~: What do you think is the best way forward?

~: What will it cost you?

~: What's the one thing that is crucial to . . . ?

Motivation Clarifying Questions

The heart-held expectations and underlying motivations of mentees are essential to understanding and standing alongside them. To have someone ask about one's driving or compelling motivations is an important gift to mentees.

~: What led you to that conclusion?

~: What do you prefer?

~: Why is this important to you?

~: What does a "win" look like for you in this situation?

How Can I Best Serve You Questions

Initially and routinely it is good for mentors to check-in with their mentees to find out what is working well in their relationships and what might be adjusted.

~: Has this time been useful to you?

~: What can I do to help?

~: What do you need from me?

~: What should I/we stop doing, start doing, keep doing?

Finally, we advise that mentors follow up with "second questions" of probing, asking for examples, paraphrasing, listening actively, following a question-response with another question, listening to responses, allowing for silence (so they can hear themselves), patience in waiting for responses (letting the question sit and stew a bit), and so on. The discipline of not answering for the protégé and the disciplines of listening and silence are important for the development of mentor effectiveness.

Concluding Remarks

We acknowledge that the act of mentoring takes place in countless circumstances (formal and informal; intentional and unintentional) by a variety of persons. These persons assume a range of roles, and the nature of these developmental relationships vary widely (hierarchical, serendipitous, network, convenience, peer, friendships, team ships, common workplace, particular expertise). Some relationships begin as casual and evolve to more structured arrangements; some just the opposite. In some cases the mentoring seems to be most about the needs of mentees or protégés (i.e., to learn a particular set of skills, attitudes, or knowledge about life, leadership, tasks, or all three). And in other cases it is more about the needs of mentors (i.e., fulfilling duty, acquiring power, asserting status, or simply the need to be needed). All said, it is obvious that each encounter, moment, and exchange will be dependent on a vast number of factors. There is no way to say "this is how you best mentor." It depends. In fact, we learn from the likes of Fred Fielder (1967) that some mentors are likely to be more task oriented and others more relationship focused. It depends on the disposition, discernment, demands, needs, and the maturity of mentees and mentors.

The Adaptive Mentorship Model (which garners considerable attention in this book) suggests that matching the developmental state of mentees for particular competencies with the most appropriate and adapted approach is a commendable practice. As we are aware, some mentees will be operating, from time to time, in a calm or ordinary pattern of day-to-day circumstances, but there are times when they interact with mentors in the middle of a storm. These different circumstances also warrant adaptive mentorship. We all know that different people learn in different ways – we have dominant learning styles. Some people are visually-oriented, so word pictures or diagrams might work best for them. Others are auditory. Still others might learn and interact best while walking together (kinesthetic learner). We also know that we retain less of what we hear than what we ourselves discover and say out loud to another. In this chapter we set out to present a few ideas about inductive mentoring or mentoring by questions. We did so through our own stories, through a conceptualization of question domains, and providing numerous examples of types of questions that might be exchanged between mentees and mentors.

References

Alder, M. (1982). *The paideia proposal: An educational manifesto.* New York, NY: Collier.

Argyris, C. (1993). *Knowledge for action: A guide to overcoming barriers to organizational change.* San Francisco, CA: Jossey-Bass.

Bloom, B., Englehart, M., Furst, E., Hill, W., & Krathwohl, D. (1956). *Taxonomy of educational objectives: The classification of educational goals, Handbook I: Cognitive domain.* New York, NY: McKay.

Fiedler, F. (1967). *A theory of leadership effectiveness.* New York, NY: McGraw-Hill.

Hargrove, R. (1995). *Masterful coaching: Extraordinary results by impacting people and the way they think and work together.* San Francisco, CA: Pfeiffer.

Luft, J., & Ingham, H. (1955). *The Johari window: A graphic model of interpersonal awareness.* Paper in the Proceedings of the Western Training Laboratory in-group Development, University of California, Los Angeles.

Schein, E. (1988). *Organizational psychology* (3rd ed.). Englewood Cliffs, NJ: Prentice Hall.

Schon, D. (1987). *Educating the reflective practitioner.* San Francisco, CA: Jossey-Bass.

Part Two

Implementing and Adapting the Adaptive Mentorship Model

Chapter Sixteen

The Adaptive Mentorship© Model and Its Potential in Professional Development

Edwin G. Ralph

ORGANIZATIONS OF ALL TYPES AROUND the world are recognizing the critical need for leadership development, especially because a large cadre of current leaders are retiring, and a considerable number of neophytes across all occupations is preparing to replace them (Blanchard, 2010; Miller & Homan Blanchard, 2010). A significant aspect in this need for leadership development is related to the mentorship of this emerging body of new leaders (Rose Ragins & Kram, 2007; Thompson, 2008). The study of leadership and mentorship in organizations has grown to span all disciplines (Steers, Sanchez-Runde, & Nardon, 2010) – from the business and commerce sectors (Bauer & Erdogan, 2009) through to the social sciences, humanities, and applied sciences, including such fields as teacher education, health care, law, engineering, and theological/clergy preparation (Allen & Eby, 2007; Carnegie Foundation for the Advancement of Teaching [CFAT], 2010; Carpenter, Bauer, & Erdogan, 2009; Ralph & Walker, 2011).

To illustrate this expanding attention being paid to mentorship, we conducted a Scopus library, 29-month search (from January 1, 2009 to May 30, 2011) using the terms *mentoring research*. From it we retrieved 717 documents (refereed articles, conference papers, research reviews, and editorials) spanning all professions, with approximately 50% of the sources from the social sciences and psychology, 38% from the health professions, and 13% from business and management. We conducted a similar EBSCO Host library search for the15-month period from January1, 2010 to April 30, 2011, and retrieved 800 documents, also representing virtually every professional discipline. The latter search, however, revealed a predominance of publications from the health care sector (approximately 60%).

A major purpose in researching mentorship across these sectors relates to the development of both the theoretical knowledge of mentorship within the field of leadership and the practical knowledge, skills, and values of novice personnel entering these occupations (Rose Ragins & Kram, 2007). Achieving this purpose will in turn enable particular units or organizations to function effectively and efficiently (Scott, n.d.).

Both the research literature and individuals' personal experience in organizational life have confirmed over time that one of the best ways to help new leaders internalize the generic functions of leadership in any field (i.e., planning, organizing, leading, and managing/controlling; Javed, 2009) is through mentoring them (Allen & Eby, 2007; Ellsum & Pedersen, 2005). The literature shows that there is no single definition of mentorship, and that every discipline has unique terms to describe this helping-developmental process (Chu, 2005; Ralph, Walker, & Wimmer, 2009).

Yet, mentoring programs may be ineffective because participants may have been inadequately prepared or trained to implement and/or sustain a sound mentorship approach (Schoonover, 2002; Ralph, 2004; Ralph & Walker, 2010a; Ralph, Walker, & Wimmer, 2009). During the past two decades we have developed and researched a mentoring model called *Adaptive Mentorship* (AM) that has been shown to overcome some of these obstacles (Ralph & Walker, 2010b, 2011). Our research has shown that implementing the AM model can enhance the mentorship process across the entire educational/training sector. We further contend that AM – which we formerly called *Contextual Supervision* (CS) (Ralph, 1998, 2005), and which we developed from contingency and situational leadership approaches (Hersey & Blanchard, 1988; Fiedler & Garcia, 1987) – is worthy of consideration for application in *any* mentorship situation (Ralph & Walker, 2010a, 2010b; Ralph, Walker, & Wimmer, 2008, ,2009).

Description

Adaptive Mentorship (AM) is a model that guides mentors in adjusting their mentorship response to appropriately match the task-specific development level of protégés whom they are assisting in the learning/work situation. We describe the AM model in Figure 1.

The outer border of the diagram represents the context within which the mentorship process functions, and this context includes physical, psychological, organizational, social, and cultural elements. Many of these influences cannot be changed by the mentor or the protégé; however, the aspect which the participants *can* control is their own behavior. On the one hand, mentors can modify their mentorship actions, which consist of two dimensions shown in the A-grid of Figure 1: their "task" response (i.e., the degree of specific direction given to their protégé regarding the technical, mechanical, or procedural aspect of the latter's performance in the task in question) and their "support" response (i.e., the degree of "human" or psycho/social/emotional encouragement they provide regarding the protégé's learning).

On the other hand, the factor over which the protégés have most control is their personal task-specific developmental level. This developmental level likewise consists of two dimensions, as shown in the D-grid of Figure 1: a protégé's "competence" level (i.e., the actual

Figure 1

Adaptive Mentorship. (The Mentor Matches his/her Adaptive Response to Coincide with the Skill-specific Developmental Level of his/her Protégé.)

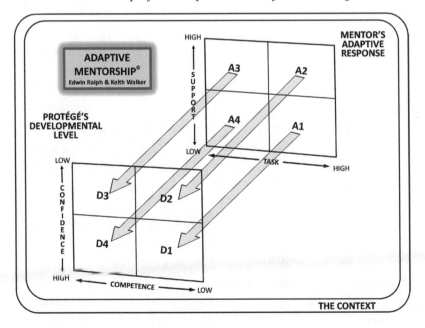

technical ability to perform the task or skill set in question) and his/her "confidence" level (i.e., the degree of self-assurance, composure, psychological comfort, and feelings of security and/or safety in performing the task in question).

The key area of the AM model is represented by the larger arrows linking the D-grid with the A-grid, each of which portrays the mentor's matching of one of four typical adaptive "A" responses with a similarly numbered "D" developmental level characterizing the protégé's performance of the particular skill/competency. It is important to note, here, that there are more than four positions in each grid; there is a broad continuum of possible A/D combinations. However, for conceptual and analytical purposes, we highlighted the four typical matchings simply to reflect common possibilities within each quadrant.

Implementing Adaptive Mentorship

The application of AM consists of three phases or steps enacted by the mentor/protégé pair, as described below:

1. **Ascertain protégé development level.** First the pair determines the existing development level of the protégé to perform the specific competency, skill set, or task being practiced at the time.

As illustrated in the "D grid" of Figure 1, a protégé's skill-specific level of development consists of both his/her *competence* and his/her *confidence* levels in performing that task. The D1 quadrant reflects an individual with "low competence" and "high confidence" to accomplish the task (i.e., he/she does not know exactly *how* to perform it but is confident, willing, and eager to do so). A protégé at D2 is low on both the competence and confidence dimensions in performing the skill; a protégé at D3 shows high competence and low confidence in it; while a protégé at D4 is high on both dimensions for the particular skill.

A protégé's developmental level may be ascertained in three ways: (1) by the mentor's formal and informal observations of the protégé's actual performance of the skill set/task, (2) by the pairs' informal conversations about the protégé's specific progress in it, and (3) by the protégé's answers to the mentor's direct questions about his/her mastery of that skill set. These levels of a protégé's development are task-specific, changeable over-time, different for different competencies, and temporary indicators of a protégé's professional progress (Ralph, 1998, 2000, 2004, 2005).

2. Match mentor's response. After determining the protégé's task-specific level of performance, the mentor must appropriately adapt his/her mentorship response to correspond to the existing developmental level of the protégé regarding the skill set in question: A1 matches with D1, A2 with D2, and so on. This matching process represents the essence of AM.

As depicted in Figure 1, the mentor's adaptive response to the protégé's developmental level also has two dimensions. The first is the amount of *support* the mentor provides (i.e., the human-relationship aspects of encouragement, positive reinforcement, praise, and emotional bolstering of the protégé as he/she attempts to develop the particular skill being learned). This support consists of genuine, positive words and/or actions. The other response element is the *task* dimension (i.e., the extent of directive action provided to the protégé regarding the technical or mechanical component of mastering the competency in question), in which the mentor's response varies along a continuum of lesser to greater amounts of specific advice or direction about the protégé's performance. This task dimension involves such behaviors that could range from direct telling or demonstrating, to making suggestions, to asking questions of the protégé, to discussing possible options, to delegating the final decision to the protégé regarding the task at hand. The mentor's *task* response, however, embraces more than helping protégés' refine their functional performance tactics; it also encompasses the broadening and deepening of protégés' holistic understanding of professional/ occupational identity and its attending social, ethical, and moral aspects.

The key principle in correctly matching the A and D quadrants is that the mentor's *task* response must be *inverse in magnitude* to the extent of the protégé's competence level, and simultaneously, the extent of the mentor's *support* is similarly *inversely proportional* to the novice's level of confidence in performing the skill set. That is, the degree of the mentor's response is opposite to that of protégé's development level. For example, if the protégé has *high* confidence in performing the skill, the mentor responds by providing *low* support;

however, if the protégé's confidence in carrying out the task is *low*, the mentor reciprocates by bolstering it by giving a *high* degree of psycho-emotional support. In a similar way, if the protégé demonstrates high competence in doing the task, the mentor responds with low levels of direction; and correspondingly, the latter gives high task/direction if the protégé possesses low competence. The mentor's response is inversely proportional to the protégé's developmental level.

3. Monitor protégé's development. The mentorship pair continually and mutually monitors the protégé's ongoing level of development in each professional category, while the mentor accordingly synchronizes his/her adaptive response to match, in inverse proportions, the protégé's changing level(s).

Rationale Supporting Implementation of Adaptive Mentorship

One factor supporting the application of the AM model is, as we emphasized above, the expanding body of research being conducted on various aspects of the mentorship/supervisory process (Allen & Eby, 2007; Westlander, 2009). This research has indicated that although the relationship between mentors and protégés is typically positive (Linn, Howard, & Miller, 2004), increased diligence will be required (a) to maintain effectiveness in the process and (b) to reduce the chances of having inadequate or inappropriate guidance, unproductive mentoring responses, unacceptable supervisory interventions, or poor leader communication that often arise (Lortie, 1975; Ralph, Walker, & Wimmer, 2009; Taherian & Shekarchian, 2008).

A second factor related to supporting the AM model was the published endorsement of the model by one of North America's most respected management/leadership educators, Dr. Barry Posner. He acknowledged the model's research record and issued a public call to scholars and practitioners in management, organizational operations, and human resources to consider the model's further application (Posner, 2004).

A third influence supporting program organizers' consideration of Adaptive Mentorship is the current initiative of the Carnegie Foundation for the Advancement of Teaching (CFAT) (2010), which has given oversight to a large-scale project called the *Preparation for the Professions Program* (PPP). CFAT's ongoing research regarding the enhancement of the preparation of professionals in six fields (i.e., clergy, engineers, lawyers, nurses, physicians, and teachers) was supported by our own investigations (Ralph 2004, Ralph & Walker, 2010a, 2010b, 2011; Ralph, Walker, & Wimmer, 2010), all of which identified the mentorship program, within the clinical and practical phase of undergraduate professional education, as being a critical factor in protégé learning but also as needing bolstering.

Initial Research Findings

Much of the previous research on Adaptive Mentorship (Contextual Supervision, Ralph, 1998, 2005) was conducted with pre-service K–12 teachers and their mentors. However, research on the model was conducted in other fields as well: early childhood education (Watt, 1998), agricultural education (Fritz & Miller, 2004), and business management (Posner, 2004). With respect to mentorship in nursing, Hersey and Weaver Duldt (1989) reported using the Situational Leadership approach (Blanchard, 2010), a well-respected contingency model to which we referred in developing our AM and CS model. In our own research, we studied mentors' use of the model during the pre-service internship in teacher education, in which protégés developed their instructional proficiency in K–12 school settings under the guidance of classroom-based and faculty-based mentors, which have also been variously called advisors, supervisors, co-operating teachers, or facilitators, according to the terminology preferred in various organizational settings.

Over the past two decades, we have conducted research and disseminated our findings. These reports have documented initial findings of the model's application, subsequent refinements to its implementation, recent research results, and caveats for implementing it in practice (Ralph, 1993, 1998, 2004, 2005; Ralph & Walker, 2010a, 2011). Results from this research indicated that the AM (CS) models did in fact assist mentors and protégés in more clearly conceptualizing the whole mentoring process and in guiding mentors' leadership responses in the relationship. Conditions necessary for successfully implementing the AM model were similar to those identified in previous research (Fullan, Hill, & Crevola, 2006; Garvey, Stokes, & Megginson, 2009) regarding the adoption of other professional development initiatives. For instance, mentors obviously needed to have adequate training and sufficient time to become acquainted with the particular model being employed.

Ongoing Research

As a consequence of our recent receipt of a federally funded Public Outreach Grant from the Social Sciences and Humanities Research Council of Canada, we are, at the time of this writing, just completing a disseminating project, the mandate of which was for us to circulate the AM model both by means of (a) face-to-face presentations at selected centres across Canada, the United States, Europe, and the South Pacific and (b) the publication of documents, reports, and/or articles regarding the AM model and its related research.

At this juncture, we have conducted a series of 31 forums, workshops, or presentations at scholarly conferences, professional seminars, practitioner meetings, and academic conventions. At these gatherings, which ranged from one to 12 hours in length, and which were attended by groups ranging in size from two to 105 participants, we described the AM model, its rationale, its application, and its research record. In the longer workshops, attendees were able to practice using the model and/or to engage in simulated interactions applying its principles. At these sessions we collected evaluatory feedback concerning the AM model from 421 respondents, who volunteered to provide us with a written critique of the AM model. The confidentiality and anonymity of these respondents and their locations were maintained, and they were representative of a wide range of professional disciplines from several countries.

Respondents who chose to divulge their location/department/ unit represented the following fields: pre-K–12 education; higher education; institutional human resources divisions; post-secondary education registrar's offices; post-secondary teaching and learning or instructional development centres; post-secondary faculties of Business/Management, Dietetics/Nutrition, Education, English-as-an-Additional-Language, Engineering, Law, Medicine, Nursing, Pharmacy, and Theology; national banks; police and military training academies; and various departments in government, business and industry. Several individuals who were in private professional practice, in consulting firms, or who were graduate students in Master's and PhD programs also self-identified at various venues.

We provided open invitations to these meetings for personnel with an interest in or a desire to enhance the mentorship process offered in their respective units. We also assumed that attendees had been involved in mentorship programs or were interested in doing so, and by virtue of their experience/position, we thus considered them to be representative of a "panel of experts" (Wiersma & Jurs, 2005), capable of providing us with objective feedback and candid judgment regarding the efficacy of the AM model.

At the beginning of each workshop, we advised participants that we would invite them at the end of the session to provide us with a voluntary and confidential evaluation of the model. This feedback form consisted of two questions: What was positive about the AM model? and What were its pitfalls/challenges? We advised respondents not to identify themselves or their place of employment, and we reaffirmed that their comments would thus be anonymous and confidential. We also informed attendees that we would be using their comments to assist us in refining the AM model and in improving future workshops.

To this point, our preliminary analysis of the comments presented by the 421-member cross-disciplinary panel of experts has revealed the following findings: (a) there was near unanimous agreement among all respondents that AM provides a useful framework by which to conceptualize the entire mentoring enterprise, (b) these experts provided twice as many positive than negative comments regarding the model, (c) AM provides mentors with specific guidance for responding to and promoting protégé growth, (d) the model systematizes an often intuitive operation that many mentors already practice, (e) AM can help reinterpret so-called "relationship difficulties" or "personality clashes" as often being mentors' mismatching of their A-response with a protégé's existing D-level, and subsequently correcting these mismatches before such mistakes escalate, and (f) anyone intending to use the model in their practice will have to be first provided with a sound rationale, clear explanations, sufficient training, ample practice (i.e., "mentoring of the mentors" themselves) in order to derive benefit from the AM model.

Concluding Comment

Up to the time of this writing, the research conducted on the Adaptive Mentorship model (and its predecessor, Contextual Supervision) suggested that it has potential to enhance both the conceptualization and the practice of mentoring in organizations wherever practitioners apply it in formal mentorship programs across the educational landscape. Although the AM model's strengths have been consistently identified over time, a lingering concern remains regarding its apparent ineffectiveness among a limited number of mentorship practitioners who have even been trained in its application. A key question therefore remains: If the model is, in fact, as efficacious as we, its developers claim it to be, then further research is warranted to seek ways that may reduce or eliminate this small but significant limitation. We therefore repeat Posner's (2004) call for interested researchers and/or practitioners to follow his example first of trying the model, as was done at the Leavey School of Business, and then of accepting his invitation: "Let's hear from you about your own experience" (p. 151). We conclude this article by echoing that invitation.

In several chapters in Part 2 of the present volume, the authors describe either their direct experience using AM in their respective contexts or their indirect speculations regarding adapting the model to fit a variety of future mentorship settings.

Open Invitation

We also invite interested scholars, researchers, or practitioners with a curiosity in enhancing the mentorship process across all professional disciplines to consider adopting the AM model in their own mentoring settings, studying the results, and contributing to the growing research literature regarding its effects.

Acknowledgement

The authors acknowledge the receipt of a Public Outreach Grant from the Social Sciences and Humanities Research Council of Canada for the purpose of disseminating the AM model across the professional disciplines. This chapter and this book are two such dissemination outlets.

The authors also thank Dr. Anthony Clarke from the Centre for the Study of Teacher Education at the University of British Columbia, and Brenda Mergel from the College of Education at the University of Saskatchewan, for their insight and assistance in formatting the AM model in Figure 1.

References

Allen, T., & Eby, L. (Eds.). (2007). *The Blackwell handbook of mentoring: A multiple perspective approach*. Malden, MA: Blackwell.

Bauer, T., & Erdogan, B. (2009). *Organizational behavior*. Available from http://catalog.flatworldknowledge.com/catalog/editions/145

Blanchard, K. (2010). *Leading at a higher level* (Rev. ed.). Upper Saddle River, NJ: Pearson/FT Press/Blanchard Management Corporation.

Carnegie Foundation for the Advancement of Teaching. (2010). *PPP (Preparation for the Professions Program) publications archive*. Retrieved from http://www.carnegiefoundation.org/publications/ppp-publications

Carpenter, M., Bauer, T., & Erdogan, B. (2009). *Principles of management*. Available from http://catalog.flatworldknowledge.com/catalog/editions/159

Chu, C. (2005). Aid as a mentoring relationship. In K. Sanga, C. Chu, C. Hall, & L. Crowl (Eds.), *Re-thinking aid relationships in Pacific education* (pp. 394–408). Wellinton, NZ: Victoria University of Wellington, He Parekereke Institute for Research and Development in Maori and Pacific Education.

Ellsum, W., & Pedersen, C. (2005). *Does coaching work without mentorship in management development?* Paper at ANZAM 2005: Engaging the multiple contexts of management convergence and divergence of management theory and practice, 7–10 Dec 2005, Canberra, Australia. Retrieved from http://eprints.usq.edu.au/1760/

Fiedler, F., & Garcia, J. (1987). *New Approaches to leadership, cognitive resources and organizational performance*. New York, NY: John Wiley and Sons.

Fritz, C. A., & Miller, G. (2004). Supervisory practices used by teacher educators in agriculture: A comparison of doctoral/research extensive and research non-extensive institutions. *Journal of Agricultural Education, 45*(4), 46–56.

Fullan, M., Hill, P., & Crevola, C. (2006). *Breakthrough*. Thousand Oaks, CA: Corwin/Sage and Ontario Principals' Council.

Garvey, B., Stokes, P., & Megginson, D. (2009). *Coaching and mentoring: Theory and practice*. London, UK: Sage.

Hersey, P., & Blanchard, K. (1988). *Management of organizational behavior: Utilizing human resources* (5th ed.). Englewood Cliffs, NJ: Prentice-Hall.

Hersey, P. & Weaver Duldt, B. (1989). *Situational leadership in nursing*. Norwalk , CT: Appleton & Lange.

Javed, R. (2009, February 19). *Why study management?* [Online article]. Retrieved from http://www.articlesbase.com/management-articles/why-study-management-780332.html

Linn, P., Howard, A., & Miller, E. (Eds.). (2004). *Handbook for research in cooperative education and internships*. Mahwah, NJ: Lawrence Erlbaum.

Lortie, D. (1975). *Schoolteacher: A Sociological study*. Chicago, IL: University of Chicago.

Miller, L., & Homan Blanchard, M. (2010). Coaching: A key competency for leadership development. In K. Blanchard (Ed.), *Leading at a higher level* (Rev. ed., pp. 149–163). Upper Saddle River, NJ: Pearson/FT Press/Blanchard Management Corporation.

Posner, B. (2004). Reflections on experience: Editor's introduction. *Journal of Management Inquiry, 13*(2), 151.

Ralph, E. (1993).Sensitive, sensible practicum supervision: A contextual application in Saskatchewan. *The Alberta Journal of Educational Research, 32*, 283–296.

Ralph, E. (1998). *Developing practitioners: A handbook of contextual supervision*. Stillwater, OK: New Forums Press.

Ralph, E. (2000). Aligning mentorship style with beginning teachers' development: Contextual supervision. *The Alberta Journal of Educational Research, 46*(4), 311–326.

Ralph, E. (2004). Developing managers' effectiveness: A model with potential. *Journal of Management Inquiry, 13*(2), 151–163.

Ralph, E. (2005). Enhancing managers'supervisory effectiveness: A promising model. *Journal of Management Development, 24*(3), 267–284.

Ralph. E., & Walker, K. (2010a). Enhancing mentors' effectiveness: The promise of the Adaptive Mentorship model. *McGill Journal of Education, 45*(2), 205–218. Available at http://mje.mcgill.ca/index.php/MJE/article/view/4653

Ralph, E., & Walker, K. (2010b). Rising with the tide: Applying Adaptive Mentorship in the professional practicum. In A. Wright, M. Wilson, & D. MacIsaac, (Eds.), *Collection of Essays on Learning and Teaching* (CELT Vol. 3, pp. 1–8). Hamilton, ON: Society for Teaching and Learning in Higher Education.

Ralph, E., & Walker, K. (2011). Enhancing mentoring in management via the Adaptive Mentorship model. *The International Journal of Knowledge, Culture and Change Management, 10*(8), 35–43.

Ralph, E., Walker, K., & Wimmer, R. (2008).The clinical/practicum experience in professional preparation: Preliminary findings. *McGill Journal of Education, 43*(2), 157–172. Retrieved from http://mje.mcgill.ca/article/view/682/2242

Ralph, E., Walker, K., & Wimmer, R. (2009). Deficiencies in the practicum phase of field-based education: Students' views. *Northwest Passage: Journal of Educational Practices, 7*(1), 74–86.

Ralph, E. Walker, K., & Wimmer, R. (Eds.). (2010). *The practicum in professional education: Canadian perspectives.* Calgary, AB: Detselig Enterprises.

Rose Ragins, B., & Kram, K. (Eds.). (2007). *The handbook of mentoring at work: Theory, research, and practice.* Los Angeles, CA: Sage.

Schoonover, S. (2002). *Six sigma leadership: The key to sustaining contemporary quality programs.* Retrieved from http://www.slideshare.net/Sixsigmacentral/six-sigma-leadership-the-key-to-sustaining-contemporary

Scott, J. (n.d.). *The purpose of management.* Retrieved from http://www.jonathantscott.com/supplemental-material/ the-purpose-of-management

Steers, R., Sanchez-Runde, C., & Nardon, L. (2010). *Management across cultures: Challenges and strategies.* New York, NY: Cambridge University Press.

Taherian, K., & Shekarchian, M. (2008). Mentoring for doctors: Do its benefits outweigh its disadvantages? *Medical Teacher, 30*(4), 95–99.

Thompson, H. (2008). *Coaching: A global study of successful practices.* Available from http://www.amanet.org/training/articles/ Coaching-A-Global-Study-of-Successful-Practices-02.aspx

Watt, S. (1998). *An examination of contextual supervision in a preschool practicum setting* (Unpublished master's thesis). Simon Fraser University, Burnaby, BC.

Westlander, G. (2009, August). Book review [Review of the two books, The handbook of mentoring at work: Theory, research and practice by B. Rose Ragins & K. Kram, and Coaching and mentoring: Theory and practice by B. Garvey, P. Stokes, & D. Megginson]. *International Journal of Evidence Based Coaching and Mentoring, 7*(2), 82–96. Retrieved from http://www.business.brookes.ac.uk/research/areas/coachingandmentoring/ documents/vol07issue2-bookreview-01.pdf

Wiersma, W., & Jurs, S. (2005). *Research methods in education: An introduction* (8th ed.). Boston, MA: Pearson Allyn and Bacon.

Chapter Seventeen

The Effect of Adaptive Mentorship© on EAL Students' Writing Development

Roya Khoii

WRITING IS A DIFFICULT SKILL for learners of second or additional languages (L2) to master. According to Richards and Renandya (2002), the difficulty lies not only in generating and organizing ideas but also in translating these ideas into readable text. These authors argued that the skills involved in writing are highly complex and that L2 writers have to focus on the higher cognitive level skills of planning and organizing as well as the lower-level skills of spelling, punctuation, word choice, and so on. The difficulty becomes even more pronounced if student writers are at a low level of language proficiency.

The complex nature of writing has led some researchers to focus on L2 writers and specifically on L2 writer variables. These variables have been divided into five basic categories: L2 variables, first language variables, transfer variables, psychological and sociological variables, and demographic variables (Leki, Cumming, & Silva, 2008). Given the variety inherent in each of these categories, one can see how differently each individual writer might approach a writing task and how the differences among different students might affect their learning to write and production of written texts. Dörnyei and Skehan (2005) concluded that individual differences in L2 learning have generated the most consistent predictors of overall L2 learning success.

In the field of learning and teaching additional languages, learning to write fluently and correctly seems to be of prime importance as a gate-keeping activity. Moreover, judgments of the performance of an individual may have consequences for the writer, such as exclusion from or successful entry into a specific discourse community. Also, writing is an important skill in supporting other learning experiences in that it is a means of recording, assimilating, and reformulating knowledge and of developing writers' own ideas. Not only that, but writing is often a means of personal discovery, creativity, and self-expression.

Considerable research has been conducted in order to explore the effect of various techniques on helping L2 learners become better writers. There are many factors that can be studied regarding the complex nature of this skill, such as the diversity that characterizes FL writing in terms of writing processes, the variety of textual outputs and pedagogical approaches (Manchón, 2009), the interplay of social, linguistic, and cognitive variables that shape the development of writing ability over time in L2 contexts, and the multilingual nature of L2 writing. However, it seems that all such studies tend to focus on the effect of these techniques on the overall performance of a given group of students rather than on how each individual benefits from the techniques in the specific context in which individuals are learning to write.

I have advocated a more individualized approach to teaching L2 writing, and I thus conducted the present study to examine the effect of applying a certain mentoring/teaching model, called Adaptive Mentorship (AM) (Ralph & Walker, 2010a, 2010b), on the development of writing among L2 students.

Writing in English

According to Cumming (2009), two interrelated changes have occurred in education internationally – namely, the global spread of English and the increasing prominence/value of written communications. There has also been a corresponding expansion in expectations for writing L2 education. Since the 1980s, the research on L2 writing has greatly expanded professional knowledge about learners' writing abilities and the multiple components and processes involved in learning to write. Cumming argued that L2 writing may represent a set of skills distinct from reading, listening, and speaking skills – unlike how they are commonly considered today in curricula and assessments.

However, the dimensions of writing skill entail numerous micro and macro components and processes that complement and interact with one another in complex ways and at multiple levels of texts, in a variety of language systems, with individual writers, and within numerous educational and social contexts. He believed that understanding these elements and their interrelationships would help identify and clarify what specifically needs to be learned to acquire writing abilities in L2.

At a micro level are the linguistic elements, text forms, learner attitudes, and thinking processes that a person must acquire control of in order to write in a L2. At a macro level are a host of influencing factors such as (a) educational and professional policies, (b) local, national, and international resources and standards applied to implement these policies, (c) established norms for writing genres of specific discourse communities, and (d) international trends such as the increasing spread and local diversification of lingua franca languages like English (Cumming, 2009).

Approaches to Writing

Typically, teachers of writing are concerned with the final product of writing. This approach is totally teacher-centred and product- or output-focused. The weakness of this product approach is that process skills are relatively less important, so the learners' existing knowledge and skills are either ignored or undervalued.

A product-oriented approach to the development of writing favors classroom activities in which the learner is engaged in imitating, copying, and transforming models of correct language. This process usually occurs at the level of the sentence (Nunan, 1991). While useful in its own place, the product approach is not in accord with more contemporary views of language and learning that concentrates more on language at the level of discourse. In addition, as Nunan observed, instead of emphasizing only completed texts, contemporary teachers of writing have become much more interested in the processes writers go through in composing texts. Competent writers do not produce final texts at their first attempt. Writing is in fact a long and often painful process in which the final product emerges through successive drafts.

Process approaches, on the other hand, are based on the notion that writing is an iterative process. Stages of the writing process can happen in a variety of orders within different contexts. This writing process is not a rigid, step-by-step activity, and it usually involves many twists, turns, stops, and starts. In process approaches, the teacher primarily facilitates the learners' writing, placing less importance on solely providing input or stimulus. Here, the role of a teacher is less of a didactic instructor.

The idea behind process writing is not to dissociate writing entirely from the written product and to merely lead students through the various stages of the writing process but "to construct process-oriented writing instruction that will affect performance" (Freedman, Dyson, Flower, & Chafe, 1987). To have an effective performance-oriented teaching program would mean that teachers would need to systematically teach students certain problem-solving skills connected with the writing process (Seow, 2002).

Moreover, according to Zamel (1987), a writing program should take into account the learners' purposes for writing, which would transcend the focus on only producing final texts for teacher evaluation. Writing skills can develop rapidly when students' concerns and interests are acknowledged, when they are given multiple opportunities to write, and when they are encouraged to become participants in a community of writers. Finally, she suggested that teachers should themselves become action researchers in their own classrooms and apply insights from what they have learned in a meaningful and relevant way – that is, to improve instruction and learning.

Despite insights into the complexities of the composing/writing process revealed by process-oriented studies, writing classes in academic situations in the country where I conducted this present study were often based on mechanistic, product-oriented activities that research has largely discredited (Zammel, 1987). Teachers of writing often overrate the role of grammatical accuracy and complexity at the expense of fluency of writing. Moreover, in spite of the studies conducted on the important role of psychological/affective factors on the development of the writing skill (Cheng, 2004; Dörnyei, 2003; Petric, 2002), many teachers focus on the formal aspects of their students' written work, both when they are teaching and also when they are providing feedback to students. These teachers tend to pay relatively little attention to how their approach might affect the students' self-confidence, their attitude to writing in L2, their motivation to write, and their affective reactions to assigned writing tasks.

Feedback to Writing

Providing feedback to students, whether in the form of written commentary, error correction, teacher-student conferencing, or peer discussion, has come to be recognized as one of the L2 writing teacher's most important responsibilities. However, to consistently offer this kind of individualized attention is often rarely possible under normal classroom conditions (Hyland & Hyland, 2006).

Surveys of students' feedback preferences indicated that EAL students value teacher written feedback and consistently rate it more highly than alternative forms such as peer feedback and oral feedback in writing conferences (Hyland & Hyland, 2006; Leki, 1991; Saito, 1994). Leki (1991) suggested that L2 teachers may be fulfilling several different and possibly conflicting roles as they respond to student writing. When giving feedback, teachers have to choose the appropriate language and style to accomplish a range of informational, pedagogic, and interpersonal goals. Studies of L2 students' reactions to teacher feedback showed that learners remember and value encouraging remarks, and that they expect to receive constructive criticism rather than simple platitudes (Ferris, 1995; Hyland & Hyland, 2006). However, many teachers are conscious of the potentially damaging effect of critical comments on students, and this aspect can translate into a reluctance among teachers to correct errors directly. Hyland and Hyland (2001) suggested that teachers often seek to mitigate the full force of their criticisms and suggestions, taking the impact from them with hedges, questions, or personal attribution. Nevertheless, this kind of implicit approach to critique might also result in students failing to grasp the point being made and thus to misinterpret the response.

Studies of teacher commentary on student writing have highlighted a number of specific issues and implications for L2 writing instructors (Ferris, 2006), some of which are:

~: Teachers should provide feedback on all aspects of student texts, including content, rhetorical structure, grammar, and mechanics.

~: Teacher feedback should be clear and concrete to assist students with revision. At the same time, teachers need to be careful not to appropriate student texts.

~: Teacher feedback must take individual and contextual variables into account.

~: ESL writers attend to teacher feedback and attempt to utilize it in their revisions.

The needs, desires, and abilities of individual student writers with regard to feedback are often overlooked by researchers and theorists. Teachers, in their efforts to be consistent, may forget that "one size does not fit all," and that different students with different cognitive and affective characteristics may require different types of feedback and guidance in terms of their writing.

Learning is based on the individual's characteristics. The approach and teaching style of the teacher is also important in the learning process (Mark, 2009). In recent years, teaching has changed and is more centred on student needs and individual differences in learning. Teachers are encouraged to differentiate their instruction in order to accommodate all students. Various instructional methods and resources are used, such as (a) the auditory mode (e.g., lectures in secondary and post-secondary levels), (b) interactive group-work that encourage discussion, and (c) visual and tactile technologies and media.

With respect to the psychological and emotional dimension, many students require encouragement in order to boost their individual motivation to persevere in the process of learning, while others are more motivated and autonomous. Some students need the teacher's regular confirmation to gain self-confidence, while others seem to have a high level of self-esteem. Some learners may begin the process of learning with fear, apprehension, and hatred, while others exude a consistently positive attitude towards learning. One of the greatest challenges of teaching is that this whole range of individual student characteristics exists in a typical classroom, requiring teachers to work with them all.

I believe that the Adaptive Mentorship (AM) model has potential to help teachers meet these learning and teaching challenges. AM has mechanisms be that L2 teachers could apply to assist them to be responsive to the needs of individual students in the area of L2 writing.

Adaptive Mentorship

To most educators, mentorship refers to a personal developmental relationship in which a more experienced or more knowledgeable person helps a less experienced or less knowledgeable person. The receiver of mentorship was traditionally referred to as a *protégé* or apprentice, but with the institutionalization of mentoring, a more neutral word, *mentee*, seems more widely used today.

There are several definitions of mentoring in the literature, most of which include characteristics such as relationship-based communication between people with greater relevant knowledge and experience (the mentor) and persons who have less (the protégé), formal and informal interaction, psycho-emotional support relevant to work or career professional development (Bozeman & Feeney, 2007).

Adaptive Mentorship (AM), formerly called Contextual Supervision (Ralph, 1996), is a promising mentoring model that has proven effective in enhancing the mentorship/supervisory process (Ralph & Walker, 2010a, 2010b). This model has been derived from a range of contingency and situational leadership approaches (Blake & Mouton, 1978; Hersey & Blanchard, 1988; Fiedler & Garcia, 1987).

AM focuses on mentors adjusting their mentorship behavior in response to the task-specific development level of protégés they are assisting in the learning/employment situation, as represented in Figure 1.

According to Ralph and Walker (2010a, 2010b), the outer border of the diagram represents the context of the mentorship relationship, including the psychological, social, organizational, and cultural factors within the work (in my case, the instructional) setting. The researchers emphasized that many of these influences cannot be changed by the mentor or the protégé; however, the key factor over which the participants do have direct control is their own behavior. Ralph and Walker added that mentors/instructors can change their mentorship response concerning the two dimensions shown

Figure 1

Adaptive Mentorship. The mentor matches his/her adaptive response to coincide with the skill-specific developmental level of his/her protégé. Adapted from Ralph, 1996 and Ralph & Walker, 2010a, 2010b.

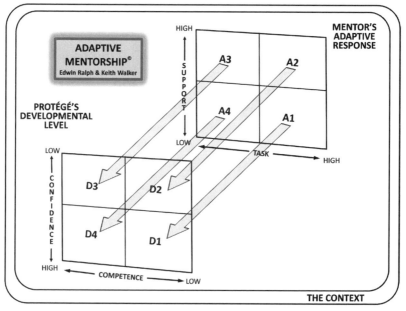

in the A-grid of Figure 1 – namely, their adaptive "task" response (the degree of direction given regarding the technical, mechanical, or procedural aspect of the protégé's performance) and their adaptive "support" response (the degree of expression regarding the "human" or psycho/social/emotional aspect of the protégé's learning).

For the protégés, the key element over which they have most control is their competency-specific developmental level in performing particular skill sets (Ralph, 1996; Ralph & Walker, 2010a, 2010b). This developmental level consists of two dimensions: the protégé's developmental "competence" level (his/her ability to perform the task or skill being learned) and his/her developmental "confidence" level (the degree of self-assurance, composure, and feelings of security and/or safety in performing the skill set). The researchers explained that the core of the AM model is represented by the larger arrows linking the D-grid with the A-grid, which portray the mentor's matching of one of four typical adaptive "A" responses with a similarly numbered "D" developmental level exhibited by the protégé in his/her performance of the particular competency. (Of course, these four combinations are simply representative of numerous matching combinations that could exist within the grids.)

Ralph, Walker, & Wimmer (2008) also argued for the transferability of AM because it may be adapted by mentors in any field to assist protégés in developing professional proficiency in their respective contexts.

Methodology

In the present study, I examined the effect of the application of the AM Model to teaching writing to EAL students in my classroom. Given the circumstances and the variables under investigation, I was the teacher who functioned as the mentor and my students were the protégés in the study.

Participants

I carried out this research in an intact essay-writing class consisting of 24 junior university students studying English Translation at Islamic Azad University, North Tehran Branch, one student of which dropped the course towards the end of the semester. Thus the N was 23.

Instruments and materials

The resource used for teaching writing in the class was *College Writing Skills*, John Langan (2004). I used the following instruments to collect the data on the variables of this study:

- ❖: a modified version of Clément and Baker's (2001) English self-confidence questionnaire used both at the outset and end of the treatment;
- ❖: the D- and A-grids of the AM Model used both at the outset and end of the study;
- ❖: a writing-attitude questionnaire adapted from Rose (1984) used both at the outset and end of the study;

~: an essay writing pretest on the topic "The Uses of Computers in Modern Life";

~: 16 essays written by students on various topics in various genres;

~: some model essays extracted from the participants' textbook; and

~: an essay writing post-test on the same topic as the pretest.

Applying Adaptive Mentorship

According to Ralph and Walker (2010a, 2010b), the application of AM consists of three phases: determine the development level, synchronize mentor response, and continually observe and adapt mentor's response. I attempted to follow these procedures in conducting the study.

1. Determine Development Level

At the outset of the study I administered a modified version of Clément and Baker's English self-confidence questionnaire and a writing-attitude questionnaire adapted from Rose (1984) to the participants, in order to ascertain their level of self-confidence and writing-attitude prior to the intervention. I then asked the students to locate themselves and their previous writing instructors (in the Advanced Writing Course, which was a prerequisite to this Essay Writing Course) in the cells on the D- and A- grids, respectively, where they believed they and their teachers had been functioning at that time. I collected and entered the data into a spreadsheet, and stored them for later analysis. I also asked them to perform a self-evaluation of their writing competence at this beginning point in my course, which helped me make a better judgment of their writing ability levels at that stage.

Based on the data obtained from the above instruments, I identified students placed at varying levels of self-confidence, attitude to writing, and competency in writing. Moreover, they provided me with their reactions regarding the affective and cognitive feedback that the students received from their prior writing instructors.

These data helped me to divide the students into subgroups in terms of affective and competence dimensions.

2. Synchronize Mentor Response

My teaching intervention started with the explanation of the whole writing process, the formal rules of writing, the different parts of an academic essay, and the significance of developing good writing abilities in one's academic and professional career. Then I provided students with a sample model essay to help them observe and learn the rules in practice. In order to measure the participants' writing competence, they were given a writing pretest on the topic "The uses of computers in modern life." I scored their essays holistically, and asked one of my colleagues to score them independently. The inter-rater reliability computed through the Pearson Product Moment formula was equal to 0.92, which was quite satisfactory. The length of each essay was also measured by using the word-count option in the Microsoft Word program.

In each class session, I assigned the students to write an essay on a given topic related to their needs, interests, and background knowledge. We did some brainstorming on the topic to help them generate ideas and share them with their classmates. There were some students who participated more in this process, while others kept silent. I tried to recognize these quieter ones by asking them simple questions or simply requesting them to write their ideas in the form of outlines and share them with the class. I purposefully encouraged their participation and expressed my appreciation when they did volunteer. I also offered more assistance (given out of the class at specific times) to students who had lower levels of self-confidence or who had negative attitudes to writing.

Altogether the students wrote 16 essays in different genres during the four-month course, and I required them to write the essays at home using the Microsoft Word program. In order to provide the necessary cognitive feedback, I assessed all essays by identifying every error and by providing the corrected form, but I scored each essay using a holistic approach. I also typed various notations at the bottom of the paper for every student. I deliberately composed these notes for the low self-confidence and lower attitude students with a more encouraging and supportive tone. Some of the good student writers had also demonstrated negative attitudes to writing, and I believed that for them, in spite of receiving adequate help for the task/competence aspect, they had not previously received enough affective feedback from their writing teachers so as to encourage them to continue writing in future. Therefore, I also expended particular effort to recognize their concerns and input, and I provided them with added psycho-socio-emotional support in order to help reduce their negative perspectives.

There were also some students in the group who exhibited computerphobia. I purposefully provided them with individualized instruction in terms of word processing, which they seemed to greatly appreciate. Because the students wrote their essays using computers, they also received continual feedback and assistance from the word processor in terms of spelling, capitalization, punctuation, grammar, and formatting of their essays. I found this extra technological support to be beneficial because of the additional individualized instruction it provided.

I met personally with all protégés/students once a week in class, but they were also free to voluntarily visit me during specifically posted times and to receive extra guidance for their writing. They could also send me their questions or concerns via email.

3. Continually Observe and Adapt Mentor Response

The students' responses regarding where they saw me functioning on the mentorship A- grid provided me valuable information regarding how to adapt my mentorship style to more accurately match the students' developmental levels. I monitored the students' progress closely in terms of their changing competence and self-confidence levels by comparing (a) their holistic scores on each successive essay with their previous performance, (b) their later patterns of participation in class discussions with their earlier ones, and (c) noting their responses to (and interactions with) me during my paired dialogs with them. These data helped me to synchronize my adaptive response to match, in inverse degrees, the students' changing development levels. As a student advanced from D1 to D2, or D2 to D3, or D3 to D4, or other combinations, I would carefully adjust my "task" and "support" behaviors with each student to try to reciprocate by matching my response to fit their then-current competence and confidence levels (i.e., by responding correspondingly with A1, A2, A3, and A4, as described in the AM model).

At the end of the four-month study, I requested the students to again fill in the self-confidence and attitude questionnaires, as well as the D- and A- grid, in order to determine if changes occurred. Furthermore, I assigned them an essay writing post-test on the same topic as the pretest to ascertain if there had been any progress in the students' writing competence as a result of my adaptive mentorship. As was the case for the pretest, the post-test papers were scored by two raters – me and a colleague. I employed the Pearson Product formula to compute the inter-rater reliability between the two raters, which was calculated to yield 0.91, which was again a desirable score.

Data Analysis

In order to determine if my mentorship intervention had been effective, I submitted the data to several statistical analyses. Initially I computed the descriptive statistics for all the instruments, and I computed the mean lengths of the writing pretest and post-test. (See Table 1.)

Then I ran a series of paired-samples t-tests in order to check the significance of the differences between the means of the first and second administrations of the different instruments used in this study. (See Table 2.)

As shown in Table 2, all the differences were significant at the 0.05 level. The students had obtained higher scores on the second administrations of the attitude and self-confidence questionnaires compared to the first ones. The differences are shown in Figures 2 and 3.

The students also obtained higher holistic scores on their writing post-test as compared to their pretest. In Figure 4 I illustrate the difference between the means of the students' scores on the writing pretest and post-test.

Table 1

Descriptive Statistics for all the Instruments

Instrument	N	Mean	SD	Min. Score	Max. score
Attitude 1	23	64.87	14.98	34	101
Attitude 2	23	73.87	10.42	52	95
Self-confidence1	23	37.29	7.48	19	54
Self-confidence2	23	42.75	8.25	30	58
Pre-test	22	11.77	2.94	8	17
Post-test	22	15.64	1.94	12	19
Length 1 (pretest)	22	344.42	79.14	187	582
Length 2 (post-test)	23	411.08	110.07	272	737

Table 2

T-test Results for Comparison of Means

Instrument	t-observed	Df	Sig (2-tailed)
Attitude Qs	5.055	22	*.000
Self-confidence Qs	4.654	22	*.000
Pretest-post-test	9.138	22	*.000
Length of pretest and post-test	3.916	22	*.001

Qs = Questionnaires * = significant at the 0.05 level

Table 3

Responses to the D-grid on the First and Second Administrations

Cells in the D-grid	First Administration	Second Administration
D1	2	8
D2	12	3
D3	7	4
D4	2	8

Figure 2

Means of the two administrations of the attitude questionnaire

Figure 3

Means of the two administrations of the self-confidence questionnaire

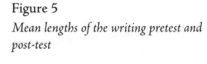

Figure 4

Means of scores on the writing pretest and post-test

Figure 5

Mean lengths of the writing pretest and post-test

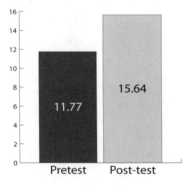

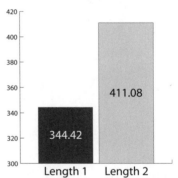

Table 4

Agreement Between D- and A-Grid Placements in First and Second Administrations

First administration	Second administration
3	13

Another interesting finding here pertained to the lengths of the students' writing pretest and post-test. As illustrated in Figure 5, the mean length of the students' scores on the pretest was 344.42, but it increased to 411.08 on the post-test. As mentioned above, the related t-test result indicated that the difference was statistically significant at the 0.05 level.

A comparison of each individual student's performances on the post-test and pretest also revealed that the weaker students' scores had contributed to the rise in the overall means on all the measures used in the study.

In the next phase of the study, the patterns of the responses of the participants to the D- and A-grids were also compared with each other. According to Ralph (1996), D1 typifies an *eager novice* or *enthusiastic beginner*, D2 characterizes a *fearful neophyte* or a *disillusioned amateur*, D3 describes a *reluctant contributor* or an *insecure leader*, and D4 exemplifies a *peak performer* or a *calm expert*.

As indicated in Table 3, on the first administration of the D-grid there were 12 disillusioned amateurs (D2), seven reluctant contributors (D3), two eager novices (D1), and two calm experts (D4). After using their responses to the A-grid as a criterion for providing my subsequent mentorship response, their self-placements on the D-grid were also studied at the end of the study. This second time there were three disillusioned amateurs (D2), four reluctant contributors (D3), eight eager novices (D1), and eight calm experts (D4).

A comparison of the responses to the A-grid on the two administrations also revealed some promising results. As shown in Table 4, comparing to only three cases of match between the cells on the D- and A-grids at the outset of the study, there were 13 cases of match at the end of the study. This finding suggested that I, in my role as adaptive mentor, had been quite successful in adjusting my mentorship response to match the developmental level of my mentees. This adaptation appeared to result in the improvement of their writing ability, the elevation of their self-confidence, and the increase in their positive attitude toward writing.

Discussion

My purpose in this study was to demonstrate that using a more individualized instructional approach to writing that was based on building human relationships could help L2 learners overcome difficulties when writing. Based on this study's findings, I am confident in suggesting that replacing traditional L2 teaching with a more individualistic style of mentoring based on the Adaptive Mentorship model can yield promising results. I found that a deeper understanding of interpersonal considerations can positively influence EAL writers both affectively and cognitively.

According to Hyland and Hyland (2006) learners vary considerably in what they desire from their teachers in terms of feedback. These authors also maintained that students have their own concerns and agendas, and it is important that teachers seek to discover these aspects and try to address them when providing student feedback. Teachers of L2 writing need to tailor their feedback comments to the needs and personalities of their students as well as to the teaching context. The application of Adaptive Mentorship assisted me to recognize the specific learning needs of my students and to provide each of them with the appropriate type of response. The results suggested that participants managed to raise their level of self-confidence, to develop a more positive attitude to writing, and to improve their overall writing ability.

A finding I found interesting was the low level of attrition in the class. My previous teaching experience prior to employing the AM approach showed that usually one third of the students left my writing classes during the first month of instruction and only half of the remainder would take the final exam. In this study, however, I was pleasantly surprised to see that the class started with 24 students and finished with 23.

Relying on a "one size fits all" approach in instructional settings often leads teachers to prejudge and marginalize some students and leads to the growth of resentment and antagonism between students and teacher or, in best cases, the existence of neutrality on the part of less self-confident and less proficient students. With the traditional approach, good writers become better writers, but the weaker ones often feel increasingly frustrated and develop a negative attitude towards the writing process, the writing course, and perhaps the writing teacher! However, from this study of applying the AM model, one sees that using a mentoring style that is more responsive to each individual student's cognitive and affective needs will lead to better results in terms of students' writing, self-image, and attitude toward writing.

Future work

The results of this study can be of interest to L2 teachers who are looking for effective approaches to solve their students' difficulties with learning to write in L2. However, the application of the AM model certainly requires some training on the part of teachers. They should also transform the conception of their own role as teachers into mentors. In other words, instead of trying to prescribe the same rules for good writing and providing the same kind of feedback to all students, they should recognize that "one size does not fit all" and should try to individualize and differentiate their method of teaching/mentoring to some extent in order to meet their students' various learning needs.

I believe that L2 teachers would do well to also consider this model in teaching other language skills such as reading, speaking, listening, vocabulary, phonology, and grammar.

Acknowledgements

This research was supported by a grant from Islamic Azad University, North Tehran Branch.

I would like to express my deepest appreciation to Professor Edwin Ralph, who greatly inspired me for conducting this research by the excellent workshop he conducted in Canada International Conference on Education (CICE 2010). He also provided me generously with all the required sources in relation to the AM Model and guided me through the various stages of this study.

Note: This chapter is an extended version of a presentation delivered at the Canadian International Conference on Education (CICE 2011) in Toronto, 4–7 April, 2011.

References

Blake, R., & Mouton, J. (1978). *The new management grid*. Houston, TX: Gulf.

Bozeman, B., & Feeney, M. K. (2007). Toward a useful theory of mentoring: A conceptual analysis and critique. *Administration and Society, 39*(6), 719–739.

Cheng, Y. S. (2004). A measure of second language writing anxiety: Scale development and preliminary validation. *Journal of Second Language Writing, 13*, 313–335.

Clément, R., & Baker, S. C. (2001). *Measuring social aspects of L2 acquisition and use: Scale characteristics and administration* [Technical Report]. Ottawa, ON: University of Ottawa.

Cumming, A. (2009). The contribution of studies of foreign language writing to research, theories and policies. In R. M. Manchón (Ed.), *Writing in foreign language contexts: Learning, teaching, and research* (pp. 209–230). Bristol, UK: Multilingual Matters.

Dörnyei, Z. (2003). Attitudes, orientation, and motivations in language learning: Advances in theory, research, and applications. *Language Learning* [Supplement], 53, 3–32. doi:10.1111/1467-9922.53222

Dörnyei, Z., & Skehan, P. (2005). Individual differences in second language learning. In C. J. Doughty & M. H. Long (Eds.), *The handbook of second language acquisition* (pp. 589–630). Oxford, UK: Blackwell.

Ferris, D. (1995). Student reactions to teacher response in multiple-draft composition classrooms. *TESOL Quarterly, 29*, 33–54.

Ferris, D. (2006). Responding to writing. In B. Kroll (Ed.), *Exploring the dynamics of second language writing* (pp. 119–140). New York, NY: Cambridge University Press.

Fiedler, F., & Garcia, J. (1987). *New approaches to leadership, cognitive resources and organizational performance*. New York, NY: John Wiley and Sons.

Freedman, S., Dyson, A., Flower, L., & Chafe, W. (1987). *Research in writing: Past, present, and future* [Technical Report No. 1]. Berkeley, CA: Center for the Study of Writing.

Hersey, P., & Blanchard, K. (1988). *Management of organizational behavior: Utilizing human resources* (5th ed.). Englewood Cliffs, NJ: Prentice-Hall.

Hyland, F., & Hyland, K. (2001). Sugaring the pill: Praise and criticism in written feedback. *Journal of Second Language Writing, 10*(3), 185–212.

Hyland, K., & Hyland, F. (2006). *Feedback in second language writing: Contexts and issues.* New York, NY: Cambridge University Press.

Langan, J. (2004). *College writing skills* (6th ed.). New York, NY: McGraw-Hill.

Leki, I. (1991). The preferences of ESL students for error correction in college level writing classes. *Foreign Language Annals, 24*(3), 203–218.

Leki, I., Cumming, A., & Silva, T. (2008). *A synthesis of research on second language writing in English.* New York, NY: Routledge.

Manchón, R. M. (2009). Broadening the perspective of L2 writing scholarship: The contribution of research on foreign language writing. In M. Manchón (Ed.), *Writing in foreign language contexts: Learning, teaching, and research* (pp. 1–19). Bristol, UK: Multilingual Matters.

Mark, L. (2009, March 25). Importance of individualized teaching. *Journal of Classroom Teaching and Learning.* Retrieved from http://joctl.blogspot.com/2009/04/importance-of-individualized-teaching.html

Nunan, D. (1991). *Language teaching methodology: A textbook for teachers.* Maylands, UK: Prentice Hall.

Petric, B. (2002). Students' attitudes towards writing and the development of academic writing skills. *The Writing Center Journal, 22*(2), 9–27.

Ralph, E. (1996). Contextual supervision: Matching supervisory styles with learners' needs. *Canadian Administrator, 35*(3), 1–11.

Ralph, E., & Walker, K. (2010a). Enhancing mentors' effectiveness: The promise of the Adaptive Mentorship model. *McGill Journal of Education, 45*(2), 205–218. Retrieved from http://mje.mcgill.ca/index.php/MJE/article/view/4653/6388

Ralph, E., & Walker, K. (2010b). Rising with the tide: Applying adaptive mentorship in the professional practicum. In A. Wright,

M. Wilson, & D. MacIsaac (Eds.), *Collection of essays on learning and teaching: Between the tides* (Volume 3, p. 3–8). Hamilton, ON: McMaster University, Society for Teaching and Learning in Higher Education. Retrieved from http://apps.medialab. uwindsor.ca/ctl/CELT/vol3/CELTVOL3.pdf

Ralph, E., Walker, K., & Wimmer, R. (2008). The clinical/practicum experience in professional preparation: Preliminary findings. *McGill Journal of Education, 43*(2), 157–172. Retrieved from http://mje.mcgill.ca/index.php/MJE/article/view/682/2242

Richards, J. C., & Renandya, W. A. (2002). *Methodology in language teaching: An anthology of current practice.* Cambridge, UK: Cambridge University Press.

Rose, M. (1984). *Writer's block: The cognitive dimension.* Carbondale, IL: Southern Illinois University Press.

Saito, H. (1994). Teachers' practices and students' preferences for feedback on second language writing: A case study of adult ESL learners. *TESL Canada Journal, 11,* 46–70.

Seow, A. (2002). The writing process and process writing. In J. C. Richards & W. A. Renandya (Eds.), *Methodology in language teaching: An Anthology of current practice* (pp. 315–330). Cambridge, UK: Cambridge University Press.

Zamel, V. (1987). Recent research on writing pedagogy. *TESOL Quarterly, 21*(4), 697–715.

Chapter Eighteen

Supervision in Nursing Education: A Canadian Perspective

Anita Jennings & Brigitte Couture

THERE IS AS YET NO full agreement regarding the concept or the practice of clinical supervision across the health sciences, nor are they articulated clearly in the literature. Our review of the databases of CINHL, Proquest Scholars' Portal, and EBSCO for the terms *supervisor, supervision,* and *clinical supervision* revealed relatively few articles, and in the ones we found, there was ambiguity concerning the terms. In addition, clinical supervision was mostly examined in relation to post-licensure, and there were even fewer articles on clinical supervision of pre-licensure nurses. Walker (2009) stated that nurse educators need to embrace evidence-based practices in pedagogy and nursing curriculum and to apply the same level of rigor to the assessment of clinical teaching and learning as is found in nursing practice and research.

Moreover, it is our view that the impact of clinical supervision on student learning and readiness to practice should be explored more methodically than it has been to this point. Much of the current literature on clinical supervision originated in the United Kingdom and focused on supervision of post-licensure nurses (Mills, Francis, & Bonner, 2005), while literature from the United States, Australia, and New Zealand addressed pre-licensure supervision. In Canada, scholarly literature related to clinical supervision, the teaching practices of clinical supervisors, and the impact of these elements on students' learning in clinical settings was rare. Ferguson (2005), a Canadian scholar, challenged nurse educators in Canada to apply evidence-based practices in their teaching strategies and to continue to develop nursing curriculum.

Usage of the terms *clinical supervision, preceptor,* and *mentor* often overlap in practice and do not lend themselves to a clear delineation of roles and responsibilities (Fowler, 1996; Lyth, 2000; White et al., 1998). Thus, in this present chapter related to the current state of knowledge of clinical supervision in nursing education, we define the terms, describe the purpose and relevance of clinical supervision and its models, outline the preparation of supervisors, and synthesize perceptions of students and instructors regarding good and bad supervision. We use the terms clinical supervisor and clinical instructor interchangeably as reflected both in the literature and in nursing practice. We also summarize key results of our recent pilot study on clinical supervision in our own nursing program.

Definition of Key Terms

Mentor and Mentoring

Butterworth, Bishop, and Carson (1996) defined a mentor as "an experienced professional nurturing and guiding the novitiate" (p. 473). Based on our experience, we believe that the term mentor and the mentor's roles and responsibilities are generally understood by most health care workers. The term *mentoring* has been defined as a teaching/learning process within a one-on-one reciprocal relationship between two individuals of different levels of knowledge and experience (Mills et al., 2005). The mentoring relationship is often a long-term one and is geared towards achieving professional goals. One of the key benefits of mentoring is the building of nursing knowledge and professional expertise (Stewart & Grueger, as cited in Mills et al., 2005). In addition, Mills et al. (2005) and Fowler (1996) added that mentoring practice has shifted over time from a focus on the career advancement of the individual to include a broader view encompassing the development of professional nursing knowledge and expertise for protégés and mentors alike.

Darling (as cited in Fowler, 1996) identified three mentoring roles: the *inspirer*, the *investor*, and the *supporter*, thus implying a helping relationship between the protégé and mentor that could be of short- or long-term duration. Unlike the terms preceptor and clinical supervisor, the term mentor appears to be more clearly described in the literature, which has recently resulted in an enhanced understanding of the process in the profession.

Preceptor and Preceptoring

The term preceptor was defined by Usher, Nolan, Reser, Owens, and Tollefson as an "experienced practitioner who teaches, instructs, supervises and serves as a role model for a student or graduate nurse for a set period of time in a formalized program" (as cited in Mills et al., 2005, p. 5). The primary objective of the preceptor is to assist the protégé in being orientated to the work environment and in acquiring essential nursing skills. Thus, the traditional teaching role is of secondary importance.

We have encountered a preceptor model in nursing for both pre-licensure and post-licensure levels. For the former, students in third and fourth year in an undergraduate nursing program typically follow a preceptor model. The student nurse works with the preceptor, who is a registered nurse in the organization. The student nurse, preceptor, and clinical instructor work collaboratively to ensure that the student achieves the course outcomes. In a post-licensure scenario, a seasoned nurse works with a novice graduate for a short period of time. The preceptor assists the novice in becoming comfortable with organizational processes and routines. In our experience, not all health care organizations offer adequate support to novice nurses; therefore, we recommend a preceptor model to assist all nursing staff who join an organization. Such preceptorship would help the newcomers become familiar with the institutional policies and procedures and to grow into competent, confident practitioners.

From our observations, most preceptor programs assign clinical staff to deliver the program. In some cases, clinical teaching associates or clinical instructors assume responsibility for supervising and evaluating a small group of students (Fowler, 1996; Mills et al., 2005). Different perspectives exist as to whether the preceptor role should include a formal evaluative component of students' performance. Because the preceptor and clinical supervisor roles both consist of supervising activities, the overlap between assisting and assessing often contributes to misunderstanding and lack of clarity both in the literature and in practice and results in both terms being used interchangeably. In our experience with pre-licensure nurses, the preceptor gives feedback to the faculty supervisor on the student's performance. The faculty supervisor has the authority to take corrective actions based on the preceptor's feedback.

However, in post-licensure scenarios, the preceptor provides evaluative feedback to the nurse manager. In most Canadian hospitals, the unit manager relies on the preceptor for feedback before making a hiring decision. In this instance, we believe that the preceptor contributes to the administrative and managerial role.

Yegdich (1999) stated that managerial supervision must be differentiated from clinical supervision and asserted that managerial supervision could take a punitive stance, whereas clinical supervision would include a teaching, nurturing stance. For instance, medication errors occur for a number of reasons. In managerial supervision, the nurse is linked to the error, and factors such as a delivery system may not always be examined. In a clinical supervision setting, the contributing factors for the error would be examined, with the underlying problem being identified and remedied. Individuals involved in both of these scenarios examine practice from a different philosophical lens. We did not deal with the managerial perspective in this paper, although we acknowledge that the differences between clinical and managerial supervision are important issues to be explored.

Clinical Supervision and Supervisor

The term supervision has been reviewed through concept analysis by Lyth (2000), who articulated the position of the United Kingdom Central Council for Nursing, Midwifery and Health Visiting (UKCC). Their definition of supervision was, "a formal process of professional support and learning which enables individual practitioners to develop knowledge and competence, assume responsibility for their own practice and enhance consumer protection and safety of care in complex clinical situations" (Lyth, 2000, p. 15). Clinical supervision was described by Butterworth and Faugier as "an exchange between practicing professional to assist the development of professional skills" (as cited in Lyth, 2000, p. 12). Upon reviewing the many definitions of clinical supervision, we prefer the UKCC definition because it identified the accountabilities and expectations of a nurse whether he or she is at the pre- or post- licensure levels. Also, this definition closely resembled the definition adopted by Canadian nursing regulatory bodies.

Fowler (1996) provided a review of the nursing literature on clinical supervision in nursing and midwifery in the United Kingdom, though the term is used mostly for post- licensure nurses. Teasdale, Brocklehurst, and Thom (2000) stated that in the USA, the term clinical supervision was generally used to describe support and guidance for student nurses prior to licensure. Mills et al. (2005) stated that clinical supervision in Australia, New Zealand, and Canada applied only to pre-licensure nurses in their clinical placement. Furthermore, Edwards et al. (2005) identified several factors that promoted the effectiveness of clinical supervision. However, we agreed with Cummins (2009) that there is a current lack of consensus regarding the definition, scope, and limitations of clinical supervision in nursing practice and in the nursing literature.

The term supervisor defines one who teaches and observes students' progress, supervising their work, and guiding them towards educational opportunities; the supervisor is a resource for students, providing them with information and advice (Lyth, 2000). The supervisor enhances the application of theory to practice and raises the awareness of the therapeutic role of the nurse (Fowler, 1996; Lyth, 2000). The role of the clinical supervisor is to ensure that students are provided with relevant experience so that they achieve prescribed learning outcomes (Fowler, 1996). Although the clinical supervision role has widespread acceptance within the profession, and many stakeholders regard this role as a positive training aspect (Fowler, 1996), we suggested that clinical supervision needs to be more consistently developed and formalized in order to provide maximum benefit for patients, nurses, and the profession in general.

Teasdale, Brocklehurst, and Thom (2000) conducted a study with 211 post-licensure nurses in eleven randomly selected hospitals and community centres. They found that the greater benefit for ongoing clinical supervision occurred with junior post-licensure nurses, which suggested that more novice nurses may need ongoing feedback and reflective exchange about their practice. The researchers also discovered that clinical supervision was not as beneficial to more advanced practicing nurses. In their study, a preceptor and clinical supervision model was employed; however, we recommend that further research is required before concluding whether novice or experienced post-licensure nurses benefit from clinical supervision.

One of the key differences among the roles of clinical supervisor, preceptor, and mentor is the power differential amongst the individuals in each role. Unlike mentoring, where there is typically minimal power differential between the mentor and mentee, in clinical supervision, the power differential is historically more pronounced, and the relationship is hierarchal and prominent (Fowler, 1996). Fowler appeared to be the only author who identified the power issues in clinical supervision.

In our review of the literature, we found differences in understanding and usage of the term preceptor and clinical supervisor, which was a source of confusion for practitioners. Second, both terms were adopted and operationalized differently in placement settings. We suggest that the terms preceptor and mentor be used in teaching post-licensure nurses and that clinical supervision be used for pre-licensure nurses. The definition of clinical supervision introduced by Lyth (2000), which included the expectations and accountabilities of pre-licensure nurses, mirrors the processes used by nursing undergraduate programs and regulatory bodies across Canada. We thus recommended that nurse educators consider using clinical supervision in relation to supervising pre-licensure nurses, thereby helping clarify the confusion presently appearing in the literature.

Purpose and Relevance of Clinical Supervision

The purpose of nursing education is to prepare student nurses to think critically and to act safely and independently (Fowler, 1996; Lofmark, Carlsson & Wikblad, 2001; Nolan, 1998). The purpose of supervision is to enable students to appropriately apply theory to practice. Although nursing theory is taught in the classroom, it can only be mastered through supervised practice (Fowler, 1996).

Severinsson (1995) contended that clinical supervision is fundamental in nursing education to enable learners to consolidate knowledge and develop a professional identity. The clinical placement offers students opportunities to apply knowledge gained in the classroom to actual practice, hence enabling them to become more independent and confident practitioners. Severinsson stated that clinical supervision is a pedagogical process where caring experiences are explained in a professional context. She found that supervisors enabled learners to gain deeper insight and understanding of the process of nursing, individual professional growth, and the development of his or her identity as a nurse.

Because nursing has moved away from a task-oriented approach over the years to a more individualized and holistic practice, clinical supervision has become more important (Fowler, 1996). The nursing profession recognizes the increased accountability and responsibility of practitioners to the regulatory body for their professional actions or inactions. Fowler further contended that supervision assists in the process of socialization of the nurse and integrating the values and beliefs of the profession.

By contrast, we have observed in our experience that clinical instructors have different roles, expectations, and performances, depending on the teaching context. We contend that because the quality of supervision may differ greatly, the impact on student learning would also vary greatly. Student nurses, upon graduation, may not be as homogenous as one may tend to believe. Ferguson (2005) stated that nursing education is still largely based on traditional teaching practices and that nurse educators do not engage in evidence-based pedagogy. Ferguson suggested that nurse educators should use best evidence to justify teaching strategies and curricular interventions, considering the needs of learners and the impact of their interventions on student learning and performance. We agree with Ferguson and recommend that nurse scholars explore key teaching, supervisory, and curricular issues in nursing education in Canada.

Models of Clinical Supervision.

Faugier and Butterworth (as cited in Fowler, 1996) affirmed that supervision models can be categorized into three main domains: (1) description of the main functions of the role, (2) description of the supervisory relationships and their main constituents, and (3) developmental processes that focus on the chat ment of the supervisory relationship. Fish (as cited in Fowler, 1996) proposed a model that included two of these elements: function and process.

Proctor's clinical supervision model (as cited in Lyth, 2000 and Teasdale et al., 2000) consisted of three elements: normative, which involved assisting nurses in the organization and provision of care and monitoring the quality of care provided; formative, which involved the education and development of learners; and restorative, which provided personal support to assist nurses cope with the pressure of work situations. We found some evidence of use of this model in the literature but not in practice.

Häggman-Laitila, Eriksson, Meretoja, Sillanpaa, and Rekola (2007) conducted a qualitative study and from it developed a model of clinical supervision. They sought input from students, preceptors, and teachers. The model identified the prerequisites for clinical supervision, its content, and its influence. Häggman-Laitila et al. stated that supervision plays a significant role in nursing education and reinforces the professionalism of graduating students. They used a preceptor model and contended that as preceptors and clinical supervisors share some overlapping functions and roles, the model could also be adapted to meet the needs of clinical supervisors. We suggest that teaching teams review the various models and discuss and adopt a model that meets their teaching needs in clinical practice.

Perceptions of Good and Bad Supervision

In our literature review, we found agreement on perceptions of good and bad supervision. Perceptions of good supervision included the characteristics of the teacher and teaching practices. The main characteristics of a good supervisor were that the supervisor is approachable, demonstrates interest in the student, and provides support to the student (Fowler, 1996; Kotzabassaki et al., 1997; Lofmark & Wikblad, 2001; Lyth, 2000). Moreover, the clinical instructor should demonstrate a knowledge of wider professional issues and a willingness to negotiate with students regarding the arrangement of learning experiences. These authors also stated that good supervision made provision for an academic and emotional dimension. For instance, academic support would include competence, knowledge, good communication skills, and constructive feedback, whereas the emotional dimension would provide support and encouragement and the ability to listen to student concerns.

In a study by Kotzabassaki et al. (1997), students and faculty identified their perceptions of the best and worst characteristics of clinical supervision. Both groups indicated that a clinical supervisor should be a good role model, enjoy nursing and teaching, and should demonstrate clinical skill and judgment. The characteristics of clinical supervision that were highly rated by both groups were that the teacher encouraged a climate of mutual respect, demonstrated clinical knowledge and judgment, listened attentively to students' concerns, enjoyed nursing, and demonstrated good communication skills. Although both groups agreed upon the worst characteristics of clinical supervisors, each group prioritized the behaviors differently. Students described the worst clinical teacher as one who was not a role model, did not provide constructive feedback or empathy, or did not direct them to useful literature. Faculty perceived the worst clinical teachers as those who were unable to use self-criticism constructively and demonstrated poor interpersonal skills.

In another study conducted by Lofmark and Wikblad (2001), students provided their perceptions of factors that facilitated and obstructed their learning in clinical settings. The students noted that the facilitating factors were practicing tasks and skills, receiving feedback, collaborating with peers and team members, and supervising on a continuous and timely basis. The obstructing factors they identified were related to weakness in the student-supervisor relationship, organizational shortcomings in the supervision, and students' personal shortcomings.

We thus understood from these sources that clinical supervision consisted of two dimensions perceived to be important by students and teachers alike – namely, academic excellence and emotional support. Students expected the supervisor to be knowledgeable, aware of professional standards, engaged in best teaching practices, and supportive of the learner in his/her personal and professional growth.

Common Beliefs and Values of Supervisors

Paterson (1994) studied clinical instructors and their central beliefs about clinical teaching. This exploratory, descriptive study investigated six nurse instructors who taught on medical-surgical wards in an urban Canadian hospital. The participants believed that clinical teaching was an integral aspect of nursing education and that they positively influenced students' learning in the clinical area. Paterson identified four themes from which clinical teachers perceive and interpret information regarding themselves as teachers and their teaching practice: the moral responsibility of the teacher, task mastery, the ability-evaluative function, and professional-identity mentoring.

We agreed with Paterson (1994) and suggested that teaching teams should describe and discuss the main beliefs that underpin their teaching practices. Furthermore, because many clinical instructors are hired for a short duration, we further suggest that clinical instructors be involved in paid professional development days where they are encouraged to explore their pedagogical assumptions and beliefs that underpin their teaching. Also by sharing teaching experiences in such PD sessions, clinical instructors would be encouraged to adopt a plurality of teaching philosophies and perspectives, thereby increasing the probability of enhancing their teaching practices.

Preparation and Training of Supervisors

Our literature review revealed that supervisors received little if any formal mentorship training (Fowler, 1996; Kotzabassaki et al., 1997; Lyth, 2000). Our experience confirmed this finding, and yet supervisors and mentors are expected to meet the learning needs of the students, the demands of the program, and professional goals of the organization and the profession. We suggest that schools of nursing adopt a formal education program for all instructors and supervisory personnel in order to enable them to share their experiences, adopt evidence- based teaching practices, and improve the quality of their supervision/mentorship activities. We suggest that the Adaptive Mentorship© model developed by Ralph and Walker (2010) is one model that could assist clinical instructors in first assessing the developmental needs of students and subsequently guiding their learning in an appropriate and timely manner.

The Authors' Study

Previous qualitative studies have identified the importance of theory integration and supervision to enhance student satisfaction in their practicum learning programs (Lofmark & Wikblad, 2000; Ralph & Walker, 2010; Ralph, Walker, & Wimmer, 2009). Yet, the extent of implementing these two factors has not been quantified to date. Considering the lack of quantitative data on this topic and the ongoing need to refine the development of a quantitative tool, we developed a questionnaire survey that sought to use both a quantitative and qualitative approach to determine the degree of students' satisfaction with their practicum/clinical program. This study was designed as a preliminary pilot to further inform the dimensions under investigation.

The pilot study took place in December 2009 with the second-year students of a collaborative nursing degree program in Toronto. Eighty-six of the participants formed the convenience sample, which represented 46% of the population. Data were collected at the conclusion of 13 weeks of clinical/practicum experience and within a class other than that taught by either investigator. Ethics approval was obtained prior to conducting the study. The print survey consisted of 26 questions (24 with a five-point Likert scale and two open-ended questions). The following research questions contained both quantitative and qualitative measures:

- ∾: Does the integration of theoretical concepts positively impact student learning in their practicum?
- ∾: Does faculty instruction impact on student learning in their practicum?
- ∾: What factors enhance or inhibit student learning in their practicum? (open-ended questions).

The questions pertaining to supervision and instruction were phrased in an indirect way and may have caused students to dilute their answers. Nevertheless, we were able to determine from the responses that students valued faculty instruction positively and that supervision did impact students' learning in their practicum. We also discovered that the integration of theoretical concepts positively impacted students' learning in their practicum. The qualitative research process also yielded important information.

The students' narratives from the open-ended questions were transcribed by our research assistant (RA). The primary investigator (PI) categorized the narrative responses into emerging themes, which were subsequently reviewed by the second investigator and further classified into sub-themes. Both investigators then reviewed their analysis together and reached a consensus regarding the themes and sub-themes.

For the first open-ended question, "What are the four factors that enhanced your learning," 64 students recorded comments. From the narratives, three themes emerged: Learning by exchanging with others, learning on one's own, and instructor emotional and academic support. In the first theme, students indicated that sharing with others included their peers, staff nurses, health care aides, and their clinical teacher(s). The sharing of information with these people seemed to help them validate their learning: "Watching and asking questions was also important." The second theme was related to the students' work to prepare for the clinical experience (such as reading, watching videos, or sharing information during post-conferences). The latter comments were cited as enhancing their learning in the clinical setting. Here, 42 comments were made, and on a few occasions the same individual made more than one comment.

The third theme related to instructors' emotional and academic support. The instructor's approach with the students seemed to be important to the students in order to help them distinguish between positive and negative feedback. Ten comments were submitted regarding the instructors' support or lack thereof. Students highlighted the importance of ongoing feedback. The academic aspect dealt with regular redirecting and suggestions to enhance the students' learning. Twenty-eight comments supported the academic aspect of the instruction. Another factor that emerged was that academic support seemed highly important only if the students felt emotionally safe and supported. A few comments were not categorized because we deemed them to be too general.

Forty-nine participants commented on factors that inhibited their learning, and a few of these participants made more than one comment. From this subgroup of narratives, four themes were generated: student issues (from being stressed to needing more practice in lab), content and practice issues, nursing staff and environment issues, and inadequate instructor teaching and support. Eleven comments were made to the effect that students had personal issues, such as not taking timely breaks due to their "own fault" or not being prepared for the clinical experience. Eighteen comments related to course content and their experiences on the unit, which they perceived as not well synchronized or appropriate for learning. Sixteen comments pertained to students not feeling supported by the nursing staff, which they felt was explained by display of a certain supervisor attitudes or by not feeling welcomed by unit staff.

Some of the comments about the placement per se may have stemmed from the fact that students in complex continuing care may not perceive their experience as valuable in contrast with students who started in acute care. For example, performing certain skills in acute care areas was highly valued over skills performed in a continuing care. Twelve comments were made about the teacher as either not being present to demonstrate a skill or not presenting enough structure.

Current Research Literature

Lofmark and Wikblad (2001) studied facilitating and obstructing factors for development of learning in clinical practice. Their students' perspectives were similar to those revealed in our study. Lofmark and Wikblad enrolled 47 degree-student nurses from two colleges and requested the participants to submit weekly diaries at the end of clinical practice. The three facilitating factors were responsibilities and independence, getting an understanding of the whole situation, and collaboration/supervision elements. Independence did not emerge as a theme in our study, perhaps because students were new to clinical practice in the second year in this program and did not implicitly feel the need for independence. However, students reported wanting to receive ongoing feedback in order to become independent practitioners later on.

The obstructing factors cited by Lofmark and Wikblad (2001) were similar to those identified in our results and were related to the following four themes: shortcomings related to the student-supervisor relationship, lack of opportunities to practice certain skills, organizational shortcomings in relation to regular supervision, and difficulties with the clinical environment including staff.

In their multidisciplinary research project, Ralph, Walker & Wimmer (2009) examined undergraduate professional education in Canada. They enrolled fourth-year student nurses from a BScN program at one Western Canadian university as well as post-practicum students from engineering and teacher education programs. The positive aspects of the practicum described by the nursing students in the Ralph et al. study were similar to those found in our study. Although fourth-year students in the Ralph et al. study were mentored using a preceptor model, and the second-year students in our study were mentored using a supervisory model, we nevertheless found similarities in the results. For example, both cohorts identified as positive their experiences of being included and accepted by unit staff, being welcomed as team-members, and developing self-confidence in their practice. Receiving effective mentorship was rated as the most positive aspect of the students' practicum in both studies. Similarly, the negative aspects in both studies included undergoing poor mentorship, being assigned unproductive tasks, having unrealistic time constraints, and receiving poor placements.

In summary, we believe that the varying supervisory and preceptorship definitions, roles, and functions need to be explored in more depth in nursing education. We suggest that clinical teachers adopt evidence-based teaching practices and integrate the facilitating factors highlighted in this review into their teaching and mentoring practice. Additionally, we urge clinical educators to research the many areas of clinical supervision in order to fill the research gap that exists in this area of nursing research.

References

Butterworth, T., Bishop, V., & Carson, J. (1996). First steps towards evaluating clinical supervision in nursing and health visiting: Theory, policy and practice development; A review. *Journal of Clinical Nursing, 5*, 127–132.

Cummins, A. (2009). Clinical supervision: The way forward? A review of the literature. *Nurse Education in Practice, 9*, 215–220.

Edwards, D., Cooper. L., Burnard, P., Hannigan. B., Adams. J., Fothergill. A., & Coyle. D. (2005). Factors influencing the effectiveness of clinical supervision. *Journal of Psychiatric and Mental health Nursing, 12*, 405–414.

Ferguson, L. (2005). Evidence-based nursing education: Myth or reality? *Journal of Nursing Education, 44*(3), 107–115.

Fowler, J. (1996). The organization of clinical supervision within the nursing profession: A review of the literature. *Journal of Advanced Nursing, 23*, 471–478.

Häggman-Laitila, A., Eriksson, E., Meretoja. R., Sillanpaa. K., & Rekola. L. (2007). Nursing students in clinical practice: Developing a model for clinical supervision. *Nurse Education in Practice, 7*, 381–391.

Kotzabassaki, S., Panou, M., Dimou, F., Karabagli, A., Koutsopoulou, B., & Ikonomou, U. (1997). Nursing students' and faculty's perceptions of the characteristics of the "best" and "worst" clinical teachers: A replication study. *Journal of Advanced Nursing, 26*, 817–824.

Lofmark, A., Carlsson, M., & Wikblad, K. (2001). Student nurses' perception of independence of supervision during clinical nursing practice. *Journal of Clinical Nursing, 10*, 86–93.

Lofmark, A., & Wikblad. K. (2001). Facilitating and obstructing factors for development of learning in clinical practice: A student's perspective. *Journal of Advanced Nursing, 34*(1), 43–50.

Lyth, G. M. (2000). Clinical supervision: A concept analysis. *Journal of Advanced Nursing, 31*(3), 722–729.

Mills, J. E., Francis, K. L., & Bonner, A. (2005). Mentoring, clinical supervision and preceptoring: Clarifying the conceptual definitions for Australian rural nurses; A review of the literature. *International Electronic Journal of Rural and Remote Health*

Research, Education, Practice and Policy. Retrieved from http://www.rrh.org.au/publishedarticles/article_print_410.pdf

Nolan, C.A. (1998). Learning on clinical placement: The experiences of six Australian student nurses. *Nurse Education Today, 18,* 622–629.

Paterson, B. (1994). The view from within: Perspectives of clinical teaching. *International Journal Nurse Studies, 31*(4), 349–360.

Ralph, E., & Walker, K. (2010). Mentoring by design: Applying the "Adaptive Mentorship" model. *Design Principles & Practices, 4*(1), 465–476.

Ralph, E., Walker, K., & Wimmer, R. (2009). Practicum and clinical experiences: Post practicum students' views. *Journal of Nursing Education, 48*(8), 434–440

Severinsson, E. I. (1995). The phenomenon of clinical supervision in psychiatric health care. *Journal of Psychiatric and Mental Health Nursing, 2,* 301–309.

Teasdale, K., Brocklehurst, N., & Thom, N. (2000). Clinical supervision and support for nurses: An evaluation study. *Journal of Advanced Nursing, 33*(2), 216–224.

Usher, K., Nolan, C., Reser, P., Owens, J., & Tollefson, J. (1999). An exploration of the preceptor role: Preceptors' perceptions of benefits, rewards, supports and commitment to the preceptor role. *Journal of Advanced Nursing, 29*(2), 506–514.

Walker, K. (2009). Curriculum in crisis, pedagogy in disrepair: A provocation. *Contemporary Nurse, 32*(1–2), 19–29.

White, E., Butterworth, T., Bishop, V., Carson, J., Jeacock, J., & Clements, A. (1998). Clinical supervision: Insider reports of a private world. *Journal of Advanced Nursing, 28*(1), 185–192.

Yegdich, T. (1999). Clinical supervision and managerial supervision: Some historical and conceptual considerations. *Journal of Advanced Nursing, 30*(5), 1195–1204.

Chapter Nineteen

Towards a Mentorship Model
for Pharmacy Students

Dawna L. Hawrysh

MANY PROFESSIONAL COLLEGES HAVE SOME form of mentoring or preceptor component in their undergraduate programs. In the health sciences, all programs require their students to complete a set number of hours in clinical placements before completing their degree. The regulatory body of each profession determines the number of hours of clinical training that must be completed. A critical part of this clinical phase is the mentorship that students receive during their practicum experiences.

The health care scene is rapidly changing from its traditional care model to a patient-centred, collaborative-care model. In the past, it was acceptable for a mentor to be merely "comfortable" in their discipline. An innovative dimension of this shift of care is the Inter-Professional (IP) aspect, wherein mentors not only have to be comfortable with coaching students from their own discipline but also with assisting the students from other disciplines who are on their IP health care teams.

At this time, there are no formal programs at the University of Saskatchewan to train these new "IP mentors," but under the Health Deans' Council there are currently two recently formed subcommittees (the Clinical Education Undergraduate Committee and the Continuing Inter-Professional Education Committee) who are collaborating to develop mentor training programs. This training would equip personnel to effectively mentor students from their own area of expertise and from other disciplines.

Mentors, with whom health care students first work in their undergraduate professional skills labs, often have a profound impact on how their students will perform their practice, how they conduct their professional relationships in the future, and influence their transformational journeys from novice to expert. Professional schools are now being mandated not only to train the clinical mentors but also to prepare mentors who work with students in their pre-practicum undergraduate labs.

Mentoring is not a new concept and can be applied across any profession. The role and function can be traced back to ancient Greek mythology in which Mentor was a wise and trusted counsellor or teacher. Mentor is an appropriate name for such a person because it probably meant "advisor" in Greek and came from the Indo-European root *men*, meaning to think (Pennsylvania State, 2008). The concept of mentoring has evolved significantly over time, first thought to be a unidirectional process with only the protégé receiving benefits from the interaction. With more research occurring in this field, scholars and practitioners recognized that mentoring is a bidirectional process with each member of the relationship gaining potential benefits. Moreover, anytime there is bidirectional interaction, one must think of how harmony can be created and maintained between the individuals involved in the relationship.

A considerable body of literature exists regarding the mentorship process, with a number of models and common themes. Loue (2011) summarized some of these themes:

> First, the mentor has traditionally been viewed as an individual who should have greater expertise in the relevant field or discipline in comparison with the mentee. Second, mentoring is a long-term interaction between at least two individuals. Third, a goal, if not the ultimate goal, of mentoring is the professional and personal development of the mentee, including his or her development of the skills necessary to succeed in the particular field and his or her socialization into the profession. (p. 2)

Stefan Schindler (2005) used the ancient Chinese philosophy of Tao to describe the process of teaching, of which mentoring may be thought of as a type or subset. His writings focused on the harmony in the teaching process. In the undergraduate setting, the mentor must balance the needs of the protégé/student with the goals and objectives that are to be met during the practicum experience; thus, harmony plays a significant role in the mentorship relationship.

Foundational Learning Frameworks Applicable to Mentorship

Schindler (2005) illustrated the role of harmony in the educational process by comparing it to the Tao symbol founded by Lao Tzu, the founder of the ancient philosophy of Taoism. A circle with both a dark and a bright side symbolizes the Tao. The two halves are connected by an S-curve in the middle. The dark side or the *yin* represented restraint, receptivity, and contraction. The bright side or the *yang* represented activity, expansion, and freedom. The S-curve between the yin and yang signified the life of harmony, ratio, and balance.

In the mentorship model the yin could be represented by the syllabus or goals of the program. These goals and objectives could be thought of as the restraints of the model. The yang could be the protégé. He or she is the eager student represented by his/her engagement in the learning activity, expansion, and freedom. The S-curve could represent the mentor, who must be able to supply the harmony required to satisfy the needs of both sides so that they are in balance.

According to Schindler (2005), "A good teacher balances the objectively imposed discipline of a syllabus with a sensitivity to the subjective needs of the students for whom the syllabus exists" (p. 47). What this means is that the mentor must be able to balance the objectives of the mentorship program with the changing needs and expectations of the protégé. One of the objectives of an effective mentorship program is to take what the student has learned in the university setting and apply it to the conditions of the real world. Because the mentor already has these real world experiences, he/she guides the protégé to make wise choices. Within a group of pharmacy clients or customers, the intern is faced with the task of working with the health care team to help diagnose certain medical conditions and prescribe drug treatment. The mentor has dealt with these matters numerous times and becomes a valuable source of information for the intern. Not only can the mentor supply information on alternative techniques/therapies, but the mentor can also facilitate access to needed information on how to go about dealing with each patient.

Albert North Whitehead (1959) discussed the idea of education being a cyclic process. His discussions centred not only on the foundation years in elementary and secondary education but also on post-secondary education. Education does not stop at the foundation years but continues a cyclic process through adulthood as well. The cyclic process that Whitehead referred to as consisting of *Romance, Precision,* and *Generalization* can be adapted both to the post- secondary setting and to the processes of mentorship found in many professional colleges at the university/college level.

For instance, students entering post-secondary education are fuelled by Romance in that they have acquired knowledge that has fuelled their interests in acquiring more knowledge in a particular field of study. A student may have been involved in a mentoring program while in high school, and his/her interests may have been sufficiently piqued to the point where he/she began to explore the area of expertise in a certain career.

The second stage, Precision, is marked by the acquisition of fact knowledge. This phase examines the discipline that the student requires for learning. Much of the acquisition of knowledge is marked by independent practice, trial and error, and mastering the subject matter individually. The acquisition of additional knowledge in the field of interest becomes a priority, and the student needs to fuel his/her own imagination.

A key stage of mastery, represented in Whitehead's (1959) third stage, is Generalization. Here, students use what they have comprehended and applied to their own knowledge. This phase is marked by creativity, which, in turn, gives way to romance. This phase naturally generates the discipline required for the phase of discovery. To Whitehead, people are intrigued by what lies in front of them and therefore desire to acquire all the knowledge they can to fulfill their aspirations regarding their future pursuits.

Whitehead (1959) described the justification for a university: "it preserves the connection between knowledge and the zest for life, by uniting the young and the old in the imaginative consideration of learning" (p. 39). A fact is no longer a bare fact. It is investigated with all its possibilities. It no longer simply remains in the memory. Individuals can now use this fact to help catalyze their dreams. According to Whitehead, a university must prepare individuals for their career "by promoting the imaginative consideration of the various general principles underlying that career" (p. 44). Thus, referring back to Schindler (2005), one realizes that learning at the university level must be one of harmony communicated by members of a faculty as they work to meet the professional development needs of their students.

Blending these two scholars' viewpoints, one could conceptualize that students enter university with the romanticism of exploring the subject matter in a field of study that they are curious about. However, if the professor/mentor does not appropriately harmonize between the course or program curriculum/syllabus and the student, then the need for precision is stifled. If a mentor ignores the romance phase and strictly focuses on precision, then the end result may produce students who memorize rather than who understand, or students who cannot solve problems, or students who cannot apply their learning to other situations, or students who do not see the relevance between what was learned to everyday or professional life.

The imaginative mentor/professor is able to adapt the program or course syllabus to the ever-changing needs of the protégés. This creativity becomes the foundation for the harmony necessary to conduct learning and understanding. As Whitehead (1959) stated, "the whole point of a university on its educational side is to bring the young under the intellectual influence of a band of imaginative scholars" (p. 150). It is this imagination that lays the groundwork to attain the harmony necessary to satisfy the needs of the learning process. The creative mentor/teacher will be able to adjust the program so as to fuel the creativity of the protégés.

A good mentor must be able to tap the creativity of the protégé to make the experience worthwhile for all participants. Protégés should be free to question, challenge, and make associations between things that may not have been usually connected, while mentors need to encourage their protégés to explore alternative solutions to emerging problems they encounter.

General Mentorship Research

Mentorship is a critical process in the area of professional development across all professional disciplines, including the health sciences, whether the professional is a clinician, researcher, or teacher. Johnson (2007) reported that there tended to be a predictable and recurring structure in most mentorship relationships. The author said, "mentoring relationships often begin cautiously with both parties testing the potential match . . . once formed, mentorships enter a relatively stable, protective and meaningful working stage characterized by personal and professional growth on the part of the protégé" (p. 97).

Johnson explored Kram's (1985) model, which identified four phases of mentorship development. Mentorship relationships move through the common phases (i.e., Initiation, Cultivation, Separation, and Redefinition), but the needs and characteristics of the protégé would shape and vary the journey through these phases.

Initiation's focus is primarily relational, in which both protégé and mentor engage in activity to adequately assess the potential match. This entry phase of development of the relationship progresses positively if both parties find something with the other to fulfill their respective needs. The mentor is attracted to the protégé by aptitude, similar interests, values, and the potential for assistance with projects. The protégé will face a number of developmental tasks during this phase; thus, the mentor must tolerate the dependence of the protégé during this initial phase.

In the Cultivation stage, the longest phase, the relationship begins to be nourished so that it can be maintained. During this time the expectations are tested against reality, and a strengthening of the interpersonal bonds typically occurs. Johnson (2007) noted that "protégés will see an increase in self confidence, professional identity . . . there is a gradual and reciprocal development of mutuality, self-disclosure and sharing of ideas and values; building of mutual trust" (p. 99). During this phase the mentor must challenge and coach the protégé. Sharing information, offering advice, and increasing challenging tasks for the protégé become the mentor's priority. During the end of this phase the mentor would affirm the protégé's competence and growing independence. Without this affirmation, the separation phase could not occur.

The Separation phase is characterized by leave-taking, which is the end of the active phase of mentoring. The mentor sets the tone for this phase by modelling openness and by taking the lead in drawing the relationship to an end. Usually a final meeting occurs to discuss the accomplishments during the time. The mentor/preceptor often also discusses ways the pair can be supportive once the student/protégé has moved on.

In the Redefinition phase there is less formality, and pair interaction becomes less frequent. The relationship becomes one of collegial friendship, in which the partners become supportive colleagues. After students graduate from professional colleges, many of them will continue to collaborate with former preceptors on various subsequent projects.

Another generic mentorship model that has potential to assist pharmacy clinicians in their mentorship of students is Adaptive Mentorship© (AM) (Ralph & Walker, 2008, 2010a, 2010b). The AM model has proven effective in enhancing the entire mentoring/

Figure 1

Adaptive Mentorship. The mentor matches his/her adaptive response to coincide with the skill-specific developmental level of his/her protégé. Adapted from E. Ralph & K. Walker (2008, 2010a, 2010b).

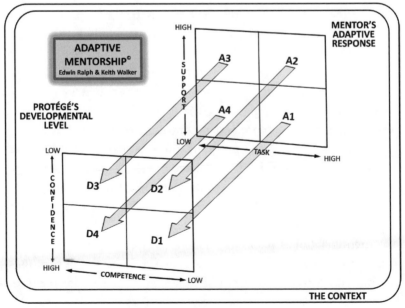

supervising process, and it requires mentors to adjust their mentoring behavior in response to the changing task-specific development needs of their protégés. See Figure 1.

The application of AM consists of three phases. In the first phase the mentor and the protégé *determine* the existing development level of the protégé to accomplish specific professional tasks. A protégé's level of development consists of both his/her competence and his/her confidence levels in performing each task or skill set at a particular point in time.

In the second phase, the mentor appropriately *adapts* his/her mentoring response to correspond to the existing development level of the protégé (e.g., A1 with D1, A2 with D2, and so on). The mentor's response is provided via two dimensions: the degree of psychological and/or emotional support, which is given in the form of encouragement, praise, or affirmation; and the task or technical dimension, coming in the form of instruction, demonstration, or procedural directions. The third phase is marked by a continual observation of the protégé's changing development level, whereby the mentor would continue to *synchronize* his/her adaptive response to match the protégé's changing development needs.

Applying the AM model to the pharmacy program, licensed practicing pharmacists in both community and hospital practices would serve as mentors in the student practicum. In the second and third year of the pharmacy programs, the students would typically function in a more technical fashion, learning about the organization(s) and performing technician functions. A mentor using the AM approach would be particularly task orientated at this stage (i.e., operating from A1 or A2, matching the neophyte students' D1 or D2 levels of lower competence and varying degrees of confidence).

In the last year of the program, the practicum occurs after all academic courses have been completed. By that stage, students' competence and confidence levels would presumably be more advanced (i.e., at upper D2, or D3, or lower D4 levels), and they would be expected to perform professional tasks as an entry-level pharmacist. The mentor would thus be expected to reciprocate by applying corresponding responses (i.e., upper A2, or A3, or lower A4 positions). At this time, the mentor would be vigilant to protect both the student and patient as the student engages in making and enacting clinical decisions under the oversight of the mentor.

Ralph and Walker (2008) identified five strengths of the AM model – namely, it helped mentors clarify their conceptualization of the general mentorship process, it replaced a "one size fits all" approach by requiring mentors to adapt their behavior according to the needs of their protégés, it was relatively easy to learn, it offered mentors a way to analyze and alleviate mentoring conflicts, and it revealed that relationship problems were often the result of mentors mismatching their "A" responses with the protégé's existing "D" development levels.

The uniqueness and simplicity of Adaptive Mentorship is the need for the mentor to be able to adapt to the competence and confidence levels of his/her protégé to perform specific professional skills. In terms of the Tao symbol described above, the mentor who uses the AM model must supply the harmony to balance the objectives of the program with the learning needs of the protégé. Likewise, just as Whitehead (1959) proposed phases of learning, and Loue (2011) proposed phases of mentorship, so too did Ralph and Walker (2008, 20010a, 2010b) propose moving through developmental phases in a cyclical manner.

In Whitehead's (1959) terms, the protégé must be romanced, which can be accomplished by the mentor serving to encourage the protégé by laying out all the possibilities that may exist for a certain context. The mentor must administer his/her responses in such a way so as to fuel the creativity of the protégé while at the same time meeting the objectives of the mentorship program. The mentor helps supply the precision of Whitehead's second phase by providing the protégé with additional expert knowledge as required to master a specific task. The protégé will then be able to generalize this information when he/she encounters a similar task in the future.

With respect to Schindler's (2005) views, he emphasized the process of teaching (i.e., mentoring) more than the process of learning. The teacher/mentor is seen as the supplier of the harmony to balance the needs of both the syllabus and the student and is tasked with creating a learning atmosphere so that the objectives of the program and the needs of his students are met. The AM model reflects the same elements described by Schindler: the objectives of the program, the protégé/student, and the mentor. Like a classroom teacher, the mentor becomes the balancing factor between the objectives of the program and the needs of the protégé. The mentor must provide the appropriate degree of support and direction required to satisfy both sides of the symbol used in the Taoist philosophy. Thus, the work of Schindler (2005) and Whitehead (1959) provide philosophical support for the AM model.

Mentorship Research in the Health Professions

With respect to mentorship research in health care settings, Elcigili and Sari (2008) explored nursing students' opinions about the expectations of an effective nursing clinical mentor. A focus group of 24 post-practicum nursing students were interviewed after their third year of nursing school. An open-ended questionnaire was used to determine the students' opinions and expectations regarding mentors and their roles. The researchers noted that students believed that effective mentors should be able to communicate without prejudice, give positive feedback, be empathetic, require students to do some research, and offer information and assistance to students as required.

Milner and Bossers (2004) investigated the evaluation of the mentor-protégé relationship in an occupational therapy mentorship program. They expanded Rogers' work (1986) on the roles of the mentor including teacher, sponsor, host/guide, exemplar/role model, and counsellor. Results of this study showed mentors and protégés strongly agreeing (95.5%) that the purpose of the mentor was to facilitate professional development. Milner and Bossers found that there was less agreement with statements related to coaching characteristics: "mentors and protégés generally and significantly agree (t-test, $p<0.05$) with the mentoring statements more than the coaching statements when reflecting on the role and purpose of a mentor" (p. 103).

Huybrecht, Loeckx, Quaeyhaegens, De Tobel, and Mistiaen (2011) studied perceived characteristics regarding mentors and the consequences of mentorship. These results were relevant for educators desiring to develop formal mentorship-training programs. The findings suggested that the mentorship relationship should be voluntary, and that to help maintain a positive attitude among all participants, the workload of mentors should be reduced to allow them sufficient time to provide feedback to their protégés. They indicated that "the training our mentors receive is theoretical. It concerns knowledge of learning styles, reflection techniques, legal and ethical issues. Future mentors also learn how to evaluate students for knowledge, skills and attitude" (p. 275).

Carr, Herman, and Harris (2005) summarized the characteristics of effective mentors as being: trustworthy, tactful , flexible, consistent, informal, willing to share information, demanding as required, willing to engage in active and open learning, willing to listen, facilitative, respectful, and committed to providing time to be with the protégé.

The researchers also found that respondents saw mentoring, coaching, and collaboration as shared processes, and they further maintained that the first teaching assistants, whom students met early in their educational preparation were important in assisting students in their commencement of a shared journey of commitment leading to improved learning and effective practice.

Furthermore, Welsh (2004) suggested that "effective mentors typically have knowledge and demonstrated skills in their field along with the earned respect of colleagues. They have well-developed interpersonal and communication skills, know and utilize tools to bring out others' talents, and have a clear understanding of balance between guiding and directing" (p. 61). Her research also identified a number of key mentoring skills/characteristics that administrators should expect when selecting mentors (similar to those offered by Carr et al., 2005), including attributes such as able to build trust, inspiring, willing to give honest, corrective feedback, willing to connect protégé to an extensive network, willing to help protégés take responsibility for their own development, ethical, encouraging/supportive, sensitive to protégé needs, appreciative of different personality/work/learning styles, and enjoys protégé's development.

In a recent study, which was a modest action-research investigation that I conducted within a graduate course at the University of Saskatchewan, I surveyed class members through a video-recorded focus-group discussion regarding their views of effective mentorship. The respondents included school administrators and teachers from the pre-K–12 system, who had overseen teacher candidates during the extended practicum portion of their teacher education programs.

That class discussion yielded the following definition of a mentor: *An individual in a leadership role who shares their expertise and*

Table 1

SPEP Advisory Committee's Summary of Effective Mentor Characteristics

Knowledge in	Skills/Abilities	Qualities/Attributes
1. Learning styles	1. Learn together	1. Patient
2. Adult learners	2. Critical thinker	2. Committed
3. "Generational issues"	3. Deal with diversity	3. Enthusiastic
4. IT & efficiency with new technology	4. Assessment	4. Positive attitude
5. Assessment (theoretical framework)	5. Able to challenge students	5. Be able to admit wrong
6. Contemporary Practice	6. Mentor	6. Be non-judgmental
7. Ability to "think out loud" to pass on cognitive skills	7. Efficient	7. Open-minded
8. How to be effective in more than one area of expertise	8. Conflict resolution	8. Conflict resolution
	9. Problem solver	9. Adaptable
	10. Able to teach skills	10. Approachable
	11. Able to identify different learning styles and teach to those styles	11. Confident
		12. Team player
		13. Lifelong learner
		14. Ethical
		15. Good communicator

knowledge with an individual who is learning or new to the profession or organization. This mentor is a "go to" person who coaches the protégé to grow professionally and individually. There was little difference between this class-generated definition and those found in the literature, such as the one by Carr et al. (2005) that stated:

> An exceptional developmental, caring and sharing relationship where one person invests their time, know-how, and effort in enhancing another person's growth – insight, perspective and wisdom as well as knowledge and skill – and responds to other critical needs in the life of that person to prepare them for greater productivity, understanding, fulfillment or achievement for the future. (p. 17)

Moreover, in that focus-group discussion I asked the members to enumerate effective mentor characteristics, the list of which was similar to the above-mentioned inventories with two additional aspects that my peers added regarding effective mentor behavior. These aspects were (a) being culturally sensitive (presumably identified, because several of them had been working with Aboriginal students and parents in their school communities) and (b) endeavoring to make protégés feel valued.

With respect to the health care sector, a current trend is to conceptualize mentoring programs as interdisciplinary and cross-professional initiatives in which programs are intended to bridge/link all health disciplines. At one general meeting I attended as a member of the Structured Practical Experiences Program (SPEP) Pharmacy Advisory Committee at my university, another brainstorming session was conducted to identify the desired characteristics of proficient mentors in a pharmacy setting. A key reason we generated this attribute list was to assist the college in the development of a future mentor-training program.

The SPEP Advisory Committee members' responses represented the reflections of licensed practitioners in both hospital and community practice. Each of these individuals was also actively mentoring students in their respective clinical programs. Our discussion centred on three categories that the respondents considered important for all mentors: In what areas should mentors possess knowledge?

What skills or abilities should they have? What personality qualities or attributes should they exhibit? In Table 1, I summarize the members' responses. Not only did the members' responses mirror the general findings identified by previous mentorship research (e.g., Allen & Eby, 2007; Elcigili & Sari, 2008; Rose Ragins & Kram, 2007), but their comments reflected what professional pharmacy practitioners seemed to experience in their daily routines of everyday work.

Conclusion

Prospective practitioners across the disciplines have regularly reported that the practicum/clinical experiences in their pre-service education were critical in preparing them for accepting their first position in their respective professions. I believe that the Adaptive Mentorship (AM) model shows promising results in enhancing the effectiveness of the mentoring process and that it could be easily adapted to a SPEP program. I have also shown how it fits with the theoretical structures of Schindler (2005) and Whitehead (1959) that I mentioned earlier.

I feel that the AM model would energize the mentorship process to help cultivate the inquisitiveness of the protégé through the optimum provision of task direction and psychological support. In my view, the generating of such interest would in turn prompt protégés towards a mastery of skills that they will require in the future. In this way, as the mentor fuels the process of protégé learning, the latter may also be encouraged to begin to question and challenge what is around them as well. As the protégé demonstrates higher levels of development (e.g., D3 and D4 levels in the AM model), they will experience elevated competence and confidence; they will be empowered to examine a variety of professional alternatives that lay before them. The mentor must supply the zest necessary to make the mentorship experience a "golden moment" for the protégé.

The importance of good mentorship programs, coupled with the growing shortage of professionals in a variety of fields, require that all professional education institutions give serious attention to equipping mentors to excel at performing their jobs. Ralph, Walker, and Wimmer (2008) suggested that mentorship program organizers "need to do so to meet the emerging pressure and challenges inherent to supplying well-trained professionals to enter their practice in the rapidly changing world of the twenty-first century" (p. 75). I endorse the AM model as a useful conceptual tool that has potential to enhance the effectiveness of mentoring in our pharmacy-education program, and indeed, that it be considered by other professional schools to bolster their mentorship programs.

References

Allen, T., & Eby, L. (Eds.). (2007). *The Blackwell Handbook of mentoring: A multiple perspective approach.* Malden, MA: Blackwell.

Carr, J. F., Herman, N., & Harris, D. E. (2005). *Creating dynamic schools through mentoring, coaching, and collaboration.* Alexandria, VA: Association for Supervision and Curriculum Development.

Elcigili, A., & Sari, H. Y. (2008). Students' opinions about and expectations of effective nursing clinical mentors. *Journal of Nursing Education, 47*(3), 118–123. Available from http://www.mendeley.com/research/students-opinions-about-expectations-effective-nursing-clinical-mentors/

Huybrecht, H., Loeckx, W., Quaeyhaegens, Y., De Tobel, D., & Mistiaen, W. (2011). Mentoring in nursing education: Perceived characteristics of mentors and the consequences of mentorship. *Nurse Education Today, 31,* 274–278. doi:10.1016/j.nedt.2010.10.022

Johnson, W. B. (2007). *On being a mentor: A guide for higher education faculty.* New York, NY: Lawrence Erlbaum Associates.

Kram, K. (1985). *Mentoring at work: Developmental relationships in organizational life.* Glenview, IL: Scott, Foresman.

Loue, S. (2011). *Mentoring health science professionals.* New York, NY: Springer.

Milner, T., & Bossers, A. (2004). Evaluation of the mentor-mentee relationship in an occupational therapy mentorship programme. *Occupational Therapy International, 11*(2), 96–111. doi:10.1002/oti.200

Pennsylvania State University. (2008). *The mentor: An academic advising journal.* Penn State Division of Undergraduate Studies. Retrieved from http://dus.psu.edu/mentor/homer.htm

Ralph, E., & Walker, K. (2010a). Enhancing mentors' effectiveness: The promise of the adaptive mentorship model. *McGill Journal of Education, 45*(2), 205–218. Retrieved from http://mje.mcgill.ca/article/view/4653/6388

Ralph, E., & Walker, K. (2010b). Rising with the tide: Applying adaptive mentorship in the professional practicum. In A.Wright, M.Wilson, & D. MacIsaac (Eds.), *Collection of essays on learning and teaching: Between the tides* (Vol. 3, pp. 3–8). Hamilton, ON: McMaster University, Society for Teaching and Learning in Higher Education. Retrieved from http://apps.medialab.uwindsor.ca/ctl?CELT/vol3/CELTVOL3.pdf

Ralph, E., Walker, K., & Wimmer, R, (2008). The Clinical/Practicum Experience in Professional Preparation: Preliminary Findings. *McGill Journal of Education, 43*(2), 157–172. Retrieved from http://mje.mcgill.ca/article/view/682/2242

Rogers, J. C. (1986). Nationally speaking: Mentoring for career achievement and advancement. *American Journal of Occupational Therapy, 40*(2), 79–82.

Rose Ragins, B., & Kram, K. (Eds.). (2007). *The handbook of mentoring at work: Theory, research, and practice.* Newbury Park, CA: Sage.

Schindler, S. (2005). The tao of teaching: Romance and process. *Process papers: An Occasional Publication for Process Philosophy of Education, 9,* 46–52.

Welsh, S. (2004). *Mentoring the future: A guide to building mentor programs that work.* Cochrane, AB: Momentum Learning.

Whitehead, A.N. (1959). *The aims of education and other essays.* New York, NY: McMillan.

Chapter Twenty

The Potential of the Adaptive Mentorship© Model in Teacher Education Practicum Settings

Peter Chin & Benjamin Kutsyuruba

THE CONTEXT OF TEACHER EDUCATION in the province of Ontario is different from other Canadian provinces in that Ontario Bachelor of Education (BEd) programs are either double-degree (concurrent) or after-degree (consecutive) programs – typically eight months in duration – and in most cases designed with almost half of that eight-month period devoted to practicum experiences.

The final year of Queen's BEd program is comprised of a class of approximately 700 students, about 40% of whom are *concurrent* students and about 60% are *consecutive* students. The concurrent students enter the final year after completing a four-year honors degree, one education-related course, and three one-week field experience sessions in each of the first three years of their four-year undergraduate degree. By contrast, the consecutive students apply for the final year of the BEd program once, and they are considered for admission on the condition that they can provide evidence of completing an undergraduate degree (typically a Bachelor of Arts or Bachelor of Science).

The BEd final year at Queen's is comprised of 14 weeks of on-campus coursework divided evenly between the fall and winter terms. There are also 15 weeks of practicum experiences comprised of 12 weeks of regular school-based and assessed practicum and three weeks of "alternative practicum," which can occur in any acceptable setting, and which is not formally assessed. The 12 weeks of regular practicum are further divided into three four-week blocks, two of which are scheduled in the fall term, and the remaining block coincides with the three-week alternative practicum in the winter term.

For each of the three four-week regular practicum blocks, clear criteria and descriptions of teaching expectations for Teacher Candidates (TCs) are listed in the *Practicum Handbook*. For instance, in the secondary school setting, it is expected that a TC will typically teach one period (of a four-period day) during the first practicum block, two periods of the day during the second block, and three during the third (a regular teacher's load). It is also expected that secondary school TCs will teach some part of their practicum in each of their identified teaching subjects.

In the elementary school setting, it is expected that TCs will typically be responsible for approximately one third of a regular teacher's load in the first practicum block, two thirds in the second block, and a regular teacher's full load during the third block. It is similarly expected that all elementary school TCs will teach some of their practicum in each of the two elementary school divisions (i.e., JK–3 primary, and 4–6 junior).

Two additional features of the 12-weeks of regular practicum experiences are important – namely, the Associate School model and the role of the Faculty Liaison within this Associate School model. All practicum students in the final year BEd program are placed through the Faculty's Practicum Office, and TCs are assigned to Associate Schools within Queen's designated geographic placement area. It is comprised of approximately 15 public and Catholic school districts that are spread out over an area of approximately 10 000 square kilometres.

Within the Queen's Associate School model, the goal is to place a cohort of three to five TCs in an elementary school and a cohort of six to eight in a secondary school. Thus, in any given year, the practicum utilizes approximately 120 Associate Schools throughout Queen's designated geographic area. TCs typically stay in the same Associate School for all 12 weeks of their regular practicum experiences, but it should also be noted that most of these Associate Schools do not exclusively accept TCs from Queen's BEd program; in fact, they occasionally host TCs from several institutions at the same time.

The Practicum Office tries to place TCs in one of the four school districts that they had identified on his/her practicum submission form. This goal has become more difficult to achieve in recent years because of the increased competition among universities for the finite number of available and appropriate practicum placements. This difficulty has been caused by an increase in the number of Ontario universities offering concurrent and/or consecutive BEd programs and an increase in the number of students in existing concurrent and/or consecutive BEd programs. The situation has been exacerbated by the arrival of international teacher-education programs (with provincial endorsement) as well as certain international border institutions (without provincial consent) operating within the province and also competing for practicum placements. At the time of writing, the existing demographics of the student population and the teaching population are causing an annual oversupply of approximately 5500 new teachers coming from all of these BEd programs.

The second important element of the practicum program relates to the role of the Faculty Liaison. This individual is the university's representative who is assigned to work with our TCs and their Associate Teachers within each Associate School. Within Queen's practicum program, there are approximately 35 people who annually serve in this role. The Faculty Liaison has responsibilities for the on-campus course instruction and for monitoring and facilitating the practicum experiences as they unfold in the Associate Schools. Within the on-campus portion of the program, each Faculty Liaison teaches a cohort of approximately 20 TCs who have been placed in the Associate Schools assigned to each liaison.

Within a typical 18-hour course, the Faculty Liaison will address various pre-teaching topics and concerns, such as classroom management and lesson planning, but will also offer sessions pertaining to such subjects as teacher beliefs and action research. The Faculty Liaison also uses some of this course time to create a preliminary timetable, plan, and process (that are flexible as needed) with respect to visiting his/her respective Associate Schools. In addition to coursework and face-to-face meetings on campus and in the schools, considerable communication is enacted electronically.

Within the Associate Schools, the Faculty Liaisons play critical roles in supporting the TCs, in collaborating with the Associate Teachers, and in helping to maintain and to procure increased numbers of practicum placements within the Associate Schools. Over the period of the three regular practicum blocks, each Faculty Liaison arranges to observe the teaching of each TC in two different practicum blocks. These observations are typically accompanied by lengthy debriefing sessions where feedback is provided to the TC on his/her instructional performance. As well, Faculty Liaisons are also sent a weekly report of the minutes of the weekly three-hour school-based TC meeting, where each cohort discusses pertinent teaching/ learning topics or issues as prescribed by the course materials.

The Faculty Liaison also spends time with each Associate Teacher during the practicum blocks to ensure that university expectations for each practicum block are being met. This connection is particularly important because some Associate Schools have TCs from several universities, some of whom have different expectations for the practicum. An additional member of the practicum team is the School Liaison, who is a designated contact person within each Associate School. The Faculty Liaison works with this individual to attempt to arrange the expected TC placements for upcoming practicum blocks, a task which can often prove difficult because of the limited number of available teachers willing to host a TC.

The Faculty Liaison also serves a role in informing the Associate Teachers of the rationale of our BEd program and the expectations for each practicum block. In cases where TCs experience problems meeting these expectations, the Faculty Liaison is the university's contact person for addressing such concerns, and if necessary, the Faculty Liaison will initiate remedial or withdrawal processes for TCs who will be unsuccessful in the practicum block. Overall, the Faculty Liaison is the critical link among the TCs, Associate Teachers, and University.

Mentorship Responsibilities in the Practicum

Our practicum model is rooted in the practice of mentorship. As a vital component of teacher education, the mentorship process facilitates instructional improvement and professional growth, and it is focused on the interactions between the mentor (usually an experienced educator) and the protégé or mentee (usually an inexperienced or less experienced educator) (Beach & Reinhartz, 2000; Hopkins-Thompson, 2000; Sullivan & Glanz, 2000). Lankau and Scandura

(2002) emphasized the primary role of mentorship in the personal learning of the protégé. Through the practice of mentorship, mentors provide support, advocacy, advice, help, protection, feedback, and information through acts of teaching, sponsoring, encouraging, counselling, and befriending their protégés. Besides providing professional benefits, mentoring relationships also offer personal benefits such as stronger self-confidence, reduced stress, increased motivation, and acquisition of new knowledge and skills (Allen & Eby, 2007; Cowan, 2006; Lacey, 2000).

Three sets of mentorship dimensions exist in the Queen's practicum model, the first of which is the mentorship relationship between the Faculty Liaison (as mentor) and the TC (as protégé). Second, Faculty Liaisons engage in mentor-protégé relationships with Associate Teachers; and third, mentorship relationships are established between the Associate Teachers (as mentors) and TCs (as protégés). This practicum model is best described as a "mentorship triad" (see Figure 1), wherein each of the relational dimensions possesses a unique set of mentorship characteristics.

Faculty Liaisons' primary role, according to the guidelines indicated in the *Practicum Handbook* (Faculty of Education, 2009), is

Figure 1

A conceptualization of the mentorship triad that functions in the teacher-education practicum facilitated by the Faculty of Education at Queen's University.

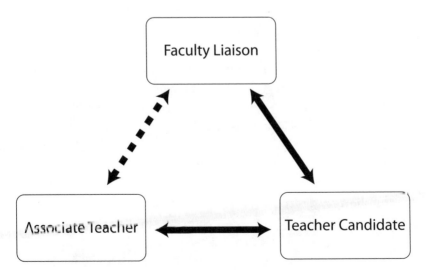

to act as consultants and advisors to TCs by distributing information, maintaining ongoing communication, and facilitating support mechanisms during the practicum. Also, Faculty Liaisons support the development of goals and processes necessary for the TCs' successful completion of assignments. Serving as "critical friends" (Costa & Kallick, 1993), Faculty Liaisons are responsible for observing TCs in their respective teaching settings and for providing them with feedback, suggestions, and assistance in focusing their professional growth. Faculty Liaisons maintain regular contact with TCs by teaching the practicum-specific course and by formally observing each candidate during two of the three teaching blocks.

At the same time, Faculty Liaisons are responsible for ongoing communication with the Associate Teachers, which entails advising, consulting, and supporting Associate Teachers in practicum matters by sharing pertinent information and discussing TCs' teaching performance and progress. Faculty Liaisons sometimes visit the Associate Schools prior to the start of the extended practicum to meet with the Associate Teachers to discuss the details of the program. These mentorship relationships are the least frequent in nature of all in the "mentorship triad."

Not surprisingly, the most frequent and intensive mentor-protégé relationships in the practicum exist between the Associate Teacher and TC. Associate Teachers are responsible for orienting the candidates to the school and its programs, for clarifying each partner's duties, and for establishing regular conferencing and open communication regarding the school's learners and curriculum. Associate Teachers act as mentors by (a) observing TCs' classroom routines and instruction; (b) providing guidance in lesson planning, unit planning, assessing, preparing timelines, and conducting classroom management; (c) providing TCs with ongoing formative and constructive feedback (both oral and written) to enhance the candidates' self-evaluation; (d) guiding the candidates in the development of effective teaching strategies; and (e) discussing with TCs their teaching performance and progress and their professional growth.

In short, interaction between the Associate Teacher and TC becomes a regular, day-to-day mentorship process, both when performance is strong and when difficulties arise. If a TC does experience problems, Associate Teachers are responsible for providing and explicating a specific teaching plan or model (focusing on areas of identified weakness) to demonstrate for the TC a diversity of methods and techniques.

Applicability of the Adaptive Mentorship© Model

In response to the call to apply the Adaptive Mentorship model to various mentorship settings (Ralph & Walker, 2010), in the following section we analyze its potential to enhance the mentorship process in the Queen's practicum mentorship triad. We describe our conceptualization of the model's fit with our particular practicum setting and explicate the analysis of the data derived from the comments and reviews we obtained from an Adaptive Mentorship (AM) workshop that we conducted with Ralph and Walker for the Faculty Liaisons at the Faculty of Education, Queen's University.

Conceptual Underpinnings

The AM seems to fit with our practicum model because it focuses on mentors' efforts to align their mentorship behavior in response to the task-oriented development level of protégés in the learning/employment environment (Ralph & Walker, 2010). Critical questions that arise are: What factors are instrumental in this mentorship process? How much effort is required in mentorship relationships between the Faculty Liaisons? Associate Teachers? TCs? In order to answer these questions, we contend that such factors as the frequency of the interaction and the nature of the working relationships between/among the parties in the triad would be instrumental for ensuring the effectiveness of the AM model's implementation.

Although the roles, responsibilities, and relationships between/among the parties are clearly described in the guidelines, not all mentorship relationships between the roles are equally identified or represented in the triad. TCs have frequent contact with Faculty Liaisons in their respective sections of the practicum-specific, on-campus course, where both parties have ample opportunities to discuss instructional and professional growth strategies. In addition, TCs receive constructive feedback and suggestions from Faculty Liaisons regarding the observation of their practicum teaching. The most frequent mentorship interactions in the triad occur between the Associate Teachers and TCs. Through everyday mentorship interactions in their schools, TCs develop their skills with the help of Associate Teachers' suggestions, advice, and feedback regarding their preparation, instruction, and professional growth. The least frequent mentorship interactions occur between Faculty Liaisons and Associate Teachers. Their interactions are limited to a few meetings a year but may occur slightly more often in cases when TCs experience difficulties in their practicum placement.

In relation to the applicability of the Adaptive Mentorship model to the practicum setting, we envision greater success of its implementation in the more frequent and direct relational dimensions of the triad (i.e., between Faculty Liaisons and TCs, and between Associate Teachers and TCs). Due to the regular and recurring nature of these relationships, the mentor-protégé pairs could first focus on determining the task-specific developmental level of the protégé and then work at synchronizing the mentor response to the protégé's level of performance. Subsequently, the mentor would continue to observe and adapt his/her mentorship response to match the fluctuating levels of the protégé's skill-specific performance. However, we anticipate that a tension might arise in the triad due to the sporadic and infrequent nature of mentorship relationships between certain Faculty Liaisons and Associate Teachers. This type of situation would make the application of the AM model more problematic. Hence, the link between these two partners in the Mentorship Triad model may not be as solid and consistent as the link between the other parties involved (thus the dotted arrow in Figure 1).

Pragmatically, we conceptualize this relational dimension between the Faculty Liaisons and Associate Teachers as representing the guiding mentorship role in the triad model. One reason for our assertion is that this Faculty Liaison–Associate Teacher dimension involves the two parties that act as mentors to the same protégés (the TCs). Second, unlike Faculty Liaisons, Associate Teachers have mentorship experience but have little to no training or professional development in carrying out mentorship responsibilities.

Finally, we believe that longevity effects in mentoring relationships must be taken into consideration. Because Associate Teachers have the most contact time with the TCs through regular in-class interactions and communication at the practicum placements, and because Faculty Liaisons only visit the schools twice, on average, it would seem most logical to us to emphasize that both partners (i.e., the Faculty Liaison and Associate Teacher) work collaboratively as joint-mentors when implementing the AM model with their common protégé.

Faculty Liaisons, who would initially possess knowledge of the AM model's specifics, would need to teach the model to the Associate Teachers in a manner consistent with the principles of the model itself. Acting as mentors to the Associate Teachers (the protégés in this situation), Faculty Liaisons could make judgments where Associate Teachers would fit in the model's D-quadrants (i.e., determine their development levels in the various mentorship skills) and then continually adapt their mentorship response and provide feedback and suggestions to the Associate Teachers as they develop their knowledge and skills to use the model.

Once the Associate Teachers had learned to apply the model (i.e., reached a D4 level of competence and confidence), the faculty and school-based supervisors would collaborate with their TCs to determine respective TCs' developmental levels and discuss what kind of feedback should be provided. Successful modelling of the AM practices between/among these parties will first help Associate Teachers develop their mentorship proficiency, and in turn, the two mentors will assist the TCs to increase their instructional competence and confidence. In this way, each member of the triad would be mentored to move to more advanced developmental levels in their respective bodies of knowledge and tasks.

We understand, however, that our conceptualization of the successful implementation of the AM model will have possible pitfalls and inevitable challenges that arise. Our mentorship triad shown in Figure 1 addressed the de-personalized, role-defined relational dimensions of the mentoring process. However, as Hanson (2003) indicated, conflicts are not only found at the formal organizational levels (e.g., intra- or inter-role conflicts), but they may also occur at the informal levels (e.g., interpersonal conflicts). Organizational roles are filled by individuals with various characteristics, interests, and preferences; Kram (1985) emphasized that relationships and organizational contexts are important influencing factors in the mentorship process. Thus, we will have to consider such relational and contextual factors in our mentorship triad format as well.

The complexity of personal styles and learning approaches influence the dynamics of mentoring relationships (Hale, 2000), and Kram (1985) further stated that individuals involved in a relationship bring a unique set of needs and concerns that have been shaped by their respective life histories. Furthermore, scholars have distinguished between mentorship as a relationship and as an activity (Bloch, 1993; Collin, 1988). Therefore, in the process of implementing the AM model, one must consider mentorship relationships based on the learning styles of the participants involved. Hale (2000) argued, "mentors and mentees should be encouraged to discuss similarities in experience and style early on in the relationship in order to encourage rapport building" (p. 233).

The continuity of relationships is another factor that must be considered. As we argued above regarding our practicum model, to establish stronger mentorship relationships between Faculty Liaisons and Associate Teachers will be instrumental in implementing AM with the purpose of facilitating TCs' professional development in their practicum placements. Yet, we must also remember that despite the benefits, developing strong ties and relationships between Faculty Liaisons and Teacher Associates may intimidate TCs in that they may not respond positively to the AM model if they sensed that a pre-existing relationship existed between their Faculty Liaisons and Associate Teachers. They may interpret such a relationship with apprehension that their mentor pair somehow possesses an unfair advantage over them.

Such a scenario would create a "catch 22" situation where a TC might perceive that the Faculty Liaison has a stronger relationship and commitment to the Associate Teacher than to the TC. If such a relationship existed prior to, and will no doubt continue after, the TC's own practicum, the TC may perceive that the larger program needs and the long-term relationships between the faculty and the school will take precedence over the TC's interests, and as a result they may feel as if the mentors are "ganging up" on him/her.

In considering the nature of the mentoring relationships in the Queen's triad, it is essential to recognize that the relationships do not exist in a vacuum. In other words, the relational dimensions in

the triad are influenced by context. Kram (1985) discussed the influence of such factors as reward systems, appraisal schemes, and hierarchical structures of the organization. Furthermore, Hale (2000)
discussed gender and age as characteristics that may or may not facilitate the development of mentorship relationships. Gender as a
dynamic in the mentoring relationship was examined by Kram in
relation to how stereotyping was used to reduce uncertainty, how
males and females assumed their stereotype role, and how role
modelling was difficult to implement in cross-gender relationships.
In addition, the dynamic of hierarchical distance needs to be considered in order to try to identify whether there is an optimum level
of distance between the mentor and the protégé to support learning
(Hale, 2000).

In the Queen's practicum context, the complexity of such issues is
exacerbated by the fact that multiple organizational contexts are involved. Specifically, in addition to the differences between university
and school contexts, within Ontario the vast majority of schools in
larger urban areas have TCs on practicum from several universities
(both Ontario-based and out-of-country based) at the same time
throughout the year. For example, one school had TCs from seven
different universities representing different program structures, purposes, lengths, and intended experiences for the practicum setting,
and in one school, an Associate Teacher worked with three candidates from different universities throughout the year.

Practical Underpinnings

In addition to our conceptualization of the potential of using the
Adaptive Mentorship model in the practicum setting, we further
analyzed the comments and reviews obtained from the AM workshop with the Faculty Liaisons. At the end of the workshop, participants were asked to assume the role of a panel of experts to assess the model, and they submitted anonymous written comments
evaluating it. The attendees all endorsed the multi-dimensionality,
flexibility, and transferability of the model due to its focused, individualized, and task-oriented approach to mentorship. Due
to the important role of intentionality in the mentoring process
(e.g., intentional improvement, intentional intervention), the AM

model was deemed an appropriate framework to be used by all parties in the triad before and during the three practicum placements. Participants viewed AM as a foundational starting point for communicating with TCs because they believed it allowed for a "neutral ground," and it involved both mentor and protégé in a collaborative process. Furthermore, attendees considered that the task-specificity and the adaptability to protégés' specific needs were useful because those features were deemed effective in facilitating the mentoring process by decisively identifying the problem and the fundamental issues at hand.

Participants identified a limitation of the AM model for the Queen's program, which was that the link between the Faculty Liaisons and Associate Teachers was missing or inadequately explained. The attendees indicated that the model would be difficult to implement unless the Associate Teachers knew and trusted the Faculty Liaisons. They suggested that Faculty Liaisons needed to build credibility in the relationships before using the model with Associate Teachers. To accomplish this goal would be a time- and energy-consuming effort and might have to take place over a few years. Workshop attendees also noted that the current lack of mentorship in-service activities for the Associate Teachers in their program would have to be ameliorated. They suggested involving School Liaisons (the in-school practicum coordinators) in planning the mentorship activities and providing in-service training and professional development opportunities for Associate Teachers. These changes may also prove difficult because, as of the time of writing, the university provided no compensation for individuals in the School Liaison role.

Furthermore, Faculty Liaison attendees discussed a number of contextual factors that may hinder the implementation of the AM model. They critiqued the linear, somewhat simplistic structure of the model, which narrowed its application and situated it simply as a "location" exercise of placing participants in respective grids. We believe that the model's utility could be enhanced if it was cast as a broad analytical tool that helped identify critical entry points and then led to a systematic practice of mentorship. In fact, drawing the Faculty Liaisons' attention to any feature of the Associate Teachers' work with the Teacher Candidates would be a major step toward enhanced practicum experiences in our triad relationship.

Implications for Practice

Within the Ontario context, there have been numerous discussions about the role of the Associate Teachers and the importance of supporting them in their mentorship roles. The Ontario Teachers' Federation as well as the various affiliates (i.e., the Elementary Teachers' Federation, the Ontario Elementary Catholic Teachers, and the Ontario Secondary School teachers' Federation) have advocated for more educational support for Associate Teachers, and each of the affiliates has created resource materials to support their members who host TCs. Additional qualification (AQ) courses on mentorship are available, but few teachers are willing to pay the substantial fee to enroll in the course, and the universities are not willing to offer such courses at reduced rates as an incentive. Various universities have offered in-service workshops for their Associate Teachers, but these sessions have met with mixed results. In cases where a university is able to place most of its TCs within local-area school districts, there are stronger relationships between the school district and university. This relationship results in a higher participation rate of teachers attending the workshops, especially when the two organizations are able to find ways to provide teaching release days for such workshops.

Specific to Queen's context, only half of our placements are local, with the remaining placements in larger urban and rural settings that are up to five hours away. Although our practicum office is willing to explore possibilities to forge local partnerships, we also recognize that support for *all* of our Associate Teachers must be made available, regardless of their location.

The common element for all of our practicum placements is the Faculty Liaison, who is assigned to a cluster of Associate Schools, and this is who would play a critical role in establishing the kind of trusting relationship necessary to establish a "second-level" Adaptive Mentorship program. We also recognize that under our existing structure, the Faculty Liaison would be unable to spend more than two days in any particular school during a practicum block, regardless of whether the school was local or distant. Coupled with the fact that the Faculty Liaison currently spends considerable time observing and debriefing TCs' lessons, there would be little time to engage in the specifics of providing additional mentoring support for Associate Teachers, even in those contexts where strong relationships exist.

A recent addition to the instructional and administrative components of our BEd program has been the move to increasing the utilization of information and communication technology (ICT). As well, all practicum forms and requests are available in digital form, which are uploaded into complex databases that are used by support staff to facilitate the monitoring and placement of TCs. Another major electronic initiative that is occurring within our faculty is the creation of a *practicum portal*, which is being built within the Desire to Learn® (D2L) software, with the intention that this practicum portal will digitally support both educative and administrative functions related to the practicum for all practicum participants – the TCs, the Faculty Liaisons, and the Associate Teachers.

The administrative functions are fairly straightforward. For TCs, it entails having all standard practicum related request or monitoring forms in an electronic format which they fill out and submit to the Practicum Office. For Faculty Liaisons, we plan to create structures that would let us track visits, track placement subjects, and submit visit reports. For Associate Teachers, we plan to create electronic structures that would let them submit honoraria requests, indicate their interest in having another Teacher Candidate, and eventually, to submit their practicum assessments.

The educative functions are more ambitious and more difficult to design. Our current plan is to create a series of learning objects that would be available to all members of the triad (so that all participants could see the same information). The learning objects will centre on core principles of the AM model. These principles focus on all members of the triad enhancing the quality of the practicum experience by giving appropriate attention to the TC's professional development and to the applicable common language with which participants can converse.

The electronic education functions will need to be supported by the Faculty Liaison through appropriately modelling the Adaptive

Mentorship model and by drawing attention to the available features of the practicum portal to the members of the triad. We feel that using the language of AM in terms of the TC's developmental needs is a significant entry point. This application would allow conversations at both levels, thus modelling mentorship skills for the Associate Teachers without focusing directly on Associate Teachers' existing mentoring practices.

In a recent instance, one Faculty Liaison informed us of how he had introduced the key concept of Adaptive Mentorship to an Associate Teacher who had been frustrated with his own ability to mentor and who had explicitly invited input from the Faculty Liaison. The Faculty Liaison reported that both he and the Associate Teacher found the exercise to be a powerful step forward in their work of analyzing the performance of the TC within the practicum setting. This example highlighted the importance of the relationship of trust that needs to exist between the Associate Teacher and the Faculty Liaison. In this particular case, the Faculty Liaison had already been working with the teachers in that particular Associate School for three years, and yet, this occasion was the first time the Associate Teacher had felt comfortable enough to report his frustration to the Liaison.

This example also indicated the importance of understanding the stages and phases of the mentoring relationship (Chao, 1997; Chao, Walz, & Gardner, 1992; Kram, 1985; Mertz, 2004). In addition, it showed that, unfortunately, being a teacher with classroom experience does not automatically equate to being a successful mentor. There are critical characteristics, skills, and abilities needed by mentors in order to be effective (Galbraith, 2001; Johnson, 2006). These attributes include, but are not limited to, human relations skills, instructional leadership, and understanding mentorship as a form of instruction (Playko, 1995). Mentors must also possess enthusiasm, knowledge of the field, communication abilities, listening skills, and a caring attitude (Bey & Holmes, 1992; Daresh, 2002). Furthermore, because mentoring is a mutual learning partnership (Zachary, 2000), our approach will also emphasize the importance of protégés taking initiative in the triad relationships. Daresh and Playko (1995) suggested that the skills of "protégéship" can be acquired, in which protégés need to undertake necessary preparations before entering into a mentoring relationship. In order to take the initiative in forming a learning partnership, they need to acquire the knowledge, skills, and dispositions that would enable them to be effective protégés (Daresh & Playko, 1995; Portner, 2002; Searby & Tripses, 2007; Zachary, 2000).

By making sure that mentors' and protégés' roles have equal importance in the triad relationships, our goal is to establish a culture of mentoring (Zachary, 2005) and a successful mentoring program (Kochan, 2002) in the practicum model of our BEd program. Through the use of the practicum portal we are intending to create issue-specific scenarios surrounding typical problems that face TCs, as well as examples of the range of effective and ineffective communication that typically occurs between Associate Teachers and Teacher Candidates regarding these problems. Through the use of Second Life® avatars, we hope to be able to create gender characters that can depict the kinds of effective and ineffective communication strategies that could exist and the implications of such strategies for improved instruction. Our hope is that such Second Life® case stories could be educative to all triad members and could serve as conversation openers specific to the mentoring relationships. As these case stories are developed, we hope to conduct research on the how the practicum portal supports the development of better understandings and practices related to the practicum experiences for TCs, Associate Teachers, and Faculty Liaisons.

References

Allen, T. D., & Eby, L. T. (Eds.). (2007). *The Blackwell handbook of mentoring: A multiple perspectives approach.* Oxford, UK: Blackwell Publishing Ltd.

Beach, D. M., & Reinhartz, J. (2000). *Supervisory leadership: Focus on instruction.* Boston, MA: Allyn and Bacon.

Bey, T. M., & Holmes, C. T. (1992). *Mentoring: Contemporary principles and issues.* Reston, VA: Association of Teacher Educators.

Bloch, S. (1993, April). Business mentoring and coaching. *Training and Development, 26,* 28–29.

Chao, G. T. (1997). Mentoring phases and outcomes. *Journal of Vocational Behavior, 51*(1), 15–28. doi:10.1006/jvbe.1997.1591

Chao, G. T., Walz, P. M., & Gardner, P. D. (1992). Formal and informal mentorships: A comparison on mentoring functions and contrast with nonmentoring counterparts. *Personnel Psychology*, 45, 619–636.

Collin, A. (1988, March/April). Mentoring. *ICT*, 23–27.

Costa, A. L., & Kallick, B. (1993). Through the lens of a critical friend. *Educational Leadership*, 50(1), 49–51.

Cowan, S. L. (2006). *So you want to be mentored: An application workbook for using five strategies to get the most out of a mentoring relationship*. Amherst, MA: HRD Press.

Daresh, J. C. (2002). *Leaders helping leaders: A practical guide to administrative mentoring* (2nd ed.). Thousand Oaks, CA: Corwin Press.

Daresh, J. C., & Playko, M. A. (1995). *Supervision as a proactive process: Concepts and cases*. Prospect Heights, IL: Waveland Press, Inc.

Faculty of Education. (2009). *Practicum handbook: A guide for teacher candidates, associate teachers, school liaisons, and faculty liaisons*. Kingston, ON: Queen's University.

Galbraith, M. (2001). Mentoring development for community college faculty. *Michigan Community College Journal: Research and Practice*, 7(2), 29–39.

Hale, R. (2000). To match or mis-match? The dynamics of mentoring as a route to personal and organisational learning. *Career Development International*, 5(4), 223–234.

Hanson, E. M. (2003). *Educational administration and organizational behavior* (5th ed.). Boston, MA: Allyn & Bacon.

Hopkins-Thompson, P. A. (2000). Colleagues helping colleagues: Mentoring and coaching. *NASSP Bulletin*, 84(617), 29–36.

Johnson, S. (2006, Summer). The neuroscience of the mentor-learner relationship. *New Directions for Adult and Continuing Education: The Neuroscience of Adult Learning*, 110, 63–69. Available from http://voced.edu.au/content/ngv19874

Kochan, F. K. (Ed.). (2002). *The organizational and human dimensions of successful mentoring programs and relationships*. Greenwich, CT: Information Age.

Kram, K. E. (1985). *Mentoring at work: Developmental relationships in organisational life*. Glenview, IL: Scott, Foresman.

Lacey, K. (2000). *Making mentoring happen: A simple and effective guide to implementing a successful mentoring program.* London, UK: Allen & Unwin.

Lankau, M., & Scandura, T. A. (2002). An investigation of personal learning in mentoring relationships: Content, antecedents, and consequences. *Academy of Management Journal, 45,* 779–790.

Mertz, N. T. (2004). What's a mentor, anyway? *Educational Administration Quarterly, 40*(4), 541–560.

Playko, M. A. (1995). Mentoring for educational leaders: A practitioner's perspective. *Journal of Educational Administration, 33*(5), 84–92.

Portner, H. (2002). *Being mentored: A guide for protégés.* Thousand Oaks, CA: Corwin Press.

Ralph, E. G., & Walker, K. D. (2010). Enhancing mentors' effectiveness: The promise of the Adaptive Mentorship model. *McGill Journal of Education, 45*(2), 205–218.

Searby, L., & Tripses, J. (2007, August). *Preparing future school administrators for meaningful mentoring relationships: A comparison of processes in two universities.* Paper presented at the National Council of Professors of Educational Administration, Chicago, IL.

Sullivan, S., & Glanz, J. (2000). *Supervision that improves teaching: Strategies and techniques.* Thousand Oaks, CA: Corwin Press.

Zachary, L. (2000). *The mentor's guide: Facilitating effective learning relationships.* San Francisco, CA: Jossey-Bass.

Zachary, L. (2005). *Creating a mentoring culture: The organization's guide.* San Francisco, CA: Jossey-Bass.

Chapter Twenty-One

Integrating a Developmental Perspective with the Adaptive Mentorship© Model

Ellery Pullman

OR MANY YEARS, INDIVIDUALS WORKING with adults in the professional fields have realized the importance of mentoring from a developmental perspective. A developmental approach to mentorship is important in shaping a clear conceptualization of the overall process involved and the issues that inevitably arise within the mentoring relationship. Mentorship in such fields as higher education, business, health care, and industry calls for a complex set of leadership skills that are rooted in a developmental approach and that will enable the person in the mentorship position to provide services using best practice interventions and strategies suitable to each protégé.

Principles of Adult Learning Underlying the Mentorship Process

Mentorship is intended to be a learning process where helpful, personal, and reciprocal relationships between the protégé and the mentor are established and where a focus on growth is the aim. During the mentorship process, protégés develop their knowledge and skills through guided practice and personal dialogue with mentors. In this relationship, mentors provide feedback and share their experiences, which protégés reflect on and incorporate into their professional thinking and practice.

The process of mentorship may be viewed through different lenses. If the protégé is viewed as an apprentice, he/she will observe the mentor's practices and learn to emulate them. In a competency based approach, the mentor will give the protégé systematic feedback regarding his/her performance and progress in acquiring the specific body of knowledge and skills being learned. The intention, here, is that the protégé will continue to build on identified strengths and minimize areas of weaknesses under the mentor's guidance. The mentor helps the protégé become a "reflective practitioner," but at the same time, the mentor also learns and develops his/her unique sets of professional skills. Thus, the mentorship process may occasionally become mutual and collaborative because the relationship may provide a dynamic growth experience for both members.

Dewey (1916) emphasized the importance of individual experience in the learning process and the value of interaction in creating a positive learning environment. Later learning theorists such as Lewin (1951), Piaget (1969) and Vygotsky (1981) continued to develop Dewey's ideas. Lewin conceptualized learning as emerging from individuals' engagement with concrete experiences and from receiving ongoing feedback from others regarding their progress. Piaget contended that learning should involve individuals accommodating new concepts into their experience and, in turn, assimilating their experience into new concepts. Vygotsky introduced the concept of the "zone of proximal development," which refers to the difference between an individual solving a problem on one's own versus solving a problem with someone who is more advanced in knowledge and skills.

Knowles (1980) coined the term *andragogy* to refer to the facilitation of learning among adults. The current focus of mentoring as a process-oriented relationship that involves knowledge acquisition and reflective practice is consistent with the five andragogical principles foundational to adult learning:

1. Self-Concept: As a person matures, he or she moves from dependency to self-directedness.
2. Experience: Adults draw upon their experiences to aid their learning.
3. Readiness: The learning readiness of adults is closely related to their assumption of new social roles.
4. Orientation: As a person acquires new knowledge, he or she wants to apply it immediately in problem solving.
5. Motivation: As a person matures, he or she is motivated to learn because of internal factors.

Mentorship may be viewed as a transformational process in which a person recognizes a need for change and proceeds to develop that knowledge. Apps (1988) noted that a transformational mindset includes a creative way of looking at situations and problems that is not obvious or routine. Critical reflection occurs accompanied by asking such questions as: What are the assumptions and values underlying the situation? What alternatives need to be considered? Are the right questions even being asked? The process is built on the premise that "what we assume about something or someone influences our perceptions and in turn our actions toward that something or someone" (p. 56).

According to Apps (1988), a transformational process included the following phases: (a) developing an awareness by recognizing that something needs to change, identifying the root causes of the dissonance, and learning about the ways to address the concern; (b) exploring alternatives by realizing that change is needed in order for growth to occur; (c) making a transition by leaving the old behind and embracing the new; (d) achieving integration by putting the pieces from the transition phase back together or, as Levinson (1978) suggested, building a new life structure; and (e) taking action by putting the new ideas into operation.

This transformational process allows for movement; it is dynamic and fluid and moves back and forth between and among the phases, with the possibility that more than one phase may occur simultaneously. This process may often occur in mentoring relationships, where a number of activities and concerns could be under consideration simultaneously.

Merriam and Caffarella (1999) identified three components in transformational learning: experience, critical reflection, and development. The aspect of experience, which was the second principle in the andragogy model, is an important consideration in creating an effective learning opportunity for adults who typically represent a range of levels and stages of development. For them, the learning opportunity needs to be relevant and applicable to each person's unique set of experiences. Argote, McEvily, and Reagans (2003) also identified experience as an important factor in a learner's ability to create, retain, and transfer knowledge.

Critical reflection was the second key to transformational learning according to Merriam and Cafferella (1999) and part of andragogy's self-directed learning (Knowles, 1980). The opportunity for reflection is also essential for creating effective learning experiences for adults involved in mentoring relationships. Adult learners need time to contemplate the implications and ramifications of their learning experiences.

The third element of transformational learning was development (corresponding to the third assumption of andragogy). Merriam and Caffarella (1999) stated that "the ability to think critically, which is mandatory to effecting personal change, is itself developmental" (p. 330).

If development is to be the outcome of transformational mentorship encounters, then effective adult learning opportunities need to be created that will focus on protégés' personal development. Knowles (1980) declared that andragogical learning assumes that adults (a) need to know why they are learning something, (b) learn best by doing, (c) are problem-solvers, and (d) learn best when the subject is of immediate use.

Yi (2005) suggested three methods to foster learning for adults, each of which has applicability to effective mentorship: *Problem-Based Learning*, which seeks to increase problem-solving and critical thinking skills; *Cooperative Learning*, which builds communication and interpersonal skills; and *Situated Learning*, which targets specific technical skills that can be directly related to adults' field of work. Each of these methods is grounded in adult-learning principles in that these methods are self-directive, they are applicable to the adults' own work situations, and they are related to the learners' past experiences.

Because adults prefer this self-directed approach, mentors need to be careful to allow for flexibility when preplanning the agenda. Similarly, because adults' experiential base is a rich resource for learning, mentors must guard against focusing solely on their own experiences rather than those of their protégés. Mentors must also be careful not to project their "ways" onto protégés who are often at a different stage in the career cycle. Mentors are usually at the stage of *generativity*, the competency building stage of their careers (Erikson, 1969). Their level of learning and exploration might very well be out of the realm of reality for a protégé at the beginning stages of his/her career. The protégé may be more concerned about fitting in, being accepted, trying to stay one step ahead of the demands of life, and achieving some measure of confidence and security in dealing with the daily work issues. Mentors need to be sensitive to these needs, and to be prepared to adjust their mentoring response to match the protégés' existing developmental level rather than forcing them into some pre-fixed mold.

The Role of Transitions in Adulthood

The concept of transitions is used both by developmentalists who speak in terms of life stages (e.g., Levinson & Levinson, 1996) and those who promote a life-events paradigm (e.g., Schlossberg, 1984). Transitions are generally viewed as a natural process of disorientation and reorientation that marks turning points on the path of growth, which involve times of acceleration and transformation. Adults of all ages and stages of development continually experience transitions, whether anticipated or unanticipated. They respond to these transitions in terms of the demands present in the situation, the context in which it occurs, and the resources at their disposal for dealing with the transition.

In the Levinson models (1978, 1996), each era has its distinctive and unifying character of learning, and each transition between eras requires a change in the character of one's life that may take between three and six years to complete. Each of the four eras in the sequence lasts approximately twenty-five years and developmental periods appear within these eras. The eras and main developmental periods are as follows:

1. Early adulthood: ages 17–45
   a. Early adult transition (17–22)
   b. Entering the adult world (22–28)
   c. Age thirty transition (28–33)
   d. Settling down (33–40)
2. Middle adulthood: ages 40–65
   a. Mid-life transition (40–45)
   b. Entering middle adulthood (45–50)
   c. Age fifty transition (50–55)
   d. Culmination of middle adulthood (55–60)

3. Late adulthood: ages 60 and on
   a. Late adult transition (60–65)

Within the broad eras are periods of development, each period being characterized by a set of tasks and an attempt to build or modify one's life structure. For example, in the Early Adult Transition period, the two primary tasks are to move out of the pre-adult world and to make a preliminary step into the adult world. Similarly, during the Settling Down period, the two tasks are to establish a niche in society and to work for progress and advancement in that niche.

Schlossberg (1984) and Goodman, Schlossberg, and Anderson (2006) described how people in transition possess strengths and weaknesses, or resources and deficits, to cope with the transition. These strengths/weaknesses lie in four categories: situation, self, supports, and strategies. When strengths outweigh the limitations, the person tends to make a successful transition.

Transitions may be predictable or unpredictable, positive or negative, gradual or sudden, and entered into voluntarily or involuntarily. Different models have been developed to show how transitions can (a) be predictable, depending on the meaning to each person, (b) involve some measure of stress that may be partially controlled, (c) affect individuals differently, and (d) help people to adapt and gain from the experience.

The Adaptive Mentorship Model with a Developmental Perspective

The Adaptive Mentorship (AM) model, developed by Ralph and Walker (2010, 2011, see Figure 1) lends itself to the integration of a developmental orientation to mentoring. The AM model may be used by practitioners possessing more experience and expertise (mentors) to promote the professional development of individuals possessing less experience and skill (protégés) in this mentorship relationship (Ralph, 2003, 2004).

Ralph (1992) noted that his earlier CS model emphasized an adaptive approach rather than a "one size fits all" method, that it was intuitively appealing because it was relatively easy to understand, that it helped bridge the theory-practice gap by clarifying the conceptualization of the supervisory/mentorship process in a holistic way, and that it offered practical mentorship guidance to individuals in mentorship roles. The AM (CS) model focuses on mentors adjusting their mentoring behaviors in an intentional way to help meet the skill-specific developmental tasks and needs of the protégés they are working with in various learning and work environments.

The approach taken by AM consists of three very practical steps. In the first step, the aim is to ascertain the specific developmental level of the protégé (Ralph, 2003; Ralph & Walker, 2010, 2011), or what could also be viewed as a pre-assessment of the development stage. This step in the process would occur as the pair builds rapport with each other. At this time the mentor and protégé determines how the relationship will be conducted and what the mutual expectations are (Hay, 1995; Ibarra, 2000; Klasen & Clutterbuck, 2002).

Also, the protégé's developmental needs and concerns are identified. This process may be as simple as asking the protégé to situate him/herself in the developmental process. For instance, the pair could respond to questions such as: What life experiences have shaped his/her current world view? What were watershed learning

Figure 1

The Adaptive Mentorship model, from Ralph and Walker (2010, 2011).

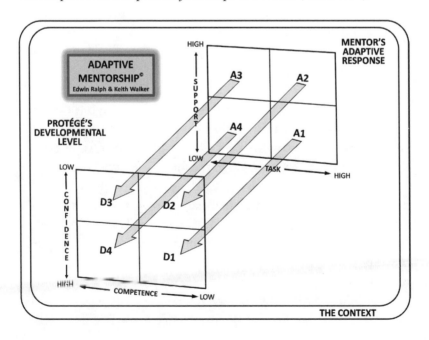

experiences, and how have they informed his/her current world view? How do age, race, gender, ability, sexual orientation, and socioeconomic status inform his/her current situation? How do all of these variables both enhance and limit him/her when interacting with or leading others? What are the gifts that each of these perspectives/orientations bring and what limitations do they pose?

A major aspect of identifying of the developmental level of the protégé is to determine as precisely as possible his/her level of developmental need. The most highly regarded "need theory" is that of Murray (1938), who defined "need" as a "construct . . . which stands for . . . a force which is organized perception, apperception, intellection, conation and action in such a way as to transform in a certain direction an existing unsatisfying situation" (pp. 123–124).

Developmental needs as they relate to mentorship processes often fall into one or more of following areas:

1. *Professional development* that emphasizes the growth of the individual as it relates to his or her professional roles;
2. *Organizational development* that emphasizes the needs, priorities, and structure of the institution or business in which one works;
3. *Career development* that emphasizes one's orientation to and preparation for career advancement; and
4. *Personal development* that emphasizes the life planning, interpersonal skills, and growth of the individual.

A key point here is to understand the life transition (i.e., events and changes) that the protégé may be facing. It is also wise to give consideration to the environmental factors that might be potentially supportive or hindering factors to the mentoring process as well.

Relationship management (i.e., the expected behaviors of the protégé and the mentor) and goal clarity are vital elements in a developmental approach to mentoring. Effective leadership abilities here would include such skills as maintaining rapport, adhering to a schedule for meetings, and being able to evaluate the direction of the relationship from time to time.

Continued clarification of developmental goals would also be important because the mentor must be able to assist the protégé to identify what he/she wants to achieve and why. Goal clarification will be enhanced when the pair can systematically analyze the available evidence and exercise decisiveness regarding follow-up action. Incidentally, mentors who find it difficult to define and follow up on their own goals will likely experience difficulty helping his/her protégé do the same. Mentors may also need to recognize that there might be times when comprehensive goal setting may have to give way to the more experientially oriented mindset of today's emerging adults, where more spontaneity might be the more desirable choice.

Once the protégé's task-specific developmental level has been determined through such means as personal reflection on the part of the protégé, a process of appreciative inquiry between the partners, observation by the mentor, or dialogue/conversation between the participants, then the mentor takes the next step. This step entails strategizing with the protégé to meet those defined needs in a specific way rather than by assuming or merely hoping that development will occur automatically with time.

At this point the AM model becomes strategic. For example, if a pair determines that a protégé reflects a level represented by quadrant D2 for a particular skill set (i.e., low in competence and low in confidence), then this individual may also be somewhat confused regarding his or her psychosocial development, particularly as it relates to identity formation (Erikson, 1963; Marcia, 1980, 2002). When in such a state, individuals often have difficulty making lasting commitments to self and have difficulty in fulfilling commitments to others. A major contributing factor here is related to a lack of self-awareness and efficacy.

On the other hand, a protégé who reflects the characteristics of quadrant D4 (i.e., high in confidence and high in competence for a task) could also be assumed to have a more established sense of identity and thus will require less encouragement and nurturing than the protégé located in D2. Chickering (1969) presented a range of psycho-social perspectives for being intentional and specific in meeting various individual needs and concerns of protégés. Perry (1970) also identified ways for mentors to be more in tune with how an individual processes the information at a particular stage of development.

At this step of strategizing mentorship responses is where Schlossberg (1984) and Goodman, Schlossberg, and Anderson's

(2006) perspectives of individuals in transition become important as well. Mentors need to recognize the situation (the environment), the self (the protégé's confidence), and the supports (environmental resources), which will also help influence the choice of mentoring strategies. With respect to the AM model, the mentor would now be seeking to ascertain the degree of task direction or procedural guidance and the degree of psycho-emotional support to administer in order to properly synchronize with the protégé's respective levels of competence and confidence for the accomplishment of a particular skill set or personal learning as a whole (Ralph & Walker, 2010).

This matching of mentor response (A1 to A4) with protégé development level (D1 to D4) is the very essence of the AM model because protégés' developmental needs can be addressed at their deepest level as opposed to the one size fits all approach that is often taken in many mentoring approaches. According to the ranges along the task and support continua, the mentor may be called upon to play a more generalist role of being a guide, sharing expertise, and encouraging and reinforcing the mentee; at other times, there may be a need for more direct instruction, telling the protégé how to proceed in a given task or process.

A key factor determining the effectiveness of the AM model rests on the accurate determination of the protégé's levels of competence

Table 1

A Framework of Protégé Competencies. Adapted from Clutterbuck, D., & Lane, G. (2005). The situational mentor. London, UK: Gower.

	Competencies	
Relationship Initiation	Relationship Management	Learning Maturity/ Disengagement
Focus; proactivity	Learn; teach	Acknowledge the debt; pay it forward
Respect; self-respect	Challenge; be challenged	Process awareness; process management
Listening; articulating	Open; questioning	Extrinsic & intrinsic feedback
	Prepare; reflect	Independence; interdependence

and confidence. Clutterbuck and Lane (2005) proposed three pairs of competencies at the *relationship initiation* level and four pairs at each of the *relationship management* and *learning maturity/disengagement* levels, as shown in Table 1.

Relationship initiation competencies include the ability to focus the mentoring relationship, to be proactive, to develop respect and self-respect, and to able to listen to others' statements and to express one's own views.

Relationship management competencies include a commitment to learning and teaching, a willingness to challenge others' assertions and to have one's ideas challenged, being open to question and be questioned, and to plan for an event and reflect during/after it as it relates to the mentoring relationship and impending outcomes. The third dynamic of the framework requires a more advanced skill set in the mentorship process called learning maturity and disengagement competencies, which involves acknowledging the skills and concepts learned through the mentorship process and implementing them. People who have had good protégé experiences often desire, in turn, to become mentors. Process awareness implies that the protégé assumes a direct role in the mentoring relationship in terms of setting his/her own goals and working toward their accomplishment.

A mature protégé, with high levels of confidence and competence, may direct the process toward established goals while less frequently relying on the mentor's knowledge and experience. On the other hand, learning from an older or more experienced mentor may provide valuable advice by which a protégé may avoid a potentially negative life situation. Learning from a mentor's successes or mistakes could help expand a protégé's knowledge base and shorten the learning cycles that experience alone would require. Living largely out of one's personal experiences may also short-circuit meaningful, relational connections that could better equip one to navigate difficult situations.

A third element, to process extrinsic and intrinsic feedback, calls for a good measure of trust between the participants, which may not always be easy to give or accept because of the sensitive nature of having to address one's weaknesses as they become apparent. A protégé must be assisted/challenged to move from a quadrant characterized by low confidence (i.e., D2 or D3) and low competence (i.e., D1 or D2) to quadrants reflecting more elevated levels.

The fourth element in the Clutterbuck and Lane (2005) framework is that of independence and interdependence. Being self-motivated, self-reliant, self-confident, and resourceful are all elements of an individual's growing sense of maturity in learning and life. The more capable protégés become as they transition to more advanced quadrants the less dependent the individual will be on the mentor. At that juncture, protégés typically develop a wider support base, depending less on the mentor's guidance and relying more on their own ingenuity. They gradually build a network of supporting colleagues, advisors, and resources that they can access as required.

A third step in Adaptive Mentorship process is to *continually observe and adjust mentor responses* (Ralph & Walker, 2010, 2011). Here the mentorship team continually monitors the protégé's changing level of development in the task being performed or skill set being practiced. The mentor is careful to adjust and synchronize his/her task and support responses to match, in reciprocal degrees, the protégé's respective levels of competence and confidence in the specific area that the protégé is seeking to develop. As the protégé advances in the D-quadrants, the mentor would adjust his/her A-grid mentoring responses to match the protégé's corresponding D position (i.e., A1 with D1, A2 with D2, and so on).

As noted earlier, developmental change or movement occurs when there is recognition of the need for change to one's current situation or circumstance. Developmental change here can entail a range of actions such as (a) resolving issues of identity formation (a sense of unity and confidence in one's beliefs), (b) integrating in a more public way the roles and commitments to specific values in emerging adulthood, or (c) navigating the transitions and challenges of young adulthood, when individuals begin to apply to themselves the information they have acquired about adult roles. Here the emerging or young adult may make a commitment to an intimate partner, have children, and/or choose and become engaged in a specific work role. In this process, young people's commitment to social institutions and to significant others typically expand and deepen. Their world view becomes more diverse, and their appreciation of the interdependence of various social systems increases. Balancing the strain of the multiple roles that many young adults face can contribute to increased stress. Effective mentors will be cognizant of these factors that may impinge on protégés' performance.

Assessment of protégés' progress helps them become more aware of their strengths and weaknesses and how others perceive them. Also, dealing with challenging experiences, even when a protégé has been considered to be strong (i.e., at D4), helps individuals to mature because such disorienting dilemmas force people out of their comfort zones and into new places. It is imperative in such situations for mentors to provide a supportive learning environment (e.g., temporarily reverting to an A3 response with high support) through which trust can be re-emphasized, encouraging the protégé to embrace future opportunities to once again take chances and experiment with new approaches.

However, a word of caution to the mentor is appropriate here. As much as the protégé's needs might be identified and the protégé has indicated a desire to move forward in a desired direction, the mentor may possibly encounter what Kegan and Lahey (2001) referred to as "immunity to change." Immunity to change is a growing understanding of the competing commitments that might keep a protégé from making the desired changes. Even with best intentions, a protégé may be simply unwilling or unable to proceed. Kegan and Lahey (1984), who were stage theorists, asserted that certain individuals may never develop past certain ways of being. How individuals see a situation is dependent upon their developmental level and previous life experiences. According to Kegan and Lahey's work, a developmental focus would be essential to maximize the benefits of mentorship for protégés and mentors alike. Effective mentoring would have to be tailored to the appropriate developmental needs of the protégé.

Concluding Remarks

I have argued in this chapter that today's effective mentors would need some measure of expertise in the fields of adult development and human systems management. My first reason for taking this position is that the mentor would be better able to "get their own house in order." He/she would be better equipped to help the protégé work toward desired outcomes. Second, the mentor would better understand how the various challenges facing the protégé could be motivating for some and dispiriting for others. Third, the mentor would realize that significant change is a cyclical theme in people's lives. They do not simply gain skills and experience over the years; rather, they change as individuals with significantly different motives and aspirations. Fourth, adult development has often been an ignored topic in much of the literature on mentorship and leadership today, but finally paying more attention to it could make an important improvement to mentorship initiatives.

Fifth, effective mentorship today calls for a thorough grounding in skills for processing the deeper issues of human beings, including a clarification of knowledge of oneself. Knowledge of how to best mentor adults in developing leadership skills for managing their lives and reaching their highest levels of impact within their spheres of influence is essential. One way to actualize this goal is to make use of approaches like the Adaptive Mentorship model that reflect this developmental perspective.

References

Apps, J. (1988). *Higher education in a learning society*. San Francisco, CA: Jossey-Bass.

Argote, L., McEvily, B., & Reagans, R. (2003). Managing knowledge in organizations: An integrative framework and review of emerging themes. *Management Science, 4*, 571–582.

Chickering, A.W. (1969). *Education and identity*. San Francisco, CA: Jossey-Bass.

Clutterbuck, D., & Lane, G. (2005). *The situational mentor*. London, UK: Gower.

Dewey, J. (1916). *Democracy and education: An introduction to the philosophy of education*. New York, NY: Free Press

Erikson, E. H. (1963). *Childhood and society* (2nd ed.). New York, NY: Norton.

Erikson, E. H. (1969). *Identity: Youth and crisis*. New York, NY: Norton.

Goodman, J., Schlossberg, N., & Anderson, M. (2006). *Counseling adults in transition*. New York, NY: Springer.

Hay, J. (1995). *Transformational mentoring*. New York, NY: McGraw-Hill.

Ibarra, H. (2000). Making partner: Mentor's guide to the psychological journey. *Harvard Business Review, 78*(2), 147–155.

Kegan, R., & Lahey, L. (1984). Adult leadership and adult development: A constructivist view. In B. Kellerman (Ed.), *Leadership: Multidisciplinary perspectives* (pp. 199–229). Englewood Cliffs, NJ: Prentice Hall.

Kegan, R., & Lahey, L. (2001). *How the way we talk can change the way we work: Seven languages for transformation*. San Francisco, CA: Jossey-Bass.

Klasen, N., & Clutterbuck, D. (2002). *Implementing mentoring schemes: A practical guide to successful programs*. London, UK: Butterworth-Heinenmann.

Knowles, M. (1980). *The modern practice of adult education: From pedagogy to andragogy* (2nd ed.). New York, NY: Association Press.

Levinson, D. (1978). *The seasons of a man's life*. New York, NY: Knopf.

Levinson, D., & Levinson, J. (1996). *The seasons of a woman's life*. New York NY: Knopf.

Lewin, K. (1951). *Field theory in social science*. New York, NY: Harper & Row.

Marcia, J. E. (1980). Identity in adolescence. In J. Adelson (Ed.), *Handbook of adolescent psychology* (pp. 159–187). New York, NY: Wiley.

Marcia, J. E. (2002). Identity and psychosocial development in adulthood. *Identity, 2,* 7–28.

Merriam, S. B., & Caffarella, R. S. (1999). *Learning in adulthood* (2nd ed.). San Francisco, CA: Jossey-Bass.

Murray, H. (1938). *Explorations in personality*. New York, NY: Oxford University Press.

Perry, W. (1970). *Forms of intellectual and ethical development in the college years*. New York, NY: Holt, Rinehart, & Winston.

Piaget, J. (1969). *The mechanisms of perception*. New York, NY: Routledge Kegan Paul.

Ralph, E. (1992, Fall). Continuous teacher development. A case for contextual supervision. *Brock Education, 2*(3), 13–17.

Ralph, E. (2003). Enhancing mentorship in the practicum: Improving contextual supervision. *McGill Journal of Education, 38* (1), 28–48.

Ralph, E. (2004). Developing managers' effectiveness: A model with potential. *Journal of Management Inquiry, 13*(2), 151–163.

Ralph. E., & Walker, K. (2010). Enhancing mentors' effectiveness: The promise of the Adaptive Mentorship model. *McGill Journal of Education, 45*(2), 205–218. Available at http://mje.mcgill.ca/index.php/MJE/article/view/4653

Ralph, E., & Walker, K. (2011). Enhancing mentoring in management via the Adaptive Mentorship model. *The International Journal of Knowledge, Culture and Change Management, 10*(8), 35–43.

Schlossberg, N. (1984). *Counseling adults in transition.* New York, NY: Springer.

Vygotsky, L. S. (1981). The genesis of higher mental functions. In J. V. Wertsch (Ed.), *The concepts of activity in Soviet psychology* (pp. 144–188). Armonk, NY: Sharpe.

Yi, J. (2005). Effective ways to foster learning. *Performance Improvement, 44*(1), 34–38.

Chapter Twenty-Two

Mentoring as Advocating

Bob Petrick

M Y AIM IN THIS CHAPTER is to unpack the notion that mentoring can be conceptualized as advocating, as practiced by the mentor and occasionally by the protégé. I developed this chapter from the perspective of a Faculty of Education liaison instructor, whose role is to collaborate in the triadic mentorship team that includes the teacher candidate or intern completing her/his extended practicum in a school-based placement and the classroom co-operating teacher hosting the intern. A role of the faculty liaison in this linking role between a teacher candidate and the school and faculty jurisdictions is often one of advocacy.

Advocacy as a Function of Mentoring Style

Reid and Jones' (1997) characterized a mentor as "not domineering, sympathetic, stimulated by new ideas, approachable, has students' confidence, good sense of humor, motivated, tactful, patient, tolerant, accepts own failings, shows humility to pupils, wishing to develop" (p. 266). Over time, words such as *advocacy* were used to describe this guidance function, particularly in the modern professional world. Its etymological origins provide elucidation of its evolving meanings over time: "pleading in support of," "speaking for another person or a proposal," "to call to a higher tribunal," "to be a patron, protector," "to be a friend or sincere collaborator," "to attend to the nurturing aspect of mentoring," "to commit to the protégé with emotional integrity," and "to anticipate, initiate, act decisively." Some of these functions appear at various times within a mentor's practice.

Roles and Functions of Mentor Advocates

I believe that mentor advocates may serve as key resources within protégés' journey to professional self-sufficiency. What I conceptualize as a "seer-like aura" may occasionally become evident in a mentor's practice in that he/she may be able to predict outcomes, anticipate actions, and create interventions on behalf of his/her protégés, and this advocacy becomes part of the concrete help offered to the protégé's along his/her transformational journey (Ackerman, Ventimiglia, & Juchniewicz, 2002). In addition, Lanier and Little (1986) suggested that a role of the mentor may be to influence a protégé's future career opportunities (e.g., by writing authentic and credible reference letters), while Johnson (2008) described a mentor/advocate as a gatekeeper. Moreover, Achinstein (2006) identified the shock that novices typically experience when interacting with new colleagues (the *micro*political phase), and when encountering varied administrative procedures and policies (the *macro*political portion, p. 127). In these situations, mentors can help protégés develop political acumen to navigate and/or negotiate the challenges that inevitably arise in the workplace. Such contextual guidance helps protégés follow unspoken "rules" of the organization, and what is often effective is for the mentor/advocate to assume a *formal status*. The formality of the relationship is enhanced through the implementation of a regime of ongoing observations, regular conversations, and coaching (Achinstein, 2006, p. 136). The mentor needs to establish appropriate standards (Goldsberry, 1998) in order to assure that the novice stays within unique boundaries and expectations. As suggested within the Adaptive Mentorship© (AM) model, the advocate needs to discern the multi-level organizational contexts involved in the protégé's world.

Johnson (2008) proposed a list of functions of the mentor. With respect to the advocate focus of this chapter, I see these functions as necessary precursors of the advocate role. Johnson's list included the mentor's encouragement, affirmation, information sharing, self-disclosure (i.e., "That incident also happened to me."), counselling, protection, and collegiality (p. 36). To illustrate the connection to advocating, one could consider collegiality to include the mentor's gestures toward building mutual trust and respect in order to displace the protégé's initial feelings of deference, insecurity, or even awe toward the mentor. Once trust is established, the novice may feel free to solicit an act of advocacy or generate an appropriate act of self-advocacy. Also because of this mutuality, the potential advocate will feel that his/her act of advocacy is justified and supportable.

Theoretical Foundations of Advocacy: Zone of Proximal Development

I believe that the need for advocacy comes from the existence or anticipation of problems, and I see the strengths of advocacy inherent in the AM model as being identified by the terms collaboration, developmental approaches, and context. Vygotsky (1978), who theorized that meaning is negotiated within a social context, recognized the importance of problem solving within the process of learning under the umbrella terms of scaffolding and the zone of proximal development (ZPD). Vygotsky saw ZPD as the distance between an individual's actual knowledge level, as determined by his/her independent problem-solving ability, and his/her level of potential development, the latter being determined through problem solving under guidance and collaboration with others possessing more knowledge (Vygotsky, 1978).

Within practicum programs in education for the professions, protégés are overseen by mentors who are presumably at a higher developmental level. The space between the mentor's and protégé's development is a dynamic one that deals with problems that typically arise in the routines of the learning setting. The mentor and protégé typically reach toward each other to collaboratively solve those problems. I discuss below how Vygotsky's theories might enable the scaffolding process to work to that purpose.

Scaffolding Based on Collaboration

Collaboration in Vygotsky's terms could be described as "co-construction," and facilitating it would be essential to the advocate/protégé relationship because collaboration could be seen as the engine that drives scaffolding. Wertsch (1995) suggested that collaboration was "a mutual task in which the partners work together to produce something that neither could have produced alone" (p. 329). An example of the efficacy of that type of co-construction could be the jamming etiquette as practiced by blues or jazz musicians. Horton (2008) described jamming as each musician being distinct and autonomous, while having the overall effect of collaborating because of the close attentiveness that each player gives to the others. In a sense, jamming becomes a metaphor for the mentorship process.

Similarly, Vygotsky's scaffold is a metaphor representing the social environment, the support system, and the interaction between collaborators. In the practicum setting, the combination of the protégé's and mentor's interactions typically helps make various inexplicit problems more explicit. This scaffolding process that occurs within the protégé's ZPD will be effective if the following enabling characteristics are present:

- ~: Intersubjectivity: Intersubjectivity refers to the creation of a common ground, through which reciprocity can be sought. To achieve reciprocity is challenging given the gap in expertise and stature between a mentor and protégé; however, an enabling strategy could involve the mentor forewarning the protégé of an emerging problem by linking what the latter already knows to upcoming challenges.

- ~: Emotional tone: Warmth, responsiveness, and immediacy of feedback are important facilitators of communications (either face-to face or electronic) between the partners once the problem has been recognized. Varying degrees of directiveness may be employed, depending on the context.

- ~: The ZPD: It is the responsibility of both collaborators to be vigilant in keeping within the ZPD of the protégé. According to AM, the mentor/advocate adjusts his/her degree of intervention according to the protégé's developmental needs and abilities. My mentorship experiences have suggested that this adaptation can be enhanced if the protégé also plays a part, even if such self-advocacy is actually directed toward the mentor rather than the source of the problem. I have found that if practicum mentors begin the year by asking protégés for weekly emails regarding progress in their work, potential problems can be minimized, and a decreasing numbers of emails are received. This process occurs within the changing ZPD.

~: Self-regulation: As the collaborators approach the A4/D4 stage, the scaffold structure changes. The mentor needs to gradually reduce the degree of support and direction, allowing the protégé to deal with new challenges. Such stepping back could occur in stages. Level one would ensure the mentor's continued involvement with immediate instructional/management concerns. Level two could help protégés focus on "the bigger picture," such as suggesting what to include in his/her professional portfolio. The third level might involve encouraging protégés to independently hypothesize beyond the limitations of immediate concerns.

Scaffolding Recognizes the Developmental View

Even though the mentor's advocacy role may involve genuine collaboration with the protégé, they both recognize that the mentor has an expert-level status by virtue of the evaluatory obligation of the position. Gay and Stephenson (1998) described many mentors as those who naturally act as "judge, jury and sometimes executioner" (p. 49). They suggested that the supporting/encouraging role was at odds with the assessment role, and Baumrind (1996) described mentors with this dual role as authoritarians. Furthermore, Wakukawa (2003) found that one of the reasons why mentoring relationships broke down was mentors being too eager to assert their authority. Maguire (2001, p. 107) found that 43% of trainees on one course felt bullied by their assigned mentors, and Cain (2009) saw this type of mentor offering "low support and high challenge" (p. 55). The AM model suggests that the mismatching of the mentor's mentoring response/style with the protégé's existing stage of task-specific competence and confidence will cause misunderstanding, conflict, and resentment. If trust has been established and maintained, the AM model suggests that the mentor's assistance and assessment roles can co-exist successfully.

Vygotsky did not perceive performance as static; the ZPD should not be measured by what people can do by themselves, solely based on what they already know. Their potential is what they can do with the help of another person acting as a mentor. The supportive and evaluator dimensions of such mentoring are not mutually exclusive.

A mentor with a developmental view toward appraising the protégé's problem-solving skill does not observe only the final solution but how the protégé approaches the issue at hand. While it is appropriate for the mentor to model specific strategies to address protégés' conundrums, the mentor should also be prepared to hear the protégé say, "No thanks, that's not right for my situation." Furthermore, once the mentor sees that the protégé is both competent and confident, then the former may take an advocate role of backing the protégé's decision. Such a stance implies developmentalism. In fact, McCafferty (2002, p. 198) stated that the implied mandate of an advocate is to anticipate development, contingent upon the context, as manifested by the setting, the discernable artifacts, and the symbolic tools already in place. Moreover, once the advocate backs up the protégé, it is likely that the protégé will be more effective and even reciprocate with similar responses.

To discern a protégé's professional readiness and maturity level requires careful observation and scaffolding. A mentorship scaffold needs to be built upon a wide variety of techniques that obtain accurate information about the protégé (Wilson, 1996). Reliability of a mentor's observations will be enhanced by their frequency and their correlations among similar observations of other members in the cohort. Nevertheless, each person's context is unique.

Contextual Considerations in Scaffolding

The nature of advocacy is idiosyncratic. Anderson and Shannon (1998) found that advocating functions, varied as they are, are conducted within the context of a caring relationship. An advocate tends to act if the need for advocacy becomes visible and justified (Orland-Barak & Rachamim, 2009) because the advocate's reputation and integrity, and those of his/her faculty or department, are at stake.

Mentors considering advocacy will typically choose one of two approaches to navigate the contexts surrounding each case. If a mentor adopts an apprenticeship approach to learning to teach, conversations between the protégé and mentor tend to address technical matters of teaching; whereas, if a mentor follows a reflective approach, he/she is more likely to encourage deeper analysis and discussion to help the protégé investigate the roots of a problem. Among Dewey's

(1933) five traditions of reflection, three of them seem applicable to mentoring teacher candidates: the academic focus, the social efficiency aspect, and the developmentalist facet.

In addition, Orland-Barak and Rachamim (2009) found that when mentors required protégés to regularly engage in reflective practice, not only did the latter deepen their professional understanding, but the former experienced greater commitment to assist protégés' deal with concerns. The more a mentor understood the context of a protégé's reflections, the more he/she was willing to advocate for the protégé. Given that an experienced mentor already has a good understanding of the contextual factors involved in school life, he/she also becomes better positioned to act as a liaison between the protégé and school personnel.

Reflecting by a protégé becomes an inward journey in which he/she attempts to address complex issues. Korthagen and Vasalos (2005) suggested that the advocate needs to identify related limiting factors and help the protégé analyze the problem, much like the peeling of an onion. The advocate gauges the extent of the act of advocacy, which in a practical way follows the AM model's approach for the mentor to adapt his/her degree of support and task-direction.

Other contextual factors that teacher educators have identified as impacting their mentorship/advocating responses are the mentor's and protégé's (a) prior experience with the mentoring process, (b) commitment level to the mentoring process, (c) awareness of and sensitivity toward the protégé's developmental needs, and (d) gender/philosophical/age differences. With respect to age differences, Johnson (2008) found that having at least half a generation age difference between mentor and protégé seemed ideal. This gap acted as a sort of natural inhibitor to encroachment of necessary boundaries between mentor and protégé, boundaries which could be inappropriately tested by the "forced" commitment to collegiality and collaboration.

Millennial Entitlement or Self-Advocacy?

If one accepts this ideal age gap in a mentoring relationship suggested by Johnson (2008), then both partners should benefit. For example, one of the teacher candidates with whom I recently worked was uncomfortable because she stated that her associate classroom teacher was "too young." She felt the closeness of their respective ages led to tension that fostered a sense of competitiveness, which she had not experienced with her former (and older) associate teacher. One of the strategies that her older mentor practiced was to gradually withdraw support, including acts of advocacy, in inverse proportions to the protégé's growing level of professional confidence. However, one caveat of this process involves potential misunderstanding between the partners, by which the protégé's demands on the good will of the advocate could possibly become excessive. On the other hand, the protégé might only consider such "excessive" demands as merely experimenting with self-advocacy. To resolve such a dilemma, the mentor would be obligated both to model and to expect clear and frank communication and to incorporate appropriate timing for these actions

Dysfunctionality in the relationship can produce counter-productive effects, as illustrated by Allen, Johnson, and Xu (2009), who identified narcissistic entitlement (NE) as "a dispositional variable reflecting preoccupation with the expectation of special and preferential treatment" (p. 385). They found that protégés scoring high on the NE variable received less support from mentors than did low-scoring NE students. Furthermore, the relationships were of a shorter duration, a lower relationship quality was reported, and a greater number of negative mentor actions were identified. Thus, poor results emerged when protégés projected excessively high expectations upon mentor/advocates.

In effective mentorship, the mentor/advocate has a mandate and the protégé has a responsibility to appreciate each other's interpretation of becoming a professional. I believe that the Boomer mentality typically sees the protégé's individuality as accountability to a greater communal purpose, whereas the Millennial mindset often sees individuality as a tool to access as many alternatives as possible and as instantly as possible. The irony of a Millennial's narcissistic attitude during the practicum is that such an outlook quickly changes within the daily realities and challenges of a school setting. The mentor/advocate's task has always been to facilitate the protégé's transition from university student to practicing professional.

Trust is Essential

The establishment of trust plays a critical role in mentoring a student teacher. Clark and Jarvis-Selinger (2005) described the significance of the emotional component of the mentor/mentee relationship and suggested that mutual trust springs from integrity in both partners. Integrity includes being predictable and honoring confidentiality. Under such conditions, each person can anticipate how the other will react if advocacy is being considered as a next step to solving a problem.

Nevertheless, Martin (1995) found that when some mentors faced awkwardness or a potential impasse with a protégé, they defaulted to ignoring the problem in the interest of professional courtesy. Occasionally, a gap appeared between what a mentor said and what he/she did, particularly in situations that were politically sensitive or personal. Similarly, protégés may have experienced difficulty between articulating what they needed and following through with appropriate action.

To illustrate this point, I offer the following rather awkward vignette from my own mentorship experience. One teacher candidate confided in me on campus that he was not comfortable projecting himself in the practicum classroom as "the excitable type" of teacher. I supported his concern by acknowledging that he was justified in teaching according to his personality style, which he described as "low key." What I did not share with him was the extra logistical commitment required from me to actualize his request.

On his first practicum, he was matched with a dynamic and dramatic associate teacher. Upon visiting that classroom, I noted the pupils close to falling asleep in his lesson. I subsequently discussed with him ways of stimulating his teaching by using media and technology, but keeping with his avowed preference to be low key and in control. The following week he emailed me, decrying the fact that his associate teacher had severely criticized his quieter approach. She wrote on his evaluation form that he was boring and unimaginative. He had subsequently countered this assertion by justifying his approach as having been sanctioned by me as representing "the university." He further asked me to intervene/advocate on his behalf before his final practicum evaluation was completed. However, I chose not to do so, describing for him instead certain steps he could take to establish a better relationship with his associate classroom teacher.

Upon reflection, I determined what I had not done in his case was to initially establish an understanding of the developmental process of collaboration, which could have prevented this complex issue from escalating. On my part, I had not put the full process of partnership into motion with the triad. I contend that such a strategy is required in order to establish clear communication of expectations among all participants.

A Process for Reaching Mutuality

Sweeney (1996) offered a process to keep the relationship between mentor and protégé true to the commitment to mutuality and validation. The steps were:

- ~: Introduction (creating a connection);
- ~: Foundation (reducing stress, promoting a team aspect);
- ~: Collaboration (establishing atmosphere of caring);
- ~: Problem solving (emphasizing critical thinking, building knowledge);
- ~: Personal framework (promoting trustworthiness, modelling by mentor);
- ~: Professional development (facilitating independence, but maintaining support); and
- ~: Transition (fostering mentor/protégé interdependence, mutuality).

The Evolving Journey of Adaptation

While AM is a developmental model, it need not follow a rigid chronological order starting at D1/A1 and progressing to D4/A4. Rather, it may be useful to compare its A/D structure to the one described by Sweeney (1996), which is developed over time. Cohen (1995) portrayed this journey in four stages: early, middle, later, and last.

- ~: Early: The relationship would develop trust, mutual acceptance, dialogue, and self-disclosure as an indicator of good faith. Without the presence of trust, the mentor would feel little obligation to risk advocating for the protégé.

~: Middle: Emphasis would be on continued exchange of information, arriving at a detailed understanding of the protégé's context. Advice would be given frequently.

~: Later: The focus would be facilitative and confrontative, if required. The protégé's beliefs would be explored, and trust would continue to be tested and reconfirmed. Based on appraisals of protégé performance up to that point, the mentor should feel free to offer alternatives and act as advocate in measure.

~: Last: The mentor would continue to model and the protégé would develop a clear vision, based on his/her critical reflection. This growth should be substantial enough to motivate the protégé to take significant initiatives. The mentor would remain ready to advocate (e.g., writing letters of reference).

Moreover, Kram (1983) suggested a four-phase model defining the development of the mentor-protégé relationship: initiation, cultivation, separation, and redefinition. For the practicum in teacher education, the stages would be:

~: Initiation: This phase is the beginning or orientation period, on campus, stressing positive relational foundations.

~: Cultivation: During the first two practicum periods in school settings, the boundaries of the relationship become clarified. Context is a factor, as reality tests the positive aspects of the relationship. Interpersonal bonds become more defined. Coaching and protection by the mentors is prevalent. The mentor/advocate remains receptive to the style and intentions of the protégé but is ready for teachable moments, often transmitting his/her own values and skills.

~: Separation: By the third practicum, the protégé needs to become more independent. Emotional separation begins, but context dictates that the mentor may be called upon to enact meaningful gestures of advocacy (being a reference).

~: Redefinition: Near the end of the practicum program, equality, if not mutuality, is actualized. In one sense, I view this final stage as being similar to the initiation period, but as occurring at a more advanced, substantiated level. The redefinition phase serves as evidence that the basic professional development has occurred and that the teacher candidate would be ready to accept his/her first teaching position.

Advocacy Scenarios

I now depict four scenarios, based on real situations, that typify developing relationships between protégés and mentors in a teacher-education practicum. I cast each of the scenarios within the A/D structure of the Adaptive Mentorship model. Following each description, I challenge the reader to analyze the scenario and offer advocacy-related alternatives for the mentor to consider.

Scenario 1 (Matching D1 with A1). In this example, a teacher candidate unilaterally attempted to change his practicum school placement without notifying me or the university practicum office. He later identified excessive travel time from his residence to the school as his reason for switching schools. On his own accord, he approached the principal of the school in which he wished to be placed, who granted him tentative permission to do so, provided that the change was cleared by the university practicum office, which was a three-hour drive from the first school.

Rather than contacting the practicum office, he later asked me to facilitate the change. Feeling surprised, but nonetheless being a central figure in this awkward situation, I believed I had three obligations: (1) to counsel the student on acceptable ways to follow protocol, (2) to inform the practicum office of his request and support his request, and (3) to contact the school principals and apologize for the teacher candidate's premature actions.

According to the AM model, the protégé reflected a D1 stage in terms of his professional conduct: he was an eager novice with elevated confidence but low competence in following acceptable procedures for school-site deportment. On campus in his courses, he was known to be bright and articulate, but he eagerly risked giving his opinions and was always animated in delivering them.

From the matching A1 quadrant, I saw that his inappropriate actions had forced me into a prescriptive mode in terms of my task-direction, but relatively low on the support dimension, because he was not only acting overly confident, but he also had unrealistic expectations of me to finish a job that he had unwisely begun. I also had to attempt to placate a hostile practicum office.

The result of this situation was that he remained at his initially designated school for the first two teaching rounds, but he was able to switch to his desired school by the third round due to unanticipated "numbers-related" factors that arose among my cohort at the previously designated site. I invite readers to analyze this scenario and offer advocacy-related alternatives that may have also helped alleviate the situation.

Scenario 2 (Matching D2 with A2). In this situation, the teacher candidate's associate teacher had transferred during practicum, but the school had initially offered the protégé little support during this transition. In retrospect, I had realized that the protégé was having difficulties finding a voice during her pre-practicum classes on campus. Because she and her subgroup had been assigned to a challenging placement in an inner-city school, I had travelled to the school prior to the practicum to meet with the school administration and associate teachers. Due to the unique context of the school, I found I had to be carefully assertive with the staff in an attempt to arrange a smooth transition for candidates.

I had visited the school at the end of the second week of the practicum to observe lessons and to conduct follow-up with candidates, administration, and teachers. At that time, the protégé in question had informed me of the difficult circumstances under which she was working as a result of her assigned teacher having been transferred on the third day of the practicum. The protégé had attempted to survive by having to deal with a series of supply teachers, a paucity of instructional materials, and a lack of consistent guidance or mentorship. She said she had been "trying to wing it," and I saw that she was rapidly declining in both her confidence and competence levels.

As her faculty mentor, I identified an array of advocacy tasks to implement: (a) to counsel the candidate and reassure her to solicit my help immediately as required, (b) to gain the assistance of the new vice principal who had also just been assigned to be the school's on-site practicum coordinator, who had not been aware that the protégé's situation had unfolded (I spent two days at the site making arrangements for the protégé), and (c) to alert the practicum office on campus of the situation and facilitate the completion of the candidate's final assessment.

The result was that the vice-principal agreed to take primary mentorship responsibilities for the protégé, a permanent teacher was eventually hired, and the completion of the protégé's formative assessment form was finalized.

From the D2 perspective, the candidate felt lost, discouraged, and incapable of resolving the situation. I wished that she had not waited so long to request assistance, because by that time her self-assurance had plummeted and she was feeling helpless. However, according to the corresponding A2 quadrant, my task was to assertively take over this situation, to spend extra time accessing the right people, and to counsel the candidate by prescribing specific strategies for her to apply and by genuinely building her weakened self-esteem. I again invite readers to analyze this scenario and offer advocacy-related alternatives to those I selected.

Scenario 3 (Matching D3 with A3). In this third example, a teacher candidate, who was later nominated for a campus student-teaching award, had asked to meet with me the day prior to my observing her science lesson with a Grade 7 class. She appeared agitated and stressed over what she perceived as her ineffectiveness in an intermediate class. She indicated her anxiety over the upcoming performance, but during our meeting I stated that it was my impression that she was a creative thinker and that her degree in Art had surely offered her ways to prepare vibrant visuals for the lesson. After she showed me her prepared materials, her dramatic introduction for the lesson, and the engaging activities, I projected my enthusiasm. During our conversation she also mentioned her history of A.D.D. as an obstacle to her functioning as well as her uncertainty of how the associate teacher viewed her performance. I ended our meeting by encouraging her to "go to the max" in this lesson, after which we would debrief the proceedings. I also promised her that I would discuss her progress with her associate teacher. (I found during that discussion with her associate that the latter had not perceived this insecurity on the candidate's part but commented on her exemplary work ethic and her successful engagement of students. When I described the protégé's feelings to the associate, she quickly realized how she could provide her with increased support.) The lesson I observed did indeed turned out to be effective. Thus, according to the D3 quadrant, the protégé was relatively competent but required considerable understanding and feedback, patience, encouragement, and trust from her mentors to build up her lagging confidence.

According to the A3 response, my initial advocacy and the subsequent support from her associate seemed relatively easy to implement, mainly because we sensed we were working with a skilled and capable individual. I also granted her an extension on the submission of her final action-research paper that was due at the end of the practicum. By offering her a collegial form of trust based on her unique context, our mutual trust was also enhanced. As in the above cases, readers may explore other ways by which the mentoring/advocating process for this protégé could have been enacted.

Scenario 4 (Matching D4 with A4). A final scenario that illustrated the A4/D4 matching involved one cohort of teacher candidates who had begun to prepare for job interviews well ahead of the normally expected time. I demonstrated my advocacy strategies on behalf of these protégés by writing early letters of reference for them and by personally contacting prospective employers for some of them.

At the beginning of each academic year, I advise my assigned protégés that I employed a collaborative means of producing and offering professional references for their upcoming job application and interview endeavors. This strategy involved emailing drafts back and forth between me and a candidate until a mutually agreeable letter was created. My challenge in this effort was to be positive, realistic, and honest, based on my accumulated documentation of each person's performance to date. Their challenge was to respectfully review my successive appraisals and provide additional context-related ideas that I had not considered.

A predicament that arose with the cohort in question was that I had not expected to receive reference requests several months before the completion of the practicum. Some protégés were seeking international jobs, and in order to meet special deadlines, they requested letters from me halfway though the school term. This situation obligated me to engage in "a leap of faith" on their behalf in that I had to make judgments before the end of their practicum. Furthermore, these protégés had not yet attended the required sessions on creating professional portfolios, thereby accentuating the significance (not to mention the increased pressure on me) to produce persuasive, yet credible, letters of reference for them. Further, some candidates wanted a specific letter for a particular job placement, while others required a more generic letter. Most of the draft exchanges were accomplished over a few days.

In terms of the D4 designation, I saw the candidates as taking responsibility to collaborate with the faculty liaison, and they recognized that I would seriously consider/incorporate their input if it was defensible and accurate. That is, they were demonstrating elevated levels of professional confidence and competence, trusting that I would treat them as colleagues – albeit novices.

From my A4 perspective, I was simply fulfilling a promise that I made at the beginning of the practicum. I was also careful to word these "early" letters such that I described their performance up to that point, and that future development (and its assessment) was anticipated. Some of these students actually did request an updated letter from me at the end of the academic year, whereupon any sense of conditionality was avoided. Readers are again encouraged to examine my mentoring strategies for this example and to suggest other possibilities.

Concluding Questions

In the light of my focus in this chapter on the advocacy component of mentorship, I pose four questions that may be of interest to scholars and practitioners wishing to conduct further research in this area. Questions that I consider worth exploring are: (a) How could the language of advocacy be integrated within the Adaptive Mentorship model? (b) Is there a conflict between being a protégé's advocate and his/her evaluator? (c) How do Vygotsky's developmental concepts of scaffolding and ZPD relate to advocacy and the unique contexts with which it is enacted? (d) How helpful is the Millennial/Boomer distinction in understanding advocacy during practicum mentorship in the professions?

References

Achinstein, B. (2006). New teacher and mentor political literacy: Reading, navigating and transforming induction contexts. *Teachers and Teaching: Theory and Practice, 12*(2), 123–138.

Ackerman,R., Ventimiglia, L., & Juchniewicz, M., (2002). In K. Leithwood & P. Hallinger (Eds.), *Handbook of education leadership and administration* (pp. 1071–1102). Boston, MA: Kluwer.

Allen, T., & Johnson, H., & Xu, X. (2009). Mentor and protégé narcissistic entitlement. *Journal of Career Development, 35*(4), 385–405.

Anderson, E., & Shannon, A. (1998). Towards a conceptualization of mentoring. *Journal of Teacher Education, 39*(1), 38–42.

Baumrind, D. (1996).The discipline controversy revisited. *Family Relations, 4,* 405–420.

Cain, T. (2009). Mentoring trainee teachers: How can mentors use research? *Mentoring and Tutoring: Partnership in Learning, 17*(1), 53–66.

Clarke, A., & Jarvis-Selinger, S. (2005). What the teaching perspective of cooperating teachers tells us about their advisory practices. *Teaching and Teacher Education, 21*(1), 65–78.

Cohen, N.H. (1995). *Mentoring adult learners: A guide for educators and trainers.* Malabar, FL: Kreiger.

Dewey, J. (1933). *How we think.* Lexington, MA: DC Heath

Gay, B., & Stephenson, J. (1998). The mentoring dilemma: Guidance and/or direction? *Mentoring and Tutoring, 6*(1), 43–54.

Goldsberry, L. F. (1998). Teacher involvement in supervision. In G. Firth & E. Pajak (Eds.), *Handbook of research on school supervision* (pp. 428–462). New York, NY: MacMillan.

Horton, S. L. (2008). Lev goes to college: Reflections on implementing Vygotsky's ideas in higher education. *The International Journal of Learning, 15*(4), 13–17.

Johnson, W. B. (2008). Are advocacy, mutuality, and evaluation incompatible mentoring functions? *Mentoring and Tutoring: Partnership in Learning, 16*(1), 31–44.

Korthagen, F., & Vasalos, A. (2005). Levels in reflection: Core reflection as a means to enhance professional growth. *Teachers and Teaching: Theory and Practice, 11*(1), 47–71.

Kram, K. (1983). Phases of the mentoring relationship. *Academy of Management Journal, 26*(4), 608–625.

Lanier, J. E., & Little, J. W. (1986). Research on teacher education. In W. Wittrock (Ed.), *Handbook of research in teaching* (3rd ed.) (pp. 527–569). New York, NY: MacMillan.

Maguire, M. (2001). Bullying and the postgraduate secondary school teacher: An English case study. *Journal of Education for Teaching, 27*(1), 95–109.

Martin, T. (1995). Giving feedback after a lesson observation. *Mentoring and Tutoring, 3*(2), 8–12.

McCafferty, S. G. (2002). Gesture and creating zones of proximal development for second language learning. *The Modern Language Journal, 86*(2), 192–203.

Orland-Barak, L., & Rachamim, M. (2009). Simultaneous reflections by video in a second-order action research mentoring model: Lessons for the mentor and the mentee. *Reflective Practice, 10*(5), 601–613.

Reid, D., & Jones, L. (1997). Partnership in teacher training: Mentors' constructs of their role. *Education Studies, 23*(2), 263–276.

Sweeny, B. (1996). *The new teacher mentoring process.* The Mentoring Leadership & Resource Network. Available from http://mentors.net/library/m_process.php

Vygotsky, L. S. (1978). *Mind in society.* Cambridge, MA: Harvard University Press.

Wakukawa, P. (2003). Mentoring as a journey. *Teaching and Teacher Education, 19*(1), 45–57.

Wertsch, J. V. (1995). *Culture, communication, and cognition: Vygotskian perspectives.* Cambridge, MA: Cambridge University Press.

Wilson, R. J. (1996). *Assessing students in classrooms and schools.* Scarborough, ON: Allyn & Bacon

Chapter Twenty-Three

Dismantling Barriers: Mentorship in Emerging Nurse-Practitioner Roles

Robert Ralph & Susan Shaw

THE IMPORTANCE OF MENTORSHIP WITHIN the practicum or clinical phase of the education of professionals is well established (Allen & Eby, 2007). However, mentorship across disciplinary lines has not been so common. In this chapter, we describe a unique cross-disciplinary mentorship initiative between the professions of Medicine and Nursing in an Acute Care Nurse Practitioner program. We describe the health care context, then discuss mentorship in general and the Adaptive Mentorship© model in particular. Throughout the chapter we share key understandings gained and personal feelings experienced in this novel journey through the mentorship process.

Canadian Health Care

In Canada, when political visionaries established the Canada Health Act, they entitled Canadians to "free" and accessible health care, which became an inherent constitutional right. However, this model of health care was not without a cost in that it has placed an increasing financial strain on federal and provincial budgets. Additional complicating factors included urbanization and aging population demographics, longer patient-to-physician wait times, increasing costs of modern technologies, shortages of health care providers, and global financial turmoil. Improving health care efficiencies has proven difficult, and facilitating cost-effective alternatives to the traditional models is a multi-level, multi-variable undertaking (National Steering Committee, 2002).

Nurse Practitioners in Canada

In the recent past, the physician-nurse relationship has dominated the face of Canadian health care. However, new professional roles have emerged, such as physiotherapists and respiratory therapists, and these have become more prominent in the health care field, occupying a niche in patient management.

The evolution of the role of Nurse Practitioner (NP) or Advanced Practice Nurse (APN) is another recent trend within the traditional group of provider roles. The reason for this addition to nursing is multi-dimensional, but a key impetus has been a financial one (Hoyt & Proehl, 2010). The Canadian Nurse Practitioner Initiative (Canadian Nurses Association [CNA], 2006, 2009; Canadian Nurse Practitioner Initiative [CNPI], n.d.) indicated that (a) the cost of health care is increasing at a rate of approximately 7% per year, a value which is incongruent with the growth of Canada's national GDP, and (b) increased health care costs are being forecast for the near future.

Several years ago, provincial government health care ministers began to address that looming financial issue and established an $800 million Transitional Health Care Fund (THCF) with the goal of increasing access to quality health care by various strategies. One strategy was the implementation and promotion of the NP role that was linked to an interdisciplinary-team approach to health care delivery. Evidence supporting this initiative was research reporting NP satisfaction in other countries such as the United States, the United Kingdom, and Australia (Jennings, Lee, Chao, & Keating, 2009).

Government and nursing bodies at the national level in Canada provided guidance to set goals for the Canadian Nurse Practitioner Initiative, and its funding was furnished by Health Canada out of THCF budget. Included in the CNPI objectives were (a) recognition and utilization of NPs in health care delivery, (b) integration and sustainability of the NP role, and (c) identification of NPs as essential health care providers. Evidence supporting these objectives was based on corroborating research conducted across the United States and the UK that indicated the addition of NPs resulted in greater patient satisfaction, reduction of wait times, and improvement in health services (Jennings, Lee, Chao, & Keating, 2009).

A trend across health regions in Saskatchewan has been to pro-mote efforts to recruit NPs into mainstream health care settings, par-ticularly for primary care in underserviced rural areas. Despite these efforts, statistics from the NP licensing body, the Saskatchewan Registered Nursing Association (SRNA, 2010), indicate that ap-proximately 130 NPs were registered for the 2011 registration year to help service the province's population of one million. Certain bar-riers to this initiative, whether actual or perceived, appear to exist.

Barriers to Nurse Practitioner Implementation

Health administrators may not realize that actual implementation of the new NP role is not a simple task. They may not understand the historical contexts that mitigate against placing an unfamiliar entity among well established health care roles (i.e., physician and nurse). For years, these have been etched in the psyche of health care providers, institutions, and members of the public (Thrasher, 2005).

It has been said that "nurses eat their young," and with only 0.7% of Canadian nurses registered as NPs (CNA, 2009), a question arises regarding the status of NPs: Will NPs have a voice in the pro-fession, or will issues concerning the RN majority take precedence over concerns related to the new NP role? Some researchers have suggested that nursing, as a profession, has been deficient in its abil-ity to engage in reasoned debate regarding the profession's position within the system (Nelson & Gordon, 2006).

Furthermore, no one disputes the fact that when health care providers build coalitions through referrals and consultations with colleagues across the disciplines, then additional competency is the result, which in turn benefits both the patient and the system. Such collaboration does not abrogate the right to treat patients autono-mously, but it maintains the goal of enhancing patient-centred care (Kohn, Corrigan, & Donaldson, 2000). With respect to the NP compared to the RN, another question arises: Will the NP be rec-ognized as an expert in the field, or will the interdisciplinary team accept the NP as a credible and accountable member?

Examining the traditional state of nursing and the socialization of nurses into the broader health care field indicates that nurses have an entrenched status within the health care hierarchy. Nursing theorists such as Patricia Benner (2001) identified an innate dual-istic and antagonistic relationship between medicine and nurs-ing – rooted in a separation between the natural and human sciences. Benner indicated that nursing has failed to produce its own body of knowledge and that it has borrowed from a variety of sciences and humanities. Yet, the nursing discipline is not relegated to the fringe, but rather it buffers against pure empiricism and the exclusive steril-ity of sole instrumental reasoning (Nelson & Gordon, 2006).

Nurses have been practicing in advanced roles since the nineteenth century (Keeling, 2007), and in times of need, nurses have been will-ing to expand their scope of practice by learning new skills to benefit the patients they serve. Often, difficult times were the impetus to precipitate role change or advancement. Keeling referred to the time when nurses faced professional prosecution for delivering anesthet-ics in the United States in the early twentieth century: "when nurses were not an economic threat to physicians – when they worked in undesirable locations or with minority populations – they were con-sidered to be competent in whatever needed to be done" (p. 48).

Thus, widespread acceptance of the new NP role will require so-ciety to view NPs as being beyond the fading white cap and garb, the female gender exclusivity, and the subservient role persona. The new NP role may well create role confusion for the general public and for many traditional colleagues alike (Thrasher, 2005). Biased or inflex-ible co-professionals working in traditional health care roles may not always welcome or accept the NP role, reinforcing the historical dis-comforts that recur with role overlap. Despite these difficulties, the future role of the NP, and of nursing, does appear to hold a pivotal and essential position in health care delivery. In fact, the immediate removal of the nursing role from within the delivery of health care could well lead to a collapse of the entire system. Thus, the future contribution of the new NP role should bolster the entire system.

Nevertheless, the emergence of the NP role may cause somewhat of a self-identity conflict within the nursing profession (Edmunds, 1999). This conflict may arise for new NPs entering uncharted terri-tory, which may engender opposition from others inside and outside of nursing. Such a situation would raise a related question: What would be needed to assist NPs to bridge this gap, to shed unhelpful traditions of the past and to acquire a broader scope of professional knowledge, skills, and practice? One strategy that would help resolve such issues would be the implementation of an effective mentorship process within the nursing and NP education programs. In such a mentorship program, protégés and mentors would learn to lay aside traditional role stereotypes and instead would empower the protégé to work in unison with the mentor toward learning goals.

The Mentorship Process

The mentorship process has been part of human learning from ancient Greece to the modern era. Examples of collaborative mentorship in the health field include the Manhattan project, the discovery of DNA, and the mapping of the human genome – all of which exemplified interdisciplinary synergy to achieve successful outcomes. Mentorship within disciplines has been routine in the educational process, but more recently, mentorship has transcended traditionally accepted roles and has reached across disciplines and professions – a less common phenomenon.

Within the mentorship process, common goals and beliefs must be shared between the mentor and protégé in order for successful outcomes to materialize. The success of such a mentorship relationship is dependent on the bond that is forged between the mentor and protégé. Research has shown that effective mentors offer their protégés a high level of career and psychological support, and that the relationship is developed on the basis of reciprocity, mutuality, respect, professionalism, and interdependence (Higgins & Kram, 2001).

A Nurse Practitioner Mentorship Experience

As a primary-care NP, I desired to further my education and complete a Masters Degree in Acute Care Nurse Practice. Living in Saskatchewan and not wanting to uproot my family, I applied to the University of Toronto's Acute Care Nurse Practitioner, Adult Stream Program, which used an online distance education format for class work and a local practicum for the clinical portion. As a prerequisite to admission, I had to provide the names of preceptors and/or clinical specialists who would commit to provide a clinical placement and mentorship for my practicum. This task, in other parts of Canada where the NP role already existed, may not have been a challenge; however, in the centre where I worked, there had not yet been any ACNP in the hospitals, nor had there been a role established for an ACNP. In fact, in that institution, some practitioners and administrators perceived this new role as unnecessary. However, I wanted my practicum to be successful, not only for my own learning, but because my experience would no doubt affect that of future students in similar program paths.

With some trepidation based on previous primary-care NP experiences, I asked Dr. Susan Shaw, Director of Critical Care in the Saskatoon Health Region (SHR) if she would consider acting as my mentor/preceptor, a role requiring her to perform duties above and beyond those of her regular responsibilities of mentoring her ICU/Anesthesia medical residents. I was pleased, somewhat surprised, and humbled at her reply: "Sure, let me know, and I will help in any way I can!" Her response not only reduced my insecurities considerably, but it instantly signalled what I considered as a significant cross-disciplinary breakthrough in our institution, in that a respected medical specialist expressed willingness to mentor a nurse practitioner in clinical practice. It was indeed a rare event.

Soon I was working with an expert in the field who was an accommodating mentor, an "out of the box" thinker, and a model of an inclusive ICU Intensivist. As I observed her accepting this new role, I noted that her mentoring responsibilities seemed impervious to some of the NP/MD issues that I have described (above). Rather, she consistently provided me with genuine support, professional guidance, and needed direction as we embarked on this unmapped journey without having a precise template or previously established set of routines to follow.

The Adaptive Mentorship Model

Dr. Shaw and I utilized a generic mentoring model developed by Ralph and Walker (2010, 2011), which they called Adaptive Mentorship (AM). We, as a protégé and a mentor, realized that we both needed some direction on how to proceed along this new interdisciplinary learning path in order to maximize our efforts. Dr. Shaw and I began by delineating program goals, objectives, and new skills that I would need to learn. Prior to initiating my clinical experience with Dr. Shaw, I referred to the AM model's *confidence* and *competence* continuum grid for protégé development (see Figure 1). On it I identified a quadrant on the developmental grid within which I thought I was functioning at that point in time in terms of my overall levels of competence and confidence in performing specific tasks related to ICU care.

The AM model was designed to facilitate an adaptive mentorship response to the protégé's developmental level for different skills, which in my case were endotracheal intubation, central line placement, insertion of invasive blood pressure monitoring lines, and conducting ICU patient consults. Some of these skills were entirely new to me – others needed practice and refinement. Due to my previous critical-care experience and related training, I had initially ranked myself within the D3 quadrant because I believed I was performing at a moderate to fairly high level in terms of my overall competence in these skills. However, I needed to bolster my confidence to perform them, especially while experiencing the triple pressures of (a)

Figure 1

The Adaptive Mentorship model from Ralph and Walker, 2010, 2011.

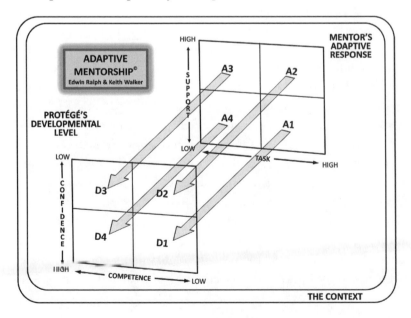

facing my new role insecurities, (b) being evaluated for graduate-program credit, and (c) embarking on this unique and innovative cross-disciplinary mentorship experiment.

I soon realized that I was engaged in a mentoring relationship that was indeed characterized by a strong bond. I believed that Dr. Shaw genuinely had my best professional interest in mind. She continually demonstrated clear communication skills, she did not dismiss or belittle the many questions that I posed, nor did she make me feel that my learning was a hindrance to her ICU routine. Rather, I felt that I was included as a contributing member of the health team.

For example, one patient, who had been extubated (i.e., removed from mechanical ventilation) in the ICU, suddenly became distressed and thus required immediate reintubation. The patient had a challenging anatomical condition, and due to the patient's relative hypoxia, became agitated. It was not possible for the team to attempt to re-insert an endotracheal tube without a chemical paralytic. I chose to use a short-acting neuro-muscular blocking agent, Succinylcholine, in order to paralyze the patient to facilitate the needed endotracheal intubation. However, at that point, I was not able to intubate the patient. I quickly glanced at Dr. Shaw, seated about 10 yards away, expecting her to be anxious or perplexed, while a second-year anesthesia resident and myself continued attempting to secure this patient's airway.

By means of her calm reaction to this situation, she actually inspired confidence between the resident and I to rely on the previous training that we had both received in our respective fields and to allow us to follow through on the procedures we had initiated. Within a short time, my colleague succeeded in securing the airway with adjunctive means. Dr. Shaw's approach of allowing us to make clinical decisions and to deal with the outcomes under her professional oversight was instrumental in bolstering our professional growth. On that occasion, and repeatedly throughout the practicum, I noted that Dr. Shaw refrained from using negative reinforcement or demeaning comments, but her response regarding my own performance, and that of my fellow protégés, consistently conveyed encouragement and support. Occasionally, if I had to abandon a procedure due to technical challenges, she would make a statement like, "You'll get the next one."

In another instance, a patient was brought into ICU after having an intracranial bleed vessel clipping and subsequent cerebral artery vasospasm. I admitted the patient, quickly intubated him, and inserted invasive blood pressure monitoring lines. When Dr. Shaw`s arrived to oversee the process, she noted that the patient was settled with the necessary interventions completed. She expressed pleasure with my progress, and I sensed a shared feeling of accomplishment between us at having achieved some of our mentorship objectives.

Detrimental Bond Relationships

Not all mentors possess this positive, empowering ability or desire to help others embrace learning and feel supported in it. In fact, I think it is unfortunate that some medical educators seem to cling to a hierarchal structure in the health professions, as described above; however, on the other hand, I also believe that it is crucial to identify objectively such obstacles and to attempt to learn from them.

One such incident occurred while I was engaged in another clinical education session during my preceptorship program in a smaller hospital. On that occasion I had the opportunity to contrast Dr. Shaw's "strong bond" mentorship style with one that was opposite. The mentorship research and people's own experiences have demonstrated repeatedly that the mentor/protégé relationship is dependent on a certain level of trust that must exist between the partners, without which effective mentorship cannot function (Hall, Otazo, & Hollenbeck, 1999). This example reinforces the importance of trust.

One day at the open desk in the hospital's busy ER, while I was reviewing a patient's case with my preceptor/colleague, a medical specialist approached us as we discussed the case. Because I had never met this physician, my colleague introduced me as his ACNP protégé. At that point, the medical specialist unexpectedly commenced what I would call a tirade against Nurse Practitioners and became louder and increasingly agitated and accusatory. He began berating me, warning me never to syringe cerumen from patient's ears, in addition to uttering several other random directives. He then questioned me as to why I was not following him into the treatment room to "learn" while he assessed his consult (a patient I knew nothing about). He next pulled a Complete Blood Count (CBC) lab report from that patient's file and, without any context, insisted that I interpret the report. Trying not to display my aggravation, I stated that the cell counts and indices on the chart were within normal parametres, which the physician forcefully refuted and gave his interpretation.

The reason I report this incident is to contrast the two doctors' mentorship styles – although I personally would not classify this individual as a mentor, nor would I consider his behavior as mentorship. I believe that demeanor of that sort does not foster learning but rather breeds tension, stress, and resentment. My reaction as a protégé would be to simply avoid that MD. As Higgins & Kram (2001) suggested, I would consequently seek information from more supportive sources, including books or online references, in order to bypass such negative communication or further confrontations. Not surprisingly, the research into this negative aspect of mentoring behavior suggest that protégés without adequate organizational and professional support will not only become less confident in their abilities, but they will likely withdraw and have a diminished sense of their own potential (Higgins & Kram, 2001).

Personal Reflections from the NP Perspective

As has been the case with other industrialized countries, the Canadian health care system has had to respond to various pressures by modifying its health care structure and the roles within it. The growth of the NP/APN role has caused a paradigm shift from the traditional MD/RN relationship and has begun to provide Canadians with an additional health care service offered by competent practitioners (CNPI, n.d.). There is also growing recognition that to provide the medical expertise needed to train this new cadre of NPs, effective mentorship is also needed. Clear mentorship models will enhance these learning relationships. Furthermore, these positive mentoring relationships can prove beneficial and highly productive not only for professional development of practitioners within each profession, but across the professional disciplines (Blyth & Croft, 2010). Individuals who engage in relational mentorship modelling obviously see the value of investing into a protégé's learning because over time the relationship will be reciprocated when the protégé, in turn, will become a mentor for other protégés. Consequently, as Higgins and Kram (2001) asserted, effective mentorship will set the stage for support and mutuality to replace toxic experiences in the learning environment. I am grateful that I experienced that phenomenon in the clinical practicum described in this chapter.

Personal Reflections of a Mentor-Physician

In the final section of the chapter, I – as the physician and mentor in this relationship – present some of my thoughts regarding this unique mentorship initiative. I describe some of my personal background, summarize my assessment of the AM model, and highlight some of my reflections and insights regarding this entire experience

Mentor Background

I was excited when Rob first asked me to supervise him for a significant portion of his two-year Master of Nursing in Acute Care. I agreed to participate because I wanted to support Rob's educational goals, and I thought it would be a fairly natural extension of my current teaching activities. After all, I work closely with nurses and undergraduate nursing students both in the operating rooms and intensive care units of the teaching hospital where I practice medicine. I also have had significant experience teaching and supervising undergraduate medical students, residents, pharmacy residents, and respiratory therapy students in a variety of clinical settings. I initially thought helping Rob would be similar to supervising one of my medical residents, an activity that I do on an almost daily basis while I work as an anesthesiologist and intensivist within an academic health sciences centre.

However, on further reflection I realized this experience was going to be different from all of my previous teaching activities. As a physician, I had little knowledge of the body of information that Rob had previously acquired both in his classroom and clinical experiences. Medical students, residents, and physicians all share a common experiential and academic base, the components of which are on a similar learning continuum/pathway. Traditionally within most faculties of medicine and nursing, nurses and doctors train in almost complete isolation from one another. Such isolation significantly contributes to a lack of understanding of each profession's core values, unique culture, and specific strengths.

Twelve years after I graduated from my own medical-school program, I was invited to present a lecture to a final year nursing class on the topic of how to work well with doctors as part of the patient's health care team. I was surprised to learn, as I was introduced to the class, that I was the first physician that had ever been invited to teach at that School of Nursing. I subsequently reflected on my own four years at medical school and realized that no nurse had formally participated in our medical training either, and yet, we as prospective physicians had quickly learned during our clinical experiences that our nursing colleagues were key resources and supports to our own medical learning.

With respect to participating in Rob's unique program, I was not only to be his teacher, but I was being asked to be his mentor. I readily understood that mentorship required the creation of a significant relationship with one's student or protégé. It also implied providing wisdom and support while modelling a high level of performance (Woodrow, 2006). I felt it was likely that I would have little to offer in terms of wisdom because I had never worked closely with a Nurse Practitioner (NP) nor did I have extensive knowledge of his learning goals and objectives.

Since the inception of the first NP training program at the University of Colorado in 1965, the Nurse Practitioner role has developed into profession firmly established in the health care systems of many countries (Buchan & Calman, 2004; Pulcini, 2010). Nurse Practitioners from a variety of countries belong to their respective professional bodies that determine practice standards and guidelines and that are responsible for self-regulation and curriculum development. As Schools of Nursing develop their respective training programs that reflect the goals and values of the Nursing profession, the whole issue of inter-professional education and practice is becoming increasingly critical and must be seriously considered by the health care enterprise worldwide.

It is clear that inter-professional practice requires inter-professional education, which occurs when "two or more professions learn with, from and about each other to improve collaboration and the quality of health care" (Centre for the Advancement of Interprofessional Education [CAIPE], 2002). If students from different professions learn together, they will likely work better together, and as result of such a relationship, the quality and delivery of care should improve (Hammick, Freeth, Koppel, Reeves, & Barr, 2007).

In the English medical education system, NP training programs have historically incorporated mentorship from physicians (Barton, 2006). Two distinct reasons for this arrangement were that (a) physicians have the clinical skills and knowledge that NPs need and want to learn and (b) such programs helped to develop a key relationship between the two professions that had traditionally separate roles, cultures, and values. However, in many institutions, the NP role is viewed as a threat to their conventionally accepted roles and authorities by the medical profession. This barrier adds to the challenge of creating a successful mentorship relationship between a doctor and a nurse practitioner student (Barton, 2006).

Considerable effort is being spent around the world to promote inter-professional education and practice as a key strategy to provide high quality and affordable health care to the populations being served (Dickinson, 2008). Preceptor development and support have been identified as core underpinnings for the successful implementation of such a strategy (CNPI, n.d.). Work done by the Canadian Nurse Practitioner Initiative has demonstrated that the mentor was a key support to an NP establishing his/her practice as was partnering with physicians. However, very little has been written about how to specifically support the mentor-protégé relationship within inter-professional education. Our experience with the Adaptive Mentorship (AM) model during this mentoring event was a possible methodology that had potential to be built into mentor development programs for inter-professional educational curriculums.

Adaptive Mentorship: A Support for
Inter-professional Education and Practice

The Adaptive Mentorship (AM) model provided a conceptual framework for our mentor-protégé relationship, despite the fact that we
began the term with a disadvantage of having little overlap between
our respective professional training programs, personal histories,
professional cultures, and knowledge/experience bases. We found
the AM framework to be sensitive to the reality that mentors and
protégés do not always have perfect learning conditions, but that the
unique context of each environment inevitably brings a host of unanticipated factors into play. This context often cannot be changed
by the mentorship participants, but what the mentor and protégé do
have power to change and control is their own behavior and reactions. The AM model served us well by allowing us to acknowledge
the variations in the context in which we were working, while at the
same time optimizing Rob's learning experience, the achievement of
his learning objectives, and the mutual development of our respective roles.

We referred to the AM model (Ralph, 2005; Ralph & Walker,
2010) to implement three general phases in the mentorship process:
(a) determination the protégé's development level, (b) synchroniza-
tion of the mentor's response, and (c) continual observation of the
protégé with necessary adaptation of the mentor's response over
time. According to the model (see Figure 1) the protégé's development level is determined by assessing his/her competence and confidence, each plotted along a continuum ranging from high to low.
In turn, the mentor's response to the developmental needs of the
protégé is adapted to be providing the appropriate amount of task-
direction and psychological/emotional support. A key point emphasized by the AM researchers is that the protégé's developmental level,
and thus the mentor's response, is task-specific rather than generic
(Ralph & Walker, 2010, 2011).

Because the AM approach functions best when applied to particular skill sets, a protégé may have different levels of competence
and confidence for each task or skill that he/she is working on or
attempting to master. As a student NP completing one of his practicum courses, Rob was expected to learn new competencies in a

variety of key areas such as patient assessment, inter-professional communication, and the performance of specific technical procedures traditionally completed by a physician. By applying the AM guidelines to assess Rob's competence and confidence levels in performing these tasks, I was able to adjust my respective task and support responses to attempt to meet Rob's task-specific needs.

I judged that Rob initially was at a D2 to D3 level (i.e., moderate to above average competence and lower to moderate confidence) for the skills that were more familiar to him due to his previous experience and skills acquired as a primary-care NP. These tasks were patient assessment and communication. Then, for new skills such as the insertion of central venous lines, Rob was at a D1/D2 level (i.e., lower competence and low to moderate confidence). Therefore, for these latter tasks, I initially spent most of my time providing mentorship support from the A2 and A1 quadrants (i.e., moderate to high task-direction to help him become more competent, and moderate to high support to build his lagging confidence). As he gained competence and confidence in performing these tasks, I reduced the amount of direct supervision and no longer had to give step-by-step instructions, particularly on the technical skills that Rob was working on mastering. With time and experience over the course of the semester, both mentor and protégé moved through the respective A and D quadrants of the AM model.

Interestingly, I noticed at times that Rob would step into the mentor role while I temporarily became the protégé. This situation would occur during occasions when I needed guidance and/or support on areas such as Nurse Practitioner roles, future responsibilities, and feedback on how our learning together was proceeding. I would describe my own initial self-assessment (as a protégé) in these areas as being between D2 (Low competence and low confidence) and D3 (High competence but low confidence). Then, Rob, as my mentor in the area of NP roles, knowledge base, and responsibilities, would accordingly provide me with the technical instruction and support that would instill in me the necessary confidence and competence to "graduate" into the D4 quadrant (high competence and confidence). I am not sure that Rob was aware that he occasionally switched from protégé to mentor, but I was!

Another insight that I gained during the mentorship experience was that I felt that the AM model was intuitive. As Rob gained skill and confidence in performing the intended medical procedures, I adapted my task and support responses to be more hands-off, which is what Rob needed in order to attain the level of professional development he will require to work independently after the completion of his Master of Nursing. The model helped us both consider the degree of competence and confidence expected of the protégé and how much direction and support should be provided by the mentor. It seemed that sometimes my mentorship response was deliberate and intentional, and at other times it was instinctive and automatic.

In short, we both found that AM was a practical framework that facilitated Rob's professional development and that helped guide my mentorship responses. We have demonstrated that having an MD involved in the training and mentoring of an NP yielded benefits for both parties.

Concluding Thoughts

We are certainly aware of the traditional "silo mentality" that has historically separated health care professions, but we are also convinced that such barriers are outdated and unhelpful. We accept that the professions of nursing and medicine have had a long history of training apart, and yet everyone recognizes that they work closely together in practice. Furthermore, the NP profession has been a relative newcomer on the health care scene, which has resulted in a redefining of the conventional jurisdictions of doctors and nurses.

Despite our disparate professional backgrounds, we have shown by our participation in this rare and unconventional experience that committed practitioners can utilize a mentoring tool, like AM, to help bridge the gap between the health care professions. We encourage educators from across all professions to consider AM's potential in enhancing mentorship practice in other cross-disciplinary settings.

Acknowledgments

R. Ralph: I thank Dr. Shaw for her willingness to "break out of the conventional mold" to undertake this atypical mentorship assignment and for her authentic mentoring style that supported my professional growth. I also wish to acknowledge and thank Dr. David Butcher, an MD in Yellowknife, NT, for the outstanding mentorship he provided me during my early nursing career. The practical knowledge, wisdom, and guidance he graciously and patiently shared with me were foundational to my ongoing development in the health care field.

S. Shaw: I would like to thank Rob for inviting me to go on this exciting journey with him. I learned more from this experience than I ever imagined. Good luck in your new career adventure!

References

Allen, T., & Eby, L. (Eds.). (2007). *The Blackwell handbook on mentoring*. New York, NY: Blackwell.

Barton, T. D. (2006). Clinical Mentoring of nurse practitioners: The doctors' experience. *British Journal of Nursing, 15*(15), 820–824.

Benner, P. (2001). *From novice to expert: Excellence and power in clinical nursing practice*. Upper Saddle River, NJ: Prentice-Hall.

Blythe, R., & Croft, W. (2010). Can a science-humanities collaboration be successful? *Adaptive Behavior, 18*, 12–20. doi:10.1177/1059712309350969

Buchan, J., & Calman, L. (2004). *Skill-mix and policy change in the health workforce: Nurses in advanced practice roles* (OECD Working Paper No. 17). Paris, France: Organisation for Economic Cooperation and Development.

Canadian Nurse Practitioner Initiative (CNPI). (n.d.). *Education framework for nurse practitioners in Canada*. Ottawa, ON: Canadian Nurses Association. Retrieved from http://www.cna-nurses.ca/CNA/documents/pdf/publications/cnpi/tech-report/section5/06_Education%20Framework.pdf

Canadian Nurses Association (CNA). (2006). *Canadian Nurse Practitioner Initiative*. Retrieved from http://www.cna-nurses.ca/cna/practice/advanced/initiative/default_e.aspx

Canadian Nurses Association (CAN). (2009). *Recommendations of the Canadian Nurse Practitioner Initiative Progress Report, December, 2009.* Retrieved from http://www.cna-nurses.ca/CNA/documents/pdf/publications/CNPI_report_2009_e.pdf

Centre for the Advancement of Interprofessional Education (CAIPE). (2002). *Defining IPE.* Retrieved from http://www.caipe.org.uk/about-us/defining-ipe/

Dickinson, H. (2008, July 14). *Why partnership working needs interprofessional training: Training together to work together.* Retrieved from http://www.communitycare.co.uk/Articles/2008/07/14/108849/Interprofessional-education-and-training.htm

Edmunds, M. W. (1999). Increasing professional tension limits NP opportunities. *Nurse Practitioner, 24*(5), 101–104.

Hall, D., Otazo, K., & Hollenbeck, G. (1999). Behind closed doors: What really happens in executive coaching. *Organisational Dynamics, 27*(3), 39–52.

Hammick, M., Freeth, D., Koppel, I., Reeves, S., & Barr, H. (2007). A best evidence systematic review of interprofessional education: BEME Guide No. 9. *Medical Teacher, 29*(8), 735–751.

Higgins, M., & Kram, K. (2001). Conceptualizing mentoring at work: A developmental network perspective. *The Academy Management Review, 26*(2), 264–288.

Hoyt, K., & Proehl, J. (2010). Nurse practitioners in emergency care: Filling the workforce gap. *Advanced Emergency Nursing Journal, 32,* 285–288

Jennings, N., Lee, G., Chao, K., & Keating, S. (2009). A survey of patient satisfaction in a metropolitan emergency department: Comparing nurse practitioners and emergency physicians. *International Journal of Nursing Practice, 15,* 213–218.

Keeling, A. W. (2007). Practicing medicine without a license? Nurse anesthetists, 1900–1938. In A. Keeling (Ed.), *Nursing and the privilege of prescription, 1893–2000* (pp. 28–48). Columbus, OH: The Ohio State Press.

Kohn, L. T., Corrigan, J. M., & Donaldson, M. S. (Eds.). (2000). *To err is human: Building a safer health system.* Washington, DC: National Academy Press

National Steering Committee on Patient Safety. (2002). *Building a safer system: A national integrated strategy for improving patient safety in Canadian health care.* Ottawa, ON: Retrieved from http://rcpsc.medical.org/publications/building_a_safer_system_e.pdf

Nelson, S., & Gordon, S. (Eds.). (2006). *The Complexities of care.* Ithaca, NY: Cornell University Press.

Pulcini, J. (Guest), & Secor, M. (Host). (2010, July 15). *The expansion of nurse practitioners worldwide* [Audio podcast in a series on partners in practice produced by ReachMD XM Radio]. Available from http://www.advancedpracticejobs.com/news.php/The-Expansion-of-Nurse-Practitioners-Worldwide/?articleID=371

Ralph, E. (2005). Enhancing managers' supervisory effectiveness: A promising model. *Journal of Management Development, 24*(3), 267–284.

Ralph, E., & Walker, K. (2010). Enhancing mentors' effectiveness: The promise of the Adaptive Mentorship model. *McGill Journal of Education, 45*(2), 205–218. Available at http://mje.mcgill.ca/index.php/MJE/article/view/4653

Ralph, E., & Walker, K. (2011). Enhancing mentoring in management via the Adaptive Mentorship model. *The International Journal of Knowledge, Culture and Change Management, 10*(8), 35–43.

Saskatchewan Registered Nurses Association (SRNA). (2010, May). RN(NP) registrants growing: Initial rn(np) licensure. *RN(NP)e-Newsbulletin, 3*(1), 1–5. Retrieved from http://www.srna.org/images/stories/pdfs/nurse_practitioner/may2010_rnnp_newsletter.pdf

Thrasher, C. (2005). *Integration of nurse practitioners into emergency departments: A mixed methods approach.* Hamilton, ON: McMaster University.

Woodrow, P. (2006). Mentorship: Perceptions and pitfalls for nursing practice. *Journal of Advanced Nursing, 19*(4), 812–818.

Chapter Twenty-Four
New Research Directions
for Adaptive Mentoring
William PS McKay & Jennifer O'Brien

I N THIS CHAPTER WE SUGGEST five new directions for research
into mentoring based upon the Adaptive Mentorship©(AM)
model. First, we discuss adding dimensions of intensity to the
model and propose a pertinent study; second, we suggest a study to
determine whether and how strongly the Hawthorne Effect might
result from such AM studies. We then present an approach to cross-
cultural AM studies as well as a possible study of brief mentoring
within medical simulation contexts. Our fifth proposal is to use the
AM model in Evolutionary Biology studies of altruism.

Study 1: The Intensity Factor

The AM model recognizes two dimensions of learning in the protégé
and two corresponding dimensions of mentor response (see Figure
1). For the protégé, *competence* is plotted on the abscissa and *confidence* on the ordinate (both increasing as they approach the origin).
The mentor's corresponding responses are task and support (both
decreasing as they approach the origin). The four larger arrows represent the *process* of mentoring. AM research to date has focused
upon identifying and improving the adaptation of the mentor's efforts to match the appropriate point on the protégé's grid (i.e., the
accuracy of the arrow). In this chapter, we refer to the arrow's path
from its origin on the Mentorship's Adaptive Response grid to its
target on the Protégés Developmental Level grid as the ideal AM
pattern.

The *process* of mentorship may also be conceptualized as having
a greater or lesser *strength*, which is a function of desire (or motivation) and effort by both mentor and protégé to achieve mutual maximum benefit from the mentoring relationship. As well, we could
conceive of a measure of the depth of their relationship, which we

call *engagement*. Furthermore, we envisage the *intensity* of the process as being represented by the size and weight or the "calibre" of the arrow. This *intensity* of the process could be modelled as the product of *strength* × *time* × *engagement*.

It is possible to further conceive of, and measure, the intensity of the mentoring process as a third useful dimension in the model. In the original version of AM as shown in Figure 1, the four larger arrows, representing the mentoring process, have the same width. However, human experience shows that the intensity of the process varies in real life, depending on the various components, and this variability can be shown diagrammatically by varying the arrows' widths, as depicted in Figure 2. Other diagrammatic depictions might be possible, but our proposed addition of the third dimension has the advantage of retaining the simplicity of the original AM diagram. Measurement of the process of intensity can be accomplished in a number of ways, the simplest of which would be to ask the mentors and protégés about their view of the overall intensity of the process or about its component parts. One could retrieve this information by posing questions, using quantitative verbal response scales

Figure 1

The Adaptive Mentorship Model. From Ralph and Walker, 2010, 2011.

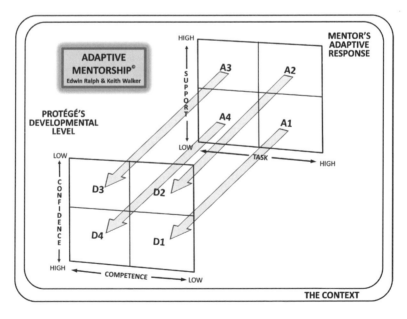

or administering visual analogue scales. Higher cost methods could be implemented, such as analyzing video recordings of interactive sessions and scoring them for one or more of *time* duration, *strength* of the interaction, and apparent *relationship depth*. These measurements could be compared to overall satisfaction reported by the participants or to objective measures of the protégés' learning. Examples of possible hypotheses of such studies might be (a) that given similar AM interaction patterns, more successful learning outcomes will be correlated with *intensity of process*; (b) that more intense interactions will correlate with better AM interaction patterns; or (c) that the components will change during the most satisfactory mentoring relationships, moving from a dominance of *strength* and *time* in the early D1/A1 and D2/A2 phases to a dominance of *engagement* in the D4/A4 quadrant.

Study 2: The Hawthorne Effect

Multiple definitions of the Hawthorne Effect have been operationally used in the literature (Chiesa & Hobbs, 2008). The most

Figure 2
A third dimension of mentorship, intensity, could be added to the AM model by representing the degree or level of intensity, shown by the comparative width or thickness of the larger arrows.

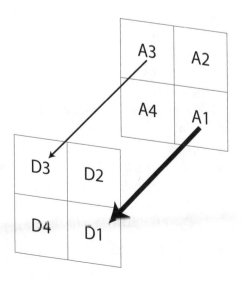

common usage, which we find most appropriate, operationally defines the Hawthorne Effect as an experimental result attributed to subjects' awareness that they are being studied. An important goal of the AM model is the improvement of mentorship by focusing the attention of both mentor and protégé on the developmental process. It would be of interest to us to compare learning outcomes of mentoring processes in a control group who did not use AM methodology with outcomes in a group who were studied while they used the AM model. The hypothesis would be the Hawthorne Effect with the studied group.

As well as difficulties of experimental design, there would be ethical obstacles to such an experiment. Experimental design challenges would lie in finding or establishing two groups who would be similar enough to minimize confounders and who would relying on a mentorship relationship for learning success. For instance, a confounding factor might be having access to resources or skills that could readily be acquired outside the mentorship relationship (e.g., printed matter or the internet). On the other hand, the practical "in-the-trenches" teaching and learning of actual skills (and lore) that is garnered in professional and clinical settings would be a more suitable environment in which to examine mentorship. To us the mentorship process is essential for novices to develop professionally, and educators should endeavor to enhance it. It must, however, be researched carefully. An experiment involving two or more professional schools, with the experimental (AM studied) group in one school and the control group in the other, would also help avoid the "cross-contamination" possibility.

The ethical issue, here, would involve the element of informed consent. In our view, the study would be cleaner and more likely to confirm or disconfirm the hypothesis if it would be allowed to proceed without the full knowledge of either group. Such a possibility could occur in Canadian institutions. The *Tri-Council Policy Statement: Ethical Conduct for Research Involving Humans* (Canadian Institutes of Health Research, Natural Sciences and Engineering Research Council of Canada, and Social Sciences and Humanities Research Council of Canada, 2010) stated:

The Research Ethics Board (REB) may approve research without requiring that the researcher obtain the participant's consent in accordance with Articles 3.1 to 3.5 where the REB is satisfied, and documents, that all of the following apply:

(a) the research involves no more than minimal risk to the participants;

(b) the lack of the participant's consent is unlikely to adversely affect the welfare of the participant;

(c) it is impossible or impracticable to carry out the research and to answer the research question properly, given the research design, if the prior consent of the participant is required;

(d) whenever possible and appropriate, after participation, or at a later time during the study, participants will be debriefed and provided with additional pertinent information in accordance with Articles 3.2 and 3.4, at which point they will have the opportunity to refuse consent in accordance with Article 3.1; and

(e) the research does not involve a therapeutic intervention, or other clinical or diagnostic interventions. (Article 3.7)

Thus, in the case of this proposal, the measurement of learning outcomes and mentorship satisfaction could be obtained by a variety of objective and subjective methods. Medical, nursing, veterinarian, and other schools for health professionals would be appropriate venues for this type of research. We think that such studies have the potential to help inform the work of enhancing the effectiveness of Adaptive Mentorship.

Study 3: Cross-Cultural Aspects

Humans are genetically similar and possess comparable distributions of "intelligence" across racial, cultural, and ethnic groups; and yet, it could be argued that cultures may be diverging. For instance, North American children of the past quarter century, Millennials, as they have been called, had generally been raised in a new way that was different from traditional child rearing practices, which were rooted in the beginnings of human history. The millennial sub-culture was typically characterized by such practices as (a) constant adult supervision and protection, both inside and outside the home (e.g., "helicopter parenting"), (b) privacy within the home (e.g., children having their own sacrosanct room, television, and computer), (c) little spontaneous play or opportunity for exploration outside the home; and (d) emphasis on self esteem (Somers, & Settle, 2010). By contrast, most children in developing counties would generally have experienced a more traditional upbringing and mentoring style at home and education at school. As a result of these differences, individuals from both groups who begin post-secondary education, tertiary training, or professional preparation will no doubt be heavily influenced by the way they were mentored in their previous contexts. Such differences may be observable in settings of professional medical education.

For example, the field in which we are involved, anesthesiology, is a medical specialty that is largely taught in a mentored environment. Moreover, the Canadian Anesthesiologists' Society is closely involved in the anesthesia residency training program (in which medical practitioners attain *specialist* status) in the country of Rwanda. In this program, a Canadian anesthesiologist, often accompanied by a Canadian medical resident (and sometimes supplemented by practitioners from the United States and elsewhere) are continually engaged in practice, training, and mentorship in the university hospitals in Rwanda on a series of one-month rotations.

We believe that this program would provide a relevant and interesting setting to study the mentorship process as experienced by Canadian Residents compared with Rwandan Residents. A hypothesis for such a study might be: applying the AM model, with the added dimension of measuring *intensity*, will yield different results in a study of Canadian Anesthesia Residents than in a comparative investigation of Rwandan Anesthesia Residents. The assumption is that the residents who had more "traditional" upbringing/schooling would require a different mentor response or style than would the so-called Millennials from North America. We readily accept, however, that it would be highly questionable to attempt to ascribe any discovered differences solely to variations between child rearing practices, especially given the differences in socio-economic status and in cultural traditions in the groups. Nonetheless, we think that many educators and mentorship personnel in professional-education programs may be interested to see what kinds and degrees of differences exist in the mentorship process as a step towards further understanding cultural differences among medical professionals and those from other disciplines.

Study 4: Medical Simulation

In medical education, we have an old aphorism that "common things occur commonly, but rare things occur." Medical education is a mixture of traditional university-based educational methods (e.g., lectures, laboratories, seminars, and small-group tutoring) and hands-on apprenticeship learning. However, a difficulty has always been to assure students' exposure to hands-on management of relatively rare events and conditions, which typically require an immediate response – the kind where there is no time to go to the books or to look things up on the internet.

An important new tool to teach appropriate responses in these types of crises has been the development of modular, high-fidelity medical simulation devices that are designed to mimic the crisis and the environment in which the practitioner will be expected to cope. These models usually consist of a life-size, instrumented, plastic "patient" and the accompanying monitors and therapeutic equipment. This package simulates what would be found in the environment in which diagnosis and treatment would ordinarily occur (in a physician's office, an emergency room, an operating theatre, or an intensive care unit). We conceive of using this simulation environment as a means to study what we might call *high-speed mini-mentoring*.

In the simulation exercise, the learner is typically plunged into a crisis situation and asked to provide optimal care to the patient. The student's efforts are often observed by peers and always by a mentor, variously termed a preceptor, supervisor, instructor, teacher, manager, or clinical guide. The simulation sessions are commonly video recorded, and the subsequent debriefing segment is a crucial part of each session. Because the students feel that they are being tested on knowledge and skill that "every physician should know how to do" (e.g., to deal calmly, correctly, and swiftly with uncommon life-threatening emergencies), and because they are performing before their peers, an expert teacher, and the unforgiving camera, students often find these simulation sessions to be intimidating and stressful (Harvey, Nathens, Bandiera, & Leblanc, 2010). In fact, many experienced physicians who "return to school" for a refresher course or workshop have also reported finding these simulation sessions more stressful than the real situation (Quilici et al., 2005). The simulator experience has thus proven to be a psychological pressure cooker for novices and veterans alike.

How the mentor prepares the learner before entering the simulator session, and how the latter is later debriefed in a manner that optimizes learning, will depend upon the mentor's methods and manner. The mentor must quickly establish a relationship of trust, a climate characterized by two-way communication, a provision to encourage learners to proceed at their own pace, a sensitivity to recognize when and how to intervene if the learner is unsure or begins to flounder, and an image that sets a professional example. Of all these essential competencies, we believe that establishing and maintaining a relationship of trust is probably most critical to success and yet most difficult to achieve. Because the simulator is expensive to operate, and because students must experience many simulation scenarios in their clinical education, mentors in these situations are not only under pressure of time, but they must practice what we termed "high speed mini-mentoring" in that the mentorship process in such sessions is relatively brief but intense. We propose that a before-and-after comparison research study be conducted in these scenarios using the AM model within the simulator exercise.

A possible hypothesis in such a study might be: better learning outcomes occur in the simulator setting after the teacher/mentors learn and apply the AM principles. An experiment with a control group and an intervention group could be designed with the follow parametres. First, the control and intervention groups could be sampled either by randomly selecting class members for each group or by taking all members from different classes. Confounding could be minimized by teaching both groups the same material that would be practiced in the simulation. The control group would receive the historically standard instructional orientation, then proceed with the simulation exercise. For the experimental group, each member would spend a specified one-on-one time period with the instructor/mentor to become acquainted and discuss the AM model and to plot where they think they fit in the axes on the AM model. The mentor would also assure each protégé that the simulation exercise would be adjusted as much as possible so that the mentor would adjust the content and his/her mentoring behavior to attempt to fit the learner's conception of their developmental level and the material being taught. At the conclusion of the simulation, data could be collected regarding changes in the protégés' mastery of the material, in participants' perceptions of their respective AM quadrant positions, and in their overall opinion of the usefulness of the AM model.

Study 5: Altruism and Evolution

Nowak (2006) believed that the process of human evolution was based on a fierce competition between individuals, and that it should therefore reward people's selfish behavior. Altruism (or Nowak's preference, co-operation), defined as giving a benefit to another person at the expense of oneself, has been a conundrum for evolutionary biologists since the turn of the last century. Simple evolutionary theory suggested that in logical terms, the organism receiving the benefit of the altruistic act should produce more offspring than the altruist. After Trivers (1971) presented his seminal work in these matters, there was considerable interest in the concepts of altruism and evolution and their relationship. Furthermore, plausible evolutionary explanations for altruism and co-operation have appeared since that time (Fehr, & Fischbacher, 2003).

The evolution of humans as hunter-gatherers of sparse and widely spread food and other necessities was theorized to depend upon a number of interconnected factors. Whereas many migratory species had developed internal global positioning systems that have allowed their annual return to familiar territory, evolution scientists postulated that human predecessors in Africa's Rift Valley similarly learned that various regions yielded nutritional abundance or famine at different times and under different weather conditions. It was felt that early people developed their ability to make these types of decisions about where to travel next, which meant that people most likely to survive had learned to observe, remember, choose, and plan where and when to go, how best to get there, and how best to preserve any surplus of resources for future lean times.

Thus, evolutionary scientists postulated that early humans evolved in their capacity for long-distance walking, thinking, and communicating. Planning required imagination, which in turn fostered development of language that would evoke pictures in the mind, which would be impossible without imagination. Because of the neural requirements of foresight and language, evolutionary scientists believed that humans evolved a large brain, which meant at birth, the child's head and body would be at an immature state, necessitating growth and development of the baby, which in turn resulted in a further requirement of intensive and selfless care of the young by the mother and/or other more mature individuals. As well, a co-operating group or tribe of humans had a greater survival benefit over solitary individuals with respect to defending against predators and hunting prey. The evolutionary benefit of co-operation, as well as the immaturity of infants that required early total care, have been invoked to explain altruism. By extension, nurturing and mentoring of the inexperienced by the more experienced has been found in all cultures and in a number of species.

The mentorship process has many of the qualities of altruism that are of interest to evolutionary biologists. For instance, it has aspects of the parent-child relationship in that the mentor's desire for the protégé to do well seems to be based on unselfish motives similar to those in parenting. Mentors universally expend time, effort, and emotional energy because they desire that their protégés do well, independent of considerations for economic gain or promotion. The fact is critical that mentors and protégés enter a mentoring relationship in which mentors talk about "their" protégés and not simply "the" protégés. The mutual wish for the protégé to perform well, and the "shared" ownership of the process, both arise from the relationship that develops between them. What may begin as merely a job to be done (e.g., instructing, teaching, supervising, coaching) often becomes a deeply held goal of the mentor for the protégé's success as well a reciprocal attachment or fondness of the protégé toward the mentor.

The determinants and distribution of altruism within a population are difficult to study because measurements of such elements as charitable donations often lack a suitable denominator. Games that depend on decisions about sharing have been devised for experimental studies of human altruistic behavior, such as sharing and/or withholding real or "play" money. This research indicated that people approach an equilibrium position in or near a "basin of attraction," a term that encompasses both the position and the likelihood of an equilibrium state affecting human altruism (Fehr, & Fischbacher, 2003).

Because mentorship includes elements of altruism, we would be interested in investigating the application of the AM methodology to studies in evolutionary biology. Typical mentorship relationships might ordinarily start in the A1/D1 quadrants and ending at the Cartesian origin – that is, in the left lower corner of the A4/D4 quadrants. The neighborhood of the Cartesian origin would be the basin of attraction of the altruistic mentorship in terms of Fehr and Fischbacher's (2003) work.

A mentorship relationship with elements of strength, time, and engagement, as we defined above, necessarily takes place between graduate students and their teacher/mentors. The academic world, towards which these types of effort are directed, is highly competitive for the new graduate with respect to future careers, positions, promotions, and resources. To us it is plausible, and may even be common in university settings, that young, newly graduated teachers of graduate students might conceive, either consciously or unconsciously, of their brighter graduate students as future competition. Further, they might have purely selfish motives for taking on a mentoring role, such as gaining recognition, seeking promotion, or attaining tenure.

These factors might skew their mentorship effectiveness by reducing or removing facets of altruism described above. On the other hand, veteran teachers who have already attained the rank of full professor would probably be unworried by thoughts of their graduate students usurping them and more likely would altruistically promote their students' careers. These older mentors may even have hopes of their protégés carrying forward the research interests on which the pair may have been collaborating up to that time.

In the light of such cases, we propose a fifth study wherein the AM principles are applied in the mentorship process of graduate students and their graduate supervisors/teachers. The study would explore how a group of neophyte teachers/mentors would supervise their graduate students compared to a group of graduate students mentored by full professors. The assumption would be that, as a group, the senior professors would be more altruistic than the novice teacher/mentors.

A possible hypothesis for such a study would be: a mentorship relationship using the AM model will finish nearer the Cartesian origin when altruism plays a significant role compared to the outcomes of mentorship not based on the AM model, where more selfish factors intrude. We envisage that such a study could be designed so that evolutionary biologists would work with medical practitioners and investigators, all of whom would be familiar with the AM approach.

Concluding Thoughts

We have proposed five new directions for research into mentorship using the Adaptive Mentorship model. We included several study hypotheses that could be tested. In our view, advancement and improvement of the AM model will require further research into its applicability across the professions. As is the case with all research endeavors, we anticipate that the participating researchers and practitioners within the experimental groups would be well versed in using the AM model. We are hopeful that our suggestions in this chapter will serve as an inspiration for future investigators from several professional disciplines who are interested not only in adapting mentorship in their respective fields, but in enhancing that process across the professions.

References

Canadian Institutes of Health Research, Natural Sciences and Engineering Research Council of Canada, and Social Sciences and Humanities Research Council of Canada. (2010, December). *Tri-Council Policy Statement: Ethical Conduct for Research Involving Humans*. Retrieved from http://www.pre.ethics.gc.ca/pdf/eng/tcps2/TCPS_2_FINAL_Web.pdf

Chiesa, M., & Hobbs, S. (2008). Making sense of social research: How useful is the Hawthorne Effect? *European Journal of Social Psychology, 38*, 67–74. doi:10.1002/ejsp.401

Fehr, E., & Fischbacher, U. (2003, October 23). The nature of human altruism. *Nature, 425*, 785–791.

Harvey, A., Nathens, A. B., Bandiera, G., & Leblanc, V. R. (2010). Threat and challenge: Cognitive appraisal and stress responses in simulated trauma resuscitations. *Medical Education, 44*(6), 587–594.

Nowak, M.A. (2006). Five rules for the evolution of cooperation. *Science, 314*, 1560–1563.

Quilici, A. P., Pogetti, R. S., Fontes, B., Zantut, L. F., Chaves, E. T., & Birolini, D. (2005). Is the Advanced Trauma Life Support simulation exam more stressful for the surgeon than emergency department trauma care? *Clinics* (Sao Paulo, Brazil), *60*(4), 287–292.

Ralph. E., & Walker, K. (2010). Enhancing mentors' effectiveness: The promise of the adaptive mentorship model. *McGill Journal of Education, 45*(2), 205–218. Retrieved from http://mje.mcgill.ca/index.php/MJE/article/view/4653

Ralph, E., & Walker, K. (2011). Enhancing mentoring in management via the adaptive mentorship model. *The International Journal of Knowledge, Culture and Change Management, 10*(8), 35–43.

Somers, P., & Settle, J. (2010). The helicopter parent: Research towards a typology (Part one). *College and University, 86*(1), 18–24, 26–27.

Trivers, R. L. (1971). The evolution of reciprocal altruism. *The Quarterly Review of Biology, 46*(1), 35 57. Retrieved from http://www.jstor.org/stable/2822435

Epilogue

Edwin Ralph & Keith Walker

WE SET THREE KEY PURPOSES for this book and for *The Forum on Mentorship in the Professions*, from which this book was derived. The first purpose was to fulfill the mandate that SSHRC had assigned us regarding the dissemination of the Adaptive Mentorship© (AM) model, which we had developed in our own mentoring and supervisory practice over the years. We believe we fulfilled that purpose, both during the forum and within the co-creation of this book. However, we hasten to say that our presentation and enthusiasm for the AM model is not suggesting a panacea for enhancing all mentorship approaches, but rather it is a potentially effective and adaptable conceptual framework worthy of consideration by mentorship personnel across the disciplines. Our aim here was to encourage interested individuals not so much to adopt AM (although a few writers did so, as documented in several chapters), but rather, as its name suggests, to *adapt* it if practitioners found that it could inform mentoring practice in specific situational contexts in their respective settings.

Our second purpose for the forum and this book was to establish a welcoming space in which traditionally separated mentorship participants could explore the wide variety of mentorship philosophies, principles, programs, and practices that their colleagues used. Our aim here was not, on the one hand, to attempt to derive a single definition or approach to mentorship that would be applicable to all professions, nor was it, on the other hand, to merely catalogue a comprehensive range of techniques used across and beyond Canada. Rather, we wanted to provide an inaugural, formal, open, cross-disciplinary venue in which a diverse group of interested scholars spanning the entire inter-professional spectrum could discuss their unique experiences as well as share and debate ideas regarding the mentorship process past, present, and future, and to thus learn from each other. We believe that the contents of the book provide evidence that this goal has begun to see fulfillment in our Canadian context.

Our third purpose in hosting the forum and co-creating the book was to affirm that (a) each professional discipline and occupation has distinctly valuable ways to conceptualize and to practice mentorship and (b) tangible effort is required to reduce the conventional silo mentality that has traditionally hindered institutional collaboration between/among professions with respect to freely sharing ideas with one another to improve mentorship. We believe we created a formal venue by which specific cross-disciplinary collaboration has begun. Through the support of SSHRC and the University of Saskatchewan that supported the forum and book ventures, we were able to help create the conditions for several individuals both to engage in a higher degree of inter-professional work on mentoring that had been evident previously and to publish and disseminate a formal record of this work.

We believe that the book effectively focused on its main theme, which was adapting mentorship across the professions to meet the diverse needs, goals, and aspirations of the participants engaged in the mentoring relationship. Rather than attempting to recommend that educational leaders adopt a single mentorship style, approach, or method – an unrealistic and unwise action indeed – the book's authors and editors emphasized tailoring mentorship to fit the particular context of each setting. Of course, such tailoring or adapting does build on the core themes of good mentoring as revealed repeatedly in actual experience and in the previous related literature (e.g., consistently demonstrating effective communication and human relations skills, seeking to meet individuals' developmental needs, fostering positive/productive relationships, and adjusting mentor behavior to supply what protégés require in terms of knowledge and encouragement).

We feel that the chapter authors and the forum attendees have achieved these goals, but what is more, in doing so, they as a group of diverse professionals have also exhibited the very attributes envisaged by the book writers for engaging in a cross-fertilization of ideas about enhancing mentorship. This group of individuals has begun to dismantle the proverbial silo barriers that have typically hindered authentic dialogue between/among professional units across the disciplines. These individuals communicated, co-operated, and collaborated in conversation, in research, and/or in documentation of these activities. Furthermore, an examination of all of the chapters in this book shows that this meaningful interchange occurred between genders, disciplines, and locations. As a group, these authors have argued that creating and maintaining effective mentorship is a worthy goal that encompasses but goes beyond one mentor/protégé pair, one department, one professional discipline, one institution, or one province/country. It is our sincere hope that the present volume will be one among several co-operative efforts regarding the enhancement of mentorship practice that interested educational leaders will initiate in the near future. We believe that such initiatives have the potential to strengthen the entire professional development enterprise. We are sincerely grateful for contributions and support of the participant authors of this text, to the Social Science and Humanities Research Council of Canada, to our home institution (the University of Saskatchewan), and to all those who have encouraged us along our own mentorship journeys.

We wish our readers well in all their efforts to refresh and foster developmental relationships through mentorship in their respective professions. All the very best to you in all these efforts may entail for you and your colleagues.

Referee Acknowledgement

Our thanks is extended to these scholars from three countries, numerous disciplines and nine institutions who provided their critical reviews for our blind reviews of selected chapters (see indication of this designation in text). We acknowledge your appreciation for your timely contributions.

- ⁓: Dr. Kirk Anderson, Associate Professor, University of New Brunswick
- ⁓: Dr. Sabre Cherkowski, Faculty, University of British Columbia – Kelowna Campus
- ⁓: Dr. Cheri Chui, Victoria University in Wellington, New Zealand
- ⁓: Dr. Susan Bens, Director of Student Services, University of Saskatchewan

~: Dr. Lynn Bosetti, Dean of Education, University of British Columbia – Kelowna Campus

~: Dr. Kent Donlevy, Associate Professor, University of Calgary

~: Dr. James Graham, Faculty, Victoria University in Wellington, New Zealand

~: Dr. Vivian Hajnal, Associate Professor, University of Saskatchewan

~: Dr. Matthew Meyers, Associate Professor, St. Francis Xavier University, Nova Scotia

~: Dr. David McIntire, Professor, Azusa Pacific University

~: Dr. Tim Molnar, Faculty, University of Saskatchewan

~: Dr. Jackie Ottmann, Faculty, University of Calgary

~: Dr. Sharon Roset, Educator, Saskatchewan

~: Dr. Kabini Sanga, Senior Fellow, Leadership Pacific

~: Dr. Anurag Saxema, Professor & Assistant Dean of Medicine, University of Saskatchewan

Contributors

WILLOW BROWN came to teacher education at UNBC with 16 years as a classroom teacher, a master's degree from Alaska, and a doctorate degree in school improvement from the University of Saskatchewan. She studies how teachers and communities learn through inquiry. She enjoys engaging and empowering learners of all ages.

SABRE CHERKOWSKI is an Assistant Professor in the Faculty of Education at the University of British Columbia (Okanagan). Her teaching and research relate to educational leadership, particularly in teacher development in learning communities. She examines the use of appreciative inquiry in school improvement, teacher leadership as confluence, and coaching and mentoring for teacher leadership.

PETER CHIN is an Associate Professor and Associate Dean of Undergraduate Studies, Faculty of Education, Queen's University, Kingston, Ontario. His research is centred on workplace learning and how novices gain experience within new settings. Particular attention is placed on understanding the differences between teaching/learning in school and in workplace environments.

BRIGITTE COUTURE, MScN, is Professor of nursing at George Brown College in Toronto and teaches in a collaborative nursing degree program (Ryerson University, Centennial and George Brown college). The author's research interest has been in team teaching within a large classroom environment, as well as in the experience of students during their practicum.

ANDREA DAVY has several years of experience as both an elementary school teacher in Prince George and a sessional instructor at UNBC in the School of Education. Her interests include mentorship and learning communities, inquiry, assessment, and curriculum and instruction in language development and second language acquisition.

NORM DRAY is the Associate Director of SELU (Saskatchewan Educational Leadership Unit), a non-profit agency that operates out of the College of Education, University of Saskatchewan, and which coordinates educational leadership development activities across Saskatchewan. Norm has accumulated extensive educational experience and practical wisdom regarding teaching, learning, and leadership.

LINDA FERGUSON is a Professor in the Faculty of Nursing at the University of Saskatchewan. Her teaching and research include mentorship and preceptorship in nursing practice and education. She is director of the newly established CASNIE program (Centre for the Advancement of the Study of Nursing Education and Interprofessional Education).

DR. JUDY HALBERT co-leads the Network of Performance-Based Schools and the Aboriginal Enhancement Schools Network. She teaches leadership studies at Vancouver Island University and is the co-author of *Leadership Mindsets – Innovation and Learning in the Transformation of Schools* (Routledge: 2009). Her interest is in transforming systems for greater quality and equity.

DAWNA L. HAWRYSH is the Projects Development Officer at Continuing Professional Development for Pharmacists, College of Pharmacy and Nutrition, University of Saskatchewan. Currently she is responsible for developing continuing education programs for licensed pharmacists in the province. Previously, she taught a number of classes and coordinated the Years 1 and 2 Practical Skills Laboratory for the undergraduate program at the College.

ANITA JENNINGS teaches nursing practice in the Faculty of Nursing at George Brown College in Toronto and in a collaborative nursing degree program (Ryerson University, Centennial, and George Brown College). Her research and teaching seek to build understanding of the issues confronting patients and the educational requirements of students.

DR. LINDA KASER is a leader of two inquiry networks in British Columbia. Linda teaches leadership studies at Vancouver Island University. She is a co-author of *Leadership Mindsets – Innovation and Learning in the Transformation of Schools* (Routledge: 2009). Her interests are in networks, leadership, inquiry, and innovation.

DEB KOEHN has a Master of Education degree from the University of Victoria. She is a regional leader for British Columbia's Network of Performance Based Schools and Network of Healthy Schools and has presented both provincially and internationally. Deb has co-instructed in the master's program at UNBC. She considers her position as a primary classroom teacher her most important one!

Roya Khoii is assistant professor at Islamic Azad University, North Tehran Branch. She received her PhD in TEFL in 1997. She has been teaching various BA and MA courses in the field of TEFL for 20 years. Her main areas of interest are teaching and testing foreign language skills.

Benjamin Kutsyuruba, PhD, is Assistant Professor, Educational Policy and Leadership, and Associate Director of Social Program Evaluation Group, Faculty of Education, Queen's University. His research interests include educational policymaking, leadership development, mentorship, trust and moral agency, transnationalization of higher education, school safety, and educational change.

Dal Lynds is an Acute Care Nurse Practitioner at the Battleford Union Hospital in North Battleford, Saskatchewan, within the Saskatchewan Prairie North Health Region. He is also affiliated with the School of Nursing at the University of Saskatchewan in Saskatoon. He has filled formal and informal roles as both mentor and protégé throughout his career.

Catherine McGregor is an Assistant Professor in Leadership Studies at the University of Victoria. Her research interests include teacher and social justice leadership, educational policy, and civic learning. She served as the faculty advisor for the Certificate in School Management and Leadership (CSML) at the University of Victoria for three years.

KELLY McINNES has spent 17 years working as an administrator in post-secondary education. Kelly holds a Bachelor of Science (University of Toronto, 1991), a Bachelor of Education (University of Saskatchewan 1994) and a Master of Education (University of Saskatchewan 2010). Kelly's academic area of interest is mentorship and other developmental relationships.

WILLIAM (BILL) P. McKAY, MD, FRCP, was a farm boy who obtained degrees in Agricultural Economics and Medicine from the University of Toronto. He did Family Practice in Paris, Ontario, then returned to the University of Toronto for specialty training in Anesthesiology. He is currently engaged in research and teaching at the University of Saskatchewan.

CATHERINE NEUMANN-BOXER is a PhD candidate in the Department of Educational Administration at the University of Saskatchewan. Catherine taught grade five and seven for ten years and was a teacher mentor for four years. Her research interests include leadership, mentorship and coaching, and dialogue.

JOSEPH KOFI NSIAH (Rev. Fr.) is currently Vicar General of the Catholic Diocese of Jasikan, Ghana. He served as assistant pastor and pastor in Ghana and Canada (Saskatchewan). Joseph holds a BA (Hon.) from the University of Cape Coast, Ghana and a MEd and PhD in Educational Administration from the University of Saskatchewan.

JENNIFER O'BRIEN received her MA in Critical Disability Studies at York University. She is the Research Assistant/Coordinator in the Department of Anesthesiology, Perioperative Medicine, and Pain Management in the College of Medicine at the University of Saskatchewan, and is responsible for coordinating all phases of the postgraduate Anesthesia resident research programme under the leadership of the Director of Research.

MARCELLA OGENCHUK, RN, PhD, is an Assistant Professor in the College of Nursing at the University of Saskatchewan. During the past 25 years, she practiced nursing in various settings including acute care and the community. Her teaching and research are in paediatrics (injury prevention in youth) and alcohol use in youth.

BOB PETRICK is an Adjunct in the Faculty of Education at Queen's University, and serves as a Faculty Liaison for teacher candidates completing their teaching practicum in Ontario schools. His teaching and research interests lie in such areas as motivating student learning, assessment of learning, Aboriginal Studies, and Aboriginal art.

JANE PRESTON is currently employed as a College of Education Position Analyst at the University of Saskatchewan. Jane taught students from kindergarten to high school while living in Taiwan, Egypt, and Kuwait. Her research and writing spotlights Aboriginal issues, community viability, rural education, and narratives on the teaching profession.

MICHELLE PRYTULA served as a teacher and administrator for 15 years prior to joining the College of Education faculty at the University of Saskatchewan. Her teaching areas include leadership, organizational theory, and educational finance. Some of her current research interests include teacher learning and induction, action research, and school leadership.

ELLERY PULLMAN, PhD, is Professor of Psychology and Leadership at Briercrest College and Seminary, Caronport, Saskatchewan. In addition to teaching full-time, he has also served in a number of administrative roles. His research and writing interests are related to the fields of adult development, faculty vitality, and organizational effectiveness.

EDWIN RALPH is a professor and internship supervisor/facilitator at the College of Education at the University of Saskatchewan. His teaching and research interests over the past 25 years have focused on enhancing the effectiveness of the teaching/learning process and its mentorship, across all levels and in all disciplines.

ROBERT RALPH recently completed his MN, Acute Care NP, and he has practiced as a Primary Care NP in Aboriginal communites in Northen Canada. He currently works in a community hospital emergency department, as well as with an air ambulance firm. His focus is on improving the quality of patient care.

KABINI SANGA is Senior Fellow of Leadership Pacific, a mentoring network and movement inspired to nurture thousands of new generation leaders in and beyond the South Pacific Region. In addition to his professorial role at Victoria University in New Zealand, Dr. Sanga is regularly called upon to facilitate and convene leadership development initiatives throughout the South Pacific.

SUSAN SHAW heads Saskatoon Health Region's Department of Adult Critical Care and is an Assistant Professor at the University of Saskatchewan College of Medicine. Susan is respected by her clinical and administrative colleagues for her focus on clinician engagement in system improvement so that patients and their families receive the best possible care.

SAREL J. VAN DER WALT is an Emergency Room Physician at the Battleford Union Hospital in North Battleford, Saskatchewan within the Saskatchewan Prairie North Health Region. Dr. Van der Walt has been both a protégé and a mentor during his professional training and in his medical practice.

ROSEMARY A. VENNE (PhD Toronto) is an Associate Professor in the Department of Human Resources and Organizational Behaviour at the Edwards School of Business, University of Saskatchewan. Her research interests include demography relating to human resource issues, including labour supply, aging of the labour force, and changing career patterns.

Keith Walker has a joint appointment in the Department of Educational Administration and the Johnson Shoyama Graduate School of Public Policy at the University of Saskatchewan. Several years ago Keith joined Edwin Ralph to further develop and disseminate the Adaptive Mentorship model across the professions and sectors. He primary interests revolve around leadership, governance and organizational development and renewal.

Denise Wilson teaches early primary in Northern British Columbia. She enjoys "learning to learn" alongside her colleagues, students, and student candidates. She believes that the learner relationship is built on mutual respect and knowledge is shared and created through focused conversation, reflective thinking and listening, and consistent implementation of research and practice.